Anti-American Myths

Anti-American Myths

Their Causes and Consequences

ARNOLD BEICHMAN

With a New Introduction by the Author

Routledge
Taylor & Francis Group

LONDON AND NEW YORK

Originally published in 1972 by the Library Press.

Published 2019 by Routledge
2 Park Square, Milton Park, Abingdon, Oxon, OX14 4RN
52 Vanderbilt Avenue, New York, NY 10017

Routledge is an imprint of the Taylor & Francis Group, an informa business

New material this edition copyright © 1993 by Taylor & Francis.

All rights reserved. No part of this book may be reprinted or reproduced or utilised in any form or by any electronic, mechanical, or other means, now known or hereafter invented, including photocopying and recording, or in any information storage or retrieval system, without permission in writing from the publishers.

Notice:
Product or corporate names may be trademarks or registered trademarks, and are used only for identification and explanation without intent to infringe.

Library of Congress Catalog Number: 92-7880

Library of Congress Cataloging-in-Publication Data

Beichman, Arnold.
 [Nine lies about America]
 Anti-American myths: their causes and consequences/Arnold Beichman; with a new introduction by the author.
   p.   cm.
 Originally published: Nine lies about America. New York: Library Press, 1972.
   Includes bibliographical references (p.   ) and indexes.
   ISBN 1-56000-590-4
   1. United States—Social conditions—1960-1980. 2. Radicalism—United States. I. Title.
HN65.B42   1992
306'.0973—dc20   92-7880
                                              CIP

ISBN 13: 978-1-56000-590-2 (pbk)

For Thomas Sowell

There is no blueprint for happiness.
Joseph Brodsky

Our power of prediction is slight, our command over remote results infinitesimal. It is therefore the happiness of our contemporaries that is our main concern; we should be very chary of sacrificing large numbers of people for the sake of a contingent end, however advantageous that end may appear. . . . We can never know enough to make the chance worth taking. . . . There is the further consideration that is often in need of emphasis; it is not sufficient that the state of affairs which we seek to promote should be better than the state of affairs which preceded it; it must be sufficiently better to make up for the evils of transition.
John Maynard Keynes,
"The Political Doctrines of Edmund Burke"

Unjust privileges prevailing in a free society can be reduced only by carefully graded stages; those who would demolish them overnight would erect great injustices in their place. An absolute moral renewal of society can be attempted only by an absolute power which must inevitably destroy the moral life of man.
Michael Polanyi,
Personal Knowledge

Contents

Introduction to the Transaction Edition	xi
Foreword	xliii
Tom Wolfe	
Acknowledgments	lix
Introduction to the Original Edition	3
1 / "America Is a Fascist Country"	15
2 / "America Means Genocide"	41
3 / "The Bomber Left Is a Moral Force"	57
4 / "The American Worker Is a 'Honky' "	81
5 / "Our Political System Is a Fraud"	101
6 / "American Values Are Materialistic"	119
7 / "America Is Insane"	137
8 / "The American People Are Guilty"	155
9 / "America Needs a Violent Revolution"	169
Reply to James A. Wechsler	217
Epilogue	231
Notes	233
Selected Bibliography	287
Name Index	297
Subject Index	305

Introduction to the
Transaction Edition

WHEN I published this book in the early 1970s, the enemy target for most of the people I wrote about was the United States. As Sidney Hook put it, "the disillusioned fellow-traveling American intellectuals have bequeathed anti-Americanism rather than pro-communism to the contemporary generation of disaffected intellectuals."[1] A virulent anti-Americanism was in the air.[2] Twenty years later, the enemy target for these intellectuals and their epigones had become Western civilization itself.[3] And by condemning Western civilization, they are renouncing its three fundamental concepts:

>1. the idea that there is such a thing as objective truth;
>2. that there is meaning to the Judeo-Christian tradition;
>3. that there is meaning to traditional moral precepts and traditional moral laws.

At precisely the time when we celebrate or should be celebrating the decomposition of the Soviet empire, of the communist-socialist ideology and the rebirth of freedom in Europe's eastern half, the lies about Western civilization by the radical egalitarians are so widespread that they have become—for the time being at least—an inseparable part of the culture of Western societies. Many intellectuals reject the core of Western values—democratic freedoms—but do not hesitate to exploit those very freedoms to further their own causes. Nevertheless, the focus of their enmity and their mythomania is still the United States. Virulent anti-Americanism is still in the air.[4]

"Whence comes this fierce hatred of intellectuals," asks Jean-Francois Revel, "for the least barbaric societies of human history and this rage to destroy the only civilizations to date that have emphatically conferred a dominant role on intelligence?"[5] Perhaps the answer can be found in the words of Michael Polanyi: "The propagandistic appeal of Marxism is the most interesting case of (what might be called) the moral force of immorality."[6]

Let me be quite clear what I include under Western civilization. Not only the Great Books, the works of philosophers, from the pre-Socratics to post-Wittgenstein; historians, novelists and playwrights, ancient and modern; scientists, physical and social; composers and musicians; sports and cuisine but also the idea of civility, the idea of freedom and above all, the idea of the rule of law.

I also include—dare I speak its name?—what Marx and Engels in the *Communist Manifesto* saw as a prerequisite to the rising of the proletariat—capitalism, that organized chaos that Kenneth Minogue once defined somewhere as what people do if you leave them alone.[7] And today we could add that it is what most people who once lived under socialism want to do for themselves.

In speaking the name, "capitalism," I am guided by something Milton Friedman once said:

> We must make people understand that the basic idea of a free society is fundamentally a humane idea. It is fundamentally the idea that people as individuals have responsibility to themselves and to one another, that those responsibilities cannot be met by turning them over to somebody else, by electing a governmental official who will take money out of your pocket in order to spend it on supposedly good objectives. . . . In spreading that basic philosophy we must go to the core of our culture, where the values and beliefs that shape our actions are formed.[8]

The peoples of the world want to emigrate to those places where Western civilization rules. They understand something which Hilaire Belloc summed up in one sentence: "The control of the production of wealth is the control of human life itself."[9] The victims of socialism, militarism a la Haiti, gulagism and the Tiananmen Squares of this world walk, ride, drive, crawl, swim, fly, hijack, in short they risk life and limb to desert a world they abominate for the world abominated by the radical egalitarians. As Lewis Feuer has written,

> To the extent that a free marketplace exists in the international system, it is American culture and the American language that are accepted as closest to the world's common culture. From Moscow to Beijing, from Johannesburg to Tokyo, it is the example of American institutions that is, consciously and unconsciously, re-shaping the world. . . . Those who, in a gesture of secession from American civilization, advocate multiculturalism on American campuses are the latest example of a malady that periodically seems to affect American academic intellectuals.[10]

For those people who flock to the West, these target lands may be denominated by America-hating intellectuals as racist, anti-foreign, anti-immigrant, anti-black, anti-brown, anti-Asian, anti-Arab, anti-African, anti-everything—yet the migrants still come or want to come to the West legally or illegally. Better to sleep on a tenement staircase in Hong Kong where there is hope than in a communal hovel in socialist Vietnam where there is none.[11]

Looking back to the 1950s, how ridiculous are the writings of Western intellectuals for whom capitalist democracies had been delegitimized and for whom the future was collectivism. Here is A.J.P. Taylor, the British historian, assuring his British audience over the BBC:

Nobody in Europe believes in the American way of life—that is, in private enterprise. Or rather, those who believe in it are a defeated party, and a party which seems to have no more future than the Jacobites in England after 1688.[12]

But for the present-day radical egalitarians (the phrase is Professor Aaron Wildavsky's), Western civilization means capitalism, capitalists and economic opportunity.[13] In the cracked camera eye of Hollywood and French filmmakers (all of them financed by the "class enemy," the bankers), the capitalist is the polluter of land, sea, and air, a junk bond salesman, a greedy yuppie, purveyor of poisoned foods and malignant medicines, imperialist exploiter of peasants in faraway lands, incipient fascist if not already a fascist, racist, rapist, male chauvinist pig, corporate raider, nuclear power fanatic, creator of the greenhouse effect and the warming universe and if we were to believe the Hollywood ideology, the assassin of John F. Kennedy.

No accusation against capitalism is too foul for movie or television scripts. But the radical egalitarians now direct their fire at Western civilization itself, its glories, its humaneness, its monuments, yes, even at the wars against the enemies of democratic capitalism. Saddam Hussein had no greater friend and ally than the radical egalitarians who populate the powerful American university establishment.

In the 1960s and later, there grew up in the arts a new modernism, the cult of the "anti"—the anti-novel, the anti-drama, the anti-theater, the anti-hero, even anti-politics, anti-memoirs and anti-history. The common denominator of the "anti" movement was a passion to destroy or at least to fragment, democratic culture, to disintegrate consensual values and traditions through a new faith, a new conformity. The cry of the anti-movement was that all doctrines, dogmas, credos are created equal but some are more equal than others. The ultimate aim of this movement, which has reached its efflorescence on the American campus, is to make democratic political systems appear absurd and inhuman even "counter-revolutionary."

And why this hatred of America and Western civilization? Because so long as the Western democracies prosper while authoritarian and totalitarian regimes founder, socialism, statism, collectivism cannot be rationally presented as the alternative to democratic capitalism. So long as the free market democracies reward entrepreneurship, invention, and innovation, so long as consumer societies exist only in non-Marxist countries, anti-Westernism will be the staple of the intellectual classes, including those semi-skilled intellectuals who dominate the so-called news reporting on television and who govern the Hollywood ideology.

Richard Hofstadter's description of the politics of the American university faculty in 1963 is even more accurate today:

> At least from the Progressive era onward, the political commitment of the majority of the intellectual leadership in the United States has been to causes that might be variously described as liberal (in the American use of that word), progressive, or radical. . . . I am not denying that we have a number of conservative intellectuals . . . but if there is anything that could be called an intellectual establishment in America, this establishment has been . . . on the left side of center.[14]

The radical egalitarians are to be found everywhere in the non-socialist world. Octavio Paz, winner of the 1990 Nobel Prize in literature, told an interviewer:

> If there is one profoundly reactionary sector in Latin America, it is the leftist intellectuals. They are a people without memory. I have never heard one of them admit he made a mistake. Marxism has become an intellectual vice. It is the superstition of the entire century.[15]

When I wrote this book, Soviet Communism was in the ascendant. This book is being republished some twenty years later when the era of Communism and its imperialist victories has come to a close. What is so startling is that the lies that were being told about the United Stats in the 1970s are still being told in the 1990s but now the lies are also about the history and the character of Western civilization itself. Even more startling is the greater power which the radical egalitarians, who were once the 1960s Left, have amassed. The 1960s Left, riding high in the 1990s, has made affirmative action and PC behavior the operating mechanism of the American university. What was once regarded as the university's sine qua non—academic excellence—is fading away. As Theodore Draper has written,

> Faced with the choice of career after the rigor mortis of the New Left, many of its former activists and sympathizers chose to get advanced degrees and ascend the academic ladder to professorships in the universities. By now a good many have gained tenure and many more are on their way. The New Left is dead, and yet it is very much alive in the very places where it was born.[16]

Mr. Draper has also pointed out that "self-styled Marxist academics are now active in virtually every discipline, especially in the social sciences." These academics, which he estimated numbered about 12,000, represent "the largest and most important cohort of left-wing scholars in American history."[17] These are "guerrillas with tenure," in Irving Howe's phrase.

Professor Kenneth S. Lynn has said that the veterans of hundreds of campus demonstrations had entered the university and "have begun to take over the colleges and universities by more subtle means than they formerly employed. In the field of history, for example, Marxism is by all odds the most fashionable mode of analysis among teachers of European history, while in American history, more and more of

Introduction to the Transaction Edition / xvii

the current scholarship is consecrated to the expression of contempt for the achievements of our civilization."[18]

Powerful and militant interest groups which were just being born in the 1970s now dominate American institutions—universities, churches, foundations, television news desks, the Democratic Party, trade unions, PBS—to an unheard of degree.[19] A word of warning or a cry of protest from gays, blacks, Hispanics, or feminists and any possible resistance among so-called ruling elites crumbles.[20] What happened to academic excellence? It has been replaced by "political correctness," or PC.[21] It has been replaced by multicultural charlatanism as in Portland, Oregon schools where children are taught that the ancient Egyptians could predict lucky and unlucky days with the help of "astropsychological treatises."[22] This kind of myth-making posing as social science has reached into our most prestigious universities, especially Stanford University in California.[23] As Emeritus Classics Professor Frank Snowden of Howard University put it:

> Many students already have been misled and confused by Afrocentrists' inaccuracies and omission in their treatment of blacks in the ancient Mediterranean world. The time has come for Afrocentrists to cease mythologizing and falsifying the past. The time has come for scholars and educators to insist upon scholarly rigor and truth in current and projected revisions of our curriculum. *Tempus fugit!*[24]

Professor Harvey Mansfield, Jr. recently described the present situation:

> [I]n American universities now . . . the evil is politicization, an ugly word for deliberate, organized bias . . . professors regarded as reactionary are isolated, their views dismissed disrespectfully, and their students out of academia. So far the evil is concentrated in the humanities but it is also felt

very strongly in the social sciences . . . politicization comes from the Left . . . the present assault on the universities comes from within."[25]

The PC movement on the American campus has threatened basic constitutional rights of non-conformist, anti-PC students and faculties. With fine irony Professor John Hart Ely, former dean of the Stanford University Law School wrote about Stanford campus attacks on the First and Fifth Amendments:

> Why not have done with it, and declare at one stroke that Stanford cannot live with the instability that necessarily accompanies *any* of the protections of the Bill of Rights? By our example we might even trigger a nationwide move for a complete abolition of that troublesome document.[26]

The radical egalitarians speak with a candor which demonstrates a sense of confidence in their academic power. No conservative or liberal would dare speak as did Professor Andrew Ross, 34, of Princeton who teaches courses on American popular culture:

> I teach in the Ivy League in order to have direct access to the minds of the children of the ruling classes.[27]

Or we have it from Professor Richard Ohmann who in a book published a few years ago disclosed the answer to something that had puzzled him: Why did society pay English teachers such good salaries to teach literature? Because thereby, he wrote, society could "insure the harmlessness of all culture; to make it serve and preserve the status quo." Professor Ohmann continues:

> We should understand what we are up against: not tests that are arbitrary, but a class society that requires such tests. No attack on these rites of

Introduction to the Transaction Edition / xix

passage can be finally successful, unless it overturns bourgeois culture, itself, and the rule of our dominant classes.[28]

What documentation for Roger Kimball's thesis:

The truth is that when the children of the sixties received their professorships and deanships they did not abandon the dream of radical cultural transformation; they set out to implement it. Now, instead of disrupting classes, they are teaching them; instead of attempting to destroy our educational institutions physically, they are subverting them from within. Thus it is that what were once the political and educational ambitions of educational renegades appear as ideals on the agenda of the powers that be. Effort to dismantle the traditional curriculum and institutionalize radical feminism . . . now typically issue from the dean's office or Faculty Senate, not from students marching in the streets."[29]

And what are some of the issues which Professor Ross might be dealing with as he exploits his "direct access to the minds of the children of the ruling classes"? Drinking, drugs, date rape, AIDS, homosexuality, government subsidies for erotic art, prayer in the schools, sexual harassment, abortion, campus speech codes, rap, evolution and creationism, condoms for adolescents. And that intellectual fraud called "multiculturalism and ethnicity." Or cultural diversity.[30]

Sidney Hook has documented that the Communist Party demanded of members who taught in universities or in public schools

to indoctrinate in classrooms, enroll students wherever possible in Communist youth organizations, rewrite textbooks from the Communist point of view, build cells within the teaching staff of colleges and universities, gain control of departments, and inculcate the Communist line that in case of imperialist war, especially if the United States was at war with the Soviet Union, students should turn their arms against their own government.[31]

Remove the word "Communist" from the list of duties and discipline which Party members once accepted and then ask whether or not we see a new "Party" discipline and "Party" duties at work in American universities. Says Hook,

> The members of the New Left make no pretense of objective teaching, sometimes asserting that the very concept of objective truth is a pretense. Far from denying that they engage in indoctrination in their classrooms, they make a virtue of it. They declare that all teaching is indoctrination, and contend that the only significant distinction that can be drawn is between good indoctrination for a classless society and bad indoctrination for American class society.[32]

Onetime Harvard President Derek Bok defined the problem of indoctrination as occurring not when the instructor disclosed his ethical values. Rather, he said, "The critical line is crossed only when a teacher attempts to force his values on his students by refusing to entertain contrary arguments or by using his power as grader and discussion leader to coerce students into accepting his views."[33] Somewhere in *The Education of Henry Adams* is the memorable sentence, "A teacher affects eternity; he can never tell where his influence stops."

The radical egalitarian *kulturkampf* is also going on in Canada where university professors have been threatened for uttering opinions that are interpreted by campus thought police as politically "incorrect." Traditional cultural values are the target of attack and, in accordance with the doctrines of deconstructionism, there are no truths, only rival interpretations.[34]

*   *   *

When I talk about the radical egalitarians, I am not talking about some fringe group of earringed, beaded sandal wearers. I am talking about administrators, departmental chairs, deans, university presidents, as well as teachers, who have accepted affirmative action in hiring, firing, promoting and grading; who have promulgated speech codes which make a mockery of the First Amendment. The damnable thing about all this is that everyone knows what is going on and yet, with a few honorable exceptions, such as President Benno Schmidt and Dean Donald Kagan of Yale University, the men and women who now run the universities and know what is happening might repeat with Hamlet:

> But I am pigeon-livered, and lack gall to make oppression bitter.

Let me recount here a shocking event at the University of Massachusetts in Amherst, a state institution. In the 1990-91 academic year the University's non-discrimination policy outlawed "discrimination on the basis of race, color, religion, creed, sex, age, marital status, national origin, disability or handicap, veteran status, or sexual orientation, which shall not include persons whose sexual orientation includes minor children as the sex object." In the 1991-92 statement the last fifteen words were deleted. Asked George Will, "Is pedophilia becoming a civil right?"[35]

Resistance to this war against Western civilization and this tide of unconstitutional repression has been undertaken by the National Association of Scholars based in Princeton, New Jersey. The NAS Research Director, Glenn Ricketts, told an interviewer, "The politically correct people want to change the entire curriculum. Race and gender have to be integral to every subject. The movement is sinister because of its flat-out totalitarianism."[36]

One of the short-lived achievements of the radical egalitarians and their followers had been their successful creation of a moral equivalence between the United States and the once Soviet Union; the idea that there was a moral symmetry between the two countries with regard to methods and policies. In other words, what the United States does is unforgivable; what the ex-USSR or any other totalitarian socialist regime does is understandable.[37] Unfortunately for the purveyors of this moral equivalence myth, the disintegration of the Soviet Union has made it a difficult thesis to pursue, especially as Soviet archives have been made public revealing even such items as that Moscow supplied hard cash to the Communist Party, U.S.A. to the tune of $2 million a year.[38]

You don't have to be a radical egalitarian to denigrate the United States and its meaning in the world today. I recently reviewed rather critically in the *Wall Street Journal* a book by William Pfaff, sometime foreign affairs contributor to the *New Yorker* magazine, syndicated columnist and longtime Paris expatriate.[39]

Mr. Pfaff is master of the Grand Cosmic Sweep, a literary device intended to validate lordly pronouncements about American foreign policy and the American character so that they sound like facts. His real focus is on a passionate indictment of America abroad, forgetful of Aristotle's pronouncement that the essence of political tragedy is to make the perfect the enemy of the good.

Mr. Pfaff seems irritated that the United States "remains an economically and socially divided nation." But what country isn't? There are some 160 countries in the world. How does the United States compare to economic and socially divided Canada, Spain, Sri Lanka, Lebanon, Yugoslavia, China, Czechoslovakia, India? Is there a modern industrial democracy which is not economically and socially divided? Mr. Pfaff talks about "the capacity of Americans for forgetting the past or acting as if the past has no relevance ... " What evidence can there be for so metaphysical a statement? How do we compare with other countries as to their capacity for forgetting the past?

"We recoil from acknowledging," says Mr. Pfaff, "the complexities and perversities of history's workings, since to do so would threaten the optimism that has been indispensable to the development of the United States itself."

Who is this recoiling "we"? For Tom Wolfe this is the "me generation." Perhaps, next time round, Mr. Wolfe could deal with the "we generation," an attribute of the modern intellectual. For it is a peculiarity of liberal journalism and high culture that whenever an American intellectual begins a sentence with the pronoun "we" or "our" and the subsequent sentences are highly derogatory to the pronominal antecedent, the intellectual absolves himself and his audience from any of the psychopathological symptoms he is ascribing to the American electorate. In our egalitarian era, the intellectual "we" has replaced the royal "we." I deal with the "we" problem in my text.

What disturbs Mr. Pfaff is the national "obsession with the ideological conflict with Communism." And that's another symptom of the "we generation," adopting reductive nomenclature to denigrate other people's political sentiments or activities. The psychopathic term "obsession" and anti-communism are inseparably linked in the vocabulary of modern liberalism. However, you can never have an "obsession" with "apartheidism," "fascism," "feminism," "militarism," "affirmative action," "povertyism," or "racism."[40]

How silly Mr. Pfaff sounds in the light of the fall of communism and the hatred everywhere of its partner, socialism. As we stare at the Soviet Ozymandias, I wonder whether Mr. Pfaff would fault the Soviet peoples for their "obsession" about Communism. And is it possible that the United States "obsession" with Communism had something to do with its collapse?

While Europeans believe in democracy, says Mr. Pfaff, "they have considered the alternatives and that scandalizes Americans." Assuming that "we" were scandalized, why shouldn't we have been scandalized? Tragically for world peace, Europeans in this century "considered" absolutism, anti-semitism, civil war, class war, clericalism, colonialism, communism, fascism, falangism, feudalism, militarism, monarchy, nazism, socialism, united frontism, as alternatives to democracy. Bismarck once said that fools learn from their mistakes, wise men learn from other people's mistakes.

Mr. Pfaff is particularly concerned at what he calls "the futility of interventions meant to dominate or check long-term historical forces of the kind at work in Vietnam and Afghanistan, and evident amid the uproar of the Middle East, the Persian Gulf, and Latin America." In his Grand Cosmic Sweep elocution, Mr. Pfaff ignores or scants the unfutile U.S. interventions during the civil war in Greece, in South Korea, the Dominican Republic, the Cuban missile crisis, Grenada, and, of course, that great interventionist machine, the North Atlantic Treaty Organization. Should the United States have allowed these putative "long-term historical forces" to have ravaged totalitarian-threatened countries or areas? Should we not have sent Stingers to the Afghan mujaheddin?

Whenever a liberal intellectual calls up the fatalist metaphor, "long-term historical forces," (the favorite cant phrase of Marxism a.k.a. "Historical Necessity") he usually means Marxist forces. Somoza, Noriega, Pinochet, Franco, Salazar were never granted the halo of "long-term historical forces" no matter how long they were in power. When applied to socialist revolutionaries, the phrase, "long-term historical forces" legitimizes socialist tyranny. Batista didn't represent "long-term historical forces." For Mr. Pfaff, Castro does. In fact, Mr. Pfaff quotes I would say approvingly an anonymous "Vatican diplomat" that Castro "from the ethical point of view, is a Christian." Senor Valladares, are you listening?

You would think that after such cosmic failures as the death of socialism, the razing of the Berlin Wall and the disintegration of the Soviet state, there would be some modesty among the new generation of radical egalitarians. After all, several members of the socialism-can-do-no-wrong school like John Kenneth Galbraith and Robert Heilbroner whom I deal with in my book seem to have recanted. Whether Professor Galbraith has modified his attacks on what he regarded as vulgar affluence, a putative concomitant of capitalism, is unknown. Nor is it known at this writing whether he still believes, as he once did, that democratic capitalism and Communist totalitarianism are converging.

The Galbraith-Heilbroner recantations reminded me of Peter Arno's celebrated full-page *New Yorker* cartoon showing a smoldering airplane which has just crashed head-first into the ground. Bystanders, including some irate generals, are looking on in horror at the pyre. And in the foreground walking away is a middle-aged man with what appears to be a set of rolled-up blueprints under his arm. Implied by the cartoon is that the man, a half-abashed grin on his face, designed the failed airplane and he is saying, "Well, back to the old drawing-board."

The memory of that cartoon came back to me as I read a news report in a college paper about a lecture by Emeritus Professor John Kenneth Galbraith of Harvard University delivered at his alma mater, the University of California, Berkeley. Mr. Galbraith is, of course, one of the most widely-known left-liberal economists in the world and has published a series, for the most part, of anti-capitalist sermons posing as economics. The lead paragraph of the *Daily Californian* story, read as follows:

> John Kenneth Galbraith, a UC Berkeley alumnus and fervent proponent of mixing socialism into a market economy, praised capitalism in a speech on campus yesterday night.[41]

Events in Eastern Europe and India, he said, had taught him that the economy he had once urged on India—a mix of socialism and capitalism—was now "economically and politically questionable." That's his phrase in quotes. (Mr. Galbraith was once ambassador to India.)

"It is a retreat, in fact, to Marx and Engels," said Mr. Galbraith. "They were adamant: Before there can be socialism, there must be the socializing influence of capitalism."

Mr. Galbraith's defection is fairly recent since it was only a few years ago that he said in a 1984 *New Yorker* article that the Soviet economy was making "great material progress." His evidence: "One sees it in the appearance of solid well-being of the people on the streets, the close to murderous traffic, the incredible exfoliation of apartment houses." The secret of such achievements: "Partly, the Russian system succeeds because, in contrast with the Western industrial economies, it makes full use of its manpower."

How anybody could have written this fellow-traveling schlock—in 1984!—when any intelligent economist knew that the day of reckoning for the Soviet economy was at hand, is really amazing. But he wasn't the only one whose scholarly methodology collapsed before the socialist illusion.

Paul Samuelson, the 1970 Nobel Prize winner in economics, and author of one of the most widely used economics textbooks in the United States was also infatuated with the Bolshevik Revolution. He wrote in the tenth edition of his textbook: "It is a vulgar mistake to think that most people in Eastern Europe are miserable." In the eleventh edition, he took out the word "vulgar." In the 1985 twelfth edition, that entire passage had disappeared. Instead, he and his co-author, William Nordhaus, substituted a sentence asking whether Soviet political repression was "worth the economic gains." This non-question Samuelson and Co. identified as "one of the most profound dilemmas of human society." To Professor Samuelson this was still a dilemma after seventy years of Lenin, Stalin, Mao, Castro, Ho Chi Minh and Pol Pot.

How could an otherwise great economist parrot idiotic Marxist propaganda? At a time when even Gorbachev was beginning to hint at the magnitude of the Soviet economic disaster, the 1985 Samuelson text said in a burst of moral symmetry:

"But it would be misleading to dwell on the shortcomings. Every economy has its contradictions and difficulties with incentives—witness the paradoxes raised by the separation of ownership and control in America. . . . What counts is results, and there can be no doubt that the Soviet planning system has been a powerful engine for economic growth."[42]

In his lecture, Mr. Galbraith criticized centrally controlled economies because they demand, he said, "trained, competent, committed and scrupulously honest administrative talent . . . an especially scarce resource."

So after decades and decades of selling socialism and centrally controlled economies as the sovereign cure for all our ills, Mr. Galbraith like another socialist before him, Robert Heilbroner, has made the great discovery, capitalism is not an absolute moral evil and socialism is not an absolute moral good. Will they then honor Hayek, von Mises, Friedman for their foresight decades and decades ago in challenging socialism for precisely the reason that Mr. Galbraith now finds socialism wanting?

As for Mr. Heilbroner, a few years ago he wrote an article titled "The Triumph of Capitalism." It began with these portentous words:

> Less than seventy-five years after it officially began, the contest between capitalism and socialism is over: capitalism has won. The Soviet Union, China and Eastern Europe have given us the clearest possible proof that capitalism organizes the material affairs of humankind more satisfactorily than socialism.[43]

Compare these statements by Messrs. Galbraith and Heilbroner with what they were writing in the ate 1960s and 1970s as I show in the text of my book. But in the end the socialist myths could still triumph, even as the Soviet Union lies in ruins, thanks to what Jean-Francois Revel calls "ideological afterglow."[44] For as Friedrich A. Hayek has written,

> If few people in the Western world now want to remake society from the bottom according to some ideal blueprint, a great many still believe in measures which, though not designed completely to remodel the economy, in their aggregate effect may well unintentionally produce this result.[45]

One of the more surprising manifestations of Revel's "ideological afterglow" is the Reuter report of some remarks made over French television in 1991 by the Prince of Wales that we ought not "consider this collapse of an ideology as the death of communism and the triumph of capitalism." And, ah yes, the old moral equivalence, capitalist societies had their faults, said Prince Charles, and that we ought "develop our perceptions of life [as an] equilibrium between the two ideologies."[46]

Taking issue with Prince Charles, Robert Conquest writes:

> He did indeed say that we "needed" capitalism, but that it should have a "more human face"; what he seems to have implied is that the socialist idea would provide the necessary humanity, and that the idea was somehow involved in the Soviet experience.[47]

It could be argued that the Samuelson-Galbraith failures in analyzing trends in the Soviet socioeconomic system might be understandable since they are not Sovietologists. But what of the Sovietologists themselves; how did they fare as experts on the Soviet Union? Terribly. A large number of American intellectuals, academic for the most part, devoted their writing and scholarly careers to proving "scientifically" that Marxism-Leninism was a viable system and that capitalism was not.

Never before have so many academics been proven abysmally wrong in virtually everything they wrote about Marxism-Leninism and the Soviet Union. In excoriating these Sovietologists, Zbigniew Brzezinski wrote:

> The whole concept of totalitarianism was under great intellectual assault. . . . Instead, the contemporary Soviet Union was actually described by scholars as governed in a manner not fundamentally different from democracies of the West.

Later some specialists even waxed enthusiastic on the reform introduced by Brezhnev.[48]

As an example of this left-revisionist betrayal of scholarship, Robert Conquest cites from the writings of Professor Jerry Hough, the dean of revisionism one might say, a passage in which Professor Hough argued that there was no famine since no one died of hunger in those pre-penicillin days, they merely contracted diseases when they were weakened.[49]

The Sovietology "left" made sharp attacks, now proven by the collapse of the Soviet empire to have been utterly unfounded against distinguished scholars like Richard Pipes, Robert Tucker, Sidney Hook, and, of course, Conquest and Brzezinski, specialists whose researches and publications about the Soviet Union and the People's Republic of China have been proven correct in virtually every particular.

There were people in the 1970s who argued that the widespread intellectual disaffection which I was writing about would quickly subside with the ending of the Vietnam war. The argument had a plausible ring. But it was not the case.

If the Vietnam war was the problem, well, it's been over for almost a score of years. The world has learned of the terrifying price which the peoples of the Soviet Union and Eastern Europe, who lived under socialism, have paid. Those in mainland China, North Korea and Southeast Asia are still paying that price. In the light of these appalling revelations, what do we hear? Here is a typical post-Cold War statement by a socialist, Philip Gasper of the left Guardian who argues that it is wrong to see the collapse of Stalinism as somehow a setback for the Left." Why? Because, he says, analysts on the Left fail to realize that "the society that Stalin built on the ruins of the Bolshevik Revolution was simply a variant of capitalism . . ." As in the West "a tiny minority controlled the economy, exploiting the mass of the population with the aim of accumulating capital." He is merely parroting the words of Mikhail S. Gorbachev.[50]

The widely accepted myth by impenitent socialists that it's all Stalin's fault is untenable. If the Stalinist model was so bad, if it was such a betrayal of true socialism, why did so many liberals and fellow-travellers of the left support Stalin and Stalinism? Why were anti-communists denounced as "red-baiters" for attacking communism? The left for the most part defended Stalin's socialism, high-mindedly agreeing that while that kind of socialism might oh! yes, appear aberrational, still Stalin, Khrushchev, Andropov were on the right track. All rather reminiscent of Leon Trotsky, Stalin's opponent, who supported Stalin's invasion of Finland during World War II because the USSR was a "proletarian" state.

Another example of unrepentant socialism is Paul Berman, who wrote an article for the *New York Times Magazine* with an editor's subtitle reading, "Despite recent events, the author argues, there remains a place for the ideals of socialism ... There is more socialism in the United States today than there was in the Soviet Union—that is, more power for ordinary people."[51] So why don't left-liberals and radical egalitarians admire the United States as a paragon of political virtue and stop reviling the United States as the epitome of capitalist greed and inhumanity?[52]

The greatest lament, of course, comes from a Communist academic like Michael Parenti: "Instead of critical analyses of capitalism and imperialism, many Soviet intellectuals are now wholeheartedly embracing bourgeois Western scholarship . . . they find excitement in the previously forbidden fruit of Western bourgeois orthodoxies."[53]

In one case, democracy's triumph in Eastern Europe is seen as a setback by one American journalist, Tamara Jones, who clearly thinks it was so much better when East Germany was ruled by Erich Honecker. She mourned the passing of East Germany in these remarkable words:

> Ten months after the new Germany merged, women in the eastern sector are coming to the

stunning realization that, in many ways, democracy has set them back 40 years.[54]

One final example of *furor socialismus*. In a recent book, a British hemi-demi-semi-Marxist, has found a new role for socialism. The author, Fred Inglis, writes: "Socialism, however disfigured by the cold war, is still the only rhetoric left with which to berate the delusions and cruelty of horrible capitalism." For him Marx still lives because Marx, among others, "diagnosed the viciousness of unbridled capitalism, the oppression and exploitation to which it inevitably gives rise, and the repellent class arrogance created in its successful bourgeoisie."[55] As Saul Bellow once said: "A great deal of intelligence can be invested in ignorance when the need for illusion is great."

I'm afraid there is no simple answer to the publicly declared war against Western civilization by Western intellectuals, concentrated primarily in American universities. And it is a war which has resonance. Meg Greenfield, the *Washington Post* editorial page editor, has written:

> A Martian reading about it [the U.S. as depicted in the U.S. media] might in fact suppose America to be composed entirely of abused minorities living in squalid and sadistically run mental hospitals, except for a small elite of venal businessmen and county commissioners who are profiting from the unfortunates' misery.[56]

I take solace in something Thomas Jefferson once said:

> It is rare that the public sentiment decides immorally or unwisely, and the individual who differs from it ought to distrust and examine well his own opinion.[57]

We cannot expect that the radical egalitarians will distrust and re-examine their opinions. As Midge Decter has said, "Being Left, means never having to say you're sorry."

But we can hope that public sentiment will remain stable and friendly to the liberties which have made the United States the wonderful country it is because we are a country unique.

What makes the United States unique is not its military power nor its huge economy, nor its vast domestic market, nor its technology. What differentiates the United States from virtually all other countries is that there is no large-scale territorial movement whose sponsors seek to secede from the country and to establish a new nation.

There is no Free Alaska movement. There is no Free Texas movement. There is no Free Any Movement except perhaps for Puerto Rico whose population, however, has voted to remain in the U.S. Did the Civil War a century ago settle the question of secession forever?

Here we are entering the twenty-first century and the cries for separatism, irredentism, secession, autonomy, independence, sovereignty, rectification of borders are heard everywhere, especially in Europe. And the cries are accompanied by gunfire and war—Serbia and Croatia, Indonesia against Acheh and East Timor, the civil war in the Republic of Georgia, Iran's war by assassination, Iraq against the Kurds.

But the cry for self-determination is heard not only in what was the Soviet Union but also in other parts of the world. The Irish Republican Army would free Northern Ireland from the British, the Scots seek a separate regime from the United Kingdom, the Basques want freedom from Spain, Quebec from Canada, Chad versus Libya, Tamils against Sri Landa, Sikhs against India, the Kurds against Iraq, Turkey and Iran, Tibet versus Communist China, Israel versus Arabdom. I'm sure I've omitted other serious inter-ethnic conflicts looming or already in being.

(Yet why is Japan, like the United States, spared from separatist movements? If there is an explanation for this phenomenon it cannot be because Japan's population mix is homogeneous anymore than it can be because our population mix is heterogeneous, that we are a nation of immigrants while Japan is not. Is it because we, like the Japanese, the

Germans and the French are blessed by a dominant single language which precludes linguistic nationalism? For the moment at least, France and Germany are free of loud cries of separatism.) One thing seems apparent—the American model of interethnic solutions, a miraculous combination of democracy and nationalism—imperfect as it is, will not satisfy the surging nationalist emotions to be observed on almost every continent of the world. Why, then, the hatred among the radical egalitarians for the United States, the hatred for Western cultures?

Perhaps here I could cite Joseph Brodsky, Russian exile, now an American citizen and our poet-laureate, who says American democracy is the best political system in the world:

> It has its ills and evils but they appear to be organic in nature, not ideological evils. And sometimes people chance upon something that works and to my eye, to say the least, this system here works. It doesn't make everyone happy, but there is no blueprint for happiness.[58]

Arnold Beichman

Notes

1. Sidney Hook, "Communism and the American Intellectuals: From the Thirties to the Eighties," *Free Inquiry* (Fall 1981), p. 15.
2. Leonard Schapiro defined anti-Americanism as " ... the cement by which the communist movement is held together, now that the unity of doctrine and disciplined allegiance to Moscow have been eroded as a consequence of the Sino-Soviet split." Statement before Subcommittee on National Security and International Operations (April 16 1970), 91st Congress.

(Washington, D.C.: Government Printing Office, 1970), p. 34.
3. Irving Kristol sees an "anti-biblical barbarism" in America as the formidable challenge to Christianity, Judaism and Western civilization. "The Future of American Jewry," Commentary 92:2 (August 1991), p. 26.
4. The once witty and urbane *New Yorker* magazine, recently wrote: "Having, as we believe, turned Europe into a danger zone, we now shun the place, leaving the Europeans to pay whatever price is paid: (9 June 1986). It is "we" who have "turned Europe into a danger zone". Not the PLO or Qadaffi gunmen, with their Rome and Vienna airport massacres, or the bombing of the West Berlin discotheque, the murder on the Achille Lauro? And is Europe today a "danger zone"? The magazine's anti-Americanism never changes. In 1949 one of its casuals opened thus: "A document describing the Russian system of exile and forced labor has been produced by the British government and is to be placed before the United Nations." It then pointed to what it called the growth of "a group of American political prisoners [who] are being marched steadily, imperceptibly, toward the queer Siberia of our temperate zone." *New Yorker* (6 August 1949). And this startling revelation, mind you, was made even before Joe McCarthy began his crusade!
5. Jean-Francois Revel, *The Flight from Truth: The Reign of Deceit in the Age of Information* (New York: Random House, 1992).
6. Michael Polanyi, *Personal Knowledge*, p. 227. H.B. Acton has made the point that "The Marxist can derive moral precepts from his social science only to the extent that they already form, because of the vocabulary used, a concealed and unacknowledged part of it." *The Illusion of an Epoch* (Beacon Press, 1957), p. 231.
7. Marx and Engels were full of praise for the achievements of bourgeois capitalism. But they weren't the only revolutionaries to appreciate those achievements.

Stalin himself wrote: "American efficiency is that indomitable force which neither knows nor recognizes obstacles; which with its businesslike perseverance brushes aside obstacles; which continues on a task once started until it is finished, even if it is a minor task; and without which serious constructive work is inconceivable." Quoted in Anders Stephanson, *Kennan and the Art of Foreign Policy* (Harvard University Press, 1989), p. 279.
8. Milton Friedman, excerpt from a lecture at the Heritage Foundation, 14 May, 1980. Mimeo.
9. Quoted in F.A. Hayek, *The Road to Serfdom* (University of Chicago Press, 1976), p. 88.
10. Lewis S. Feuer, "From Pluralism to Multiculturalism," *Society* 29:1 (November/December 1991), p. 18.
11. Or as Milovan Djilas wrote in 1983: "The Western system now, as it is, is a better system. I say this openly, not because I am a partisan for capitalism; I'm not. But this system in the West is better. It is more human. In the West you have everything you have in the East and you have something more. Political freedoms and greater possibilities. In every way it is better." *Encounter* (October 1983), p. 28.
12. Quoted by Owen Harries, "Communism, the Cold War and the Intellectuals: A Post Mortem" in *Commentary* 92:4 (October 1991), p. 14.
13. See Aaron Wildavsky, "The Rise of Radical Egalitarianism and the Fall of Academic Standards," *Academic Questions* 2:4 (Fall 1989), pp. 52ff. Also, Wildavsky, "Has Modernity Killed Objectivity?" 29:1 *Society* (November/December 1991). Nat Hentoff calls the radical egalitarians "the new Jacobins." See his article with the same name in *Reason* (November 1991), p. 31. His theme is embodied in the article's question: "Will the terror of political correctness spread from the campus to the `real world'?"
14. Richard Hofstadter, *Anti-Intellectualism in American Life* (Knopf, 1963), p. 39.

15. Alan Riding, *New York Times* (3 May 1979), "For Octavio Paz, A Solitude of His Own, as a Political Rebel."
16. Theodore Draper, "The Class Struggle," *New Republic* (26 January 1987), p. 29. Mr. Draper's article deals with a more recent myth, that the professors who were at one time Communist Party members were political innocents, that they were not following the Party line, rather the Party line was following them. His important article is a critical essay-review of a book, *No Ivory Tower* by a prominent left historian, Ellen Schrecker, which seeks to whitewash the Communist academics. An equally important essay-review of this book is by Sidney Hook, "Communists, McCarthy and American Universities," *Minerva* 25:3 (August 1987), pp. 331-48.
17. See Mr. Draper's articles in *New York Review*, 9 and 30 May, and 13 August, 1985. The articles are titled "American Communism Revisited," "The Popular Front Revisited," "Revisiting American Communism: An Exchange."
18. Kenneth S. Lynn, "After the Debauch," *American Spectator* (December 1982), p. 14.
19. PBS, which is publicly as well as privately funded, is probably more left-oriented than any major institution in the U.S. As a sample of what goes on in the PBS world, we can examine one week of prime time current affairs programming at KCET, Los Angeles, 1-7 April, 1991: left-liberal productions, 13; conservative productions, zero. *COMINT (Committee on Media Integrity)*, 1:2 (Spring 1991), p. 9.
20. In November 1991, Senator Bob Kerrey (D., Neb.), seeking the Democratic presidential nomination, "was forced to make a fool of himself to appease a powerful constituency in the Democratic coalition, militant homosexuals and lesbians," wrote Bob Tyrrell, editor-in-chief of the *American Spectator*. "So great is their power in the party, and so frivolous are their issues, that they could coerce Mr. Kerrey into a public apology for a private joke that derided Jerry Brown's flakiness,

because, alas, it referred to lesbians making love—an apparently sacred act, to be mentioned by heterosexuals only with the utmost reverence." *Washington Times* (1 December 1991), p. B1.
21. Politically correct professors, writes David Lehman, "acquiescing in the notion that disinterested inquiry is an impossibility and that every value judgment is necessarily a power play before it is anything else, they make their decisions by applying ideological litmus tests." Quoted in the London *Economist* (18 May 1991), p. 95, from Mr. Lehman's book, *Signs of the Times: Deconstruction and the Fall of Paul de Man.*
22. Albert Shanker, "Sacrificing Accuracy for Diversity," *New Republic* (9 December 1991), p. 5. Mr. Shanker is the admirable longtime president of the American Federation of Teachers, AFL-CIO.
23. Isaac D. Barchas, "Stanford After the Fall," *Academic Questions* 3:1 (Winter 1989-90), pp. 24-34.
24. Shanker, "Sacrificing Accuracy."
25. Harvey Mansfield Jr., "The State of Harvard," *Public Interest* (Fall 1990), review of Henry Rosovsky, *The University*, pp. 113-23.
26. In Stanford University *Campus Report* (20 November 1991), p. 4.
27. Quoted in Anne Matthews, "Deciphering Victorian Underwear," *New York Times* Magazine (10 February 1991), pp. 43-58.
28. Richard Ohmann, English in America (Oxford University Press, 1976), quoted in *Times Literary Supplement* (27 August 1976), p. 14.
29. Roger Kimball, *Tenured Radicals: How Politics Has Corrupted Our Higher Education* (Harper & Row, 1990).
30. As Arthur Schlesinger, Jr. has written in *The Disuniting of America*: "'Multiculturalism' arises as a reaction against Anglo or Eurocentrism; but at what point does it pass over into an ethnocentrism of its own? . . . When does obsession with differences begin to threaten the idea of an overarching American national-

ity?" Quoted in *Society* 29:1 (November/December 1991), p. 16.
31. Sidney Hook, "Communists, McCarthy and American Universities," *Minerva* 25:3 (Autumn 1987), p. 342.
32. Hook, *ibid.*, p. 344.
33. Quoted in Arnold Beichman, "Is Higher Education in the Dark Ages?" *New York Times Magazine* (6 November 1983).
34. "The Silencers: A New Wave of Repression is Sweeping Through the Universities," *Macleans's* (27 May 1991), pp. 40ff.
35. George Will, "1991, Wielding a Blackjack," *Newsweek* (30 December 1991), p. 60. In December 1991, Governor William F. Weld of Massachusetts appointed an avowed lesbian to a lifetime $80,000-a-year judicial post. According to the Boston *Herald*, this is the first open lesbian ever nominated to a State judgeship.
36. Glenn Ricketts, *Maclean's* (27 May 1991), p. 44. As of 1991, "more than a hundred universities ha[d] instituted censorship codes which typically outlaw racially and sexually 'stigmatizing' or offensive speech," writes Dinesh D'Souza, "'PC' So Far," *Commentary* 92:4 (October 1991), p. 44. Mr. D'Souza is the author of *Illiberal Education* (Free Press, 1991).
37. See Jeane J. Kirkpatrick, "Moral equivalence and Political Aims," *Society* 22:3 (March/April 1985), pp. 3-8 and her article, "My experience with Academic Intolerance." *Academic Questions* 2:4 (Fall 1989), pp. 21-29 and "Doctrine of Moral Equivalence," U.S. Department of State, Current Policy No. 580, (9 April 1984). Also Michael Novak, "Using 'moral equivalence'" *Washington Times* (31 May 1985), p. 3D.
38. "Party in the U.S. Reportedly Got Soviet Millions," *New York Times* (1 December 1991), p. 7 (national edition).
39. William Pfaff, *Barbarian Sentiments: How the American Century Ends.* (Hill and Wang 1989), passim.
40. According to Jean-Francois Revel, the left "has been using the 'fascist' peril to reconstruct the Manichean

Introduction to the Transaction Edition / xxxix

universe it needs to feel at ease." In September 1984, the European Parliament, at the request of its Socialist bloc, undertook an investigation into the "rise of fascism and racism in Europe." Since the last fascist dictatorships—Greece, Spain and Portugal—had disappeared a decade earlier, it seemed a strange inquiry. The final report showed that any alarm about European fascism was wild exaggeration. Concern about the rise of racism, said Mr. Revel, was not misplaced. However, he added, that "we tend to reduce almost all human rights violations to racism, and, furthermore, to reduce all forms of racism to that practiced by whites against other races or ethnic groups." Jean-Francois Revel, *The Flight from Truth: The Reign of Deceit in the Age of Information* (Random House 1992), pp. 61 and 79.

41. *Daily Californian*, University of California at Berkeley, 1 October 1991, p. 1.
42. Moral equivalence is an international disease of the culture. A travel writer, just returned from North Korea to England, met a professor of medicine at a party, a man of great learning. The writer, Dr. Anthony Daniels, described the ceaseless, ubiquitous and inescapable propaganda he had encountered in the country of Kim Il Sung. The professor, who had never been to North Korea, replied: "Ah, but have you considered how much power Rupert Murdoch wields in this country?" Anthony Daniels, *Utopias Elsewhere: Journeys In a Vanishing World* (Crown Publishers, 1991).
43. *New Yorker* (23 January 1989), pp. 98ff. Mr. Heilbroner was quoted as describing Marx as "the great philosophical economist of capitalism.
44. Jean-Francois Revel writes that even though Marxism "has been discredited, it still goes on influencing many of our modes of thought." *Flight*, p. xii. See also Henry F. Meyers, "Das Kapital: His Statues Topple, His Shadow Persists: Marx Can't Be Ignored," *Wall Street Journal* (25 November 1991), p. 1.
45. F.A. Hayek, *The Road to Serfdom*, p. viii.

46. Quoted in "The Rise and Fall of Lenin," by Robert Conquest in *Times Literary Supplement* (20 September 1991), p. 4.
47. *Ibid.*, p. 4.
48. Quoted by Albert I. Weeks, "The Perils of Russia-Watching," *Christian Science Monitor* (29 October 1990), p. 18. The Brzezinski article ran in *Encounter* in September 1990.
49. Robert Conquest, "The Unquiet Graves," *The New Republic* (18 & 25 September 1989), p. 42.
50. Philip Gasper, quoted in National Review, (21 October 1991), p. 6. Mr. Gasper is following the Gorbachev line: " . . . [H]ad it not been for Stalin's Thermidor in the mid 1920s, which betrayed and trampled on the ideas of the Great Revolution—a revolution that was genuinely popular and for the people, it might still have been possible to direct the country along the path of democratic progress, revival and economic prosperity.

    "People make ironical comments about the socialist choice but they do not see that the rejection of socialism in the public mind took place because socialism was associated with Stalinism . . . I am convinced that the discrediting of socialism in the eyes of the masses is a passing phase. . . . The next generation will surely return to this great idea." In Mr. Gorbachev's *The August Coup* quoted in *New York Review* (19 December 1991), p. 81.
51. Here is a fraudulent definition if I ever read one, the disarmingly simple "idea" of socialism—"more power for ordinary people." Ask the victims of socialism, how much power they have now or ever had? An even greater fraud perpetrated by the true believers is to modify the word "socialism" so as to lend it moral respectability—centrally planned, decentralized, communal, feminist, liberation, market, orthodox, peasant, reformist and, of course, African, Asian, Christian, Indian, Latin American, Gramscian, Trotskyite and on and on into the black night of totalitarianism.

52. Paul Berman, "Still Sailing the Lemonade Sea," *New York Times Magazine*, (27 October 1991), pp. 32ff. One of the more desperate attempts to salvage something from the "socialist" disaster is the apologia pro sua vita by Bertell Ollman, of New York University. Was it socialism which ruled the Soviet Union? No, it was a "Regency of the Proletariat" and the Soviet "Regent" was the Communist Party. Ingenious but—no cigar. See Bertell Ollman, "The Regency of the Proletariat in Crisis: A Job for Perestroika," *PS* 24:3 (September 1991), pp. 456, 457.
53. Michael Parenti, "The anti-Marxist Soviets," (*People's Daily World* (16 June 1990), p. 20. The publication is the official organ of the CP-USA, which at this writing has purged Angela Davis, the La Pasionara of American communism and a ranking Communist Party leader for many years, for some heresy.
54. Quoted by L. Brent Bozell III in the *Washington Times*, (11 January 1992), p. C3.
55. *The Cruel Peace: Everyday Life and the Cold War*, (Basic Books, 1991), p. 421.
56. Meg Greenfield, "Why We're Still Muckraking," *Newsweek* (25 March 1985), p. 94.
57. Quoted by Norman N. Gill, *American Political Science Review*, vol. 79 (March 1985), p. 197. I should also note that some Western intellectuals had begun in the 1970s to accept the probable defeat of the democracies by Moscow. Owen Harries quotes Daniel P. Moynihan's 1975 article in *Public Interest*: " . . . liberal democracy on the American model increasingly tends to the condition of monarchy in the 19th century; a holdover form of government, one which persists in isolated or peculiar places here and there, and may even serve well enough for special circumstances, but which has simply no relevance to the future. It is where the world was, not where it is going." Or the words of Jean-Francois Revel in his 1983 tract, *How Democracies Perish*: "Democracy may, after all, turn out to have been a historical accident, a brief

parenthesis that is closing before our eyes." Quoted in Owen Harries, "Communism, the Cold War and the Intellectuals: A Post-Mortem," *Commentary* 92:4 (October 1991), p. 15.
58. Interview, "Poetry for All: The American Dream of Joseph Brodsky," *New York Times*, (10 December 1991). p. 81.

Foreword

ARNOLD BEICHMAN takes a grimmer view than I do of the people he features in this book. His characters are serious-minded, morose, morbid to the point of gangrene, some of them . . . and quite out to lunch. They're marvelous. Their words remind me of those dotty Savants one occasionally meets in Rabelais and Evelyn Waugh; except that Beichman's people are real. They confirm my belief that hard times and heavy weather can do no injury at all to the human comedy. On the contrary, they refine it. The times, our dear solemn times, have brought to refinement one of the richest comic characters of the century. I am speaking of that boychik of the bourgeoisie who, in his zealous belief that he holds a lien on Destiny, had become the successor to Lewis' Babbitt: viz., the American Intellectual.

Despite the title, this is not a book "about America." Like Jean-François Revel's *Without Marx or Jesus*, it is a book that uses the subject of the United States as a device with which to explore the modern intellectual's retrograde habits of mind. Beichman finds nothing particularly amusing about what American intellectuals do to rationality and the English language, let alone the common weal, when they get on the subject of the United States. But I, for one, find his demonstration of the hash these men have made of the mother tongue extremely entertaining.

For example, by having the patience to rummage through the works of academicians such as Professors Andrew Hacker and Philip Slater, Beichman has isolated some new species of both tropes and *figurae sententiae,* as seventeenth century rhetoricians termed them. In one figure of speech, which might be called *data fantasia*, or the phantom degree, the intellectual uses expressions such as *virtually, immeasurably, invariably, so often, profound, more and more, larger and larger,* to cover up for the fact that, as Beichman puts it, he "has no data, has done no research, and has merely transmuted perceptions into 'facts'." A few examples: *"Virtually* every American possesses a self-esteem hitherto reserved for a privileged or talented few" (said, with some disgust, by Hacker in *The End of the American Era*) . . . *"More and more* people feel with a *larger and larger* portion of themselves that the destruction of mankind as a failed species might be a sound idea" (Slater, *The Pursuit of Loneliness*) . . . "It is no accident that hostility to hippies *so often* focuses on their olfactory humanity" (Slater again; note also "olfactory humanity"—if there exists in the British Museum a repository for catachresis, this man will be immortal) . . . "The stages through which new nations move as they establish their identities *invariably* alarm us" (Hacker) . . . As you can see, the tell-tale word also tips you off that you have just read, or are about to read, a statement that can't be proved one way or the other, in any case, and is beyond rational debate, or simply bananas.

The second Doctor Hackerism—"The stages through which new nations move as they establish their identities invariably alarm us"—is also an example of a trope Beichman has isolated and named "the intellectual we." "It is a rule uncontradicted by time," says Beichman, that whenever an intellectual says "we" or "our" or "us," and the reference is derogatory—as in "we are overfed" or "our guilt"—he makes it clear that he is talking about all Americans except himself and his fellow intellectuals. Thereby, Except Me & Co. are absolved from guilt concerning whatever seems to be wrong. Beichman has found an almost too beautiful example of this figure in the *Partisan Review*'s 1967 symposium on "What's Happening to America?" This classic included an entry by Paul Jacobs that began: "Madness surrounds us on all sides." Given the evident state of siege, it is no wonder that he lapses into that favorite high school textbook example of redundancy ("on all sides"). But the beautiful word here is *surrounds*. One immediately gets a picture of Except Me & Co. holed up in a bunker in the middle of a no-man's land swarming with twisted geeks, all writing and bubbling and babbling away out there in the craters as Jacobs attaches his communique to the shanks of the *Partisan Review* carrier pigeon.

When Jacobs says "Madness surrounds us on all sides," meaning "here in America"—that's bad. But when Frantz Fanon describes a newly independent "Third World" nation as "possessed by a kind of creative madness"—that's good, "creative" being an example of another Beichman rhetorical note, the intellectual "halo word." The halo word is a special form of antiphrasis used by intellectuals not for ironic delight (as in "the tender kiss-kiss claustrophobia of her love"*) but simply to transform the meaning of the word it is put next to. Other halo words are "revolutionary," as in revolutionary violence (good) as apposed to official violence (bad), and "human," "humanness" and "humanity," as in the aforementioned "their olfactory humanity," which is a code expression for the pungent odor of righteousness.

What bothers Beichman about all this cruel and unusual punishment of the English language is that most of it is not the work of literary intellectuals, in which case it would be par for the course. After all, the typical literary intellectual is a gentleman amateur in the nineteenth century British sense, with no more than an undergraduate education, no scholarly background, no training in the use of evidence according to either historical or scientific methods, and no more than a newsmagazine knowledge of concepts that have developed in the social sciences. But men like Hacker, Slater, Herbert Marcuse, Robert Heilbroner, Conor Cruise O'Brien, Robert Lekachman, and Kenneth Keniston are men within the academic community, respected scholars within their fields in some cases. Why do such men turn to certain subjects, such as American civilization today, and all at once surrender them-

---

* An oxymoron.

selves, like houris, to techniques they wouldn't tolerate for two paragraphs in a paper by a graduate student?

The answer, I think, is this. When these men get onto such subjects, they no longer write as scholars. They write as intellectuals. At this late date it shouldn't be necessary—but perhaps it is—to mention that the difference between a scholar and an intellectual is greater than the difference between an artist and an artiste, which is an old music hall form for a belly-dancer or a stripper. The word "intellectual" seems to have been first popularized by Clemenceau during the Dreyfus Case in 1898. From the beginning the intellectual was primarily a believer in a cause (e.g., justice for Dreyfus) who, in addition, considered himself part of the world of Culture that starred such signers of the *Manifeste des Intellectuels* as Zola, Proust, and Anatole France. The intellectual has always been a person who has set himself off from the common run of humanity by professing certain beliefs and observing certain tastes, forms, and fashions of *la vie intellectuelle*. In other words, the intellectual is a status type rather than an occupational type. What gives him his status are his values, biases, manners and style of consumption. Hence the muddle so many writers get into when they try to define the intellectual in terms of what he produces. It is not necessary for a man to produce (or even be involved in) art, literature or scholarship—except as a consumer—to be accepted as an intellectual within the intellectual community, although such accomplishments are highly prized. It is perfectly possible for a framing shop clerk, or a corporation lawyer, to be regarded as an intellectual. What is crucial is the nature of his beliefs, the style of his private life and the company he keeps. As Revel has put it, much of the life of the intellectual is devoted simply to removing himself from the mob, which in modern times goes under the name of "the middle class."

By the same token, the mere fact that a man is an artist, a novelist, or a scholar is no guarantee that intellectuals will accept him as one of them. William Faulkner lived *la vie intellectuelle,* and was regarded as an intellectual, when he was part of Sherwood Anderson's literary circle in New

Orleans in the 1920s. Later on, after writing many novels, he became a catalpa-tree recluse in Mississippi and seemed to spend his time hunting, riding, drinking bourbon, wearing dirty khakis, and hunkering down with the good old boys in the court house square—and was no longer regarded as an intellectual but as a holy beast who, like Cézanne, was capable of producing great art despite "intellectual shortcomings." Buzz Aldrin, the astronaut, happens to have a doctor of science degree in astronautics from MIT, but the intellectual community does not, to put it mildly, look upon him as an intellectual; more like a programmed laboratory animal, in point of fact ("programmed" being, as Beichman points out, the opposite of a halo word; it is a word with horns on it; as in a programmed society—bad—as opposed to a planned society —good). If he wished to, however, Aldrin could turn that situation around in no time. He would merely need to acquire a Volkswagen, some brown bread for the bread box, a set of Thonet "Corbu" bentwoods, muttonchops, a few new friends, all the Beatle albums from *Revolver* on, a lapsed pledge card from CORE, a kitchen full of recyclable bottles that nobody ever gets around to taking to the Safeway, a stack of unread *New York Review of Books* piling up in a mound of subscription guilt, and utter a few words on the subject of, say, war, or the higher priority of things here on Terra—in which case you can be sure it would be observed that his quiet reluctance to conform to the Astronaut stereotype, as well as his smoldering brilliance, had been apparent all along. Aldrin—as the scientist who is not an intellectual—is merely the extreme example of a phenomenon quite common on college faculties all over the country. Academic intellectual status groups tend to be made up largely of teachers in the liberal arts. There are also scientists who are accepted as intellectuals, but they are more likely to have to *prove* themselves . . . chiefly by showing their appreciation of non-scientific intellectual fashions and tastes.

In other words, what characterizes a man as an intellectual today differs very little from what characterized a man, in a slightly earlier age, as a theosophist, an upland

Baptist or a Swedenborgian. Hence Arnold Beichman's sense of frustration, which he expresses with considerable irony and charm. He wonders why it should be necessary to stand up and say things to educated people that seem obvious to the point of banality, such as: America is not, in fact, a fascist state ... The American political system is not, in fact, a fraud ... Americans are not, in fact, a genocidal people ... It is, in fact, pointless to say that America (or any nation) has "gone insane" ... But of course! What does he expect! Sooner than tell an orthodox American Intellectual not to believe such things—he should try telling a theosophist that there is, in fact, no Cosmic Consciousness and no Rhythm of Creation ... Sooner to have told George F. Babbitt not to be a decent go-ahead fellow who plays the game ... Such beliefs—Americans are a genocidal people, etc.—make up part of the Babbittry of the modern intellectual. Among orthodox intellectuals today such statements—or statements arising from such assumptions—are quite the opposite of shocking or daring. They are the staples of polite conversation. They have the same easy currency, and serve the same social function, as the remarks that flowed around the dinner table in George F. Babbitt's set, where it was *de rigueur* to express the view that Prohibition was undesirable among people such as themselves but good for the working classes. Such an *up-to-date* view certified that a man was a *live one* in Zenith City.

It should be amusing, and instructive, to see how intellectuals react to this book—at least judging by what has already happened in the case of Revel's *Without Marx or Jesus*. I became intrigued when I read Mary McCarthy's strange "afterword" to *Without Marx or Jesus;* so much so that I called Revel's American publisher.

"Since Jean-François is not well known in this country," his editor told me, "we felt that an afterword by Mary McCarthy would help."

Marvelous. Having Mary McCarthy introduce a book like this as a precaution against the unfamiliarity of American readers was like filling up your house with nerve gas as a precaution against burglars. Helpful Mary's explanatory essay informed the American reader first of all that the book was a joke, a put-on, in the tradition of *Gulliver's Travels*. Revel will protest and insist that he's being serious, she said, but that's just part of the gag. She described Revel as the perennial naughty schoolboy who always contradicts obvious truths just to see the astonishment on everybody's face. She wanted you to know that she found him lovable, however, like Dennis the Menace. If his little prank made him look "almost insane," ready for "a straitjacket," "absurd," "contrary," "Falstaffian" and like "an expressionless comedian" (both) and laughably biased—she was ready to forgive him all that . . . After all, he exhibited such a "joy in bias itself as an artistic form."

Just in case there remained some gullible souls who still might take the man's ideas seriously, however, Helpful Mary added that Revel was also not very bright (has only a "common garden intelligence"). Not only that, he was personally the most nondescript bourgeois lump you could imagine. She actually used the word bourgeois, adding, generously, that she meant it in an eighteenth century sense. "He has a round, flat 'Dutch' face" . . . "a moon face" . . . He wears "a gray suit and carries a brief case" . . . She wanted to introduce to the American reader a "placid, benevolent, easy-going, sentimental" homebody—a man, in short, who was anything but an intellectual.

Leaving aside the fact that almost every statement she made about Revel's book and Revel himself, right down to his clothes, was false—the question remained: Why such an elaborate and bizarre exercise in condescension? (Unless she was simply getting even for the time Revel told a *New York Times* reporter, in passing, that her apartment in Paris was "small, quiet and provincial.")

I was struck by the fact that almost every shot she got off about Revel was one I had heard before . . . somewhere . . . Whereupon it all came back . . . I had heard precisely the same line on Revel from French and Italian intellectuals when I was in Europe early in 1971. The book had been published in France in 1970 under the title *Neither Marx Nor Jesus*. Prima facie, it presented the United States as the freest and most progressive nation on earth. It was a book that sent French intellectuals into spasm of anger. The instinctive defense—"he's right-wing"—was simply not available. Revel's opposition to de Gaulle had been too well known; beside that, he had run on a socialist ticket. Even Mary McCarthy paid homage to his fight against de Gaulle, as if in evidence of her good will. The line I heard over and over took the form of reductionist ("nothing but") logic: such as, "Revel is nothing but a *provocateur*" . . . Revel is nothing but an anti-conformist" . . . or, as Mary McCarthy repeated it: He "only cares that his 'slant' should run counter to respectable culture and received opinion." None of these exercises, however, and least of all hers, could disguise one thing: the resentment underneath.

Why such resentment? It was not simply because here was a man who seemed to be saying nice things about the United States. Almost everyone, friend and enemy, saw at once that Revel's book is not really a book about the United States at all. But neither is it a book, as Mary McCarthy put it vaguely, about "France," or even the "French Left." Revel's real subject is: intellectuals. He had in mind a hidden subtitle that comes through immediately: "Our Retrograde Intellectuals."

His purpose is to use the subject of the United States, or anti-Americanism, to illustrate the mentality of intellectuals in his own country. It is a fascinating and amusing picture. Revel presents a gallery of French intellectuals who have such notions as: Eldridge Cleaver's *Soul on Ice* was boycotted by white Americans but became a best seller anyway because so many Negroes bought it . . . If you ask a New York policeman for directions, he will threaten you with his nightstick . . . The leading New York restaurants try to exclude Jews . . . American capitalists fought the California grape strike by importing grapes from Israel . . .

I couldn't help but notice how well most of the things Revel has to say about French intellectuals (aside from such Parisian *bijoux* as the above) apply to American intellectuals. Point for point, as he describes them, the habits of thought are identical: the irrationality, the fear of change, the hostility to new ideas, the antique versions of Marxism, the use of revolutionism as an instrument of fashion rather than of progress, the snobbery even toward likely allies, the distrust of freedom, not to mention the gorgeous displays of ignorance.

Revel says that anti-Americanism is not merely a part of latterday Marxist ideology but something essential to the French intellectual's very psychology. French intellectuals regard the United States as the final fascist monster created by the death throes of capitalism. This belief is essential to the intellectual, says Revel, in order to relieve the pain of his "wounded leftist chauvinism," his resentment of the fact that the United States is not merely the most powerful Western nation politically and economically but is also the focal point of Western culture in the arts and in science . . . and in that status intangible, "excitement" . . . the new Athens, the new Rome, the new Paris . . . the place where, in the last half of the twentieth century, one must go if one wants to be where "things are happening," just as ambitious Italian artists moved to France in the eighteenth century for the same reason.

This "wounded chauvinism," says Revel, leads intellectuals into the following piece of logic. America is the final bastion of capitalism-fascism. So the world divides irrevocably into those who support America and those who resist her. The more one resists her, the more truly revolutionary one is. And, as everyone knows, to be truly revolutionary is to be creative, innovative, daring, progressive. Therefore, an anti-American, revolutionary posture certifies one as a progressive person in many areas, including the arts and literature, regardless of aesthetic considerations.

Already, of course, one can see the uncanny way in which Revel's strictures about French intellectuals fit our own. Anyone who has followed the New York art and literary scenes for the past five years will be able to cite cases of artists and writers, and critics, who have taken up radical politics like a sort of miracle pill, an instant substitute for experiment or discovery in the formal sense. To cite only the most obvious example: Since 1963 *The New York Review of Books* has continually dismissed or, more often, ignored new novelists and poets. It has also fought the experiments in nonfiction of the past decade (for example, see Alfred Kazin's recent reprimand of Capote and Mailer for straying from The Novel), while at the same time hailing a Hasty Pudding production like *MacBird* as a breakthrough in the theater arts. This literary journal now dwells upon works cast in the form of the nineteenth century English essay. In short, it has become one of the most reactionary forces in American letters—yet preserves a veneer of "progressivism" among literary intellectuals simply by following an orthodox political line.

It was an irresistible logic that led *The New York Review of Books* to choose for its attack on *Without Marx or Jesus* . . . right . . . Mary McCarthy's afterword to the book itself. Nor do the curious concentric circles around this book stop there. At one point Revel writes:

> Ever since I was old enough to tell the difference between Europe and America on the map, I have heard predictions of the growth of the fascist Right in America and of the socialist Left in Europe. If these forecasts are correct, we are confronted by One of the great mysteries of contemporary history. We will never be able to understand why, in the last fifty years, so many millions of Europeans have fled to America to escape persecution, and so few Americans have fled to Europe.

I happened to have read the above lines in a Xeroxed copy of the publisher's English-language typescript. After the phrase "so few Americans have fled to Europe," an American editor had written a note in the margin to Revel: "J.F.R.: Quite a few leaving now—ought to mention them."

Splendid! Outside of a few Army deserters in Sweden—whom some might portray as victims, but hardly of "persecution"—I couldn't even imagine whom the note referred to, unless it was émigrés such as . . . S. J. Perelman and Mary McCarthy, who cast themselves as fugitives in London and Paris . . . not from the knout or the gas chamber, however, but from . . . Bad Taste . . . Like Harold Stearns fifty years ago, they have discovered that Americans do not comprehend the art of living. Revel's next lines, following the marginalium, happened to be: "Unfortunately, we tend to judge the United States and the rest of the world by different standards."

I should add that in the printed edition Revel has obligingly included a footnote indicating that he is aware that there are American deserters and draft resisters in Europe . . . and wearily pointing out the fatuity of comparing this to the exodus of Hungarian Jews or Spanish Republicans.

To all such arguments, says Revel, the orthodox intellectual answers: Yes, but the right-wing reaction has already begun in America; a military-industrial oligarchy is swallowing up America's birthright of democracy and freedom. In the minds of intellectuals, says Revel, the dark night is always about to fall in the United States . . . but mysteriously never does. Extreme right-wing movements succeed only in Europe, in the United States they always collapse as fast as they rise (he mentions Joseph McCarthy and Barry Goldwater). The fact is, he says, the momentum of the United States is in precisely the opposite direction. He goes on to demonstrate, in some detail, that American citizens have—and exercise—greater freedom of information, freedom of expression, and freedom to dissent, than any people in the history of the world. Americans have —and exercise—greater civil liberties than any people in the history of the world. He says the United States government has become unique among governments in taking on a burden of public guilt for its own "crimes against humanity"—first in the 1954 Supreme Court school decision committing the government to make amends for past injustices to Negroes, and later in such things as the Calley case. No other government, he says, would feel compelled to bring murder charges against soldiers involved in a military action. Not only that, says Revel, "the United States is one of the least racist countries in the world today." He argues that Europe's colored immigrants (North Africans, Portuguese, Jamaicans, Pakistani, Senegalese) are not only more repressed than American Negroes but also have far less hope of ever improving their lot.

Intellectuals ignore all such evidence, says Revel, because it is vital to their position to see only rightist tendencies in America. If necessary, they simply take the position that "everything American is, by its nature, more horrible than the most horrible thing that exists elsewhere." Thus the French film critic Pierre Marcabru can say of a newsclip of an American dance marathon of the 1930s: "I don't think I've ever seen anything more tragic, even in films on concentration camps." If that seems like a caricature, it could easily be matched by any of scores of gems from American intellectuals during 1969 and 1970, such as charges of "cultural genocide" against universities that refused to establish open admission policies for Negro applicants.

French intellectuals are even reluctant to give the United States credit in such seemingly nonsensitive areas as science, says Revel. This is because it is essential to the intellectual to believe that America's achievements are due to natural resources, historical accident, or barbaric greed; or, in any case, not intelligence. That was why Jean-Jacques Servan-Schreiber's *American Challenge* aroused such a furor among European intellectuals. Servan-Schreiber's thesis was that American successes were due more to intelligence than to force or riches. French intellectuals were used to joking about American business and scientific techniques as colossal forms of boorishness known as "American management." The news that America had accomplished something was the signal for intellectuals to say that the accomplishment was worthless.

Many European intellectuals, says Revel, now reject growth, technology, and science itself *in toto*. "These intellectuals have great prestige and influence; and they are dominated by an obsession with the past and a hostility to science." They disparage science with an ingenious mixture of Marx, Freud, and ancient cultural gods. They are moreover permeated with an anachronistic sense of their own cultural superiority. For them, as for the medieval cleric, culture is a means of separating themselves from the rest of mankind . . . They have created an identification of leftist feelings with anti-scientific and anti-technological feelings: "Science equals capitalism; that is the slogan to which it is all leading."

Revel's description, of course, can be transferred to the United States without altering a line. Here we have seen the phenomenon of the intellectuals' amazing hostility to NASA's success in reaching and exploring the moon. For example, two American intellectuals with curiously identical ideas on many subjects, Norman Mailer and Peter Schrag, have both characterized the space program as "tasteless." Schrag meant it in the sense of "bad taste"; Mailer meant "without taste." He complained, for example, that the NASA facilities in Houston are odorless. This seems like a piece of pointless crankiness until one realizes that "odorless" is a code word for "sterile." In fact, his long and involved book on the first moon flight, *Of a Fire on the Moon*, was nothing more than an announcement that the whole enterprise was sterile. Like their European counterparts, Schrag and Mailer were saying: They (these Americans, these nonintellectuals, *rustauds, goyim*) may have accomplished a feat—but the feat was worthless.

Intellectuals are wed to a romantic dream of the past and never want to abandon it. They have an unquenchable nostalgia for the great scenarios of nineteenth century Marxism, such as the Paris Commune of 1871 . . . a glorious moment! . . . and a total failure. The intellectuals of the left are, in fact, determined to accomplish . . . *nothing*.

They avoid realistic strategies because they are not really working for revolutionary change at all. Quite the opposite. French intellectuals make a point of insulting and alienating the French lower-middle class, ridiculing their ("American-style") love of consumer goods, etc., even in the very moment when these "shopkeepers" have joined them in the most difficult political achievement (e.g., the toppling of de Gaulle in 1969). The analogy to American intellectuals' snobbery toward "the hard hats," "the white lower-middle class," "the rednecks," is too obvious to require elaboration. The last thing that intellectuals in France or the United States want is an alliance with unions or petty tradesmen because that would involve the onerous and unromantic business of realistic political strategies.

If the intellectual of the left does not want political success, then what is he after? Preservation of his status, says Revel. The status of the intellectual is not rooted in revolutionary tradition, but in feudal tradition, in the ancient role of the priest and the literatus as the "stewards of culture." True socialist revolution could seriously injure the status of the traditional intellectual, particularly insofar as he continues his rearguard action against science.

Thus, says Revel, the intellectual plays a charade in which all that he really hopes to gain is applause. "Decisions," he says,

> are made less on the basis of what it is possible to accomplish than of what it is fashionable to believe . . . The indispensable prerequisite of a goal then becomes not that goal's attainability, but its laudability.

I could pursue that theme, too, as it applies to American intellectuals . . . but forgive me if I sum it up in a single phrase: "radical chic."

The intellectual is, among other things, one who "loves peasants and fishermen but cannot stand middle-class people," says Revel.

In an interview in *The New York Times Book Review* earlier this year Revel drew Mary McCarthy into concocting a solemn and utterly loony conceit about the American-style deep-basted frozen turkey as a symbol of the approaching "death of nature." The sloven laziness of the middle class presumably led to its preference for frozen turkeys over fresh-killed and to turkeys already injected with vegetable oil to the "natural" kind one bastes in the oven . . . so that within two years, probably, a person such as herself would be unable to buy a proper turkey . . . The

Death of Nature, of course, follows, just a link or two down the chain of logic . . .

So M. Revel has been good enough to introduce us to one star of the American cast in this on-going *opera bouffe*. And now our local impresario, Arnold Beichman, brings on scores more. I don't know what orthodox intellectuals will make of Beichman. As with Revel, Beichman's credentials are too strong for them to use the instinctive retort: "He's right wing." He was for three years city editor of the major ornament of Left daily journalism in New York, the newspaper *PM*. He was a pioneer in international labor journalism and has been involved with the international trade union movement for 15 years. He was among the first American correspondents to cover the Algerian rebellion against the French, wrote the first stories about the FLN in any Western newspaper, and (as a correspondent for *Newsweek*) predicted that the French would lose, because of the strong anti-colonial feeling among the people—a view that at the time (1957) seemed unbelievable. He covered South Africa in 1965 and briefed the late Senator Robert F. Kennedy before his trip to South Africa. When he applied for a visa to accompany Kennedy, the South African government turned him down because of what he had written. A later application for a visa to South Africa was also refused. He covered Kenya and other newly independent African nations in the early 1960s, was a friend of the late Tom Mboya and remains close to many African leaders. Beichman is currently teaching political science at the University of Massachusetts, Boston, and has finished his doctoral dissertation.

Which is to say only that Beichman is approaching the contemporary Left intellectual not as an outsider but as that most hated of creatures, the heretic, the backslider, the dissenter, the non-conformist. He is not even attacking the Left in general nor intellectuals in general but, rather, what George Orwell after a similar career, described as Left intellectuals' tendency toward "smelly little orthodoxies." In fact, the state of mind that Beichman has isolated is precisely that which Orwell described in "Politics and the English Language" and "Notes on Nationalism." Orwell, of course, was writing about the 1930s. That this marvelous form of Savonarolism has endured for four decades through two epochs of intellectuals, is a matter that should fascinate psychologists and sociologists. I think it is up to them to have the last word.

Meanwhile we have the work of the apostate Beichman. And, as we are about to see, he is saddled with a whole set of traits unbefitting a modern American intellectual: logic, clarity, a sense of humor and a connoisseur's eye for (in Tennessee Williams' image) the great grey cockaloonie bird overhead.

TOM WOLFE
January, 1972

Acknowledgments

I want to thank a number of people who have helped make this book possible, although I assume full responsibility for the effort and its shortcomings. Such friends as Robert Conquest, Kingsley Amis, Anthony Hartley, David Rees and Tibor Szamuely of the Tuesday luncheon club in London and Irving Brown in New York gave me much in the way of ideas and political analysis. A man whose views had a large influence was the late Elliott E. Cohen, *Commentary*'s first editor. Despite our occasional disagreements (or perhaps because of them) Irving Kristol has helped sharpen my political perceptions; his wife, Professor Gertrude Himmelfarb, taught me much, particularly the pleasure of scholarship. I have profited greatly from the writings of Sidney Hook and Daniel Bell. The writings of Richard Hofstadter were of enormous meaning to me. A. M. Rosenthal knows how much I am indebted to him for his rather unsentimental view of some of my ideas which compelled second looks at them. (I might just as well say it here: no matter how much the *New York Times* is criticized and attacked, its indispensability as a continuing source of information is only realized when one sits down to write my kind of book.) I want to thank Melvin J. Lasky, who saw the possibilities of a book in my *New York Times Magazine* article, 6 June 1971. (A shorter and somewhat different version of the article first ran in *Freedom at Issue,* the Freedom House publication.) Without the unfailing sympathy, limitless patience and good editorial sense of Carroll Aikins Beichman, I don't think I'd have made it.

I must also express my deep gratitude to Mrs. Joan Selby

who made available to me the rich resources of the Library of the University of British Columbia and who did the final checking of the manuscript. Thanks also to the Library staff of the University of Massachusetts (Boston).

ARNOLD BEICHMAN

There is a hierarchy of deceptions.

Near the bottom of the ladder is journalism; a steady stream of irresponsible distortions that most people find refreshing although on the morning after, or at least within a week, it will be stale and flat.

On a higher level we find fictions that men eagerly believe, regardless of the evidence, because they gratify some wish.

Near the top of the ladder we encounter curious mixtures of untruth and truth that exert a lasting fascination on the intellectual community.

Walter Kaufmann, "I and You, a Prologue,"
in *I and Thou*, by Martin Buber, 1971

"No," said the priest, "it is not necessary to accept everything as true, one must only accept it as necessary." "A melancholy conclusion," said K. "It turns lying into a universal principle."

Franz Kafka, *The Trial*

Introduction to
the Original Edition

THE CULTURE of a free society becomes seriously corroded when lies—I am not talking about dubious hypotheses, metaphysical statements or half-truths: I am talking about lies—circulate as unchallenged truths. When an unsupported assertion is accepted as a statement of fact rather than as something to be proven, when the line between probability or possibility and certainty becomes invisible, then, in short, we have to do with the institutionalized lie.

In political discourse, one expects lies, half-truths, and credibility gaps. Politicians and statesmen are not, after all, philosopher-kings, nor do we expect them to be such.[1] In culture, however, when lies begin to be accepted as worthy of discussion—not refutation—by our powerful social critics and literary intellectuals, a crisis in values must follow. Culture cannot long withstand the perversion of truth because culture *is* truth. When culture becomes politics, revolutionary politics in particular, there can be no criterion for truth and its inseparable companion, rationality:[2] for then every man is his own judge of truth with the right, if he so chooses, to enforce his version of truth on the refractory.[3] As André Malraux once wrote, "the path that leads from moral reasoning to political action is strewn with our dead selves."

A lie in culture is not only, nor can it ever be, a mere misstatement of fact. A lie in culture is easy to accept and hard to refute because one gets trapped by "meta-facts"; there are no empirical data around. Take for example this line from *Book World* (16 January 1972) that "this nation is perilously close to collapse." What does the word "collapse," in this context, mean? Revolution, anarchy—collapse into what? Is America more perilously close to collapse than, say, Ghana, Bulgaria, Ceylon, China, Albania? When a distinguished writer says that "the great virtue of economic depression is that it combined a very low degree of opportunity with a very high degree of motivation," it is not something refutable; it is a rather ghastly perversion of human values. When President Kingman Brewster of Yale said a few years ago that he doubted that a "black revolutionary" could receive a fair trial in America, that was not only a misstatement of fact but a lie in culture. When another university president says white America has "embrace[d] Hitlerism" and a *New York Post* columnist says America and South Africa are about the same, are these just misstatements of fact or a disagreement over values? These are some examples from my book of not merely willful misstatements of fact but willful distortions of reality.

I am sure a good case could have been made out for Hitler's allegations about Jewish control of the German economy. Were they any less a lie because they contained a bit of "truth"? The devilish thing about lies in culture is that they are designed not to be refuted. A man who says that the United States is "perilously close to collapse" is using a marvelous physical symbol whose content is nil because a statement that cannot be refuted cannot be demonstrated.

The state of America today is that of a country about which more lies are told by Americans than were ever dreamt of in Moscow, Peking or Havana. There is nothing new about lying in culture except that the lie is today called the "counter-culture."[4] The earlier high-water mark of such mendacity came in the 1930s when leading American intellectuals transformed a nauseating tyrant into a democratic socialist and the pontiff of a "proletarian" culture which they found far superior to "capitalist" culture. Within the memory of many, there were young people (and their elders) in the English-speaking democracies who swore they would not fight for King and country—the famed Oxford pledge—while at the same time they demanded a system of collective security against fascism —but, of course, without rearmament.[5]

What is new is that lying through the perversion of language or distortion of fact is now widely accepted as a normal state of affairs, so long as these lies are created by "progressives" around "progressive" issues. Consider a little lie—the misuse of the phrase "underground press" to describe the left-radical-counter-culture newspapers, all of which are obtainable on most 42nd Street newsstands or on streetcorners from the East Village to Haight-Ashbury. The phrase underground press once defined a publication which had to circulate secretly, from hand to hand, lest a repressive and ruthless government arrest and punish the editors. There was an underground press in tsarist Russia as there is one today in communist Russia.[6] An underground press existed in France during the nazi occupation. These publications weren't displayed at any kiosks in Moscow or Paris. Our "underground" papers and books are sold openly and widely with full instructions on how to make a Molotov cocktail or how to put in false claims for "lost" travelers' checks so you can live on "no dollars a day." About the worst fate which can befall the publisher of our "underground press" is bankruptcy due to lack of advertising from manufacturers of clothing, "posters, electronic strobes, jewelry, buttons, bells, beads, blacklight glasses, dope pipes and assorted 'head equipment,' "[7] or what Henry Fairlie has called "the salesmanship of the gutter." Why, then, is it the fashion to refer to it as the "underground press" when so clearly it is not?[8]

Or take the word "blind," a one-way adjective which is attachable only to unprogressive political positions. Professor Robert Heilbroner likes to talk about "blind anti-communism"; but no true progressive would ever, for example, say "blind anti-fascism" or "blind anti-racism." On the contrary, one must *always* condemn a fascist dictatorship but one need only condemn a communist dictatorship once a year—say, the anniversary of the second invasion (1968) of Czechoslovakia; the first Soviet coup d'état (1948) has long been forgotten—or during some particularly horrendous event like the 1970 suppression of

Polish shipbuilding workers in Gdansk. To keep harping about communism makes you a "blind anti-communist." To keep harping about fascism (especially in America, a Big Lie I will deal with later) makes you a "progressive."[9]

To praise a communist or totalitarian "socialist" revolution as a significant modernizing force is to be a realist and a scholar; to be doubtful is to be "blind" to reality. Professor Heilbroner wrote a few years ago:

> It is [China's] herculean effort to reach and rally the great anonymous mass of the population that is *the* great accomplishment of Communism—even though it is an accomplishment that is still only partially accomplished. For if the areas of the world afflicted with the self-perpetuating disease of backwardness are ever to rid themselves of its debilitating effects, I think it is likely to be not merely because antiquated social structures have been dismantled (although this is an essential precondition), but because some shock treatment like that of Communism has been administered to them. (Italics in original.)[10]

This passage is replete with one-way adjectives, nouns, and concepts, and I will be dealing with them in a later section as part of the Big Lie pattern about America (see chapter 9). There are other adjectives which, when coupled with a certain noun, will evoke one kind of response; change the adjectives and the response goes from negative to positive. For example, Alain Touraine talks about "this programmed society."[11] By rhetorical convention, the word "programmed" is now a boo word. However, if one were to substitute for this word another adjective—say "planned"—there would instantly be widespread approval. There is no need to explain precisely what one means by a programmed society as against a planned society, or to ask: planned by whom? Programmed—bad; planned—good.[12]

Again, by progressive convention, no sooner does a self-proclaimed socialist seize power over any country than his success is predetermined no matter what he does, no matter how wicked, immoral, or inhuman. No other judgment is conceivable or possible. On the other hand, a military or fascist dictator can never benefit from this doctrine of "inevitable success" because, by progressive convention, he is *corrupt, blundering, inefficient, feudal, backward.* Communist dictators are never corrupt and their blunders always turn out to be great leaps forward.

Robert Skidelsky is another practitioner of the one-way concept. He has expressed his horror at the "active identification of a large and influential segment of the academic community with the forces supporting the *status quo.*"[13] Describing the condition of Britain in the 1950s, he said that "in renouncing a critical or visionary role, the political scientists, by implication, aligned themselves with the *status quo.* Their concern was with describing and explaining how the political system worked rather than with suggesting alternatives and improvements."[14] Skidelsky, a competent British historian of good scholarly attainments, never gets around to defining what he means by the *"status quo."* By progressive convention, the status quo in democratic countries is bad and those intellectuals who support this status quo, whatever it is, are selling out. The status quo in socialist countries is rarely challenged by Western progressives except for an occasional criticism of some detail of "untidy" administration. Neither Marx nor Engels made clear what kind of institutions would be established after one status quo is replaced by another status quo. When the Marxist dialectic is finally realized as the synthesis, will history stop, will that status quo be forever? While progressives are always bemoaning the status quo in America, Britain and other Western-type democracies or the status quo in fascist countries like Greece or Spain, few ever demand a change in the status quo in Russia, China, Cuba, North Korea and North Vietnam. The status quo in these countries is cheered as a paradigm of progress. To be for the "status quo" in America (or in any democracy) is to be precisely for those freedoms like the Bill of Rights which, as part of the status quo, make possible change in the status quo.

In actual fact, to be against the status quo, in progressive rhetoric, is really to be against only *one* status quo

—that which exists in the Western democracies or in certain fascist or militarist states. The status quo in socialist or communist societies is normally accepted by Western critics (if not by the people who live in those societies) as part of some long or permanent revolution. On occasion something dramatically unpleasant happens in one of these "progressive" countries which leads to a momentary "disillusion" and a conscience-saving statement of criticism. Western progressives are always being surprised and disenchanted at what sometimes happens in a communist country. The most recent such disaffection was expressed by sixty Western intellectuals over Fidel Castro's mistreatment of the Cuban poet, Heberto Padilla.[15] The signers of this protest included Jean-Paul Sartre, Simone de Beauvoir, Marguerite Duras, Carlos Fuentes, Alberto Moravia, Alain Resnais, Claude Roy, Nathalie Sarraute, and Susan Sontag, among others.[16] Their letter to Castro pleaded with him to " 'spare Cuba dogmatic obscurantism, cultural xenophobia, and the repressive system imposed by Stalinism on the socialist countries.' " They wanted " 'the Cuban revolution to return to what made us consider it as a model in the realm of socialism.' "[17]

The lying which went on about Castro and his revolution was not fundamentally different in character from the lying which went on over Stalin's Russia. Saul Landau once demonstrated how a communist tyranny can be transformed into a "socialist" miracle. In an interview, he solemnly declared:

> Fidel did promise elections. But he quickly found out that the Cuban people did not want them—for very good historical reasons. . . .
> You must remember the desire, the terrible desire for unanimity on all decisions. They don't want things to be just a majority rule, they want it to be all the way. . . .
> . . . To the Cuban worker free speech meant very little. The revolution to them is absolute good . . . Anybody who opposes the revolution is absolute evil. It's quite as simple as that. . . .

> . . . You see, Fidel hasn't had to use police just as he didn't have to impose censorship on the press —they did it themselves. The workers in the print shops and so on.
>
> . . . you could say that Fidel as a personality is one of the most tolerant people. He does not judge people. He trusts people until they defect. . . .
>
> . . . Cuba is the first purposeful society that we have had in the Western hemisphere for many years . . . where men have a certain dignity, and where this is guaranteed to them. And one of the best guarantees to make a man a man is a gun in his hand.[18]

One wonders how Miss Susan Sontag can, in the light of her signature on a protest to Castro, justify her essay on Cuban poster art, wherein she singled out Cuba as seeking "to raise and complicate consciousness—the highest aim of the revolution itself [and] perhaps the only current example of a communist revolution pursuing that ethical aim as an explicit political goal." It was to the credit of the Cuban revolution that the two potentially antagonistic views of art—one expressing and exploring "an individual sensibility," the other serving "a socialpolitical or ethical aim"—remain an unresolved contradiction. And in describing the revolutionary posters ("their beauty, their stylishness, and their transcendence of either mere utility or mere propaganda") she said that they "give evidence of a revolutionary society that is not repressive and philistine." To her, the posters demonstrated nothing less than that Cuba "has a culture which . . . is relatively free of the kind of bureaucratic interference that has blighted the arts in practically every other country where a communist revolution has come to power." And if one would understand why Miss Sontag has so entrapped herself, it is because she has adopted the view of Antonio Gramsci, the Italian Marxist who (as she defines it) affirms that "culture, more than the strictly political and economic institutions of the state, is the medium of this necessary civil revolution."[19] And now she is just one more disillusioned intellectual (the disillusion, one can be sure, is only temporary) who, despite all the history of the last half-century and its climatic Stalinism, was unable to predict, when she became a Castro sectary, what would happen to Padilla, as it had happened to Mandelstam or Sinyavsky, if he dared express and explore his "individual sensibility."[20] In a totalitarian society, artists flourish best in exile.

I have devoted this space to Susan Sontag and her "willing suspension of disbelief" because her kind of zealotry always awaits a new god which, this time, please, will not fail; yet the new god always seems to fail. It is exactly this species of zealotry which leads to Big Lies about American democracy, in fact about all democracies. What happened to Padilla in Cuba could not happen to Padilla or Sontag in America and if, by the remotest chance, it did, then the protests and legal action forthcoming would not be from faraway observers, but here at home from American intellectuals.

Existence of widespread persecution of political prisoners in Cuba is hardly some recent revelation. The Inter-American Commission on Human Rights in 1970 reported that while it had several times requested information about charges of human rights' violations in Cuba, the request had never been honored. The commission report, made to the Organization of American States, charged:

1. That there are many persons in Cuba, including women and children, who have been jailed for political reasons and executed without prior trial or after a trial in which the accused did not enjoy the guarantees of due process.
2. That the situation of political prisoners in Cuba, sentenced to imprisonment after having been arbitrarily arrested and subjected to trials in which the guarantees of due process have not been observed, continues to have extremely serious characteristics incompatible with the principles set forth in the Charter of the Organization of American States,

the American Convention of Human Rights, the American Declaration of the Rights and Duties of Man, and the Universal Declaration of Human Rights.²¹

Is there no relation between Padilla's tribulations and the absence of democratic liberties in Cuba? The Sontag zealotry ignores such questions because it prepares to measure reality against an ideal-in-being, an ideal-that-never-was, and an ideal-that-never-will-be until men are like the gods themselves. By the perversion of such words as "ethical" and "transcendence," millions of people are condemned to enslavement and death, to the applause of Susan Sontag and Jean-Paul Sartre who, when it all turns out to have been a colossal error, can blame it all on an aberration called "Stalinism," can proceed to issue a conscience-easing letter of protest, and then go on to collect their illicit royalties in publicity and respect for their integrity.

Social critics, like Susan Sontag, who despise America remind one sadly of the spirit of anti-Weimarism about which Professor Fritz Stern wrote so sharply in describing the *Vernunft-Republikaner* of pre-nazi Germany:

> Theirs was a resentment of loneliness; their one desire was for a new faith, a new community of believers. . . .
> . . . they denounced every aspect of the capitalistic society and its putative materialism. They railed against the spiritual emptiness of life in an urban, commercial civilization . . . They attacked the press as corrupt, the political parties as the agents of national dissension, and the new rulers as ineffectual mediocrities. . . .
> . . . They ignored—or maligned—the ideal aspirations of liberalism, its dedication to freedom, the hospitality to science, the rational, humane, tolerant view of man. . . .

> . . . They were not concerned with compromise; they sought to destroy the present.[22]

And perhaps even more dispiriting, we have intellectuals like Sartre who can declaim that " 'to keep hope alive one must, in spite of all mistakes, horrors, and crimes, recognize the obvious superiority of the socialist camp.' "[23]

Although I have in these introductory remarks focused on what appear to be issues peripheral to my main theme, I have done so in order to demonstrate the organic relationship between the lies in culture circulated by American social critics and the lies about so-called socialist or communist countries, usually by the same critics. There is an enormous difference when some communist hack like Gus Hall makes invidious comparisons between America and the Soviet Union and when Miss Sontag does. We judge Gus Hall's words differently from Susan Sontag's; we must.

I will discuss in the following chapters Nine Lies about America which are subsumed in nine categories—Fascism, Genocide, Violence, Labor, Political System, American Insanity, American Guilt, Human Values, Utopianism and Revolution. I do not intend in this discussion to make the usual obeisance to "progressive culture" which demands that a defender of political democracy must preface his defense with a full prior confession about America's faults, its imperfections, its obtuseness. I regard such admissions, while factually quite often correct, as a form of cant. In a reasonable community of readers and writers, it can be assumed that to analyze the strictures of our puissant social critics is *not* to suggest that America should be immune from criticism for its foreign policy failures (notably in Southeast Asia), for the urban crisis, the race crisis, or any other crisis. But I simply refuse to concede that any one, or all, of these crises either proves that democracy no longer exists in America or that democracy would be improved by its destruction.

The logic of the rebel is to want to serve justice so as not to add to the injustice of the human condition, to insist on plain language so as not to increase the universal falsehood, and to wager, in spite of human misery, for happiness. Nihilistic passion, adding to falsehood and injustice, destroys in its fury its original demands and thus deprives rebellion of its most cogent reasons.
Albert Camus, The Rebel, 1956

We had fed the heart on fantasies,
The heart's grown brutal from the fare,
More substance in our enmities
Than in our love.
William Butler Yeats, "The Stare's
Nest by My Window," The Tower, 1928

These professors . . . see no merit in the good, and no fault in the vicious, management of public affairs; they rather rejoice in the latter, as more propitious to revolution. They see no merit or demerit in any man, or any action, or any political principles, any further than as they may forward or retard their design of change: they therefore take up, one day, the most violent and stretched prerogative, and another time the wildest democratic ideas of freedom, and pass from the one to the other without any sort of regard to cause, to person, or to party.
Edmund Burke, Reflections on
the Revolution in France, 1790

Dans tout pédagogue, il y a un démagogue qui sommeille.
(In every teacher, there is a demagogue . . . sleeping.)
Raymond Ruyer, Les nuisances
idéologiques.

1

"America Is a Fascist Country"

**America is already a fascist country or
is on the road to fascism.**

THIS IS a thesis which unites a number of influential literary intellectuals and publicists in agreement. There is only some small dispute as to how soon it will be before it all becomes *real* fascism. Nor is this as absurd as it sounds. After all, when a polemicist freely announces over radio and television, in newspapers, magazines, and a best-selling book, that America is indeed a fascist land, the man making such a statement could be considered an odd case of divorcement from reality. So this troublesome problem is avoided by distinguishing between "fascism" and "real fascism" in words without ever making clear the distinction between the two in fact. Or else, quotation marks are placed around the dark word itself, or perhaps a paradoxical adjective before the word "fascism," thereby raising the statement to the level of metaphysics where the realm of fact presents no challenge. But challenge there must be.

Professor Herbert Marcuse, for example, has said that "as far as I'm concerned, one can speak with complete justification of an incipient fascism" in America. In the same interview, a few sentences later, he disclosed the existence in America of "preventative fascism." The *Harvard Crimson,* in Fall 1970, announced with dramatic precision that America will be living under "real fascism . . . before three years are over." Charles Reich tells us that America is at "the brink of an authoritarian or police state" and that "today [in America] both dissent and efforts at change are dealt with by repression." Professor Philip Green has written that "the evidence suggests it may be that America is pioneering in a new political system: of formal democracy for the many, and a kind of informal Fascism for the few."[1] Professor Philip Slater of Brandeis University has written that "liberals will be given the choice, during the next decade or so, between participating in some way in the new culture and living under a Fascist regime." Mel Wulf, legal director, American Civil Liberties Union, offers these formulations: "though we are not yet a fascist state in general," or "though we are not now a police state in general." Alfred Kazin, in an interview a few years ago, was asked whether he thought there was a "totalitarian threat to the artist in this country comparable to the one you've described abroad." Kazin replied:

> I certainly do. It is occurring more subtly and doesn't yet seem so acute and disastrous. But there has been the same collapse of ideals along with it and a gradual diminishing of intellectual freedom and speculation. . . . The sense that we must necessarily support the established system gets more demanding.

Andrew Kopkind wrote some time ago, "if some kind of 'fascism' comes to America—as too many of all persuasions now fear and hope, as a way of self-vindication—it will be because institutional therapy failed to cure a complex of morbid 'social diseases.' " In his book, *Trial*, Tom Hayden refers to America's " 'inflexible fascist core' " and insists that " 'we are now living in 1984.' " Professor John Tytell of Queens College argues that since the functions of the House Un-American Activities Committee are now in the Department of Justice, "then we are ten nervous steps closer to oligarchic fascism." William L. Shirer has said that "we may well be the first people to go fascist by the democratic vote." Dotson Rader, who edits a radical review, wrote that the aim of New Left terrorism is "to make the latently fascist nature of the American system overt . . . to make apparent to the American people what already exists." Kenneth Lamott has described California as "our first para-fascist State." The Black Panthers, in their newspaper, have published articles equating zionism with fascism. A weird formula for fascism in America was described by Daniel Sisson:

> Simply taking one example—the adults' attitude towards drugs—it is not implausible to estimate that by 1980 85 per cent of the young will be felons while the other 15 per cent will be Fascists, trained to keep them under control.[2]

One of the most atrocious smears of American history, one which borders on the wilfully blind, was made by Dr. James Cheek, president of Howard University, who declared:

> In twenty-six years since waging a world war against the forces of tyranny, fascism and genocide in Europe, we have become a nation more tyrannical, more fascistic and more capable of genocide than was ever conceived or thought possible two decades ago. We conquered Hitler, but *we have come to embrace Hitlerism.* (Italics added.)[3]

A few paragraphs further on, Dr. Cheek announces the sovereign remedy—"what the nation now needs is rebirth of morality." How a people who have "come to embrace Hitlerism" can suddenly find the ethical resources to create a "rebirth of morality," I leave to Dr. Cheek to explain.

Bertram Gross, Distinguished Urban Affairs Professor at Hunter College, recently predicted that "It" could happen here—not quite as it came to Germany and Italy, but as "an outgrowth of peculiarly American conditions." His article presented an image of neo-fascism "American style" which he described as "techno-urban fascism." It would be, he said, "a new form of garrison state, or totalitarianism, built by older elites to resolve the growing conflicts of postindustrialism." This would be a pluralistic "friendly fascism" which Gross epitomizes as *"a managed society* [ruled] *by a faceless and widely dispersed complex of warfare-welfare-industrial-communications-police bureaucracies caught up in developing a new-style empire based on a technocratic ideology, a culture of alienation, multiple scapegoats and competing control networks."* (Italics in original.)

The Bertram Gross image of what he calls "American totalitarianism" would have, so far as I can see, all the hallmarks of American democracy. Let me quote him:

> Pluralistic in nature, techno-urban fascism would need no charismatic dictator, no one-party rule, no mass fascist party, no glorification of the state, no dissolution of legislatures, no discontinuation of elections, no distrust of reason.[4]

Perhaps a better name for this cross-eyed vision would be "democratic fascism" or "liberty-loving fascism" or "Lockean fascism" or even "anti-fascist fascism."

Walter Lippmann is also a propounder of this paradox of what I call "non-fascist fascism." He was asked in an interview, "Do you see the danger of fascism in America?" He replied to his questioner, Ronald Steel, "There will be a danger. I don't think there will be fascism on a national scale—the country's too big for national fascism. But I think there will be local fascism. In local communities, majorities or strong minorities will rise up if they think they're threatened. And they'll use violence ruthlessly." Why can't Lippmann call it, say, "lynching" which seems to have disappeared in America? Why must it be dressed up in nonsense verbiage like "local fascism"?

Professor Gross, unwittingly, supplies an answer. In presenting his neo-fascist nightmare, he said that he was doing it "without discussing *any* of the factors that might bring it—or prevent it from coming—into existence." (Italics in original. *New York Times,* 4 January 1971.) This is the most significant explanation of his essay because it demonstrates that Professor Gross has no *theory* of fascism in America, any more than the Communist Party had when it proclaimed in 1933 in its official organ:

> It is now necessary to point out that the Roosevelt "new deal" program represents not only the strengthening of the open fascist tendencies in America, but also that it is quite consciously and systematically supporting and developing social-fascist ideas, organizations, and leaders. Roosevelt has a very special need for the social-fascists.[5]

Professor Gross has a set of attitudes, metaphysical in nature, in that they can neither be verified nor falsified; being metaphysical, these attitudes are congruent with any statement whatsoever. Nor do any of our culture critics who, like Professor Gross, declaim about the imminence or omnipresence of fascism in America, have any theory whatsoever to explain how it will come or has come to America, a theory with even a modicum of empirical data. That is why they use all these qualifying adjectives, although they never make clear what *real* fascism is or how *fascist* fascism would take shape. The reason they have no theory is *(a)* that they have either deliberately misunderstood the ingredients of fascism or *(b)* that they have not the faintest conception of what constitutes fascism, both suppositions highly improbable in the case of a Distinguished Professor at Hunter College.

Do those polemicists who call America "fascist" mean Italian, German, Spanish, Peron "fascism"? There is no generic concept of "fascism." In actual fact, half a century after Mussolini's March on Rome, there still isn't an acceptable working definition of fascism, although several scholars have designed a fascist model. The "agent theory" of Marxist-Leninists—Hitler and Mussolini were mere tools of "finance capital"—has long been discredited. As Professor Henry Ashby Turner, Jr., has written:

> Anyone who reads many studies of fascism as a multinational problem cannot but be struck by the frequency with which writers who begin by assuming they are dealing with a unitary phenomenon end up with several more-or-less discrete sub-categories. Regardless of what criteria are applied, it seems very

difficult to keep fascism from fragmenting. In spite of this, there has been a general reluctance to consider what must be regarded as a definite possibility: namely, that fascism as a generic concept has no validity and is without value for serious analytical purposes ... The generic term fascism is in origin neither analytical nor descriptive.[6]

Professor N. Kogan has proposed as a fascist model one with these attributes: *(1)* it depends on a "mass base" supporting a charismatic leader; *(2)* it is a modernizing and revolutionary rather than a traditionalist and conservative movement; *(3)* it rejects the egalitarian ethos and extols hierarchy and discipline, all of which is reinforced usually by a single-party system; *(4)* it seeks the creation of a psychologically conditioned New Man; *(5)* it glorifies terror and violence as a matter of principle; *(6)* it expresses a distinctive "integral nationalism." Professor Kogan insists that these traits must all be present and interrelated if a political system is to be categorized as fascism. Franz Neumann has listed five essential characteristics of a totalitarian fascist system: *(1)* it is a police state; *(2)* there is a concentration of power in the State; *(3)* there is a monopolistic State party; *(4)* social controls are total, and *(5)* a state of systematic terror is the norm.[7]

Is it not peculiar that Professor Gross quite explicitly excludes the Kogan or Neumann parameters from his pluralistic "friendly fascism"? Not only is there no fascism in America by any empirical standard, but the likelihood of its coming to America is real only to those intellectuals and progressive critics who look upon democracy as a regressive form of government, or to those critics who seek a sustaining elitehood for themselves through a crypto-authoritarian politics under their management.

What makes the accusation about a fascist *Amerika* so utterly irrational is that any empirical data to disprove it can always be dismissed by America's accusers as frivolous, no matter what the evidence. For example, what other government in the world could permit anti-war propaganda to be broadcast to its troops fighting a war overseas? Or when in history has it been done? On 3 May 1971, I listened to former Congressman Allard Lowenstein on a "Meet the Press" program denouncing the war in Vietnam on the highest moral grounds. It was as informed, provocative and persuasive an attack on the American military action in Vietnam as I have ever heard. *But I was not listening to the broadcast over the normal commercial network. I was listening to it on the shortwave broadcast facilities of the American Forces Radio and Television Network which covers overseas military bases, including South Vietnam.*

This is fascism?

In Washington itself, leaflets were distributed to employees of the Department of Health, Education and Welfare in mid-March detailing the projected peace activities of the "May Day Movement." The following events took place under the auspices of "HEW Peace Activities"—

April 7, Indochinese Film Festival featured a movie which portrayed "the effects of the war on the Indochinese civilian population" and presented "the May Day Movement's threat, 'if the Government won't stop the war—we'll stop the government.' " Where was this film shown? Room 1137-North, HEW Building.

April 8, Rennie Davis, National Coordinator of the People's Coalition for Peace and Justice spoke in the North Auditorium on anti-war activities "and how HEW employees can become involved."

On subsequent days, films made in Hanoi were shown in Room 1137-North, including one "produced by the National Liberation Front to show the struggle for liberation in South Vietnam and to show the health services provided by the NLF." On April 21 in Room G-751 North, a group described as "a panel of Washington activists [who] have recently met with Vietnamese and Laotians [spoke] of the changing characteristics of the war."

Rather bemused by these leaflets, I wrote to then-HEW Secretary Elliott Richardson for further information about these meetings. In a letter to me dated 22 July 1971, Secretary Richardson wrote:

No reprisals have been taken against any of the employees of this Department who were involved. It may be of interest to you to know that the activities were sponsored by two employees groups, the HEW Action Project and the Thursday Discussion Group. Neither group enjoys official standing within the Department's structure, nor are any of the groups' activities officially approved or promoted.

The use of Departmental meeting space for nonofficial meetings of employee groups is permitted under regulations of the General Services Administration. These regulations are applicable to all GSA-controlled property, including the HEW North Building Auditorium. The regulations are supplemented by provisions of a Secretarial Order issued on November 1, 1969.

The groups sponsoring the "peace activities" routinely made proper application for, and were granted permission for the use of, meeting space for their various activities in accordance with the procedures outlined in GSA regulations and the Secretarial Order. The present state of the law generally does not permit the Department to censor speech or speakers in connection with nonofficial meetings of employee groups. On two occasions in the recent past, courts have restrained the Department from prohibiting use of facilities for particular "peace" activities; *Tabor v. Cohen*, D. C. Cir. No. 22, 512, Order of November 21, 1968; *Reiss v. Finch*, 419 F2nd 760 (1969). In those cases, the Department's attempts to deny use of meeting space were deemed unjustified prior restraints on free speech.

Once again, this is fascism?
No rational person would suggest that there is fascism in America or that we are on the road to fascism in the face of all the obvious substantial evidence to the contrary. Why, then, do some of our most august academicians and

publicists believe—or say they believe—that fascism exists or is on its way in America? Why, for example, do they not warn us against the coming or arrival of some other American species of *totalitarianism*—why only fascism? There are some obvious reasons and some not so obvious for this strange aberration.

The idea of fascism is so abhorrent to us that to call a person or a political system "fascist" is immediately to endow the accusation with a semblance of authenticity. (A half century ago, Walter Lippmann wrote in his *Drift and Mastery,* "There is in America today a distinct prejudice in favor of those who make the accusations.") The usefulness of this kind of accusation is that it is such a Big Lie, no evidence is needed to prove it; or better yet, everything is proof. It is the Mount Everest approach to political analysis: How do you know? Because it is there.

Recently handy evidence was found in Trudeau's Canada, following the kidnapping and murder of the Quebec minister of labour, Pierre Laporte, by self-pronounced revolutionary terrorists of *Le Front de Libération du Québec* (FLQ), and the kidnapping of the British trade commissioner, James Cross. Prime Minister Trudeau's government, at the request of Quebec Premier Robert Bourassa who asked for emergency powers, invoked the War Measures Act which *(a)* declared a national emergency and *(b)* outlawed the FLQ; that is, it would no longer enjoy protections provided by the law.

> Until October 1970 members of the FLQ had enjoyed a rather anomalous status. On the one hand, they were dedicated to the overthrow of the constitutional system of Canada; on the other hand, they enjoyed the protections of that very system.
>
> On October 16, the Federal Cabinet cleared away this ambiguity: the FLQ was no longer to be treated as being within society. The normal laws of society were to be suspended. The government was in fact declaring war on the FLQ. It was doing to the FLQ what the FLQ had long ago done to it.[8]

For seven years the FLQ had claimed responsibility for bombings throughout Quebec. In a document made public in 1963, the FLQ said that it was "a revolutionary movement of volunteers ready to die for the political and economic independence of Quebec." Its members called themselves "suicide-commandos."[9] What was the reaction among American progressives to Trudeau's resistance? A correspondent for the *New Republic,* writing from Montreal as a self-described "draft-refusing" American, reported that "on the morning of October 16 . . . the country chosen as a refuge and whose government all praised for its tolerance had suddenly, without warning, become a police state."[10] The *New Republic* correspondent never got around to explaining how the police state of Canada only a few months later became just as suddenly an unpolice state. You didn't have to prove that the Trudeau decrees were fascist; the mere declaration that they *were* fascist meant there was no need to prove they were. What is more, to call them fascist was to imply that these decrees were forever and that, therefore, Canada was (and is still) disastrously embarked on the road to fascism. And since America is Canada's overbearing next door neighbor, and since Canada dare not sneeze without first obtaining America's imperial permission, fascism's next stop is naturally America.[11]

Thus by constant reiteration that America *is* pre- or proto-fascist, America *becomes* fascist and all the scholarly qualifiers—like "incipient" or "preventative" or "not yet a fascist state *in general*" (or how about "creeping fascism"?)—get blurry and redundant. The transition is simple because any unpleasant or awful single event in America—say, the Attica jail riot and killings—can be transformed into living documentation that we now live in *Amerika.* Such demonology can so easily turn a doubtful future into a doubtless present. I think so, therefore it is. This sort of "non-cognitive" cognition was ably defined by Georg Lukács, the eminent Hungarian Marxist:

> It is the Stalinist tendency to exclude everywhere so far as possible any sort of mediating concepts and

to bring into direct connection the crudest matters of fact with the most abstract theoretical positions.[12]

The lie about fascism is not confined only to the United States. It is one heard whenever and wherever a self-described revolutionary movement explodes within a democratic society and where that society acts to protect itself along the firm and intelligent principles laid down by Arthur O. Lovejoy, the eminent American philosopher and founder of the American Association of University Professors:

> The believer in the indispensability of freedom, whether academic or political, is not thereby committed to the conclusion that it is his duty to facilitate its destruction, by placing its enemies in the strategic positions of power, prestige or influence. ... The conception of freedom is not one which implies the legitimacy and inevitability of its own suicide. It is, on the contrary, a conception which defines the limits of its own applicability; what it implies is that there is one kind of freedom which is inadmissible—the freedom to destroy freedom. The defender of freedom of thought and speech is not morally bound to enter the fight with both hands tied behind his back. And those who would deny such freedom to others, if they could, have no moral or logical basis for the claim to enjoy the freedom they would deny.[13]

In France, during the events of May 1968, the cry of fascism—and nazism and gestapoism—was heard among French progressives and student revolutionaries. In some cases, it was expressed politely, restrainedly; witness Alain Touraine:

> The repression that [the revolutionaries] denounced was not directly police repression but the kind of repression that knows how to appeal to the police when it is threatened; repression in the name of order

that calls itself reason, repression in the name of modernity that calls itself the bypassing of conflicts, the repression of the State that takes itself for society.[14]

Nice prose, same accusation—except it also criticized the young revolutionaries for accusing the dean at Nanterre University of being "a Nazi and a Gestapo agent" which, of course, he was not. But Professor Touraine criticized them because they should have had "a more mature political judgment." And he also criticized the student marchers who "shouted 'C.R.S. = S.S.' " (as if the French gendarmerie were a Hitlerian guard), or " 'De Gaulle—Fascist.' "[15]

Surely it is a phenomenon of some magnitude that in most democratic countries, there are influential voices always warning about the imminence of fascism or that it has actually arrived. Where does this kind of Big Lie come from?

It has to do with a peculiar habit of the modern political mind, namely "guilt by category"; and one can trace it back to the French Revolution or to the Bolshevik notion of "objective guilt" about which Lenin wrote in 1902:

> *All* worship of the spontaneity of the working-class movement, all belittling of the role of "the conscious element," of the role of Social-Democracy, *means quite independently of whether he who belittles that role desires it or not, a strengthening of influence of bourgeois ideology upon the workers.* (Italics in original.)[16]

Perhaps, more precisely, this spurious cry of fascism is the omnipresent infection among progressives on the left: it goes back to the "social-fascist" slogan of Lenin which was used later by Stalin's Comintern. This communist line, enunciated at the Fourth Comintern Congress in 1922, blamed the Italian Socialist Party for Mussolini's victory. A young Earl Browder was quoted as saying that "we may expect the real fascist leadership in America to spring from the Gompers bureaucracy [in the American Federation of Labor]." Zinoviev asked, " 'What is Italian Social-Democracy?' " and answered his own question, " 'It is a wing of the fascists . . . International Social-Democracy has now become a wing of fascism.' " In 1924 Stalin said, " 'Social Democracy is objectively the moderate wing of fascism. . . . They are not antipodes, they are twins.' " Otto Kuusinen, the Finnish communist, argued that the more " 'social-fascism' " developed, the " 'closer it came to being "pure" Fascism.' " How vividly Browder and Kuusinen foreshadow today's distinction among our progressive critics between fascism and "real" fascism.[17]

Theodore Draper's analysis of the "ghost of social-fascism" has vast relevance to the American progressive's *cri de coeur*. As he wrote:

> For the theory of social-fascism was based on the proposition that "bourgeois democracy" and "fascism" were merely different norms of the "dictatorship of the bourgeoisie." One was "masked," the other "naked." The "democratic form" of the bourgeois dictatorship was considered by far the more dangerous and detestable of the two because it was supposedly harder to expose.
>
> The real enemy, then, was "democratic forms." The theory of social-fascism made the German and British Social-Democrats of the period the main carriers of this contagious disease. . . .
>
> The theory was intrinsically designed to destroy the "democratic forms" of bourgeois society, not to hold back fascism. It succeeded in doing the former far better than it did the latter. It was intended to justify a Communist dictatorship in the name of the proletariat by making the alternative a "masked" Social-Democrat dictatorship or a naked fascist dictatorship, both equally in the interest of the bourgeoisie.[18]

If one extends the disastrous social-fascism line of the communists to our present progressives, one need not for a moment imply that when they preach the lie about fascism in America they are acting as communists. Obviously, they are not; but, given their narrow ideological resources and limited historical knowledge, they have taken over lock, stock, and barrel the Comintern line which, without doubt, did help bring Hitler to power.[19]

To suggest that America is fascist, or is going fascist, is to suggest that the American government, the political parties, the trade unions, the press and other media, and the majority of the people (or a large and strategic minority) are all either fascist or pre-fascist—with the exception, of course, of the person who is making the accusation and his valiant band of true believers. This is a form of irrationalism which Marx described in 1875 when he condemned those of his followers who argued that "in opposition to the working class, all other classes form only a homogeneous reactionary mass." Engels, seven years later, wrote of this semi-intellectual childishness:

> The idea that the coming revolution will *begin* on the basis that "here is Guelph and there is Ghibelline" is clearly a childish one—the idea that the whole world will be divided into two armies—on one side ourselves, and on the other the whole "single reactionary mass." This is as much to say that the revolution must begin at Act V, and not Act I. (Italics in original.)[20]

In discussing the tragedy-producing idiocy of the Stalinist Comintern which smoothed the nazi road to power, Professor Sidney Hook has written:

> And if there were no important difference between the Social-Democracy and Hitler, it followed *a fortiori* that there could be no important differences between Hitler and Schleicher, Schleicher and Papen, Papen and Bruening [Hitler's reactionary but non-fascist predecessors]. . . .
>
> . . . The Communist Party characterized Bruening's regime as already Fascist, then Papen's regime, then

Schleicher's regime, so that when the Fascist Hitler came to power, theoretically it was not prepared for the difference in political *quality* which the difference in political *degree* had brought about. It was only on the eve of its destruction that it woke up to the political importance of the differences between a regime which permitted mass organizations of the working-class, *including the Communist Party,* to exist and one which did not. (Italics in original.)[21]

Why are the prophets of fascism in America so certain that it will be fascism, and not communism or a form of "friendly" communism, "informal" communism, "incipient" communism, "preventive" communism? Because fascism—not communism—is regarded by progressives on the left as anti-historical, anti-progressive and therefore more easily overthrown. It was a German communist leader who declared in the Reichstag on 14 October 1931, "We are not afraid of the fascists. They will shoot their bolt sooner than any other government." Draper, who quotes this, observes:

> Inherent in this fatal reasoning was a still more suicidal implication—that Hitler was "unconsciously" serving the cause of the proletarian revolution by tearing the mask away from bourgeois democracy. However reactionary he appeared to be, according to this logic, his historic role was "objectively" revolutionary.[22]

One generation never learns from the previous one. In 1968, during the second uprising at Columbia, I did a television interview with two SDS (Students for a Democratic Society) leaders for the Canadian Broadcasting Corporation. I asked one of them how he was reacting to newspaper reports that white workers were "flocking" to the George Wallace candidacy. (It turned out after the 1968 election that these reports were highly exaggerated.) He answered that the fact that workers were going to vote for Wallace was good "because it shows the workers' disaffection from the System." I suggested that the last time workers had shown such disaffection from the System, it was the Weimar Republic, and they had bought Hitler instead. "That only means we must lead this disaffection into left channels," he said. How? The defiant answer was, "By conducting wildcat strikes among workers and radicalizing them." It is now years later and the SDS or any other radical involvement with American workers, hard hats or soft collars, is minimal.

This kind of fantastification about fascism as the precursor of the "great cultural liberation" is a modern form of Blanquism, which Friedrich Engels defined as "the phantasy of overturning an entire society through the action of a small conspiracy."[23] The laws of history, as expounded by the progressive left, provide that American politics is fundamentally reactionary; from reaction, one can slide without difficulty to fascism; from fascism, one can then visualize the Better World, even Walden Two. Time has no meaning, space no existence, nothing much can be done about it—so relax and despair and dream blithely about all kinds of horrors to come.

Today it is the Nixon-Agnew-Kissinger fascist threat. If I ask: Does anybody really think that President Nixon, Vice-President Agnew and Dr. Henry Kissinger would dare impose a fascist regime on America or that they are contemplating such a coup d'état—the answer from a left progressive audience would be meaningful silence. Merely to doubt the existence of such a conspiracy is to reveal oneself as highly reactionary or at best, naive, or to be smeared by Harriet Van Horne in her *New York Post* column (18 June 1971) as "an apologist" for the Nixon administration. Not to believe that the nation's elected leadership, the Pentagon, the power elite, the military-industrial complex are planning a fascist takeover is to demonstrate that one has been brainwashed into a state of political cretinism. To demand objective proof of such conscious plotting is to place oneself solidly in the camp of the enemy. The argument that there is a world of difference between a fascist plot (or "incipient fascism") and a Republican president desperately anxious to be re-elected, might elicit a grudging concession, "Well, maybe Nixon hasn't gotten there yet but give him time and you'll see." While it is permissible to add up every act of injustice committed by the United States government as proof of the existence of fascism, to use a similar "ethical calculus" about other countries in which acts of injustice are systemic rather than episodic, is impermissible.

There is a more scholarly and objective way to pin the fascist label on America, and it involves blurring the distinction between this country and the Soviet Union. For example, Professor Howard Zinn has written:

> When the United States defines the Soviet sphere as "totalitarian" and the West as "free," it becomes difficult for Americans to see totalitarian elements in our society, and liberal elements in Soviet society. Moralizing in this way, we can condemn the Russians in Hungary and absolve ourselves in Vietnam.[24]

This passage exemplifies precisely what I mean when I refer to lies in culture. Let Professor Zinn's Russian peers try to organize a "March on Washington" to the Kremlin to demand an end to Soviet occupation of foreign territories or an end to discrimination against ethnic minorities, and he would quickly perceive the difference between "totalitarian elements" in America and totalitarian elements in the Soviet Union. Or let *Izvestia* or *Pravda* attempt to publish some inside stories about the Soviet Pentagon and the Kremlin (as did the *New York Times* in June 1971 when it published the secret Vietnam story) and he would see the difference between the Soviets and the United States. Perhaps Professor Zinn senses all this—and yet he persists in repeating the same wearisome equation: American totalitarian elements = Soviet liberal elements.

The most diligent purveyor of the fascist canard about America is the mythopoeic Professor Marcuse, whose phrases "repressive tolerance" or "the democratic educational dictatorship of free men" remind one of Robespierre's defense of the Terror, *"Le gouvernement de la*

Revolution est le despotisme de la liberté contre la tyrannie [The revolutionary government is the despotism of liberty against tyranny]." When one begins to tell lies in culture and to turn culture into revolutionary, totalitarian politics, the rhetoric of paradox is a most useful weapon. Among the favorite phrases of the New Left are "creative disorder," i.e., preventing a pro-Vietnam meeting from taking place at Harvard; or "creative vandalism," i.e., destroying ten years of a professor's research notes during a building occupation; or describing, as Tom Hayden did, student revolutionaries as "guerillas in the field of culture."

Revolutionary politics is full of this kind of paradoxical linguistics. B. F. Skinner has written that "while I recognize that [Walden Two] is a form of despotism, we must use it temporarily to achieve a better government for all."[25] Andrew Kopkind, whom I quoted earlier, makes anything America does bad by definition. He says that "America is cleverest when it protects its opposition and neutralizes them. . . . Repressive tolerance is an exquisitely subtle game." Thus if America allows oppositions to function, it's a clever tactic. If America sends out the police, the National Guard, the sheriff and his deputies, it proves that America is going fascist.

This is an old trick whereby one tries to win arguments in philosophy and culture. C. Wright Mills tried that in his book, *The Power Elite*, in which he wrote:

> Whether they [the power elite] do or do not make such decisions is less important than the fact that they do occupy such pivotal positions: their failure to act, their failure to make decisions, is itself an act that is often of greater consequence than the decisions they do make.[26]

To which Professor John Bunzel responded:

> The difficulty here is that there is no way of testing this assertion. If the "power elite" make decisions, this shows they are powerful; if they do not, this also shows they are powerful because they decided not to

make decisions. Either way Mills' notion of a "power elite" is established. [But, as Bunzel has already pointed out,] any proposition that is not capable of being refuted is not scientifically acceptable.[27]

When Skinner concedes that his Utopia would be "a form of despotism," he is not conceding (and he would be highly offended at the suggestion) that he might be peddling a form of fascism; after all, the despotism would be merely temporary, aimed at creating "a better government for all." How, then, could one reject Mussolini's definition of fascism—"'organized, concentrated, authoritarian democracy on a national basis'"?[28] How nicely Skinner's prose dovetails with Lenin's, who declared in March 1920 that "the Soviet Socialist democracy is in no way inconsistent with the rule and dictatorship of one person; the will of a class is at times best carried out by a dictator, who alone will accomplish more and who is often more needed."[29]

What I am suggesting is that those intellectual and academicians who decry an invisible fascist epiphany may themselves be fascinated by the cultural meaning of fascism. This view has been sharply delineated by Benjamin Barber:

> The symptomology indicated by rightist and leftist discontent may hold out promise for an eventual revolutionary cure, but it also suggests the pathology of fascism. The danger is not simply that rebellion may invite repression. . . . The danger is that the rebels are themselves driven by needs for which fascism provides one kind of answer.[30]

Joachim Fest, the German historian who has written the history of the nazi leadership, has discussed the relationship of the student protest movement to fascism. He has argued that "at a deeper level a close basic kinship exists. For fascism as a historical phenomenon was part of the romantic counter-revolution characteristic of the age, and it is the continuation of the latter that we are witnessing in

San Francisco, Berlin or Woodstock; fascism was its most radical, powerful and desperate manifestation." Fest says that it would be incorrect to dismiss the protest movement adherents as fascists or to argue that "the movement as a whole was a contemporary version of fascism." He continues:

> But common to both are pessimistic disbelief in reason and total rejection of the existing order. Gregor Strasser's lapidary remark that Nazism meant *das Gegenteil von dem was heute ist* ("the opposite to what exists at present") has something in common with Marcuse's statement that the existing order "as a whole is always bad."[81]

To have argued at this length about the Big Lie of fascism in America may appear as a waste of time and energy. Yet this Big Lie is one of the most pervasive on the American campus today. Students who know little about Hitler or Mussolini or, for that matter, Stalin or Lenin, talk with much fluency and little knowledge about American fascism. It is already *here,* so no proof is necessary to substantiate its existence. Still, I must return to a most important question previously raised.

Why do our apocalyptic intellectuals only see "fascism" as the likely fate for America? Why, as I asked earlier, don't they ever say that a form of "totalitarianism" is coming to America—or a variety of brutalitarian communism? After all, whatever traditional liberties would disappear under a fascist regime would disappear as completely under a communist regime. The concentration camps which are "on the way" are as much part of communist totalitarianism as they were of nazi totalitarianism.[82] The police state nightmare is far more the order of the day in the Soviet Union than it is in most other countries, even in "proto-fascist" countries like America. Is it so unbelievable that, after more than half a century of the Bolshevik Revolution, a great writer like Alexander Solzhenitsyn must publish abroad and tell us:

> This book cannot at the present time be published in our native land except in Samizdat [privately circulated typescript] because of censorship objections unintelligible to normal human reason and which, in addition, demand that the word God be unfailingly written without a capital letter. To this indignity I cannot stoop. The directive to write God in small letters is the cheapest kind of atheistic pettiness. Both believers and unbelievers must agree that when the Regional Procurement Administration is written with capital letters or K.G.B. or Z.A.G.S. [the secret police or city registration bureau] are written in all caps then we might at least employ one capital letter to designate the highest Creative Force in the Universe.[33]

It is a marvel that despite all the evidence of the permanent war of the Soviet dictatorship against the peoples of the Soviet Union, America's dissident intellectuals can only foresee one enemy of intellectual freedom—America—and only one future, fascism, for America. Why fascism? Was Mussolini's fascism that much more wicked and bloodthirsty than Stalin's bolshevism? All one need do is to examine the authoritative study by Robert Conquest of Stalin's reign of terror[34] to see the difference—at least in human lives—between Mediterranean fascism and Eurasian communism.

The fact is that while these and other of America's critics may be opposed to fascism, they most certainly are not opposed to a totalitarian dictatorship so long as it has a so-called socialist, or self-proclaimed socialist, orientation or is accepted as socialist by either Moscow or Peking, or both. It is not a defense of Batista's dictatorship to ask how much worse it was than Castro's more durable dictatorship. I have no answer, but for those who are convinced that Batista's dictatorship was far worse than Castro's, the question must be put as to how they measure the moral superiority of the one against the moral inferiority of the other. Why this fear of fascism, which in any modern manifestation can hardly be said to exist since the fall of Hitler, of Mussolini,[35] of Peron (unless one wants to point with flesh-creeping horror at the world peril of falangism or the Greek colonels) and so little concern about a Russian tyranny with nuclear power, a roving Mediterranean fleet and tremendous intervention capability?

In this spirit one of the more flagrant debasements of the English language was perpetrated by Senator Walter F. Mondale of Minnesota. Speaking before the 1971 Institute of the NAACP Legal Defense and Education Fund, the Senator declared:

> The sickening truth is that this country is rapidly coming to resemble South Africa.
>
> Our native reserves and Bantustans are the inner city. And our apartheid is all the more disgusting for being insidious and unproclaimed.[36]

Either Senator Mondale doesn't know what apartheid is (in which case he ought to learn), or he does know—in which case he deserves the censure of his colleagues. I have been to South Africa as a journalist. My dispatches and articles must have offended Pretoria because when I sought to get a visa to reenter South Africa, once with the late Senator Robert F. Kennedy (whom I briefed on conditions there before his trip to South Africa in June 1966) and later without him, I was refused on both occasions. (The South African government barred U.S. reporters from accompanying the Senator, so the first refusal was a blanket rejection. The second refusal, however, was made in a letter to me from the South African consulate in New York and was reported in the *Rand Daily Mail* in July 1966.) I have visited the Transkei, the first Bantustan, and interviewed the Bantu leaders. I have interviewed the present prime minister, J. B. Vorster, and South African black labor leaders like Mrs. Lucy Mvubelo.[37] To suggest that America is "rapidly coming to resemble South Africa" when we are in the throes of the most democratic reappraisal of traditional race relations since the Civil War, is demagoguery, particularly using the easy, paradoxical trick of suggesting that "our apartheid is all the more disgusting for being insidious and unproclaimed," as Senator Mondale has done.

Apartheid in South Africa for blacks, coloreds and Asians is a form of totalitarianism since it intrudes on the private lives of all non-whites: it determines whom they may marry, with whom they may have sexual intercourse, which theaters and concerts they may attend, where they may live regardless of what they can afford, where they may work and at which jobs. Only a man whose mind is so resentment-ridden that he would mock whatever attempt is made to extirpate the curse of racism, could accuse America of "rapidly coming to resemble South Africa."[38]

Nor do I regard Mondale's charge as "just politics," any more than I regarded Senator Joe McCarthy's Big Lies as merely political. It is men like Senator Mondale, far more than the Southern racists in the Senate, who make a solution to racism in America more difficult than it is.

I want to conclude this chapter with one final example of how pervasive is the Big Lie about fascism in America. Three Iowa public school pupils were suspended in 1968 by school authorities because they wore black armbands as a symbolic protest against U.S. policies in Vietnam. The majority opinion held that under the First and Fourteenth amendments, the students had the right to wear the armbands. In an astounding piece of reductionist hyperbole, the Supreme Court said:

> In our system, state-operated school may not be *enclaves of totalitarianism.* School officials do not possess absolute authority over their students. (Italics added.)[39]

In other words, if the right of school authorities to ban wearing of black armbands had been upheld, our public schools could now be quite properly called "enclaves of totalitarianism." What might happen to the educational process if all students took to wearing armbands or other insignia as "symbolic speech" for different causes, is something which the Court overlooked—but it could warn about schools becoming "enclaves of totalitarianism."

The intellectual malady of our time has become infectious indeed when the contagion has spread even to such august precincts as the Supreme Court of the United States.

Genocide means any of the following acts committed with intent to destroy, in whole or in part, a national, ethnical, racial or religious group, as such:
- *(a) Killing members of the group;*
- *(b) Causing serious bodily or mental harm to members of the group;*
- *(c) Deliberately inflicting on the group conditions of life calculated to bring about its physical destruction in whole or in part;*
- *(d) Imposing measures intended to prevent births within the group;*
- *(e) Forcibly transferring children of the group to another group.*

United Nations, Convention on the
Prevention and Punishment of the
Crime of Genocide, 1948

I am informed, every morning when I awake, that some general and eternal law has just been discovered which I never heard mentioned before. There is not a mediocre scribbler who does not try his hand at discovering truths applicable to a great kingdom and who is very ill-pleased with himself if he does not succeed in compressing the human race into the compass of an article.

Alexis de Tocqueville,
Democracy in America, 1835

2

"America Means Genocide"

America means genocide; America is guilty of genocide; American history is genocide.

IF ONE HOLDS that genocide refers to tragic historical phenomena of the magnitude of Auschwitz or the Katyn Forest,[1] then the argument has an instructive shift. America is guilty of "cultural" genocide, "ethnic" genocide, "psychic" genocide—all of which are held to be *ipso facto* as bad as physical genocide. It is in essence the same linguistic technique used in disseminating the Big Lie about fascism in America, namely, the adaptation of an adjective as a seeming qualifier to a noun with an absolute meaning. If by similar debating standards, it is argued that China's seizure of Tibet[2] or persecution of the Uighur people in Sinkiang—or Stalin's seizure of the Baltic countries[3] and the dispersal of their populations, or Soviet counterrevolutionary invasions of East Germany, Hungary, Poland, and Czechoslovakia—might conceivably be defined as cultural or ethnic genocide—or that the Kremlin's suppression of Russian intellectual life might amount to metaphorical genocide—then there would be forthcoming the unfriendly riposte that this is Cold War propaganda. If the debater is too young to have heard about the Cold War, the answer may be, "So what? Russia is bad but America is worse."

Usually the favorite rebuttal is that the debater knows nothing about Russia, China or Cuba and is only interested in his own country, America, and her infamies. To talk about Russia or other foreign countries, about which the debater knows only what he reads in an untrustworthy press, is considered diversionary. Yet a little later the same debater, who has just proclaimed ignorance and disinterest in Russia and China and Cuba, somehow evinces an extraordinary amount of knowledge about the dictatorship of the Greek colonels which America is said to be supporting with enthusiasm; he is an expert on Franco's Spain going back to 1936, and an authority on Thailand, Brazil, the Dominican invasion, and all the dictatorships "allied with American imperialism." Any knowledge of "people's democratic" dictatorships has either escaped his notice or their evils are regarded as irrelevant to America's genocidal crimes.

This kind of moral standard is easily attained if you believe that fascist-military-capitalist dictatorships, unlike communist or Third World or socialist dictatorships, are unprogressive, backward looking, anti-historical. Thus Dr. Conor Cruise O'Brien in a recent essay, wrote:

> It is not enough to say that an underdeveloped country has the right to be nonaligned; it is necessary to recognize its rights to "go Communist," if that is the tendency of the political and social forces inside the country itself.[4]

But suppose the political and social forces wanted to go fascist, theocratic, anarchic or, heaven forbid, capitalist; or if, after the underdeveloped country had gone communist, the people decided they had erred and attempted to throw out communism, what then? Obviously that would be nothing but another CIA-inspired plot; for otherwise who would ever want to surrender the pleasures of a socialist paradise, unless, that is, he were bribed or being blackmailed?

The charge of genocide can be raised against America in another fashion. As Susan Sontag has written, opposite to, but in the spirit of Houston Stewart Chamberlain, Richard Wagner's son-in-law and white supremacist philosopher:

> The white race *is* the cancer of human history; it is the white race and it alone—its ideologies and in-

ventions—which eradicates autonomous civilizations wherever it spreads, which has upset the ecological balance of the planet, which now threatens the very existence of life itself.[5]

This racist drivel was published in a leading American literary magazine whose editors have recently become deeply concerned over what they regard as the disappearance of civility in cultural debate and in politics. Curiously, the *Partisan Review* editors and Miss Sontag who have been worrying privately about civility have failed to inquire publicly whether the Sontagian nightmare contributes to civility in culture. One might assume that when a magazine publishes a libel based on color against a large part of humanity, then it regards such a libel as worthy of debate—but, of course, the passage is only a metaphor, a self-fulfilling piece of metaphysics. If Miss Sontag had been writing rationally, she might have found it difficult to attack the white race and "its ideologies," one of which happens to be the very ideology she espouses, namely Marxism-Leninism.

Another count in the genocide indictment is the American war in Vietnam. Yet one can say that a government which fires rockets and mortars, downs Phantom jets, holds prisoner several thousand Americans, inflicts vast casualties on its enemies, which kept a war going successfully for almost thirty years against the soldiers of Japan, France, America, Australia, New Zealand, Korea and the Philippines; a government which refused to negotiate except on its own terms and in time, no doubt, will control South Vietnam, is hardly a government, a nation or a people who are victims of genocide. It has been a cruel war and, finally, an absurd war, with all kinds of atrocities on both sides but when someone calls the war in Vietnam genocide, I ask how many mortars, tanks and howitzers did European Jewry have and how many rifles did the Katyn Forest victims own?

The Big Lie about American genocide is one which has spread widely among apparently reasonable intellectuals. It turns out to be something which, like fascism, exists within the American people, as some genetically transmitted ethos. Never mind proving so monstrous a charge. Just say it, that is enough. Here we have the science editor of WCBS-TV News, Earl Ubell, uttering some, I suppose, scientific thoughts on the subject of America and genocide:

> We are a nation with the blood of genocide on our hands. For those who think that America cannot go the way of Nazi Germany, we have only to recall that we have already been down that road. That's what makes the whole black-white situation so frightening. Will white Americans somehow find their way back to the rationale of destroying whole peoples in the name of God, capitalism and law and order?[6]

The former book reviewer of the *New York Times,* Eliot Fremont-Smith, not only made the charge of genocide, but insisted that America's genocidal proclivities were "facts." In discussing John Hersey's book, *The Algiers Motel Incident,* he wrote:

> What is finally devastating about the book is that it shows America to be deeply—and unknowingly to most of its citizens—genocidal. The analogy to early Hitler Germany has been hitherto dismissed by "reasonable" men as irresponsibly naive and extreme. One now thinks that this is because reasonable men have been ignorant of the facts. Yet the facts have been around for quite a while. It would seem that they can at this late date be only wilfully avoided.[7]

What facts, one must ask of Fremont-Smith? Are you genocidal "unknowingly"? Is a whole people genocidal "unknowingly"? If most of America's citizens are unknowingly genocidal, how did Fremont-Smith and his journalist allies who slander human beings in this fashion manage to escape this taint? These are questions which to Fremont-Smith would only prove that I, too, as the propounder of such "reasonable" questions, am genocidal, unknowingly, of course. And so it is said, so it is published, so it is read, just another little observation about the life of the Average Genocidal Man in America.

In 1971 a group of college and university students (from Harvard, Yale, Cornell, Michigan, Amherst, Antioch, Oberlin, Chicago, Syracuse, Rochester, Illinois and Berkeley) spent a year as interns in New York City government. After their year they issued a report published under the auspices of the American Assembly, about their experiences and estimates of the future. It contained this paragraph:

> In the 1960s, the nation enacted a blueprint for a great society by providing comprehensive legislation to insure equal rights and opportunity for all Americans; yet *we recognize that everyday government is a party to genocide by its inaction and the active intent of its agents.* This genocide is as much the government's systematic failure to provide vital services such as health, justice, housing and income in the ghettos as it is the outright persecution and killing of minorities across the land. (Italics added.)

Professor Morton J. Tenzer, director of Urban Research, University of Connecticut, pointed out in a letter to me that the Urban Fellows "came to this startling conclusion after a year's experience observing firsthand the activities of the urban government [New York City] most devoted to providing services and to helping minorities of any in our country." He added:

> If after a year spent not in libraries or labs but actually working in city government, they can still conclude that somehow everyday government in the United States is guilty of committing genocide and that this is as much a business of actual commission, e.g., the "outright persecution and killing of minorities" as its omission "to provide vital services," it is trivial to say perhaps there is a gap in communications between the generations.

The *New York Times Book Review,* in its 1968 "summer reading" issue, had a special section entitled "A Question of Commitment." James Baldwin was one of those who participated in this symposium. He wrote that "the truth can no longer be ignored—white America appears to be seriously considering the possibilities of mass extermination." And guess what James Baldwin was going to do in this summer of 1968? He told the readers of the *New York Times Book Review* what he was going to do in this fascist, racist, genocidal United States:

> I intend to survive the summer because I am working on the screen version of "The Autobiography of Malcolm X" and hope to be shooting it, come the long, hard winter.

For saying that America plans mass extermination and that American leadership is out to control the world, Baldwin conceded he "may be dismissed as paranoiac [but] so were those unhappy people (shortly to be reduced to corpses) who saw the real significance of the Reichstag Fire. (We may already have had ours.)"

The whole point about the genocide accusation against "white America" is to make it appear that it is Americans who are genocidal, not merely their government and that, therefore, Americans are unredeemable. That is why Baldwin can write, in 1972, that Americans are "the most dishonorable and violent people in the world" and why he can play his own little "genocidal" game—"[I]t is not necessary for a black man to hate a white man, or to have any particular feelings about him at all, in order to realize that he must kill him."[8]

Stokely Carmichael also said in February 1968, "Many of us feel—many of our generation feel—that they are getting ready to commit genocide against us."[9]

It is only to be expected that the communist movement would help spread this libel against the American people; for example, in its publicity for the autobiography of William L. Patterson, *The Man Who Cried Genocide.*[10] It was Patterson who presented a petition to the United Nations charging the American government with genocide against the Negro people. It is to be expected that the *New Statesman* could run a book review in which the writer would say:

> In the ghetto schools you can see children who have been destroyed by white America; psychological and cultural genocide does not seem an exaggerated description of the process. I find it difficult not to feel that anything, anything at all—racial hatred, voodoo, millenarian myths, communism—that restores to these victims a sense of dignity and self-worth is amply justified and worthwhile.[11]

It is to be expected that Professor Philip Slater should, with his American self-hatred, write that "Americans have always been a people with marked genocidal proclivities," or that "We have become a dangerously irritable people."[12] What is not to be expected is that responsible American publicists and journals should collaborate in this grievous nonsense. But this is what happens. A Big Lie begins to circulate, then it becomes common currency. It becomes part of the radical chic culture and before long the Big Lie has become so ordinary that nobody even notices what is being said. In that, of course, resides our basic protection; but it does serious injury to a free culture and the public mind when something as awful as the crime of genocide is attributed to a whole people, a whole society, and when few commentators think it even important enough to argue about.

An example of what happens when a Big Lie begins rolling and develops a momentum of its own, is the story of how the Black Panthers became "a victim of American genocide" and how major American dailies, like the *New York Times*, the *Washington Post* and the *Christian Science Monitor* all accepted as something beyond the need for proof the report that twenty-eight Panthers had been murdered by police.[13] In December 1969, Charles R. Garry, the lawyer for the Black Panthers, said that within that very year, a pattern of genocide had been established against the organization. The *New York Times* reported on 7 December and 9 December, 1969, that twenty-eight Panthers had been killed by police. This was totally incorrect. On April 26, 1970, the *Times* again reported that twenty-eight Panthers had been killed by the police. This was incorrect. In between, the *Times* reported that Garry had put the number of Panthers killed by the police at twelve. This was also incorrect.

This story, which appeared in the Times, 21 December 1969, was, as Edward Jay Epstein has written, "unfortunately inadequate." The *Times* reporter cited six incidents in which Panthers were killed by police. The reporter, however, neglected to mention that in four of these incidents, fourteen police were shot or killed by Black Panthers. There were other half-truths in this story.

What is most important about the original report is that Garry's assertion about twenty-eight Black Panther deaths at the hands of police was published 7 December, 1969 as, according to Epstein, "as established fact, without giving any source for the figure or qualifying it in any way." Two days, later, the *Washington Post* stated that twenty-eight members of the black militant group had "died in clashes with the police since January 1, 1968"; and even a paper as cautious as the *Christian Science Monitor*, after a telephone interview with Garry, cited the Panther charge of "police murder" and "genocide" and expressed "a growing suspicion that something more than isolated local police action was involved."[14]

Garry theorized about "a national scheme . . . to destroy" the Panthers and this unsubstantiated statement was repeated in the *Times* by John Kifner, who asserted that Nixon administration statements "appear to have at least contributed to a climate of opinion among local police . . . that a virtual open season has been declared on the Panthers." *Time,* 12 December 1969, reported that the gun battles between police and Panthers amounted to "lethal undeclared war," and concluded, "Whether or not there is a concerted police campaign, the ranks of Panther leadership have been decimated in the past two years."[15] In its next issue, *Time* repeated Garry's allegation that twenty-eight Panthers had died in police gunfire and asked, "Specifically, are the raids against Panther offices part of a national design to destroy the Panther leadership?" *Newsweek* in a news report headlined, "Too Late for the Panthers?" asked, "Is there some sort of government conspiracy afoot to exterminate the Black Panthers?"[16]

Quite naturally, Negro civil rights leaders like Roy Innis, Ralph Abernathy, Julian Bond, and the late Whitney Young condemned the alleged plot against the Panthers. The story spread from Garry to the newspapers, and then to the magazines, and then to civil rights leaders—until it finally became embedded as a formal finding of incontrovertible authenticity.

Epstein only did the obvious—but it was something no other journalist did, an achievement for which the *Wall Street Journal* paid him a curiously backhanded compliment.[17] Epstein simply went out and researched every one of the twenty-eight Panther deaths in Chicago, Seattle, New Haven, Los Angeles, Oakland and San Diego. He found that no twenty-eight Panthers had been killed by the police. Even the Panther lawyer, Garry, who had initiated the story, finally conceded it was only nineteen. But when Epstein examined the nineteen cases, he found that the police had had nothing at all to do with nine of the slayings. Of the remaining ten on Garry's list, six Panthers, Epstein reported, "were killed by seriously wounded policemen who clearly had reason to believe that their own lives were in jeopardy." In the four remaining cases, two Panthers confronted policemen with weapons. The writer concluded that *in only one instance*—the shooting by police on 4 December 1969, of Fred Hampton and Mark Clark—were Panthers attacked "by policemen whose lives were not being directly threatened by those men."

Even more significant is Epstein's rebuttal of the John Kifner article in the *Times* that Nixon administration statements had "at least contributed to a climate of opinion among local police . . . that a virtual open season has been declared on the Panthers." Epstein wrote:

This is historically inaccurate since five of the ten Panther deaths that can be directly attributed to police action occurred before the Nixon administration took office.

One would have thought that after jouralism's miserable experience with Senator Joe McCarthy's "numbers game" about communists in Washington, the American press would be somewhat wiser. Not at all. The Associated Press reported that twenty-seven Panthers had been killed; United Press International said twenty had been killed in "cold blood" by police. *Life* in one issue (6 February 1970) published three different Panther mortality figures. It gave Eldridge Cleaver as its source for twenty-eight murders, declared on its own that nineteen Panthers "are dead," and added, "it is uncertain that more than a dozen have died of police bullets." Articles in the *New Republic, Ramparts, New Statesman* used the figure twenty; the executive director of the American Civil Liberties Union said twenty-eight. Nicholas von Hoffman of the *Washington Post* wrote a column using the twenty-eight killed as the figure given out by the Panthers, adding that "there is no strong prima-facie reason to disbelieve them."

When Epstein talked to Charles Garry in September 1970, the Panther lawyer explained that he had chosen the number twenty-eight when reporters called him for a statement after the shooting of Fred Hampton and Mark Clark because that "seemed to be a safe number." Epstein remarked on this:

> You know, if Garry had picked a number ending in zero, he wouldn't have been as effective as he was by saying twenty-eight. The number he picked was low enough so as to sound plausible and effective. It was like Joe McCarthy when he waved his list of Communists in the State Department and said there were 146 or whatever number it was.[18]

The Black Panther affair—and more importantly, the Epstein reportage—is extraordinary even in a country which is attacked habitually by some of its own citizens as "fascist," "racist," "genocidal." For almost two years this venomous libel circulated about police "genocide" against the Black Panthers without a single leading newspaper or press agency (with the exception of *Newsday*) ready to investigate the charge made on the authority of a person who, by definition and position, was a special pleader for the Black Panthers. Not until the *New Yorker* came along did the true story finally emerge.

Why did the press believe this Big Lie? Why did they take the word of a Black Panther lawyer without checking his figures? Is not skepticism supposed to be the honest journalist's weapon against special pleaders and propagandists? Why did a *Times* reporter blame the Nixon administration for murders which had occurred—and which were not even due to police "genocide"—before President Nixon took office? And why was there nobody on the *Times* or *Washington Post* copy desks to check so flamboyant an accusation which should have had, at least, some chronological accuracy?

If any one episode demonstrates the power of our culture critics over the press and magazines in America on social issues, it is this sickening story about police "genocide" against the Panthers. Facts are irrelevant. *Si non é vero, é ben trovato* (even if it isn't true, it could be). Epstein put it very well in his conclusion:

> Four deaths, two deaths, even a single death must be the subject of the most serious concern. But the basic issues of public policy presented by the militancy of groups like the Panthers and by the sometimes brutal police treatment of angry and defiant black people in general can be neither understood nor resolved in an atmosphere of exaggerated charges—whether of "genocide" against the Panthers or of "guerrilla" warfare against the police—that are repeated, unverified, in the press and in consequence widely believed by the public.[19]

The cry of genocide in America is part of the spirit of "revolutionism" which informs our powerful social critics. As I will show, they look upon America as hopeless, as unredeemable, as doomed. When one says that a democratic country is capable of being genocidal or is on the way to a state of "friendly fascism," the intent of these Big Lies is not to improve but rather to destroy that democracy. For the fabricators of a Big Lie, to say America means "genocide" is really a kind of Big Truth—because their aim is to bring about the Republic of Virtue, a new order, a new society, a new state, a new everything. In other words, truth must, in this ideology, depend on the *motive* behind the Big Lie. A noted psychologist once wrote:

> The scientists involved in espionage have been very few, indeed, and misguided as they *may* have been, *they have acted on principle and not for personal gain.* (Italics added.)[20]

Thus if one is motivated by a particular ideal or ideology, everything can be readily forgiven.

The genocidal Big Lie is raised in a different fashion by Professor Philip Slater, when he writes in his *Pursuit of Loneliness* that a fascist coup "might well be combined with a right-induced nuclear war. . . . when the old culture falls it may take the entire world with it." Not long ago some Western intellectuals were intoning their slogan for survival, "better red than dead," that is to say, better to exist under a communist dictatorship than to have the world destroyed in the name of some decadent ideology. In the light of Professor Slater's disclosure that the old culture is led by thermonuclear psychopaths, would he and other intellectuals who share his opinions and who claim total political power by the right of eminent alienation, dare say: "better fascist than dead"? After all, Professor Slater truly believes such a "right-induced nuclear war" is probable; as he says, "more and more people feel with a larger and larger part of themselves that the destruction of mankind as a failed species might be a sound idea."[21]

These quotations from Professor Slater can be understood or defended as legitimate philosophical speculations out of which great theories of human nature may some day derive. What cannot so easily be defended, however, are the great newspapers and mass circulation magazines, whose editors pretend to some intellectual rigor, having no compunctions about publishing Big Lies as relevant truths and making little old-fashioned effort to check the accuracy of what they publish. A. M. Rosenthal, one of the most distinguished and wisest editors I know, explained to me why this problem exists:

> There is room in this country for all kinds of journalism, political journalism, and the kind of objective journalism we try to practice. But I believe that advocacy journalism should be written for journals of advocacy and not for newspapers which tell their readers that they try to be objective.[22]

The Black Panther Big Lie is an example of what happens when ideology replaces honest reporting. When well known writers can so casually compose as horrifying an indictment of a country and a people as "guilty of genocide" and when such an indictment finds resonance among intellectuals, in and out of the academic community, it can be said that in American culture, as in some sectors of American journalism, we have entered the Age of the Manifesto.

"Do you realize that we are very powerful already? Our party consists not only of those who kill and burn, or fire off pistols in the classical manner. . . . Such people are only in our way. . . . Listen, I've summed them all up: the teacher who laughs with the children at their God and at their cradle is ours already. The barrister who defends an educated murderer by pleading that, being more mentally developed than his victims, he could not help murdering for money, is already one of us. . . . The juries who acquit all criminals without distinction are ours. A public prosecutor, who trembles in court because he is not sufficiently progressive, is ours, ours. Administrators, authors—oh, there are lots and lots of us, and they don't know it themselves. On the other hand, the docility of schoolboys and fools has reached the highest pitch; the schoolmasters are full of bile. . . . Do you realize how many converts we shall make by trite and ready-made ideas? When I went abroad, [the] theory that crime is insanity was the vogue; when I returned, crime was no longer insanity, but just common sense, indeed, almost a duty and, at any rate, a noble protest. . . .

". . . Oh, if only we had more time! The trouble is we have no time. We shall proclaim destruction—why? why?—well, because the idea is so fascinating! But—we must get a little exercise. We'll have a few fires—we'll spread a few legends. . . .

". . . And the whole earth will resound with the cry: 'A new and righteous law is coming.' "

Fyodor Dostoyevsky, *The Devils,* 1871

Unlike any other type of society, capitalism inevitably and by virtue of the very logic of its civilization, educates and subsidizes a vested interest in social unrest.

Joseph Schumpeter, *Capitalism, Socialism, Democracy,* 1942

No society offers and tempts men so much as does an egalitarian society and in no society can one find so much frustration.

Alexis de Tocqueville, *Democracy in America*, 1835

3

"The Bomber Left Is a Moral Force"

The Bomber Left in America is a moral force.

THE BOMBER LEFT may be guilty of something, but the guilt is pardonable. It is only a legal, not a moral, guilt—because (*a*) America is a violent country,[1] (*b*) violence is the Bomber Left's agonized answer to the need for a moral response to America's counterrevolutionary refusal to "change" and (*c*) nobody gets hurt during a bombing except by accident. So the bomb becomes a psychedelic abstraction destroying another abstraction: a computer center (at the University of Wisconsin where a student was killed); a faculty club (at the University of California, Santa Barbara, where a custodian was killed); a university hall (at Pomona College, Claremont, California, where a secretary was blinded and otherwise severely injured when she opened a time bomb package). This is the syndrome.

Political frustration ascribed to the Bomber Left usually evokes deep sorrow among avant-garde social critics. It is significant that a similar indulgence for the "Goldwater Right" is unthinkable; any violence arising out of despair on the "Wallace Right" is, by avant-garde convention, backward looking and contemptible. Violence on the Bomber Left is taken to be an aberrant yet somehow progressive step towards the New Jerusalem.[2] Thus it comes to pass that Bomber Left violence can be understood as "non-violence" while Bomber Right violence, where it happens, becomes fascist brutality.[3] The Bomber Left is a victim of American society; the Bomber Right *is* American society. Q.E.D.

In Spring 1970, the Alma Mater statue on the 116th Street campus of Columbia University was bombed during the night. The next morning a distinguished academician was heard to say, sadly, as he looked at the damaged hulk:

> These kids have a higher priority—social justice—and if we had social justice, these things wouldn't happen.

The academics who find extenuating circumstances for the violence are, in my opinion, as culpable as the dynamiters themselves: for it is they who supply the essential moral cachet. These latterday *narodniki* have been encouraged to feel that any punishment for what they have done is a violation of their civil right to bomb and proves that this is a repressive society.[4] Consider the gallery of rationalizers.

Professor Douglas Dowd of Cornell University is one of those who has explained away the Bomber Left:

> Violence on the left by the people who are trying to change things has to be understood for what it is. It is in the first place being practiced by people who have tried many other kinds of things, whether you're speaking of Weathermen now or bombers. They're serious, committed people, and the other characteristic is that they're desperate. They've given up on the idea that a movement can get any place *without* violence. (Italics in original.)[5]

Dr. Benjamin Spock has said that he opposes violence because it "wins damn few people to your side." The news report continued sympathetically:

> He hastened—characteristically—to qualify this judgment, however. "I don't want to imply that I'm morally superior to the Weathermen—I'm certainly not as

courageous and maybe not as sincere. But that doesn't make them right necessarily."[6]

A rather startling pronouncement came from Wayne O'Neil, Professor of Humanities at the Massachusetts Institute of Technology:

> Recently, in the face of men who believed that X should not be promoted because of his strongly held and activist political position, I argued *in abstracto* the injustice of my voting against the tenuring or promotion of Y simply because he carried on chemical and biological warfare research, provided that his research was good, that he was a fine teacher, and that the university supported in principle work on CBW. On the other hand, I would have no compunctions about bombing Y's CBW lab as long as no one got hurt.[7]

Professor Tytell, whom I quoted earlier, has written:

> The New Left has searched for surgical antidotes in an era of hysteria. Existentially refuting the perennial liberal plea for patience . . . the New Leftists advocated radical change through direct action. They have publicized their new bravado with courageously reckless insistence.[8]

Professor Richard Poirier's apologies are reminiscent of those pro-Stalin liberals in the 1930s and 1940s whose favorite riposte to some documented outrage in the Soviet Union was: How can you talk about slave labor in the Soviet Union when there are outhouses and pellagra in the South? Is Dr. Poirier any more sophisticated than were the pro-Stalin intellectuals when he can write:

> Before asking questions about the propriety and programs of young militants who occupy buildings, burn cars and fight the police, let's first ask what kind of world surrounds these acts.[9]

Another distinguished academician, Professor Robert Lekachman, felt impelled recently to speak "some word of appreciation of SDS." As he expressed it:

> SDS has played the role of the farmer who clubbed his balky mule over the head with a two-by-four. When reproved by a humanitarian bystander, he replied that the first necessity of the case was to get the animal's attention. Although I care as little for the illegal occupation of buildings as I do for the clubbing of mules, I must also note the obvious: Both techniques do genuinely attract the attention of their targets—mules or university administrators.[10]

The violence at our universities is evidently no worse than hitting a mule with a stick: in fact, the violence is progressive because it leads to good things for future generations. As the *New Statesman* once wrote in defending the purges of Stalin, "A social revolution is accompanied both by violence and by idealism."[11]

A rather more philosophical defense of violence is to be found in the writings of Herbert Marcuse. For example, he argued in a recent lecture:

> The violence of revolutionary terror, for example. is very different from that of the White terror, because revolutionary terror as terror implies its own abolition in the process of creating a free society. . . .
>
> How one can prevent revolutionary terror from turning into cruelty and brutality is another question.[12]

Tolstoy was once asked if he didn't see the difference between reactionary repression and revolutionary repression. He replied that there was, of course, a difference: "the difference between cat shit and dog shit."

Defense of the Bomber Left is based on disregard of what its votaries are actually saying, or if not disregarded, then this is depicted as nothing more serious than a prank or in the jargon of the day, a put-on. Here, for example, is a statement which, as part of a "strategy of creative disruption," calls for what might—given an error in dosage—be regarded as criminal poisoning:

> We can stop the defense research being carried on under university auspices.... Students could infiltrate the office staffs of the electronic accelerators and foreign policy institutes, and hamper their efficiency. *The introduction of a small quantity of LSD in only five or six government department coffee-urns* might be a highly effective tactic. (Italics added.)[13]

Tom Hayden has an even more brilliant tactic:

> Perhaps the only forms of action appropriate to the angry people are violent. Perhaps a small minority, by setting ablaze New York and Washington, could damage this country forever in the court of world public opinion.[14]

So we have here another useful abstraction—"the court of world public opinion," whatever that may be—which, in order to be influenced, demands wholesale arson of two cities and, I suppose, the incineration of their populations purely by accident. Then there is Marcus Raskin, who knows what most of the world is thinking:

> [America] is now viewed as the world's primary enemy by the poor and the young.[15]

How young is young? How poor is poor? What countries think so? How do you know? Does a reader have a right even to ask for the data which "prove" this allegation?

A special school of explicators of left violence now exists, whose adepts compose *apologia pro sua bomba* texts in a spirit resembling that of the young parricide who, deploring his present stage of orphanage, beseeched the court's mercy. Members of this school are recognizable by a giveaway sentence which usually begins, "And yet . . ." This phrase is invariably preceded by a catalogue of admitted sins—bombing, arson, days of rage, sabotage, malicious mischief, ascent from *engagé* to *exalté* to *enragé* —and the fog-banks of nauseating verbiage descend:

> And yet, after all these criticisms have been made, the realities to which the new terrorism has been a response must not be ignored. . . . In moments of bitterness, it sometimes seems as if America has spawned the radicalism it deserves. It is easy enough to castigate the terrorists for forgetting the creative side of legitimate *praxis*. What is more difficult is to recognize how rapidly attempts to construct alternative life-styles within the current society are swallowed up, how the "liberated zones" of the counterculture have been almost immediately "reenslaved" by the mass media. *And to remember that their rejection of the American working class as a force for social change did come after several years of largely futile community organizing.* [So the terror is all the fault of George Meany and an unresponsive American working class.] It is also easy to express horror at the irresponsible violence of the terrorists without at the same time seeing it in the context of America's increasing "legitimate" use of violent means at home and abroad. (Italics added.)[16]

It is worth examining this piece of prose and other sentences which I have not quoted. The aim, of course, is to blame the terrorism on the System, on Us, on society, on the Establishment, on the working class—"realities . . . must not be ignored. . . . America has spawned the radicalism it deserves . . . perhaps most disturbing is . . . can be partly understood . . . what the terrorists have grasped in their desperation. . . ." (It's not their fault, poor kids, they are desperate and they are trying to tell us something.) Then there are the sentences to shame you out of your middle-class stuffiness—"it is easy enough to castigate the terrorists," or "it is also easy to express horror," or "so, too, is it simple to register indignation." The sign of the literary intellectual is to see exculpatory complexities in a flower child's gelignite.

Dr. Kenneth Keniston is another votary of the "I-don't-condone-violence-and-yet" school, about whom Professor Joseph Adelson has written:

> [Keniston] is all too eager to believe anything he is told. His respondents tell him they are non-violent; he believes it. They tell him they act only out of the highest moral principles; he believes it. No doubt if they told him they could walk on water he would believe that too.
>
> If there is anything which has characterized the Movement, which has distinguished it from expressions of American radicalism in this century, it has been the infatuation with violence. . . . To say that Keniston has been insensitive to the presence of violence is, if anything, to understate the case. In his view, young radicals are not only free from the disposition to violence, they are in fact entirely opposed to it; they are victims rather than instigators.[17]

What I find extraordinary about this so-called fascist *Amerika* is the freedom for those who want to publish praise of revolutionary violence and political assassination. Their words manage to circulate as if they were the Gideon Bible. I am not here even remotely suggesting censorship of the media. I would merely like those purveyors of the fascist *Amerika* Big Lie to tell me in what other country in the world, progressive or reactionary or whatever, would the leading newspaper publish the following statement by a revolutionary, in this case, Eldridge Cleaver:

> There are . . . advantages to political assassination, not that this can eliminate the function, but you know that the man will be replaced, and it has great educational value. It teaches the people to kill the enemy and hate the enemy. It would give me great satisfaction if Richard Nixon should be killed. I would consider that an excellent thing.

Let's skip the footnote reference. This was published in the *New York Times Magazine,* 1 November 1970, as part of an interview with the self-exiled American Negro revolutionary by Sanche de Gramont entitled, "Cleaver Speaks." (On 1 August 1971, the *New York Times Magazine* published a long interview with George Lester Jackson, another black revolutionary, while he was still serving an indeterminate one-year-to-life sentence in San Quentin after three convictions for robbery. He was quoted by the interviewer, Tad Szulc, as saying that "the political leadership in the United States must be 'neutralized and corrected as effectively as possible . . . and by correcting I mean killing them.' " [Ellipsis in quote.] Jackson, who was killed 21 August 1971 in what was described as a jail-break in San Quentin, was one of the three "Soledad Brothers." Three prison guards were also killed at the same time.) I am not sure what I would have done had I been the editor, and I am certain that the editors were torn between Cleaver's democratic right to express himself and the responsibility of a great newspaper published in a country where assassinations of presidents and presidential candidates are, one might say, with a bow to H. Rap Brown, "as American as cherry pie."[18] I do know that if I were Robert Coles I might have swallowed hard when reading this Cleaver unction. It was Coles who, reviewing Cleaver's book, *Soul on Ice,* described him as a man "full of Christian care, Christian grief and disappointment, Christian resignation, Christian messianic toughness and hope."[19]

In several major newspapers I read analects from Carlos Marighella's *Minimanual of the Urban Guerrilla.* Marighella's advice has an uncanny resemblance to what has been happening in America:

> It is necessary for every urban guerrilla to keep in mind always that he can only maintain his existence if he is disposed to kill the police and those dedicated to repression and if he is determined to expropriate the wealth of the big capitalists, the latifundists and the imperialists.[20]

The following statement was also published in a widely circulated magazine which goes through the U.S. mails, and is sold openly on newsstands although it poses as part of the underground press:

> I thought of the President being gunned down in the War Room while his astonished generals waited their turn at death, and mobs of angry blacks, free at last, roared through the White House, like the Winter Palace, entering into an orgy of violence . . . tearing into the Congress and slaughtering the members one by one on the Senate and House floors while galleries packed with tourists from the Middle West watched in horror. Rage moving and thundering through the federal bureaucracies and mowing down the civil servants, the blood flowing in the streets, sparkling in the bright sunshine. . . . A revolution bigger than the Russian or the French, more beautiful, wider, bloodier, bringing down the final, sweet fire on all our heads.[21]

A new paperback magazine, called *Defiance*, is being distributed and sold on American newsstands (I purchased mine at Boston's Logan Airport) with this enlightening analysis:

> However appealing to concepts of guerrilla warfare, the extolling of violence and martyrdom in the struggle for liberation in America would be viable except for the fact of despair. It is the deadly knowledge that the American statist political arrangement is utterly corrupt, irredeemably false, that it is riddled with bad faith and hypocrisy, that the entire corporate-military system is facing disintegration, anomie, that entices the young to appeal to violence as the only efficacious means to freedom. Incontrovertibly, the corruption and anti-democratic nature of the political arrangement in this country have given birth to the terrorist.[22]

There have been thousands of meetings against the war in Vietnam at universities, there have certainly been hundreds at Harvard University. In Spring 1971 some pro-Vietnam students decided to hold a public Harvard meeting in support of the war. The meeting was broken up by students who announced in advance that they were coming to the Harvard auditorium to break it up. And they did, despite appeals from Harvard administrators that, in the name of free speech, they allow the meeting to go on. When a move was made to punish the anti-war students for their actions, it was argued in the University student newspaper that any punishment would violate the rights of the student anti-war protesters. To lend this argument the highest respectability, Professor Warner Berthoff of Harvard's English Department published a letter a few days later which said:

> Like those on the platform, those in the audience [i.e., those who broke up the meeting] came to say something. They said it. In the circumstances of a political rally, wherever [it] happens to be staged, the right to shout down speakers is embraced by the same principle of freedom of speech and expression as protects the speakers in their efforts to make themselves heard.[23]

One of the most recent rationalizers of student violence is, sadly enough, a man who as a former Hungarian communist suffered at the hands of Matyas Rákosi and later participated in the 1956 Hungarian uprising. He is George Paloczi-Horvath. After watching the Polish October, the Prague Spring and all those regrettably futile attempts to bring a breath of freedom to Eastern Europe, Paloczi-Horvath now finds that repression in Western countries is as bad as, if not worse than, it is in the Soviet Union or the satellite countries. And what is his convenient solution? Youth, that amorphous category which is everything and nothing, before which Paloczi-Horvath bows as presumably he once bowed before the Marxism-Leninism-Stalinism he now abjures. As mythopoeic as Marcuse, he talks vaguely about how "various vicious circles were in effective operation" in the West, so that "academic youth [has] been forced to resort to violence in self-defense [and] hundreds of thousands of students fought in effect for the restoration of truth and wisdom." He concludes:

> The overwhelming majority of the revolutionary student groups were convinced that their fight for the destruction of the present obsolete university system and the creation of a new one was the precondition of creating a wise and good social order that would imply less frustration, less waste, less pain and less violence.[24]

And suppose that one happens to disagree with this idea about the social value of destroying the "obsolete university system." Would one be allowed to resist the revolutionary student groups? Would one be given an opportunity to argue, to dissent, to vote? Alas, Paloczi-Horvath never gets around to the wisdom and truth of the rights of the opposition. In fact, he is rather dismissive about people who disagree; they represent "conformist majorities [who] refuse to consider the ultimate consequences of their actions and behavior." This writer acknowledges his debt to the Center for the Study of Democratic Institutions in Santa Barbara, California, for sponsoring the book and to Laurance S. Rockefeller for his "most generous grant."

As one ponders this rationalization of violence in the cause of revolutionary change, one is moved to ask a disagreeable question. Why don't Marcuse, Rader, Paloczi-Horvath, Dowd and other progressive intellectuals issue a call for violence in countries which they might also feel are "betrayers of the faith," viz. the orthodox communist countries in Eastern Europe or in Soviet Russia itself? Why are only democratic countries the target of *le propagande par le fait* (the cult of the deed)?

There are several reasons, I think, for our present crisis of violence, one of them described a long time ago by H. G. Wells:

It chanced, too, that a wave of moral intolerance was sweeping through London, one of those waves in which the bitterness of the consciously just finds an ally in the panic of the undiscovered.²⁵

The Wellsian epigram surely describes the unconditional surrender during the 1968-1970 campus insurrection of these academics who had long ignored students in favor of other more lucrative commitments and were now intoning: *mea culpa, mea maxima culpa*. Another reason is the radical saw, "no enemies on the left," or as Marcuse once put it in an interview when asked, "Are you arguing that there can be no enemy to the left?"

The situation is such that an enemy on the left is rather hard to imagine. We have so many enemies on the right.²⁶

One reason why the revolutionary left ignores the logic of liberating, humanizing violence against communist dictatorships is because in communist countries the advocacy of anti-System violence is defined as treason and as "counter-revolutionary," while in democratic countries, the advocacy of anti-System or personal violence is regarded as an essential part of civil liberties. Marcuse concedes this point quite contentedly:

The establishment has a legal monopoly of violence and the positive right, even the duty, to use this violence in its self-defence. In contrast, the recognition and exercise of a higher right and the duty of resistance, of civil disobedience, is a motive force in the historical development of freedom, a potentially liberating violence.²⁷

How have we come to this moment in America in which we see the growth of what Richard Hofstadter called the "mystique of violence on the left"? As Professor Hofstadter noted:

[We] are never surprised at violence cults on the right. . . . What has been more arresting is the decline of the commitment to non-violence on the left, and the growth of a disposition to indulge or to exalt acts of force or violence.[28]

What has caused this paralysis of will among men of learning and decency that they can offer the most abstruse rationalizations for this mystique of violence on the left? Is it, perhaps, the very idea of Youth in its current neo-romanticization as the essence of purity, freedom, virility and the future? How is it that the teenage student seems to so many of them to hypostasize the virtues of the charismatic leader with mission announced and obedience demanded? It could be that youth does seem virtuous and incorruptible to those professors whose prestige is measured by how little time they devote to teaching and to office hours for students. It is not the first time in history that the guilt-ridden old have sought redemption in the young. But the young also have their psychological disorders, and only a Freud of political neuroses could diagnose the point at which they both meet. Nothing from the past—neither Rousseau's youth cult, nor Bakunin's nihilism, nor even Spengler's vision of a new barbarian horde of young urban vandals—satisfactorily explains the sorrowing indulgence for the Bomber Left.

Professor Adelson has suggested that what he calls "the images of victim and visionary control our current perception of youth." He adds:

More often than not the two images coalesce. Either the young are oppressed because of their visionary capacity, because they see fully what the established powers fear to see at all; or because their victimization, the very posture of humiliation they are forced to endure, allows them a prescience beyond the common understanding. The figure of the prophetic victim, though it draws upon traditional religious imagery, and though it resonates with earlier

American archetypes . . . becomes the dominant image of the young in the postwar era. . . .

And in the 1960s, we note an important change. The young victim now transcends his victimization; he overcomes his passivity and in doing so achieves strength and heroism. He is the prophet armed, his rebellion justified by his prior oppression, his vision of a better world setting the goals of his movement. Indeed in this decade the themes of oppression, prophecy, and rebellious heroism become the dominant motifs of collective fantasy, as the metaphor of victimization is politicized, and as other groups . . . are defined, by themselves, or more often through self-appointed spokesmen, as victims, visionaries and revolutionary heroes.[29]

Until recently nobody mistook violence for, of all things, cherry pie. Until now, few literary intellectuals attended to George Sorel's distinction between "force" (the instrument of bourgeois oppression) and "violence" (the instrument of proletarian liberation). Today one of the most popular subjects and examination questions in any university sociology or political science course is that of political, or social, violence. For some academicians and progressives —who resemble those footloose revolutionaries of tsarist Russia described by Engels as "officer candidates without an army"—the idea of violence has become the "in" concept because there is, they say, "no other way." The former head of SDS has written:

> The rebel is an incorrigible absolutist who has replaced all "problems" with the one grand claim that the entire system is an error, all "solutions" with the single irreducible demand that change shall be total, all diagnoses of disease with one final certificate of death. To him, total change means only that those who now have all the power shall no longer have any, and that those who now have none—the people, the victimized—shall have all. Then what can it mean to speak of compromise? Compromise is whatever ab-

solves and reprieves an enemy who has already been sentenced.[30]

With such final alternatives in so total a form, there can be only one next step. This apocalyptic rage so afflicts an important sector of the student-academic intellectual left that as sharp a critic of American society as Professor H. Mark Roelofs of New York University has been moved to say:

> The radical not in communion with the society he would remake is condemned to inanity and to thinking and talking in a fantasy world of his own devising.[31]

Yet it is this fantasy world, born out of what Nietzsche described as "the weariness that wants to reach the ultimate with one leap," which has seized the imagination of young men and women and persuaded them that there is no way out but destruction. It is the very way prescribed by Nechayev in his *Catechism of the Revolutionist:*

> The revolutionist is a doomed man. He has no personal interests, no affairs, sentiments, attachments, property, not even a name of his own. Everything in him is absorbed by one exclusive interest, one thought, one passion—the revolution. Day and night he must have one thought, one aim—inexorable destruction.[32]

There is very little that is new in this kind of desperadoism, this Bakuninist "creative destruction," this *culte de moi* which claims that civil disobedience can only be meaningful if its votaries can plant bombs at such times and places of their own choosing, if they can act as executioners of those whom they have defined as guilty for all the world's sins.[33] James Joll has described how between 1880 and 1914 there were an extraordinary number of anarchist outrages against "the symbols of power and corruption in existing society"—the kings, the prime ministers, the legislators. He writes:

> Bombs were thrown into fashionable theatres and restaurants as a protest against bourgeois society. And in one famous case in Paris in the 1890s, a man threw a bomb into a very ordinary café where workers as well as members of the bourgeoisie were drinking, on the assumption that nobody is exempt from guilt and that in attacking society anywhere you are bound to hit some guilty men. This is certainly an argument used by some radicals today. Any section of existing society contains guilty people who are responsible for the whole, and therefore you may as well start your revolution right away and throw your bombs at whatever is the most immediate target that presents itself.[34]

The present-day outburst of violence is proving to be as meaningless as the *fin de siècle* violence. It has accomplished little, nor for that matter was it probably ever intended to "accomplish" very much. Over and over again the Bomber Left and its avatars have been asked: What is it that you want? The answers have been along the same lines as in these two incidents:

> One university student in Rome was asked what he and his rebels wanted. He replied: "No demands, no delegations, no deals, no dialogue: the occupation continues." Another [said] "The battle was no objective, it *is* the objective." (Italics in original.)

> "We refuse to give proposals for what comes after the revolution. We'll discuss that then. In 1789 the Third Estate in France didn't have any proposals. They just said: 'We are nothing. We want to be everything.' "[35]

During the Spring 1968 uprising at Columbia, I asked a young leader of SDS to define the organization's program.

"The Bomber Left Is a Moral Force" / 73

Buildings had already been occupied by students, and an associate dean had been imprisoned in his office. Hundreds of students were milling about in the spring sun as we stood near occupied Hamilton Hall, a Columbia classroom building. Short and heavily moustached, the young revolutionary grinned at me and waved his hand at the throng of students and onlookers:

> "Program! Do you think we could get a crowd out here like this if we had a program? Programs are divisive. What we have are demands, demands, not programs."[36]

We had all this decades before when fascism was the new spirit of the age. There was Drieu La Rochelle, a follower of the renegade Communist, Jacques Doriot, who had founded the Fascist PPF [French Popular Party]. Drieu La Rochelle wrote in 1936:

> It is not the program that counts; what counts is the mentality of the party that proposes the program. Do not ask us first what is our program, but what is our mentality. The P.P.F. spirit is a spirit of life, of action, of speed.[37]

How reminiscent it all is of the dialogue in Turgenev's *Fathers and Sons:*

> "We shall destroy because we are a force," observed Arkady. ". . . Yes, a force is not to be called to account."
>
> "Allow me, though," began Nikolai Petrovitch. "You deny everything; or speaking more precisely, you destroy everything. But one must construct, too, you know."
>
> "That's not our business now. The ground wants clearing first. The present condition of the people requires it," added Arkady, with dignity; "We have

no right to yield to the satisfaction of our personal egoism."³⁸

Paradoxically, the indulgence of the Bomber Left may well have actually achieved something which the bombers themselves could not have anticipated: a greater regard for national stability than ever before. In a huge, sprawling country like ours, with power both centralized and decentralized, the opportunities for *l'acte gratuit*, the individual act of meaningless violence, are enormous. And that itself may be responsible for the failure of the "days of rage" to initiate anything revolutionary. As has been stated by two long-time students of violence:

> If individual acts of aggression are sufficiently abundant to provide an outlet, stability may occur in the face of systemic frustration.³⁹

This insight may be usefully coupled with another, applicable to Bomber Left violence:

> To qualify as revolutionary, violence must be *centralized;* it must attack and conquer the central seats of political and administrative power. In Colombia violence has been scattered, local, decentralized. (Italics in original.)⁴⁰

It has been quite clear that the Bomber Left violence has been uncentralized and unorganized, that it has lacked the important ingredient of modern revolution—an *apparat*. And it has lacked the strategic *apparat* because it is an anarchistic, not a totalitarian, movement, no matter what its ideological proclamations may say. Revolutions are not made by slogans like "participatory democracy" or "up against the wall." They are made, or not made, by revolutionaries who understand organization. Recall all the dramatic events of May 1968 in Paris—the marches and parades in the Champs de Mars and along the Champs Elysées, the factory occupations, mass meetings, propaganda barrages, fires, barricades. When it was all over, what remained? There in all its old conservatism, was the *apparat:* the French Communist Party with its cadres and *les durs,* the hard-core militants, who are subject to call with or without notice. The would-be revolutionaries and their sympathizers, like Alain Touraine, failed to understand that the French Communist Party, the key to mass insurrection, was not going to commit itself to revolutionary adventurism and student "spontaneity."[41] Daniel Cohn-Bendit, the student leader of the May revolt, rushed into print with a book about "obsolete communism." But where is Cohn-Bendit? In revolution, survival, as the Abbé Sieyès implied, is all.

The "days of rage" were little more than a modern version of Blanquist putschism. The strategy of street warfare by an urban guerilla is worthless in modern postindustrial society where a barricade is hardly more of a nuisance than the average traffic jam during the rush hour. And as for the urban guerilla himself, he seems to resemble what psychologists have described as a "gesture-child."[42] The more serious question is this: Why did many otherwise intelligent intellectuals (particularly those involved with the sciences, social and natural) and university administrators believe that their *crise de nerfs* could conceivably infect the rest of America? Their behavior, as they surrendered to little groups of radicalized students, resembled that of Alexandre Ledru-Rollin during the 1848 revolution in France when he said, *"Je suis leur Chef; il faut que je les suive* [I am their leader; I must follow them]."

Dr. Staughton Lynd seems to me the modern Ledru-Rollin. In August 1970, a bomb was exploded in a U.S. Army research building at the University of Wisconsin killing a young physicist who was working there late at night. In February 1972, Karleton Lewis Armstrong, 25, was arrested in Canada and held for extradition. At the extradition hearing Lynd argued that the bombing was a political act, no matter how misguided. He said that the bombing was similar to others designed to rid universities of complicity with the American government in the Vietnam war. He requested the Canadian court to deny extradition. Judge Harry Waisberg upheld the U.S. extradition claim and said:

> I find it significant that none of these witnesses, all of whom freely admitted political activity of the kind they suggest is associated with the bombing, requires political asylum. That speaks eloquently for the fact that the respondent [Armstrong] is sought only for the enforcement of the criminal law.[43]

Samuel McCracken, who reviewed my book, has criticized my views of the Bomber Left by arguing that "the moral content of a bomb is more perplexing than [Beichman] makes out." He said:

> ... I am convinced that some [Bomber Leftists] really believe they are rebelling against an illegitimate government, and see themselves as a sort of *maquis*. That they believe this does not say much for their intelligence, but it does not of itself discredit their moral purpose.[44]

"Moral purpose"? Without intelligence, there is no rationality and without rationality can there be "moral purpose"? Moral purpose—for what? Human conduct without intelligence is a defense of *l'acte gratuit,* of thinking with the blood. Intelligence and moral purpose would seem to me inseparable, otherwise every political assassin—including the killers at the Munich Olympics in the summer of 1972—or those like Eldridge Cleaver who merely encourage assassination, would have a moral case. I must take issue with McCracken's use of the word "maquis," whose connotation did not incorporate, during the French Resistance, terrorism. Professor A. L. Goodhart has written, *maquisards* "never attacked peaceful travellers gathered at an airport nor did they kill a group of unarmed athletes waiting to take part in the Olympic Games." He adds:

> There is a vital distinction between guerrillas and terrorists.... In the past, members of irregular armed forces were regarded as belonging to illegal organisations, but in the present century they have been accepted as legitimate combatants. (See the Geneva Convention 1949). To be recognized as guerrillas they must comply with four conditions, the most important of which is that "they must conduct their operations in accordance with the laws and customs of war." Stated shortly, guerrillas must fight a war against their armed enemies as regular soldiers do. They must not attack non-combatants. On the other hand, terrorists seek to obtain their object by killing or injuring non-combatants who may have nothing to do with the conduct of the war.[45]

Professor Daniel Bell argues that "what the rhetoric of revolution permits—both in the new sensibility and the new politics—is the eradication of the line between play-acting and reality, so that life (and such 'revolutionary' actions as demonstrations) is played out as theater, while the craving for violence, first in the theater and then in the street demonstrations, becomes a necessary psychological drug, a form of addiction."

The "new sensibility" has a name, says Professor Bell: the counter-culture armed with an ideology. "The main tendency of that ideology—though it appeared in the guise of an attack on the 'technocratic society'—was an attack on reason itself." In place of reason would come some form of "pre-rational spontaneity," like Charles Reich's "Consciousness III" or the "shamanistic vision" of Theodore Roszak. But does not the older radical tradition detest this "new sensibility"? Is it not a synonym for hated irrationalism? Yes, but the fact is that this older tradition "intellectually and esthetically" accepts the premises of "modernism." Daniel Bell names, *inter alia,* Philip Rahv, Robert Brustein, Lionel Abel, Irving Howe as allies of modernism and adds perceptively:

Yet all the new sensibility has done is to carry out the premises of modernism through to their logical conclusions.⁴⁶

It has been, at moments, a terrifying logic, as we move from the old literary explosions of small intellectual coteries to the infatuation of a new young avant-garde with the power that comes out of the barrel of a gun. Small wonder that a weary European man of letters in America was moved to make the bitter joke, "When I hear the word gun, I reach for my culture."

If experience has established any one thing in this world, it has established this: that it is well for any great class and description of men in society to be able to say for itself what it wants and not to have other classes, the so-called educated and intelligent classes, acting for it as proctors, and supposed to understand its wants and provide for them. A class may often itself not either fully understand its wants or adequately express them; but it has a nearer interest and a more sure diligence in the matter than any of its proctors and therefore a better chance of success.
Matthew Arnold, "The Future of Liberalism,"
in *Irish Essays and Others*, 1882

The damned impertinence of these politicians, priests, literary men and what not who lecture the working-class socialist for his "materialism"! All that the working man demands is what these others would consider the indispensable minimum without which human life cannot be lived at all. . . . Not one of those who preach against "materialism" would consider life livable without these things. . . . How right the working classes are in their "materialism"! How right they are to realize that the belly comes before the soul, not in the scale of values but in point of time.
George Orwell, "Looking Back on the Spanish War,"
in *England, Your England, and other Essays*, 1953

The doctrines which men ostensibly hold do not become operative upon their conduct until they have generated an imaginative symbolism.
Leslie Stephen, *History of English Thought
in the Eighteenth Century*, 1927

If experience has established any one thing in this world, it has established this: that it is well for any great class and description of men in society to be able to say for itself what it wants, and not to have other classes, the so-called educated and intelligent classes, acting for it as proctors, and supposing that they understand its wants and provide for them. A class may often not either fully understand its wants, or adequately express them; but it is in a sounder interest, and on a more solid footing, when it learns to press its wants for itself than when it has them expressed by others.

Matthew Arnold, "The Future of Liberalism," in *Irish Essays and Others*, 1882

The damned lie in the use of these politicians, priests, literary men and what is it so father them is a sentimental socialism for his "materialism." All that the working man demands is: what these others would consider the indispensable minimum without which human life cannot be lived at all... No one of those who preach against "materialism," would consider life livable without these things... I saw right the working classes are in their "materialism." How right they are to insist that the belly comes before the soul, not in the scale of values but in point of time.

George Orwell, "Looking Back on the Spanish War," in *England, Your England and other Essays*, 1953

The doctrines which men openly hold do not become operative upon their conduct until they have generated an imaginative symbolism.

Leslie Stephen, *History of English Thought in the Eighteenth Century*, 1927

4

"The American Worker Is a 'Honky' "

The American worker is a "honky."

THE AMERICAN WORKER—white, that is—is a retrograde, decadent, selfish creature: a honky.[1] Or as A. H. Raskin, assistant editor of the *New York Times,* has described him:

> The typical worker—from construction craftsman to shoe clerk—has become probably the most reactionary political force in the country.[2]

Astonishingly a *New York Times* editorial (undoubtedly written by Raskin, it was so knowledgeable) four years later, 19 July 1972, denounced AFL-CIO President Meany for seeking to "sit out the Presidential campaign." The editorial warned about Meany's "steamrollers" and "strongarms," fumed about "the nabobs of labor," described them as "autocrats" because they were "uninterested in even the most perfunctory appraisal of rank-and-file sentiment." And all this because the AFL-CIO leadership proposed to stay neutral.

I said "astonishingly" because the *Times* editorial was implying that Raskin was wrong in his description of the American worker, that the American worker might not, after all, be "the most reactionary political force in the country" since if he were to be consulted he might opt for Senator McGovern—the *Times* candidate—and repudiate an imposed neutrality. Quite obviously the *Times* was not suggesting the rank and file be consulted so that they would get a chance to demand a *Nixon* endorsement.

(I wonder if the "typical worker" is the most reactionary force where the John Birch Society might fit in the Raskin continuum.)

Other views of the American worker are that he revels in racial discrimination, imperialist wars, fascism, anti-intellectualism, "blind" anti-communism and other political bloodsports. Instead of producing a race willing and capable of serving High Culture, these latterday industrial troglodyte parvenus of the affluent society have created a life-style far inferior to the thousand-dollar-eight-channel-hi-fi-stereo-Fiat-Spider-BMW-Triumph-Easy-Rider-acid-head-Midnight-Cowboy-progressive-labor-pot-life-style of their critics.

Surprisingly enough, these same proctor-intellectuals who condemn the dollar imperialism of the American worker find it intolerable that there should be any poverty in America. But what if poverty were finally to be eliminated? Would not the *nouveau riche* workers then become, in the eyes of their self-styled liberators, reactionary, racist, imperialist, puritanical honkies and all impatient to become high-priced hard hats?

Equally astringent feelings are prevalent among intellectuals about workers in other Western countries. For example, Theodore Roszak wrote:

> Even the factory workers [in France] who swelled the students' ranks from thousands to millions during the early stages of the May 1968 General Strike seem to have decided that the essence of revolution is a bulkier pay envelope.[3]

Edward Hyams recently wrote a hymn of hate against British workers for the failure of socialism to take hold in Great Britain. He said in what is surely one of the most arrogant displays of sectarian temper in a long time:

> But to get back to Britain, the reasons for its [socialism's] failure, and for the present triumph of the basest kind of knife-in-the-back, kick-in-the-balls capitalism, are clear enough, of course: *the cap-*

touching social cowardice of the British working class which a century ago astonished observers as different as Karl Marx and Hippolyte Taine. . . .

The victory of the bourgeoisie, the capitalists, not only over us, the people, but over the policies of the Social-Democratic parties' policies [*sic*] since, say, 1848, is not hard to understand, though what capitalism stands for is old, ugly and base; and what socialism stood for was young, handsome and noble. (Italics added.)[4]

When Hyams talks about "us, the people," one can only wonder who he is talking about—what people, the cap-touching cowardly British workers, all twenty-five million men and women? It reminds me of what Bertrand Russell once wrote as to why Marx and Bakunin could not work together. "Marx hated Slavs, Bakunin hated Jews"[5]— but how they loved the proletariat.

Hyams' bitterness has a historic parallel. A little more than a century ago, Friedrich Engels, one of the earlier proctor-intellectuals, watched with dismay the results of the 1868 British general election and wrote a letter (18 November 1868) to Karl Marx:

What do you say to the elections in the factory districts? Once again the working class has discredited itself terribly. . . . Everywhere the working class is the rag, tag and bobtail of the official parties, and if any party has gained strength from the new voters it is the Tories. . . . It all shows up the disastrous political ineptitude of the English working class. The parson has shown unexpected power and so has the *cringing to respectability*. Not a single working-class candidate had the ghost of a chance but my Lord Tom Noddy or any *parvenu* snob could have the workers' votes with pleasure. (Italics added.)[6]

The Big Lie about the American worker arises from the problem of elites in America versus the "mass society." It derives from a deep ambivalence about the people.

Two attitudes prevail side by side: the Hamiltonian suspicion and contempt (Alexander Hamilton once said, "Take mankind in general, they are vicious, their passions may be operated on"); at the same time, the glowing Populist confidence as one intones, "All power to the people." It has its origins too in the assault on Bohemia's enemy number one, the hated bourgeoisie. It was Charles Baudelaire who wrote that " 'the real saint is he who massacres the People for the sake of the People.' "[7] Its most recent form was exemplified by Daniel Cohn-Bendit when he said (with some surprise, I imagine):

> The industrial proletariat, far from being the revolutionary vanguard of society [is] its dumb rearguard. In May, 1968, the most conservative, the most mystified stratum of society, the one most deeply ensnared in the traps of bureaucratic capitalism, was the working class.[8]

Cohn-Bendit's insights into the character of the industrial proletariat were perhaps better expressed, and more directly, in a bit of dialogue recorded during the events of May. It is between a Citroen factory worker and a student activist:

> "Where are your parents right now?"
>
> "Spending the weekend in the country."
>
> "I wish I had the money to go to the country."
>
> "What good would it do you if we're still being exploited by the capitalist system? You've got to think beyond a 10 per cent wage increase."
>
> "First I'd like to have the wage increase. I've got three kids."
>
> One student to another, *sotto voce:* "They can't see any further than their daily bread."[9]

This elitist, class-conscious contempt for the worker was expressed with an affecting innocence by a Kent State University student, following the tragic killing of four students in May 1970. In an interview, Jeffrey Zink (then twenty-one, and a senior planning to enter law school) said:

> [If] you get out of your little shell and out into the general public, you'll realize that Spiro Agnew is probably the most popular man in the nation. If you want to live in a democracy and go by votes, then I'd say without a doubt Agnew and Nixon are in the lead. Everybody didn't go to college. Everybody hasn't read the books we've read. They earn their $8000 a year and have their own little home, their car and their job and they don't really care about anything else. That's the majority.[10]

This, again has historical parallels. Most nineteenth and twentieth century revolutionaries shared a similar contempt for the "people," the general public who, as our Kent senior said, "don't really care about anything else." (Not even their children, their families, their pleasures and sacrifices? Pure materialists, these lower orders, subhuman, faceless, who deserve no better epithet than "they.") Filippo Buonarroti, survivor and historian of Babeuf's Conspiracy of the Equals in 1796 and a patron saint for the pre-1848 revolutionaries, was openly contemptuous of the masses and their opinions as expressed through popular suffrage. He believed that if the masses were allowed the vote after a revolution, they would invariably vote reactionaries back to power. For Proudhon, "Universal suffrage is the counter-revolution." Auguste Blanqui opposed elections to the National Assembly.[11] Bakunin wrote:

> Universal suffrage, as long as it is exercised in a society where the people, the mass of workers, are economically subject to a minority, can produce only fake elections, anti-democratic in essence and

absolutely opposed to the needs, instincts and the real will of the people.[12]

More recently, Professor Marcuse has indicated that "liberation would mean subversion against the will and against the prevailing interests of the great majority of the people."[13]

The problem for the "defender of the people" is always the people's own will and interests. The people, afraid to follow the true path forward, is a cowardly beast about whom Lenin's precursor, P. N. Tkachev wrote:

> Neither in the present nor in the future can the people, left to their own resources, bring into existence the social revolution. Only we revolutionists can accomplish this . . . social ideals are alien to the people; they belong to the social philosophy of the revolutionary minority. (Ellipsis in quote.)[14]

These proctor-intellectuals remind me of the priests about whom Stendhal wrote in the opening pages of *The Charterhouse of Parma:*

> For the last half-century, as the *Encyclopedia* and Voltaire gained ground in France, the monks had been dinning into the ears of the good people of Milan that to learn to read, or for that matter to learn anything at all was a great waste of labor, and that by paying one's exact tithe to one's parish priest and faithfully reporting to him all one's little misdeeds, one was practically certain of having a good place in Paradise.

This animosity towards the working class is, of course, to be seen (although expressed in the name of the working class) in so-called socialist countries. For example, the Central Committee of the Soviet Communist Party became quite exercised at a film, *The Great Life,* which portrayed the reconstruction of the war-ravaged Don Basin with the leading role assigned to rank-and-file workers and miners. It adopted a resolution (4 September 1946) which thundered:

> The movie *The Great Life* propagates reaction, lack of culture and ignorance. The mass promotion to leading posts of technically illiterate workers with backward outlooks and tempers, as shown by the producers, is entirely insincere and incorrect. They [the producers] did not understand that now, after Soviet power has created its own intelligentsia, only modern cultured people who know their work well, and not backward vulgar people, are highly valued and boldly promoted. It is foolish and strange to represent as a favorable phenomenon the promotion to leading positions of persons who are reactionaries devoid of culture.[15]

The contempt and even the hatred for the American worker is far greater than anything that the National Association of Manufacturers could ever dream up. Echoing Susan Sontag's racism, we have Murray Kempton writing that " 'the AFL-CIO has lived happily in a society which, more lavishly than any in history, has managed the care and feeding of incompetent white people' and adds [with the usual Kemptonian flourish] 'Who better represents that ideal than George Wallace?' "[16]

Paul Goodman has written that "from its beginnings, the American workingmen's movement had accepted the role assigned to it by management, of being wage-slaves, and its demands were *merely* for shorter hours, higher pay, and safer and more dignified conditions; it was not syndicalist, seeking power, and it was not anarchist, seeking workers' management." (Italics added.)[17]

Unlike Engels or Marx, Lenin knew precisely what to do to prevent the workers from "discrediting" themselves as they had appeared, so distressingly to Engels, to have done. He abolished trade unions, and anathematized collective bargaining as "economism." He knew that the real proletariat—and not the fictional protagonists of the Marxian drama—is indeed unrevolutionary, that without a so-called proletarian vanguard, workers would "only" seek more money and better conditions of work. Inside each proletarian there is a counterrevolutionary wildly signaling to be let out. As Lenin wrote:

> The history of all countries shows that the working class, exclusively by its own effort, is able to develop only trade-union consciousness. . . . The theory of socialism, however, grew out of the philosophic, historical, and economic theories elaborated by the educated representatives of the propertied classes, by intellectuals . . . altogether independently of the spontaneous growth of the working-class movement; it arose as a natural and inevitable outcome of the development of thought among the revolutionary socialist intelligentsia.[18]

To come to power at the head of a revolution as designed by Lenin and Engels one needed an "angel in marble," —the Worker, *der Arbeiter*—willing and submissive about the mission wished upon him by nineteenth and early twentieth century "scientific socialists," the proctors of the proletariat, self-appointed, self-anointed, and objectively speaking (in their favored phrase), the would-be new class of the modernizing revolution. For Lenin, in backward, non-proletarian Russia, it worked; but for no one else since. The working class in democratic, pluralist societies has refused to rise to the revolutionary bait. Even Fidel Castro's revolution in non-democratic Cuba was middle-class in origin.[19] When in the Spring of 1958, he proclaimed a May Day general strike, it was not Batista's thugs who frustrated Fidel's call to arms; it was the hard fact that the revolutionary, middle-class intellectuals around Fidel simply had no relationship to the workers or peasants and, consequently, their manifestos fell on deaf ears.

It is this immunity to revolutionary slogans among workers and trade unionists which so enrages the left progressives. And this immunity is demonstrable by a simple fact: revolutionary socialism or communism has yet to be established in an industrial country through electoral victory. Where revolutionary socialism or communism has been imposed, it could only be maintained by the destruction of trade unions and of collective bargaining. Is it not striking that the significant worker revolutions of the 1950s and 1960s have been in East Germany, Poland, Hungary, Czechoslovakia? The overthrow of Nkrumah in Ghana and Sukarno in Indonesia had worker support. And is there any question but that the East European revolutions would have been just as successful as those against Nkrumah and Sukarno had the Soviet Union not been a border power, a next door neighbor? And could the East European revolutions have gone as far as they did had not there been—here, at last!—an open, irrefragable alliance between workers, students, and intellectuals?

It is precisely this kind of alliance which is non-existent in Western industrial countries. While there may be a kind of loose synergistic process among revolutionary students and professors, the most essential ingredient for the realization of the dreams of revolutionary students and professors—a mass audience, "unconscious masses," or even a *Lumpen-proletariat*—is lacking. Because there is no base, there is no effective ideology, only a frenetic "socialist" rhetoric, à la Régis Debray, and terroristic Nechayevian bombings.

Against whom is this terror and this metaphorical revolution directed? No longer at the university, because even after an academic administration has collapsed, what do you have, what have you changed (that is, if you are a revolutionary student or radicalized professor) in the world outside? Very little. Today militant action must be directed against the non-revolutionary worker and his trade unions. The Weathermen faction which controlled the SDS, regarded white workers in America as "inherently counterrevolutionary, impossible to organize, or just plain evil—'honky bastards.'" Weathermen leaders derided white workers for "desiring better homes, better food, and better lives."

Such sneers are to be found not only among the revolutionary students but also among aging middle-class journalists and intellectuals who, as the phrase used to go, never had it so good. This phenomenon—the separateness of workers from student revolutionaries and from radicalized academicians—has been remarked upon by a proctor-journalist, Henry Brandon of the London *Sunday Times,* who reported from Washington (11 May 1969) that "the SDS efforts to enlist support among industrial workers has failed so far. They are too fat and conservative." Missing from this analysis was a list of reasons why industrial workers should have supported the SDS and why not Mr. Brandon himself? I have not heard that he has taken up the SDS banner or crusade. Why must the worker do what Mr. Brandon need not do? If the revolution is so much in the interest of the worker, would it not be in Mr. Brandon's interest too?[20]

The spendable average weekly earnings of a production worker with three dependents in 1968 was $95.28, according to the U.S. Bureau of Labor Statistics. In 1969, it was a little under $100. In 1970, it was $104.86 and as of May 1971, $110.34. One can be sure that the "fat and conservative" workers' wages are far lower than Brandon's regular remuneration plus expense account and other amenities. This "fat and conservative" predicate seems to have been inspired most recently by Dr. Marcuse, who argued that the " 'new working class' [what he calls the 'instrumentalist intelligentsia'] could disrupt, reorganize, and redirect the mode and relationships of production. However, they have neither the interest nor the vital need to do so: they are well integrated and well rewarded."[21]

The assault by the proctorial intellectuals against the American labor movement is quite understandable. American workers were just as heedless of appeals by Stalinist or Trotskyite intellectuals inside and outside the labor movement during the 1940s and 1950s as they are deaf today to the New Politics, including (despite Murray Kempton) the race politics of George Wallace. It was quite clear then, as it is now, that workers had long rejected the role, assigned to them by Marx, as the "gravediggers of capitalism," or of acting (as C. Wright Mills put it) as "the historic agency of change." Mills rejected "the notion that the labor movement is a progressive force in contemporary history." He argued that this " 'labor metaphysic' " was a legacy " 'from Victorian Marxism that is now quite unrealistic.' "[22] In rejecting the working class as the revolutionary transmission belt, Mills found the "intellectuals—as a possible . . . agency of change."[23]

The American-worker-is-a-honky Big Lie burgeoned in the 1950s when it became quite clear that American labor was not merely anti-fascist, but that it was also anti-totalitarian, that the struggle against Hitler's crusade for world domination did not cease with his defeat but necessarily extended as a struggle against Stalin's more "rational" crusade for world domination. It meant a trade union rejection of Henry Wallace's third party campaign in 1948, support for the Marshall Plan, the North Atlantic Treaty Organization and other pillars of American foreign policy. Perhaps even more significant in the growth of the "honkyism" Lie among American progressives, was labor's support for nascent trade union organizations in the Third World as part of the opposition to communist totalitarianism. For many progressive intellectuals this was labor's gravest offense.[24]

More curious than the attack on the American worker from the left is the attack on the worker and his trade unions from such center and right proctor-intellectuals as William F. Buckley, John Kenneth Galbraith, and Irving Kristol. Buckley has for a long time been possessed by a Manichean view of trade unions. When their leaders speak on domestic issues, they are devils seeking to impose some form of dastardly collectivism on America; when they speak on foreign affairs, they are saints and Buckley cheers.[25] Professor Galbraith has written:

> As the trade unions retreat, more or less permanently, into the shadows, a rapidly growing body of educators and research scientists emerges. . . . It is possible that the educational and scientific estate requires only a strongly creative political hand to become a decisive instrument of political power.[26]

Actually, Professor Galbraith put his disenchantment with American trade unionism less metaphorically and more succinctly at Harvard in a student "rap" session in 1971:

> Let me say a word in defense of traditional liberalism. There were about five or six of us ... who first started the opposition to the [Vietnam] war. We didn't have any help from the communists in those days, we didn't have any help from the left, we didn't have any help from the labor movement. I've been on George Meany's shitlist ever since for that. The labor unions pulled out of ADA [Americans for Democratic Action] when I became chairman, largely because of my stand on the war.[27]

Irving Kristol, whose views I have over many years usually found quite congruent to my own, has argued that "trade unionism has become that most dangerous of social phenomena: a boring topic." Trade unionism, he says, has lost its legitimacy and relevance. As so-called evidence he offers the undeniable fact that the *New York Times* (about whose journalistic competence he raised serious doubts a few years ago in the magazine, *The Public Interest,* which he co-edits) no longer carries any serious labor reportage; that *Fortune* magazine some time ago discontinued its "Labor" news department; that *Time* and *Newsweek* only occasionally report on trade union affairs; as for television, labor is on camera only during a tumultuous strike.[28]

Such "evidence" proves little about American labor. What it does prove is the incompetence of American news media to report with any foresight and analysis about what is going on in the minds of working people. The postal workers' strike in Spring 1970 received banner headlines in the daily press, and pages and pages of reportage in the newsweeklies, and tens of thousands of film footage on television. Yet on the day before (or the week before) the unprecedented postal strike, not a single daily, or weekly, or television station forecast what might happen.²⁹ How is it that the media didn't know this was going to happen? Can it be that it is our newspapers and journals which are the bloody bore? What makes Professor Kristol's attack so unusual and unexpected is that, as an identifiable Burkean Whig, he wants some kind of drastic but undefined alteration in a labor-management-government system which seems to have worked in recent decades about as well as, if not better than, any similar system I know. As Edward Banfield has written in another but relevant context:

> A political system is an accident. It is an accumulation of habits, customs, prejudices and principles that have survived a long process of trial and error and of ceaseless response to changing circumstance. If the system works well on the whole, it is a lucky accident —the luckiest, indeed, that can befall a society. . . . To meddle with the structure and operation of a successful political system is therefore the greatest foolishness that men are capable of. Because the system is intricate beyond comprehension, the chance of improving it in the ways intended is slight, whereas the danger of disturbing its workings and setting off a succession of unwarranted effects that will extend throughout the whole society is great.³⁰

Furthermore, how can a social movement which brings together millions of workers into associations where they can work out their own economic advancement be "a bore"? Obviously, it must be a dreary thing to frustrated revolutionaries, like the Weathermen, and to cynical proctor-intellectuals like Professor Galbraith, that a teamster or a garment worker or an electrician obstinately refuses to surrender his autonomy as a human being to become part of an abstraction called "a class," or to expand his role as a union member to include that of revolutionary conspirator and heroic transvaluer of values.

The history of American trade unionism is studded with the most violent episodes—the Homestead strike, the

1921 steel strike, the Molly Maguires, the 1937 Memorial Day massacre in Chicago—but it never became revolutionary violence. This should not be misunderstood. I am not celebrating the American worker as my own private "angel in marble," nor am I hypersensitive about criticism of trade unions. What is undignified is the disdain for working people, the *ad hominem* generalizations about them by scholars who feel no need to supply a bill of particulars for their indictment. What I marvel at is the sudden and excessive assault on trade unionism and workers by so varied a political spectrum, at a time when workers in Western countries are demonstrating a stubborn resistance to eloquent invitations to bring down the house on all of us. I am particularly mindful of the fury of the intellectuals on the occasion of the hard-hat violence in downtown New York in May 1970, and how all construction workers suddenly became "labor fascists" because of a stupid, anomic outburst of violence against some local students. It hadn't happened before, such violence, and it hasn't happened since; but nobody among left progressives indulged the hard hats *their* little fling, sympathized with *their* frustrations and their "moral purpose," nor explained away *their* little sin. The unwashed had dared lay hands on New York intellectuals-to-be and fascism and racism were already on the march in Wall Street.

Samuel McCracken, whose review of my book I referred to in the previous chapter, taxes me with not having dealt successfully with "the more plausible charge that the working classes tend to be racist."[31] Here is just what I am arguing against, the creation of an abstraction called "the working classes" and imputing to this vast number of people an ethos called "racism." It is the particular sin of this "class" just as its other sin is a lust for money and material possessions since they should be "liberators" not spenders. And why shouldn't the "working classes" be racist just like any other "class"?

In America there is no one "class" more racist than any other. The whole "class" concept in American society is so full of pitfalls that the concept itself borders on a kind of "racism." Stanley Ossowski in his *Class Structure in the Social Consciousness* has argued that our society is characterized by "non-egalitarian classlessness," something which Professor Earl Latham has defined as "a form of social inequality without social stratification, with much overlapping, without clearly differentiated social and economic functions, unlike the concept of class with which Marx worked."[32] Why, then, does fashionable liberal opinion still talk about the "working classes"?

When the American worker refuses to join these summer soldiers of revolution, he is showing good sense. The utopian promise is always that things will be *better* for him, but the worker has always grasped with a fine instinct that the revolutionary program actually means that the average man will not have it better but *worse*. The dialectical ploy is always, of course, that the real worsening of living conditions is only "temporary" and that the sacrifices are for the "next generation." Half a century after Lenin's seizure of power, you can, as far as the workers in most industrial countries are concerned, kiss all the ploys goodbye. Only the wilfully blind can fail to see the tragic import of Che Guevara's refreshingly candid thesis in "Notes on Man and Socialism in Cuba":

> The vanguard group is ideologically more advanced than the mass; the latter understands the new values, but not sufficiently. While among the former there has been a qualitative change which enables them to make sacrifices to carry out their function as an advance guard, the latter go only half way and must be subjected to stimuli and *pressures of a certain intensity*. That is the dictatorship of the proletariat operating not only on the defeated class but also on individuals of the victorious class. (Italics added.)[33]

Here is the perfect casuistry of the new class of proctors; they alone are advanced enough to see things whole, they alone have the right to impose sacrifices, to institute (how Orwell would have loved the phrase!) "pressures of a certain intensity." We have the same candor from Lenin, who—like Marx, Engels, Bakunin, Tkachev, Guevara, and all the others—knew that the revolution would not be a free and self-conscious act of the proletariat. As Lenin said:

> When we [the Bolsheviks] established the dictatorship of the proletariat the workers became more hungry, and their standard of living went down. The victory of the workers is impossible without sacrifices, without a temporary worsening of their situation.[34]

Why, then, do the proctors always assume that the workers do not know their own true and best interest when they turn rudely away from the apocalyptic prophets of the new democracy and the people's economy? Are they so wrong when they sense that things will actually become worse and that, as a consequence of the worsening, the revolutionary program for the "new democracy" can only mean that people—yes, the People—will have fewer, if any, democratic rights? For obviously, a new movement, a revolutionary movement which stands for material decline in the economic and political achievements of the masses, can hardly expect either to get the consent of the majority (hence the minority putsch for power) or popular approval when the revolutionary elites take power (hence totalitarian police controls).

And how hypocritical these confessions of Lenin and Che are. After all, according to Marx, things could get worse only under capitalism; the pauperization of the worker was inevitable:

> The modern laborer, on the contrary, instead of rising with the progress of industry, sinks deeper and deeper below the conditions of existence of his own class. He becomes a pauper, and pauperism develops more rapidly than population and wealth. And here it becomes evident, that the bourgeoisie is unfit any longer to be the ruling class in society, and to impose

its conditions of existence upon society as an overriding law.[35]

When our left progressives denounce the American worker with his disgusting life-style—cars, color television, motorboats, leisure time—they are attacking that which Marx said could not develop within the framework of bourgeois democracy, the abomination called "the consumer society."

What is said about the American worker and the American labor movement by intellectuals, both conservative and progressive, is more than just a Big Lie. It is a contempt for the working people of America, Britain, France, Canada and other democracies for refusing to share the discontent of the intellectual classes with the prevailing order of democratic societies. This was amply confirmed by a veteran television producer for one of the big networks, the National Broadcasting Corporation. Said Fred Freed:

> The blue and white collar people who are in revolt now do have cause for complaint against us. We've ignored their point of view. It's bad. It's bad to pretend they don't exist. We did this because we tend to be upper-middle-class liberals. We think the poor are "better" than the middle class. We romanticize them. The best thing that happened to me was a month I spent working in the Detroit slums after the riots. I stopped romanticizing the poor.[36]

Contempt for white workers was expressed by Professor Andrew Hacker of Cornell, who was absolutely ecstatic that he could announce America's approaching "terminal hour." Its doom, he said, was inevitable. Even if America "could end poverty and bigotry, diffuse its pyramids of power, and suppress its imperial tendencies, there is no reason to believe that such a society would contain a greater quotient of talented people." He also announced that "the egos of 200 million Americans have expanded to dimensions never before considered appropriate for ordinary citizens."[37]

As George Orwell once said about similar hyperbolic nonsense, "You have to belong to the intelligentsia to believe things like that: no ordinary man could be such a fool."

> Democracy in itself is neither lofty nor beautiful; it is just a necessity. But History seems to indicate that, to a higher degree than any other form of society, it is potentially capable of deflecting explosions into creative channels, and of coaxing the beautiful and sublime out of the common tastes of the common man.
>
> Arthur Koestler, "Culture in Explosion," in Drinkers of Infinity, 1960

> As in private life we distinguish between what a man thinks and says of himself and what he really is and does, so in historical struggles we must distinguish even more carefully the catchwords and fantasies of parties from their real organism and their real interest, their conception from their reality.
>
> Karl Marx, The Eighteenth Brumaire of Louis Bonaparte, 1852

> The actual shaping of policy is in the hands of elites; but this does not mean to say that the society is not democratic. For it is sufficient for democracy that the individual citizens, though prevented from taking a direct part in the government all the time, have at least the possibility of making their aspirations felt at certain intervals.
>
> Karl Mannheim, Ideology and Utopia, 1929

Democracy in itself is nobody's idea of beautiful. It is just of necessity, and History seems to indicate that, to a higher degree than any other form of society, it is reluctantly capable of defending, organising its 'creative minorities', and of creating the freedom contradiction out of the common tasks of life common to man.

Arthur Koestler, 'Chance his greatness'
In Defence of infinity, 1968.

In private life we distinguish between what a man thinks and says of himself and what he really is and does, so in historical struggles we must distinguish even more carefully the addresses and fantasies of parties from their real organism and their real interest, their conception from that reality.

Karl Marx, the eighteenth Brumaire
of Louis Bonaparte, 1852.

The actual shaping of policy is in the hands of cliques; but this does not mean to say that the society itself democratic, for it is sufficient for democracy that the individual citizens, though prevented from taking a direct part in the government, should all the time, have at least the possibility of making their aspirations felt at certain intervals.

Karl Mannheim, Ideology and Utopia, 1936.

5

"Our Political System Is a Fraud"

Our political system is an utter fraud, particularly the two-party system.

THIS Big Lie is essentially an attack on the system of government which we call democratic. To refer to America as a democratic country is not only to ensure a cynical smile in response but even to raise questions as to the sanity of anybody who suggests that America is a free country. Professor Robert Paul Wolff, a philosopher, wrote a few years ago:

> Anyone who still imagines that the United States is the land of opportunity and the bastion of democracy is a candidate either for a mental hospital or for Richard Nixon's Cabinet.[1]

I am not suggesting that there is anything particularly sacred about a two-party or a multi-party state nor that such a state is beyond need of reform. Professor Allan C. Brownfeld has written a most effective critique of the two-party system.[2] There are many other useful critiques, but they do not masquerade as being something they are not. A good deal of the attack on the American political system is not an attempt to change it but rather to overthrow it in the name of some vague, progressive paradise in the future, based on a Christ-less soteriology.

Professor Wolff has argued strongly against elections that they are ceremonial and little more:

> Even the periodic election becomes a ritual in which voters select a president whom *they* have not nom-

inated to decide *issues* which have not even been *discussed* on the basis of facts which *cannot be published*. The result is a politics of style, of image, of faith, which is repugnant to free men and incompatible with the ideal of democracy. (Italics added.) [3]

This is nonsense, and will remain nonsense until Professor Wolff offers us an existing model which comes near his democratic ideal so that we can judge the usefulness —and the true relevance—of his criticism. It surely is not true that our politics are "repugnant" to free Americans, unless he, of course, insists on controlling the meaning of the word "free." I take it that Professor Wolff wants an electoral system by which voters select the man whom they have first nominated. Yet one can suggest that the voters "nominate" the man whom a plurality or a majority want to see as president. What are presidential primaries for?

Is it conceivable, for example, that the two major parties (or, for that matter, a third or fourth or fifth party) would seriously nominate a candidate who was anti-Catholic, anti-Semitic, atheistic, anti-labor, anti-health care, anti-capitalist, anti-Soviet, pro-communist, pro-fascist and anti-Negro? Of course, George Wallace fits part of the bill as a racist—but then Adlai Stevenson was often criticized during and after his presidential campaigns for being lukewarm on civil rights, pro-French colonialism during the Algerian war, and pro-Taft-Hartley law. Stevenson tried to seize the center but Eisenhower had preempted it. In American pluralistic politics, which Professor Wolff abominates, you can run for the exercise or for election to office; it is difficult to do both. What Professor Wolff does is to confuse the literalness of the nominating process with the actuality, what in politics has been referred to as the "living system."[4] What does Dr. Wolff want? Everybody in the smoke-filled room at once? No one can claim that the present system of presidential nominating conventions is an ultimate good. It is not a matter of saying: if it exists, it is perfect. But we are a people, and our politicians exemplify this, with multiple group affiliations, with interlocking circles, with several establishments. In a political democracy, as Anthony Sampson put it, "no one man can stand in the centre, for there is no centre."[5]

Clinton Rossiter once suggested, "we live under a persistent, obdurate, one might almost say tyrannical two-party system. We have the Republicans and we have the Democrats, and we have almost no one else." To which James Reston replied:

> No one else, that is, except George Wallace of Alabama, and Eugene McCarthy of Minnesota. . . . Both parties are clearly losing the allegiance of many of their voters, and while splinter parties cannot yet attract a triumphant majority of independents, they could easily hold the balance of power between the two major parties and decide who wins.[6]

In actual fact, the Wolff criticism of the party system in America is based on a concealed premise. A functioning multi-party political system with fairly strong civil rights makes radical or revolutionary overthrow of a democratic state quite difficult. Wolff argues that for him, "pluralist democracy, with its virtue, tolerance, constitutes the highest stage in the political development of industrial capitalism. Interest-group politics [is] a domesticated version of the class struggle."[7] This definition, of course, holds only if one looks upon Americans as enjoying a single role status, no matter how many other group affiliations they visibly possess. Our periodic elections are part of a system which "thanks to judicial review" has "domesticated" revolution (as Professor Alpheus T. Mason once put it) and "brought [it] within the four corners of the Constitution." As he wrote:

> Brought into juxtaposition are three essential buttresses of freedom: Right of Revolution, Bill of Rights, Judicial Review. Oppression of individuals and minorities may encourage resort to the moral right of revolution, a right no American can gracefully query; an independent judiciary, by courageously interposing its judgment against majorities

bent on infractions of the Constitution, advances the cause of peaceful change.[8]

Peaceful change, that's the rub. It prevents the fiction of "the class struggle" from reaching a bloody conclusion, or as Professor Ted Gurr has expressed it in a somewhat more academic formulation:

> The likelihood and magnitude of civil violence tend to vary inversely with the availability of institutional mechanisms that permit the expression of nonviolent hostility.[9]

C. Wright Mills in one of his essays bemoaned the fact that neither in the United States nor in the Soviet Union "are there nationally responsible parties which debate openly and clearly the issues which the world now so rigidly confronts. The two-party state is without programmatic focus and without organizational basis for it. We must recognize that, under some conditions, the two-party state can be as irresponsible as the one-party state."[10] Now the late Columbia sociologist was no enraptured admirer of the Soviet Union, but it is arrant humbuggery to talk about how "under some conditions" a two-party state can be as "irresponsible" as a one-party state—like one which produces a Stalin? Can a mild adjective like "irresponsible" apply with equal force to one-party totalitarianisms and two-party pluralisms? What Mills failed to grasp was that the Communist Party of the Soviet Union (as Richard Pipes has pointed out) "is not a political party nor even *the* political party, but the country's permanent administrative corps." (Italics in original.)[11] The future of Russian politics, he said, "is in large measure identical with the future of the Communist Party of the Soviet Union." The future of the United States does not hang on the future of either the Republican or Democratic Party:

> Who wins an American election may make very little difference to the way the United States is governed, for there are few differences of principle dividing the Democrats and Republicans. But the very fact

that there are two parties competing constitutionally for power prevents the governors of the USA from persuading themselves that their own political survival and the safety of the state are identical objectives.[12]

In other words, if the two- or multi-party system has any merit at all, it is in this simple idea: that no men or group of men will ever become infected with the idea that they are so indispensable to a country that it would be treason for them to surrender power, election or no election, to a successful democratic opposition. As Seymour Martin Lipset has pointed out:

> The defeat of the Federalists in the elections of 1800 represented *the first occasion in modern politics in which an incumbent political party suffered an electoral defeat and simply turned over power to its opponents*. (Italics in original.)[13]

Was it a mere circulation of elites which allowed something so unprecedented in world history to occur, a transfer of power simply because of an electoral poll? Was this expression of "arithmocracy" just a little ritual plotted by John Adams and Alexander Hamilton to fool the people?

One of the academics who is an unquenchable advocate for what he calls "extraparliamentary movements" is Professor Richard Flacks. He must take as his inspiration the slogan "the worse, the better" à la Lenin. He has written:

> The principal source of energy for all that has been most creative and promising in the past decade has been supplied by the *failure* of the political system even to give the appearance of being an effective instrument of change. (Italics in original.)

His extra-parliamentary movement might form, as the "only acceptable coalition," one that was "substantially anti-imperialist, anticorporate, and supportive of community self-determination"; and then he added, in that peculiar linguistic mixture of shorthand, argot, euphemism, and cover-up that is so characteristic of left progressive prose:

> If by some chance such a coalition could come to power nationally, it would not have the power to implement very much of its program by conventional means. There would still be a need for mass movements in the streets.

I would assume that Professor Flacks, a founder of SDS in an earlier epiphany, was not talking about turning urban streets into pedestrian malls. He was writing in the centenary year of the Paris Commune and I suspect he was talking about street barricades. Behind the vague rhetoric was the promise of guns and executions in an up-against-the-wall-this-is-a-stickup *Götterdämmerung* for *Stalag Amerika*.

The animus towards the United States' political system, the anti-Americanism or the loathing for their own land and its institutions to be found among the left progressive ideologues, amounts to such a serious loss of cool, that it is the surest guarantee of their continued failure to influence the course of American politics in what they consider a desirable direction. I am particularly moved by Professor Flacks' urging that "the disparate forces of opposition [must] begin to 'reach' the white working class. . . . Students and intellectuals could do infinitely more than they have to approach factory workers directly and with concrete proposals for cooperative action."[14] Now Professor Flacks, I am sure, really means what he says; but, alas, neither he nor his disciples will lift a finger to help organize, as professional organizers, workers who are either in racket unions or in badly managed unions with exploitative, "sweetheart" contracts.

I have tested this proposition on a number of occasions. I have talked at length both to fellow students at Columbia University (where I was a graduate student during the 1968–69 uprisings) and, later, as a guest lecturer at student meetings at Harvard. Whenever I heard about the need for winning over the factory workers to the side of revolutionary change, I always tried to make the following proposition.

> I will obtain for any student who wants it, a job—with pay—as a union organizer in any one of the toughest situations in the New York metropolitan area. AFL-CIO unions have unsuccessfully tried to crack a racket-infested factory area which exploits black and Puerto Rican workers, many of them women, via "sweetheart" agreements. Organizers who have tried to approach workers in this Bronx-Yonkers borderland have been beaten, two seriously enough to be hospitalized. No arrests were made by the police. Attempts to break the "sweetheart" contracts have failed in the courts.

I have made this offer innumerable times. It has never been accepted. Obviously, it is easier to listen to speeches at Harvard's Leverett House, or to take over Grayson Kirk's office, or to call Andrew Cordier Lumumba's "murderer" than to take on a tough organizing assignment outside there, in the real world. I make this same offer to Professor Flacks, and if he is too busy studying pedestrian traffic flow, perhaps he can suggest some revolutionists who want to get out of the parlor and do a little useful liberating of exploited workers.

The Big Lie about the American political system is the usual elitist-based analysis which naïvely regards "practical politics" as an immoral sellout, a two-party system as the destruction of democracy and a deflection from authentic ideals and values. What they seek is a single-issue party, a no-politics system. In fact, they seek to create, to use Dr. John Bunzel's book title, "anti-politics in America."[15] And if one wants to see the model of anti-politics, I am afraid that New York City is the paradigm, where flourishes "a condition of war of all against all," the Hobbesian nightmare world come true. What were once normal political lines of fracture in the New York polity seem to have become unbridgeable. It was once a legitimate, though imperfect, political system, one which created a consensual politics, and it has disintegrated. The disintegration—the crumbling legitimacy of urban governmental institutions—is to be seen throughout the city. One basic reason for this exhaustion of legitimacy is the disappearance in any real sense of responsible party government in New York City—that process by which recognized political parties, preferably no more than two or three, nominate and compete for office and by which, at periodic intervals, they are held accountable for their activities.

The dislike of political parties is nothing new in America, particularly among ideologues. In fact, ideological politics demands the expulsion of practical politicians—that is, non-ideological elements—from positions of influence. We have James Madison's famed *Federalist Paper Number 10* with its abomination of parties, which for him meant "the violence of faction."[16] Washington, in his Farewell Address, warned against " 'the baneful effects of the Spirit of Party.' "[17] The American party system, which developed during the early nineteenth century, is wholly extra-constitutional, even though parties are an integral part of our civic culture.[18] It was the shocking corruption of party machines in the late nineteenth and twentieth centuries, and the consequent failure of local government, which led to the great municipal reform movement against the "bosses," against Tammany. Political parties were dismantled in the cities by reformers in order to get rid of the corrupt district leaders and police officials who were living on the proceeds of vice and gambling. Well, New York does not have the political parties but it still has the vice and gambling and corrupt police officials.

In New York City, traditional party government was crushed in the La Guardia years. In its place arose what Professor Theodore Lowi has called "the bureaucratic city-state," the powerful professionalized urban government agencies which became the beneficiaries of the permanent reform era and party-less urban governance. These agencies, the housing bureaucracy, the urban development authorities, the welfare agencies, insulated from competitive party politics, run the city—except during crisis and chaos when nobody runs it. As a result of the replacement of the Old Politics by the New Anti-Politics, political power is today diffused among innumerable and unmanageable interest groups, both within, or tangential to, government. Each group is capable of generating effective pressure, primarily upon the mayor, to achieve its own aims or, at the very least, to prevent the effectuation of another group's aims.

There is, of course, nothing new in special interest groups; they are the stuff of politics. What is new in New York City, however, is the startling increase of fragmented special interest groups—particularly in the black community and among white liberal intellectual groups—and the qualitative change in their operational code which now includes the omnipresent threat of violence and civic disruption. Many of these are—and this is the danger of anti-politics, or ideological politics—single-issue pressure groups. None of them constitutes a political majority nor can any of them become a political majority because of the ideological cleavages among them, the utter irreconcilability of their apocalyptic objectives, the zero-sum game quality of their competition (whatever I win, you lose), the absence of linkages among them. Such chaos is always created by what Edmund Burke once called "metaphysical politics."

What I am suggesting is that such irreconcilable factions and interest groups make effective majoritarian or pluralitarian government impossible. Faction politics is anti-politics because ideological commitment prevents prudential, compromisable "muddling through." The factions which dominate New York's anti-politics begin life with great cohesion because of their single-issue dedication. Their cohesion increases as they attack each other and thus prevent bridge-building or negotiation. Where is the location of political power—the ability to make authoritative decisions on public policy—in New York City? Legally, of course, in Albany; but even Albany must pay heed to the factional anti-politics of the fissionable special interests.

Of one thing we can be sure: political power does not flourish in city hall nor in the City Council, the Board of

Estimate, Albany, Harlem, Bedford-Stuyvesant, the Patrolmen's Benevolent Association, the United Federation of Teachers, the Conservative Party, the archdiocese, the Central Labor Council, or the Chase Manhattan Bank. What seems to have developed are "islands of functional power" (in the words of Professor Wallace Sayre), each of which owns a piece of the action with veto power over the others who have their own veto power—and, together, they all have veto power over the city's chief magistrate.

Instead of politics of bargaining, we have the politics of confrontation. Instead of party brokerage politics, whereby grievances may be incorporated and processed by government on some priority basis, the city has a mayor victimized by a charter which has successfully separated him from political leadership and party government. Early in his first administration, Mayor Lindsay attacked "power-brokers" (without daring to name or define their role). He thus failed to recognize that governing a city without functioning, viable political parties meant that everybody was a "power-broker" with his own mandate for collecting and processing grievances. And where everybody has power, nobody, not even the mayor, has authority. He quickly learned that the city charter grants him the semblance of authority but with remarkably few sanctions, negative or positive. Thus the mayor, whose office is regarded as the second most difficult in the country, is not only *not* an accepted leader, but, even worse, he can maximize neither his power nor his authority in emergencies as can the president or the governor.

Who, in the era of anti-politics, speak for New York City, who is listened to, who is heard—as, like it or not, Mayor Richard Daley is heard in Chicago where he rules as a *politician,* not as some would-be *primus inter pares* ideologue? Everybody speaks in the New York City clamor and everybody is heard; but, despite his formal power, the mayor is powerless when emergencies erupt. Someone once said, "Sovereign is he who decides in the emergency situation." Can the mayor or anybody else decide in the emergency situation? A whole host of interest groups can create emergencies; almost none can decide how to end them. Can the democratic process, the unending search for a majority, function through anti-politics, that is, "job action" politics?

The weakening of the party structure in New York City and its replacement by the "bureaucratic city-state" began with La Guardia, was halted for a while during the O'Dwyer administration, began anew with the Wagner administration, and has continued through the Lindsay regime. Out of such counterproductive, anti-politics reforms (viz. "proportional representation"), from the proliferation of splinter parties (during his political career, La Guardia ran under *nine* different party labels in New York City) and from quaint bits of intellectual folklore (cities like New York can be run without politics and should be run "scientifically"), was created the ungovernability of New York City. And with it came a corruption and looting far exceeding the old Tammany limit of "10 per cent of the contract." All these were the unintended consequences of the worthy anti-corruption movement of the recent decades. Urban government can be run "non-politically" when its concerns are non-ideological. Perhaps La Guardia was right when he said back in the halcyon 1940s that there was no Democratic or Republican way to clean the city streets. Today with a powerfully organized sanitationmen's union, there is an organized labor way to clean the streets; if that way is not dealt with, the city streets become a city dump until the sanitationmen's union obtains a strike settlement.

What has happened to New York City, a sharply divided city, is not a limited polarization—which is acceptable—but rather an unlimited atomization. This makes for the kind of dangers for an existing polity which John Stuart Mill once wrote about:

> A state never is, nor, until mankind are vastly improved, can hope to be, for any long time exempt from internal dissension; for there neither is nor has ever been any state of society in which collisions did not occur between the immediate interests and passions of powerful sections of the people. What, then,

enables society to weather these storms, and pass through turbulent times without any permanent weakening of the ties which hold it together? Precisely this —that however important the interests about which men fall out, the conflict does not affect the fundamental principles of the system of social union which happens to exist; nor threaten large portions of the community with the subversion of that on which they have built their calculations, and with which their hopes and aims have become identified. But when the questioning of these fundamental principles is not an occasional disease, but the habitual condition of the body politic; and when all the violent animosities are called forth, which spring naturally from such a situation, the state is virtually in a position of civil war; and can never long remain free from it in act and fact.[19]

Any elected political leader or professional politician knows that his survival and personal advancement depend upon his ability to keep together a party or a coalition, an alliance of people willing to work together on some common basis, not through "all-or-nothing" politics. By what mechanism can a politician or an elected official like the mayor of New York City strengthen himself, his party, his coalition? His personality is insufficient; his "charisma" can disappear. To strengthen himself he needs a party mechanism to mediate between himself and aggrieved groups. Thus it is the mayor, in the absence of politics, who is always on the receiving end of police department pickets chanting "blue power," Negro militants chanting "black power," or stock exchange executives fighting proposed city taxes with low-key references to "money power." Walter Bagehot once said that a man could not bargain on his knees. Too often, the mayor—and it could be almost any citizen in New York City—is on his knees.

The mayor lacks power because no party system exists with an interest in transforming his opinions into action, legitimate action. It is, in reality, in nobody's interest that the mayor and his administration should be successful.

One doesn't will a political party into existence, but one can create the conditions so that there is motive enough for regeneration of moribund urban political institutions.

We have seen in recent years what can happen to a great city when politics disappear, when a party system disappears. It didn't happen by design and conspiracy. It happened because of an off-with-their-heads monocausal approach to the delicately functioning political system of a great city.[20]

Today the cry is against pluralism, that traditional liberal concept which demonological progressives have transformed into the obstacle to their vision of true progress. And yet when one examines the concept of pluralism, one quickly discovers it has certain indispensable values under certain circumstances. For example, when a progressive announces that a socialist dictatorship is showing signs of "liberalization," he means that it is undergoing some structural change in the direction of pluralism, a sharing of power by hitherto excluded groups in the population. Now if "liberalization" is a good thing for the Soviet Union (we have not yet heard about "liberalization" in Mao's China and, most likely, we won't for a long time), why isn't it a good thing for America? Why is pluralist "liberalization" wonderful in communist countries where it doesn't exist and a fake in democratic countries where it does exist? Is America less democratic today than it was, say, half a century ago? Of course, among some progressives the answer would be "yes, less democratic." But there are people with experience of both political systems who speak differently:

Jean-Jacques Servan-Schreiber: Mr. Loebl, if, as I believe, you remain a convinced Communist, would you rather live in Soviet Russia or in the United States to achieve the human values to which you have devoted your life?

Eugen Loebl: I would prefer to live in the country nearer the ideals of socialism, and that, permit me to say, is the United States.[21]

It is one of the paradoxes of America's left progressive thought that the very intellectuals who mock the two-party or multi-party state and say it is a fiction are at the same time the staunchest supporters of the one-man-one-vote concept for territories under colonial domination. And yet as soon as the one-man-one-vote status is achieved in a liberated colony, the same intellectuals are suddenly transmuted into the staunchest supporters of one-party states, so long as these can boast a Marxist-Leninist-Maoist inpiration.[22] In America they deride the multi-party system, alleging that it prevents the people from having more say in their affairs, but for the one-party socialist dictatorships, which expressly bar popular participation (including the right of dissent), they have nothing but an indulgent understanding. They are tolerant of communist one-party systems or African socialist one-party systems where elections always end up with 99 per cent plus for the incumbent one-party regime. Fascist one-party states, like Spain and Portugal, never benefit from this tolerance nor do boring no-party states in Africa like Liberia or Houphouet-Boigny's Ivory Coast. Since these countries are avowedly non-socialist, their one-party (or no-party) regimes are definably reactionary, and not progressive like the Cuban regime.

The American political system, with its many virtues, is something less than perfect. Agreed. I am quite prepared to heed the argument that the American political party system "as it exists today, is admirably suited to the segment of the public that it serves—those who identify with middle-class values," that the party system "does not encompass the entire populace," one-fourth to one-third of whom "have not been socialized to middle-class standards." It is arguable that the party system does not "serve their interests nor is it responsive to their needs."[23] Our problem is not the valid criticisms of the various institutions, but rather the overkill ambition of some left intellectuals who would overthrow the entire system in the name of what they childishly call socialism or some variant of Marxism. While it is possible to build a *better* two-party system out of an already existing two-party system, it is difficult to build any kind of a multi-party system out of a one-party system. In this connection, Nikolai Bukharin once said with nice bolshevik wit, "We might have a two-party system, but one of the parties would be in office and the other in prison."[24] Why not a genuine two-party system as a goal, why not a kind or understanding word for a two-party state which has on occasion become a three- or four-party system? Why is a one-party socialist state which produces a Stalin, a Rákosi, and a Novotny preferable to an imperfect two-party state which does not? Do the left progressives who now despise democratic politics in the United States truly want to see a revolutionized society in which a mere handful of dedicated men could impose an unshakeable tyranny over the American people? Merle Fainsod, in his magisterial study of the Soviet Union, has offered the "generous estimate" that in March 1917, the Bolshevik Party membership was about 23,600.[25] Is such a minority seizure of power what the left progressives seek for America? I am inclined to say that this is the issue which they will be forced to face since the present system of governance prevents widespread popular conflict, obstructs a power seizure by a single minority, encourages adaptation to changing circumstances ("a Catholic can't get elected president"), and discourages either left or right "politics of unreason."[26]

There are, I repeat, serious criticisms to be made about American politics. But what must be made clear by critics is, it seems to me, whether they seek reform or revolution. Often it is difficult to understand what the critic seeks because of a lack of definition of terms used or an explanation of how alternative proposals will work. For example, a radical observer of American politics, Grant McConnell, has argued that the dispersion of public power (both functionally and geographically) has, instead of preventing tyranny, acted to create greater tyranny.[27] What has happened is that the power, now decentralized, has been appropriated by non-governmental special interest groups, and by local governments; instead of the emergence of a broad national constituency, small constituencies now exercise absolute power. A sharp-eyed critic of Professor McConnell's book has noted:

> Yet it is curious that he does not analyze the New Left which, while sharing his democratic goals, pursues a diametrically opposite strategy of radical decentralization and local direct action.

Professor Kesselman examines the McConnell solution—the "alchemy" of the broad constituency that transforms "base parochialisms and particularisms into something higher"—and finds it thoroughly unconvincing. Professor McConnell fails to answer such basic questions as:

> How does the large constituency remedy the shortcomings of power exercised in small units? What are the workings of the alchemical process? How do you identify the "something higher"? What kind of political actions does he consider democratic? If a vigorous executive is the remedy, is not democracy diluted in consequence?[28]

These questions which Professor Kesselman has raised can apply equally to even more extreme critics than Professor McConnell. What will happen after the Big Change? How will it happen? Marx never told us, nor did Engels. As Bertram Wolfe has put it, "a critique of capitalism is not a blueprint for a future society, as Lenin was to discover with dismay after he took power." He quotes a frequent plaint in Lenin's works:

> It did not even occur to Marx to write a word on this subject; he died without leaving a single precise quotation or irrefutable instruction on this. That is why we must get out of the difficulty entirely by our own efforts.[29]

Lenin had a momentary dream of a state "withering" away but the dream was short-lived. He consoled himself with a maxim of Napoleon—*on s'engage et puis on voit* (let's try it out and see).

No, I am afraid that will not do at all.

The new treason of the intellectuals is what we have shared **and even** contributed to the current loss of faith in the power of the human mind to cope with human problems, faith in the worth of reasoned discussion, faith even in the possibility of objective truth.
     Abraham Kaplan, "The Travesty of the Philosophers,"
     Change in Higher Education, 1970

This is the curse on salvationist creeds: to be born out of the noblest impulses of man, and to degenerate into weapons of tyranny. An exclusive creed cannot admit opposition. It is bound to feel itself surrounded by innumerable enemies. . . . Political Messianism is bound to replace empirical thinking and free criticism with reasoning by definition, based on a priori collective concepts which must be accepted whatever the evidence of the senses.
  J. L. Talmon, *The Origins of Totalitarian Democracy*, 1960

The sector of public opinion generally most vulnerable to ideological propaganda is constituted by that peculiar class, concentrated in the great cities, called the intellectuals. Their principal characteristic is a preoccupation with ideological formulations, a preoccupation that tends to blind them to what actually is as opposed to what is said. They live in the Socratic world of ideas, a nominal world that is more real to them than the real world.
     Louis J. Halle, *The Cold War as History*, 1967

6

"American Values Are Materialistic"

American values are wholly materialistic, intended to bolster a decaying economic-social system rejected by the rest of the world except for a dwindling handful of American "client states."

PRECISELY what many American intellectuals condemn about America—its emphasis on accumulation of goods in a consumer society—is what so obviously the people of Poland, Czechoslovakia, Hungary, East Germany and the USSR and, I suppose, every other country in the world crave, and crave badly enough to revolt or to threaten to revolt when their hope of obtaining these satisfactions is frustrated.

Does anybody really believe that the uprisings in Eastern Europe during the past two decades have been inspired by a desire for, say, more communism, or more collectivization? Is anybody really persuaded that if Eastern Europe could free itself from Soviet Red Army occupation, or threat of occupation, the Soviet system would continue to exist? Or that those bourgeois values so thoroughly condemned in the West by the progressive intellectuals would not be embraced and cultivated by the peoples of Eastern Europe? I am not suggesting that what might replace Soviet communism in Eastern Europe after a successful revolt would be something that we call laissez-faire capitalism, but I do suggest that a liberated working class or peasantry would seek the *embourgeoisement* which Western intellectuals affect to despise.

What do the Russian intellectual dissenters seek if not the "bourgeois" freedoms that the radical left denigrates?

When Dr. Marcuse talks about "repressive tolerance," I am sure that the Andrey Sinyavskys and the Yuli Daniels, and other dissenters, would welcome a little of the very treatment which Dr. Marcuse finds so unbearable.

I recall a meeting of Eastern European exiles which I once attended as a foreign correspondent in Europe. The speaker was the American trade union leader, the late Walter P. Reuther, who declaimed that he did not want to fight either for Stalin or for Standard Oil. A middle-aged Romanian trade union official in exile muttered nearby, "If only I had a chance to fight for Standard Oil against Stalin!"

It may sound strange to define East European revolutions in terms of material wants, but this is purely because we have become so "intellectualized" that it is difficult to believe that people want not only freedom but material satisfactions as well. I take my text in this matter from Alfred North Whitehead:

> The essence of freedom is the practicability of purpose. Mankind has chiefly suffered from the frustration of its prevalent purposes, even such as belong to the very definition of its species. The literary exposition of freedom deals mainly with the frills. The Greek myth was more to the point. Prometheus did not bring to mankind freedom of the press. He procured fire, which obediently to human purposes cooks and gives warmth. In fact freedom of action is a primary human need.[1]

It is another of the paradoxes of our time that what our advanced and affluent culture critics loathe most about their fellow Americans is precisely that which is considered desirable by the rest of the world. It is surely extraordinary that this attack on American values comes from the most successful, the most prosperous, intellectual class in modern history. A career as a literary intellectual during the 1930s was as close as one could come to a vow of poverty without taking holy orders. And, paradoxically, this was the time that the literary intellectual had an enormous influence in culture. Since then, fate has dealt most cruelly with him. He has been given everything—money, fame, prestige, status, audience, even influence. He has become a permanent cover story in our popular magazines.

Ideas in America no longer "trickle down" over a period of time. Today, let some new notion like camp, or pop art, or Women's Lib, or "sex" bloom, and instantly newspaper and magazine editors, obeying some editorial tropism, accord it the most respectful hearing with color photographs as well. Literary avant-gardistes in America are in permanent danger of being overrun by their own eager middle-class followers. No wonder the literary and progressive intellectual is discontented with America. If you cannot *épater le bourgeois* and if the workers ignore you, what remains? So you write about politics in terms of moral pronouncements and the presently fashionable apocalypticism.

In the 1930s, intellectuals regarded poverty-stricken Americans as *their* people and America as *their* country. Even the Stalinists among them found it not uncongenial to adopt the slogan, "Communism is twentieth-century Americanism." Today these intellectuals, and the younger ones among them who believe that the only way to make history is to ignore it, complain that America presses down upon them; "mass culture" is a disease; the "working class" they once helped, or so they fancy, to "liberate" is now crude and materialistic.[2] *Whatever* progress America makes in civil rights, health care, poverty, minimum wages, educational opportunities, the progress is just not good enough and, at the same time, is an example of vulgar materialism. This alienation from America is not due to Vietnam and the bitter aftermath. It was there with the 1948 Truman Doctrine on Greece and Turkey; it was there with the Bay of Pigs; it was there in the nuclear confrontation in 1962 in Cuba.[3]

It has been noted by scholars of Russian history that the Russian *intelligent* in the nineteenth century suffered from a double alienation. As Professor Marc Raeff has explained it, the *intelligent* was alienated from his country, his government, his fellow countrymen; and secondly, he was alienated from the rest of the world, even from Western Europe, in which he had even less faith. I suspect that this double alienation is what today is most characteristic of our intellectual *frondeurs,* particularly in the academic world. There are few foreign political heroes available any longer —no Nkrumah, no Sukarno, no Stalin, no Castro, not even Mao really. About all that may be left in the way of a hero is Marx and only the youthful Marx at that.

Not only is there no foreign political avatar or revolution for many of our progressives, but they are even a bit embarrassed that all the hopeful predictions of the better society under a new socio-economic regime seem to have disastrously misfired in most areas of the world where the new order of things has been imposed. In Eastern Europe there are today different forms of ownership and economic management, according to Milovan Djilas; there are no collective state farms in Yugoslavia and Poland; socialism has become risky in Eastern Europe. As Djilas says:

> Parties in all Eastern European countries are caught in this dilemma: if they permit an increasing autonomy within the economy, enterprise becomes available to parasites; while if they retain the controls, even through state agencies [as distinct from the party apparatus—translator's note], the ensuing waste, disproportions, and inefficiency generates social unrest. The modes of economic management in Eastern European countries are drifting persistently toward Western European efficiency and profitability.[4]

I raise the question of Eastern Europe not because there is any vast cult of admiration among left progressives for the economies of these Soviet-controlled lands. I mention these economies because at least we can see in them what the future would be like under a post-revolutionary regime, and have thus a measuring rod of the virtues and vices of pre-revolutionary bourgeois democracy. How much disagreement is there, really, with the following official Soviet point of view among our left progressives? The words are Khrushchev's, in 1963:

> A bourgeois republic, however democratic, however hallowed its slogans purporting to express the will of the people or nation as a whole, or an extra-class, will, inevitably, remain in practice—owing to the existence of private capitalist ownership of the means of production—a dictatorship of the bourgeoisie, a machine for the exploitation and suppression of the vast majority of the working people by a handful of capitalists.[5]

I would suspect not very much disagreement. In fact, Khrushchev's words are applied to America or to any other democracy by most left and non-communist periodicals published wherever a free press is allowed to exist.

Now why is there this attack on American—or democratic—values? It has only a little to do with actual American misdemeanors, with rules and regulations that are violated by fools and knaves and government officials. Whence this definition of American values as wholly materialistic, and part of a decaying system?

The attack on American values and their definition as materialistic is, of course, directed against the American worker and his family who have moved into the middle class. The American economy, as most Western economies, despite recessions and shake-outs and inflation-deflation cycles, has managed to avoid mass unemployment. (I think there would be wide agreement on that without for a moment detracting from the argument that unemployment of 7 per cent of the work force is intolerable.) And it is precisely this relative immunity from depression and mass unemployment which has irritated one distinguished American intellectual, Professor John W. Aldridge:

> The great virtue of economic depression is that it combines a very low degree of opportunity with a very high degree of motivation. It creates limits within which one is forced to function, and in cutting down the range of available choices it dispels the confusion about where best to apply one's energies.[6]

The author of this paean to mass unemployment and national depression reminds me of a friend of mine who thought the one advantage of a good depression would be that taxicabs would become more available on New York streets. He is now complaining that taxi fares are too high.

Another academic who has turned angrily on the middle-class American worker might better have titled his book *The Nightmare World of Andrew Hacker*. Like all nightmare worlds, the fantasy and horror have a basis in reality but no more than that. Professor Hacker, to whom I referred in chapter 4, exemplifies a saying among lawyers —whatever is admitted need not be proven. His rhetoric is full of "admissions" and little proof. Unlike Edmund Burke, who said that he did not know "the method of drawing up an indictment against an whole people," Dr. Hacker does.

While Dr. Hacker echoes many of the radical left plaints, in actual fact he is a conservative who mourns the fact that too many Americans have so risen in status, income, and literacy, that the concept of an elitist society run by culture critics and academics is no longer possible. For him, America is no longer "a nation [but] has become simply an agglomeration of self-concerned individuals; men and women who were once citizens are now merely residents of bounded terrain where birth happens to have placed them."

It must be remembered that Dr. Hacker is one of our leading university figures, a specialist in political science, a field of study which presumably concerns itself not merely with airy speculations but with rigorous testing of concepts. The trick in all his generalizations is to leave premises unexamined, to speak in terms of helpless outrage, and to do all this with such lightning rapidity that, before you know it, you are in full agreement that it's all over for America. I want to examine some of his statements.

> Virtually every American possesses a self-esteem hitherto reserved for a privileged or talented few.

Self-esteem is hard to measure in absolute terms. What about comparative terms? How about "virtually every Chinese" or "virtually every Brazilian" or any other human being in any other country and his self-esteem? The Hacker trick here is to use the adverb "virtually." All sentences which begin with the adverb "virtually" imply that the writer is about to assert something as fact rather than something to be proven or to be researched. The adverb "virtually" applies to sentences where any kind of verifiability is precluded by the meaninglessness of the proposition.

> Yet the very fact of being freed from traditional controls brings a transformation in human character; and the rapid liberation of so many Americans carries serious—and unanticipated—consequences for the society as a whole.

This sounds awesome, but all social acts carry with them unanticipated consequences, as noted by Professor Robert Merton who formulated the concept of the "unanticipated consequences" some three decades ago and even earlier by Max Weber. To test the emptiness of Hacker's proposition, one need only ask: suppose there had not been "rapid liberation of so many Americans"—what would have been the serious and unanticipated consequences of that? Can Professor Hacker say? Can anyone? History does not present its alternatives.

> There eventually arrives a time when a preoccupation with private concerns deflects a population from public obligations.

What does this mean? How great a preoccupation deflects a population from public obligations? Deflects how many? What are these private concerns? Do public obligations and private concerns differ from country to country?

> The majority [in America] exercises its power by creating an atmosphere which makes life uncomfort-

able for those who disregard **accepted precepts of** conduct, and it enforces these **sanctions not only on** deviant outsiders but also over its **own members.**[7]

On the contrary! Never has a middle class been less secure about its accepted precepts of conduct; never has a middle class been so eager to listen to and to read about its villainies and debaucheries. Never has there been a middle class in all history with so little confidence in itself, in its right to exist, and in its own legitimacy. As Norman Podhoretz said some time ago:

> The American middle class now routinely says of itself what its worst enemies have always said of it: that it is crassly materialistic, fixated on selfish goals; it now sees itself as an abomination to its children, as a passive supporter of racism and exploitation and oppression at home, and a passive supporter of imperialism and genocide abroad. It says all this about itself and it applauds everyone who attacks it in these terms.[8]

And, in our current period of pornography—with sensuous men and women studiously reading about fellatio, cunnilingus, annilingus and necrophilia—any serious enforcement of sanctions by the majority against anybody has become impossible. I return to Dr. Hacker's assertions:

> Outwardly the new middle class seems content with corporate citizenship and is not bothered by the fact that political affairs are in the hands of others. Yet is this really the case? Studies of the new suburbia show that neurosis and feelings of helplessness are endemic; a sense of isolation and powerlessness is having profound social and psychological effects. [Use of the word "profound" is common among writers who want to sound profound but who cannot explicate their own profundity or the symptoms they denominate as "profound."] Problems of mental health cannot be cured by political participation [whoever

said they could?], but the democratic theory has always assumed that self-government can create the environment in which mental and moral health are most likely to flourish. The middle class, in divorcing itself from politics . . . has weakened itself immeasurably.

Earlier, the author was ascribing to the middle class enormous power over those who disregard "accepted precepts of conduct." Now the middle class has "weakened itself immeasurably." ("Immeasurably" is another word which indicates that the writer has no data, has done no research, and has merely transmuted perceptions into "facts.") Dr. Hacker concludes this passage with the ominous sentence:

> If a crisis arises, even a relatively mild one, can we be sure that this group will continue to adhere to democratic values?[9]

And if I were to say that I am certain that the "middle class" will indeed continue to adhere to democratic values, and if I offered as much proof for my certitude as Hacker has for his doubts, would Hacker feel any better about the middle class?[10] To what other values does he foresee the middle class moving? Fascist, communist, socialist, Luddite, Judaeo-Christian—what? If anything is true it is that the middle class is more politically involved than ever before, simply because most public issues involve more people than ever before and because the great issues of a post-industrial society are more and more—unavoidably—public issues: taxes, roads, ecology, airports, employment, agriculture, safety, armaments, housing, race. It might even be arguable that over-participation of the middle class in politics may be responsible for "neurosis and feelings of helplessness" and, perhaps what is called for today is a strong dose of political apathy. Says Hacker:

> This revolution—with or without violence, whether from the left or from the right—will be averted only if corporate America can make room in its environs

> for those who demand entry.... Thus far, corporate America has escaped open attack because the victims of new technology do not yet outnumber its beneficiaries. But technology advances according to rules of its own.

This sort of metaphysical mumbo jumbo is a favorite of people who want to sound both earnest and profound; one deifies technology into some kind of anthropomorphic entity without ever spelling out what one means. I have no objection to metaphor. But metaphor is neither politics nor social analysis.

> America is in a struggle between two identifiable classes. The Marxian model of bourgeoisie-versus-proletariat may no longer apply: but the confrontation is real and its peaceful resolution remains unlikely.

If the Marxian confrontation model may no longer apply, then how is the confrontation "real"? Real between whom, the affluent majority against the non-affluent minority? If the Marxian model doesn't apply, what other model does? And why is it so unlikely that a peaceful resolution could ensue?

> Black Americans have yet to mount the kind of rebellion typical of people victimized by alien oppressors.... Only a dozen or so young, committed men and women in any slum of several hundred thousand are required for a series of symbolic acts. Why, for example, have no white policemen been found in ghetto alleys or tenement hallways, their throats slit ear to ear?... This sort of violence prevailed in Europe throughout the German occupation, in Palestine during the British mandate, and in Algeria prior to the French withdrawal.... The failure of black America to produce even a score of men willing to display such resistance shows how strong are the controls which have held that race submissive for so long.

Only a man with a somewhat fevered politics would compare the United States with nazi-controlled Europe, British-occupied Palestine, French-occupied Algeria, especially when he has written that America "is now a freer and more democratic society *than at any time in its history*. . . . And as the nation's technology has grown more sophisticated, the more *deeply* have Americans been penetrated by the democratic temper." (Italics added.) And, if you please, Dr. Hacker adds even higher praise: "America is the *first nation in history* to have succeeded in bestowing material comfort and *moral equality* throughout the majority of a population." (Italics added.) And further, "I am suggesting that the nation is fundamentally democratic because it has liberated its citizens from hitherto prevailing controls, enabling them to create new and heightened estimates of their qualities and capacities."[11]

Is it possible that the reason most black Americans have not engaged in symbolic acts of murder, assassination, or arson is because they believe as Dr. Hacker does, that America is today freer and more democratic, has bestowed a sense of moral equality, has liberated its citizens better than any other country in the world?

Professor Martin Kilson of Harvard University, whose credentials may weigh a bit more heavily than Dr. Hacker's on the subject of the American Negro, has pointed out that his data would indicate that there is no "popular Negro desire to alter the system fundamentally [nor that] blacks feel their adequate inclusion into American society precludes democratic means." He cites a 1969 Gallup Poll which found that 76 per cent of Negroes were satisfied with their jobs, although in 1966, the figure was 69 per cent and in 1963, when the riots began, 54 per cent. He adds that another set of data suggests that most blacks, "though nursing strong feelings of relative deprivation and thus harboring militant inclinations, have not acquired evaluations of the system that are qualitatively different from those held by the white majority." He cites a poll conducted by Northwestern University's Center for Urban Affairs in 1969, which asked Negroes how they characterized themselves in social terms. The answer:

> *Most black Americans now identify themselves as middle class* [and] *on all items except housing, more than half the black respondents said they were better off. In no case did as many as 10 per cent say they were worse off*[!] (Italics in original.)[12]

To continue with Professor Hacker's analects:

> American marriages cannot be counted among the nation's more successful institutions. Not only do a high proportion end in divorce or desertion, but few of those which continue intact are love-filled or light-hearted relationships. How many American marriages can stand the strain of having two fully fledged human beings living under a single roof?[13]

How can Dr. Hacker possibly know that "few" marriages are "love-filled or light-hearted"? And how few are few? What are fully fledged human beings? What do we know about French marriages, Syrian marriages, Congolese marriages? How do they fit the fully fledged requirement? Now it is true that the 1970 divorce rate jumped 40 per cent over the rate in the 1960s. During the 1960 decade, the rate was about ten divorces per one thousand marriages. Suddenly in 1970 the statistics indicated fourteen divorces per one thousand marriages; Jack Waugh wrote in the *Christian Science Monitor:*

> However the signs look worse than they are. They ignore the basic stability of most American families.... The more accurate measure isn't divorces matched against marriages of a given year; it's divorces matched against the total marrriage pool in the country.
> There are 50 million married couples in the United States. And out of that pool only 14 out of every 1000 last year were divorced. That is 700,000 divorces.... It is no small figure and it is the highest in the Western world. But the number of families that

still stay together in the face of the changes sweeping the country is still the overwhelming statistic.

On the basis of opinion polling by Samuel Lubell, the *Monitor* writer concluded that "the majority of American families, far from restlessly seeking new styles and alternatives, still prize the old; and they want desperately to hold themselves together in the face of change."[14]

In two hundred pages, Dr. Hacker has contradicted himself innumerable times. I have quoted his unrestrained admiration for American democracy and then his reprobation, as when he talks about "the all-too-evident shortcomings of the American democracy [which] disqualify our system as an object of emulation." Suddenly, somewhere else, there is a broadside from out of nowhere: "Another encumbrance—hardly new in our history—is that we tend to regard all foreigners as inferior to ourselves." But is it really true that we have not become the least bit less xenophobic since the days of Trollope, Wilde, Dickens? Not improved by one jot or tittle? Again, "the stages through which new nations move as they establish their identities invariably alarm us." ("Invariably" is another one of those non-cognitive words which one uses when facts, research, data are lacking; who would dare argue with an adverb like "invariably"?) Or, "we cry out with horror at the summary justice that condemns local landlords to be strung from lampposts or shot in village squares." Shouldn't one cry out with horror at lynching anywhere? Or is capital punishment an evil only under capitalism?

An *amicus curiae* of the progressive left will reply to my attack on Hacker that criticism like mine reveals "a lack of open-mindedness towards large generalizations." Yet it is difficult to remain open-minded when one reads what is really a description of America as a sort of "slobocracy," ruled by slobs for slobs and not for fastidious intellectuals, who recoil in horror at the idea that they might be middle-class. As Eugene Ionesco once said, "Often, alas, the most detestable kind of bourgeois is the anti-bourgeois kind of bourgeois."

My reply to those who defend the "large generalizers" like Dr. Hacker is that they make serious political theorizing and speculation impossible because they sound so foolish, so ridiculous, so at variance with what one sees and hears. America is a fascist country? The branch of political theory to which Dr. Hacker belongs is what I could call the "Anything is Possible" school. This school, in its attack on American values or humanistic values, clouds its concepts with romantic rhetoric; its hypotheses are bestrewn with tautologies, and its adherents can leap from "is" to "ought" and never even know they have done so; their ethics are really nothing but disguised commands.

Of course, in a sense everything is indeed possible—American can become a fascist state, the American people can become more bloody-minded than they have ever been since the Civil War, the world can go to hell in one explosion. Jean Harlow and Marilyn Monroe will return to lead Women's Lib when the trumpet sounds, Bobby Seale may someday become president of the black United States with Mark Rudd as his ambassador to white Americans—it is all a possible fantasy, but is it political thinking? In the country of the blind, the one-eyed man is king and in the country of the deafened, the noisiest, loudest, most raucous apocalyptician gets the hearing.

The final passage in Voltaire's *Micromegas* describes how the giant of Sirius promises his earthly visitors a book of philosophy, written with full details for their use in which, by reading, they could see the end of things and all the secrets of nature. Upon their return to earth, they deliver the volume to the Academy of Science in Paris. And when the secretary of the Academy opened the book, "*Il ne vit rien qu'un livre tout blanc; 'ah,' dit-il, 'je m'en étais bien douté.'* [*He only saw blank pages; 'ah,' he said, 'just as I suspected.'*]" So with Dr. Hacker, and his book.

Anyone who has read Samuel Butler's *Erewhon* will recognize once more the truth of the saying about nature imitating art. Butler describes in his Utopia the study of "hypothetics" in which one imagines a set of "utterly strange and impossible contingencies." To Erewhonians, the study of "hypothetics [is] reckoned the fittest conceivable way of preparing . . . for the actual conduct of their affairs." This course of study took place at "the Colleges of Unreason where under the professorships of 'Inconsistency and Evasion'" there was the "deliberate development of the unreasoning faculties." Writes Butler:

> The more earnest and conscientious students attain to a proficiency in these subjects [inconsistency and evasion] which is quite surprising; there is hardly any inconsistency so glaring but they soon learn to defend it, or injunction so clear that they cannot find some pretext for disregarding it.
> Life, they urge, would be intolerable if men were to be guided in all they did by reason and reason only. Reason betrays men into the drawing of hard and fast lines, and to the defining by language. . . . Extremes are alone logical but they are always absurd.[15]

Would it be in order to categorize Professors Hacker, Reich, Marcuse, Gross, and others I have quoted as charter members of the Unreasoning Faculties?

The study of national character can produce almost any conclusion.
Adam Ulam, *The Bolsheviks,* 1965

Yet the doctrine that madness is health, and that madness is liberation and authenticity, receives a happy welcome from a consequential part of the educated public. And when we have given due weight to the likelihood that those who respond positively to the doctrine don't have it in mind to go mad, let alone insane—it is characteristic of the intellectual life of our culture that it fosters a form of assent which does not involve actual credence—we must yet take it to be significant of our circumstance that many among us find it gratifying to entertain the thought that alienation is to be overcome only by the completeness of alienation, and that alienation completed is not a deprivation or deficiency but a potency.
Lionel Trilling, *Sincerity and Authenticity,* 1972

If the development of civilization has such a far-reaching similarity to the development of the individual and if it employs the same methods, may we not be justified in reaching the diagnosis that under the influence of cultural urges, some civilizations, or some epochs of civilizations—possibly the whole of mankind—have become "neurotic"? An analytic dissection of such neuroses might lead to therapeutic recommendations which could lay claim to great practical interest. I would not say that an attempt of this kind . . . was absurd or doomed to be fruitless. But we should have to be very cautious and not forget that, after all, we are only dealing with analogies and that it is dangerous, not only with men bu also with concepts, to tear them from the sphere in which they have originated and been evolved. Moreover the diagnosis of communal neuroses is faced with a special difficulty.

In an individual neurosis we take as our starting-point the contrast that distinguishes the patient from his environment, which is assumed to be "normal." For a group all of whose members are affected by one and the same disorder no such background could exist; it would have to be found elsewhere.
Sigmund Freud, Civilization and Its Discontents, 1930

7

"America Is Insane"

America is insane, Americans are insane the whole country is insane.

THIS SENTIMENT has become fairly common among an extraordinary number of men of letters, so much so that it is taken as conventional wisdom in everyday intellectual discourse, particularly on the left. Even though the thesis is more frequently rhetorically put than, shall we say, factually expounded, there is fierce competition among social critics for more and more lurid evidence of mass insanity in America. One writer, whom I will quote, suggests that the best way to beat the insanity of "the System" and the masses is for sensitive spirits to become insane in response. I will cite a few examples of the kind of rhetoric I mean.

In their Winter 1967 issue, the editors of *Partisan Review* published a symposium on the theme, "What's Happening to America." One could be certain, even without reading the number, that, with such an open-ended title, a guarantee of publication in *Partisan Review,* and inclusion of some really way-out social critics, many of the answers would sound like a politicized updating of the Book of Revelation. I read the volume carefully. Here is the opening sentence in an article by Paul Jacobs: "Madness surrounds us on all sides."[1] One can assume that Jacobs is not talking about himself, nor his friends and political allies, and certainly not youth ("I am personally optimistic about youth"). After all, if he and his friends were mad, who in all sanity could have been around to answer the *Partisan Review* questionnaire? The evidence for the indictment of America or the American people as "insane" is assembled in this manner: select every bit of nastiness and horror and clumsiness that may happen in a subcontinent like ours in any given calendar year; sprinkle the findings with words like "frantic," "frightened," "vulgarize"; cite a few especially stupid television commercials; describe topless shoeshine girls in San Francisco; reiterate "the madness of the country is reflected, too, in its President." There you have it—a clinical indictment of a whole nation!

Harold Rosenberg, a founder and leading member of the Apocalyptic Set, wrote in the same issue that "the American public is out of its mind, lucid at moments but subject to fits of apathy and nose-thumbing." And then in a sputtering burst of metaphors, he continued:

> If the country doesn't collapse or blow up it is because strings pulled from different angles behind the scene cause a temporary balancing of stresses.[2]

Whose strings, which angles, and how long is temporary? Who, as the saying goes, is loony now? This politics is being played out in the theater of the absurd.

The ineffable Nat Hentoff has suggested that to achieve social reconstruction, students should go crazy. One question bothered him:

> Should not every student develop a cultural paranoia in which every professor is viewed as a potential agent or tacit supporter of the murder factory and every academic system is seen as set against the student's mental and social health until he finds out differently?[3]

Susan Sontag found that "the unquenchable American moralism and the American faith in violence.... constitute a full grown, firmly-installed national psychosis, founded, as are all psychoses, on the efficacious denial of reality."[4]

In his famous pamphlet entitled *The White Negro*, Norman Mailer apotheosized the "hipster" as a "philosophical psychopath." Comparing the psychotic ("legally insane") to the psychopath (who is not), he contended that the psychotic is "almost always incapable of discharging in physical acts the rage of his frustration, while the psychopath at his extreme is virtually as incapable of restraining his violence."[5]

Theodore Roszak went a little further in his "psychoanalysis," an elaborate system of non-thought which is really the leftovers of dog-eared paperbacks wrapped up as political analysis. Roszak declared:

> A suicidal pathology is at the root of our politics. . . .
> . . . We must fight our way out of the moiling, suffocating arena of politics so that we can with distance recognize the essential sickness of the games that are played there.
> . . . our world is not beset by problems to be solved, but rather by a disease to be cured.[6]

The Right Reverend Paul Moore, Bishop Coadjutor of the Episcopal Diocese of New York, also availed himself of the privilege of acting the role of pulpit analyst. He too is an expert in the psychopathology of everyday American life:

> The health of a democracy can be judged by its debonair tolerance for dissent. A sick state, lacking in confidence, quivers at the sight of opposition. Is our Government verging on paranoia, the most dangerous of psychoses?[7]

One of the most flamboyant suggestions of mass therapy has come from Allen Ginsberg:

> I will make a first proposal—on one level symbolic, but to be taken as literally as possible, it may shock some and delight others—that everybody . . . try the chemical LSD at least once, every man woman and child American in good health over the age of 14—that, if necessary, we have a mass emo-

tional nervous breakdown in these States once and for all, that we see bankers laughing in their revolving door with strange staring eyes. . . . I propose, then, that everybody including the President and his and our vast hordes of generals, executives, judges and legislators of these States go to nature, find a kindly teacher or Indian peyote chief or guru guide, and assay their consciousness with LSD. . . .
The LSD I am proposing is literal. I hope it will be understood as not THE solution, but a typical and spiritually revolutionary catalyst.[8]

The founder of *Crawdaddy!*, the magazine of rock, is Paul Williams and he had his metaphorical fling about American insanity:

As everybody who writes for *The Village Voice* seems to know, this country is crazy. Freaked. Out of touch with reality. Nothing that goes on in the U. S. can be put in perspective, because there's no framework left. We've built up a system of irrelevancies based on misinterpretations based on inaccuracies, and we can't get back to Start to try again. . . . We pretend not to notice the bars on the windows.[9]

The delight in sidewalk psychoanalysis of a people is itself a striking phenomenon. Almost everybody I know goes about analyzing the country and its people. The passion that some intellectuals have to psychoanalyze Americans—always, of course, to uncover serious mental pathologies! I have never known a sidewalk analysis of American national character which is not bleak, despairing and apocalyptic—sometimes taking the form of prophecy, as, for example, Jack Newfield's look into the crystal ball:

America is threatening to become a giant lunatic asylum. . . . there is the possibility that the best of this generation will be jailed, or driven underground, in a paranoid paroxysm of repression.[10]

What is startling is that this infantile kind of pseudo-scientific, irresponsible scribbling posing as prose is even to be found among centrist intellectuals and journalists. John Scott, a *Time-Life* executive in 1960, once wrote:

> We are overfed, overindulged egocentrics. We are pampered, petulant, and selfish individualists, suspended in a state Reinhold Niebuhr calls "sophisticated vulgarity." We are unwilling to implement the ritual we mouth on Sundays and share with our neighbors. We have contrived a series of deals with pseudo-truth which has left us bloated with food and drink but ideologically naked.
>
> For too many of us the brotherhood of man has degenerated into a glorification of the rugged individual and his ability to acquire and keep more material goods than the neighbor he does not love.

This was quoted by Harry Schwartz, the *New York Times* editorial writer, who was reviewing Scott's book. He preceded the quotation with this statement: "Consider, for example, this harsh—but, unfortunately, accurate—description of our society with which Scott closes his book."[11] So we have the spectacle of *Time-Life* and *New York Times* writers of some serious reputation and influence playing ghoul with a putrid, egocentric American, dead in body and soul.

I want here to interpose what, in my own overfed, egocentric way, I have chosen to call Beichman's Law. It is a rule, as yet uncontradicted by time, that whenever an intellectual says "we" or "our"—as, for example, "we are overfed" or "our guilt," etc.—and the subsequent sentences are highly derogatory to the pronominal antecedent, the intellectual absolves himself and his immediate audience from any of the psychopathological symptoms he is describing, and, consequently, from any responsibility for what is happening or is about to happen. This is known as the "intellectual we" which has replaced the now passé "royal we." It is also a modern editorial form of selling indulgences.

Stewart Alsop, the columnist, was recently the hero of a teaser institutional advertisement placed by his sponsor, the Columbia Broadcasting System. A quotation was printed on one page of a magazine with a "Who said that on the CBS Radio Network?" The quotation read:

> I think it's possible to date precisely the onset of our madness. November 22, 1963. The murder of John Kennedy was a traumatic shock to this nation, from which we haven't fully recovered even yet.[12]

Of course, the Kennedy murder was a traumatic shock; that is merely emphasizing the obvious. But how can anybody, even Stewart Alsop, know the date when "our madness" seized us and know that "we" haven't yet "fully" recovered? And what kind of "madness" is it, and how does Alsop know we're not getting better? The chart is what we want to see.

Let me cite another lay analyst who shares these views and those of the left lay analysts:

> The whole country [United States] is one vast insane asylum and they're letting the worst patients run the place.[13]

The author of that diagnosis which sounds like Jack Newfield's which I quoted earlier, is Robert Welch, founder of the John Birch Society.[14] This is almost bordering on madness: when everybody begins to declaim that everyone else is mad.

Sometimes the Big Lie about American madness is a grim generalization about some American phenomenon which—if true—could well be defined as an act of, or demonstration of, madness. Take this statement by Alexander Campbell:

> When the people of Arkansas learned that some prison inmates there had had nutcrackers and electric apparatus applied to their testicles and had been murdered, their reaction was to inquire if the per-

sons who exposed these conditions wished crime to pay.¹⁵

The white voting-age population of Arkansas in 1968 was 850,643. Does Campbell mean that all—he must certainly mean a large majority—of the people of Arkansas had the same reaction? How does he know? Was there a public opinion poll? Can Campbell really believe that 850,000 adult whites (there is also a 192,626 Negro voting-age population, but I assume Campbell excludes them as part of "the people of Arkansas") all held this same opinion? Would it not be proper to offer one scintilla of evidence?

Professor Daniel Bell has noted that the major preoccupation of those American novelists "who have touched the nerve of the age" was the theme of madness. As he has written in a brilliant essay:

> When the social life has been left behind, and the self, as a bounded subject, has been dissolved, the only theme left is the theme of dissociation, and every important writer of the 60's was in one way or another involved with this theme. The novels are hallucinatory in mode; many of their protagonists are schizoid; insanity, rather than normalcy, has become the touchstone of reality. Despite all the social turmoil of the decade, not one novel by these writers was political; none (with the exception of Bellow's *Mr. Sammler's Planet*) dealt with radicalism, youth or social movements.¹⁶

What Professor Bell says about some of our novelists is even truer for those intellectuals, academics and journalists who are not novelists, at least by definition and marketplace acceptance. Or, rather I should say that while a good many of them do deal with radicalism, youth, and social movements, their writing is all (to use Bell's language) "hallucinatory in mode." Nor is this all. If we are to believe the lay analysts, America has succeeded in building madness in one country. In a world where, in the space of a few days, Asian and African mobs led by political and military elites can kill, maim, destroy tens of thousands, if not hundreds of thousands of their fellow countrymen in the name of what is known as "nation-building"; in a world where peaceful coexistence can sometimes mean Russian missiles in Cuba and Russian missiles in Egypt; in a world where crowds can go berserk at sporting events and do each other grave injury; in a world where Arab guerrillas flee into Israel for protection from butchery by their brothers; in a world where the Soviet Union forbids one of its greatest writers to leave the country merely to collect a Nobel Prize for literature—it is Americans alone who are crazy, Americans alone who are paranoid. Presumably the rest of the world is sane.

There are, of course, an infinite number of ways of implying an emotional unbalance in a people. One of them is to keep your two little eyes open and take in the big picture. Generalize about facial expressions as you pass pedestrians in the street. These faces do not necessarily have to belong to persons you have seen before. You have a right to interpret and make a relevant generalization because they are, after all, fellow Americans. For example, Professor Slater (with whom I want to deal later in this chapter) has given us his impression on returning to these shores:

> Reentering America [from abroad], one is struck first of all by the grim monotony of American facial expressions—hard, surly, and bitter—and by the aura of deprivation that informs them.

Charles Reich keeps his eyes open in railway stations:

> Stand at a commuter train station and see the blank, hollow, bitter faces. Sit in a government cafeteria and see the faces set in rigidity, in unawareness, in timid compliance, or bureaucratic obstinacy; the career women with all their beauty fled, the men with all their manhood drained.

Paul Goodman, in a Canadian radio broadcast, used his eyes in this way:

> The American faces that used to be so beautiful, so resolute and yet poignantly open and innocent, are looking ugly these days—hard, thin-lipped, and like innocence spoiled without having become experienced. For our sake, as well as your own, be wary of us.

Tom Seligson's observations are in a somewhat different milieu:

> America, that stunning, painted, dying whore, had wrinkles under the skin cream and corruption in the heart.[17]

I suspect that nothing is more tempting for a literary intellectual, interested in making a quick, flamboyant point, than to try to prove a large case with a little evidence; what might be called "proof by anecdote." Even one fact, if one is desperate enough, can be made to go a long way. You see what you want to see, and ugliness, like beauty, is in the eye of the beholder. What makes these particular portraits of America and Americans so outrageously dishonest is that facial expressions, even those of Messrs. Slater, Reich, Goodman and Seligson, tell almost nothing at all about an individual. But this is of no matter when one is seeking any kind of documentation to prove the unprovable.

Dr. Ray Birdwhistell of the University of Pennsylvania, is the inventor of "Kinesics"—described as the study of nonverbal communication patterns. For some time, he has been studying the American smile; and he has recently reported his findings:

> Almost as soon as I started to study "smiling" I found myself in a mass of contradictions. From the outset, the *signal* value of the smile proved debatable. Even the most preliminary procedures pro-

vided data which was difficult to rationalize. For example, not only did I find that a number of my subjects "smiled" when they were subjected to what seemed to be a positive environment but some "smiled" in an aversive one. . . .

As I enlarged my observational survey, it became evident that there was little constancy to the phenomenon. It was almost immediately clear that the frequency of smiling varied from one part of the United States to another. . . .

. . . The term "smiling" as used by American informants covers an extensive range of complex kinemorphic constructions which are reducible to their structural components. . . . I have learned that "he smiled" as a statement on the part of an American informant, is as non-specific and uninformative as the statement on the part of the same informant that "he raised his voice."[18]

When a scientist can find that something as seemingly demonstrative as a smile tells you nothing, one would think that a little modesty among social scientists about other facial expressions might be in order. But this is of no matter when one is seeking to dehumanize people, to dehumanize Americans. How easy it is when you are angered at a "people" to find confirming evidence for your resentment. Peer at the faces of the English, the French, the Turks, the Russians, the Moroccans, the Afrikaners—any people anywhere in the world at airports and railroad stations, and you will see what you want to see. During the Stalin era, pro-Soviet correspondents at the height of the Stalin-induced famine could look outside railroad windows passing through towns and villages where people were starving to death, and they could see happy, rosy-cheeked peasant girls waving gaily.

To call everybody else crazy is an example, I submit, of the primitive mind at work; it is an ancient form of exorcising devils and witches. The "primitive mind" of our day uses an updated version of the *Malleus Maleficarum*[19] and exaggerates every human defect into instant and inexorable evil. No more frightful example of this primitivism at work is to be found than in *The Pursuit of Loneliness,* the recent volume by Professor Philip Slater (late of Brandeis University, where he was head of the Sociology department). His work reminds me of something Edmund Wilson once wrote about H. L. Mencken's *Notes on Democracy,* whose basic theme was that the human race was composed of "gentlemen" and "boobs." Although the work pretended to be a systematic inquiry into democratic government, "it is Mencken's same old melodrama, with the gentleman, the man of honor, pitted against the peasant and the boob." Wilson wrote:

> We are not told what makes people gentlemen or what makes people boobs, or of how it is that both these species happen to belong to the same human race, or of how it is that we often find them merging or become transformed into one another. With his fierce inflexibility of mind, Mr. Mencken is capable neither of the sympathy of the historian, of the detachment of the scientist nor of the subtlety of the philosopher. And his new book is not to be taken as a contribution to political science: it is simply another of his "prejudices" treated on a larger scale than the rest.[20]

To overturn America, one must first attempt to dehumanize Americans. And this is the function of Slater's book of hate.

These are harsh words: I mean them to be. In the nature of documentation, let me offer first a chrestomathy of Slater's ideas, the sum of which recalls Cyril Connolly's description of Ronald Firbank: "like most dandies, [he] disliked the bourgeoisie, idealized the aristocracy and treated the lower classes as his brothel."[21] Some of my quotations from Slater's volume are in context, others are abbreviated and might be considered out of context, but the rhetoric and sentiment is characteristic throughout.

We know something about the hopes that tinge the old maid's search for a ravisher under her bed, but we need to understand better the seductive impact that informs our enraged fascination with the revolutionary currents of American society.

We seek more and more privacy, and feel more and more alienated and lonely when we get it.

We die from our own machines, our own poisons, our own weapons, our own despair.

We interact largely with extensions of our own egos. We stumble over the consequences of our past acts. We are drowning in our own excreta.

Americans have always admitted being lawless relative to Europeans.

Americans have always been a people with marked genocidal proclivities.

We cannot avoid asking the question, do Americans hate life? Has there ever been a people who have destroyed so many living things?

We pride ourselves on being a "democracy" but we are in fact slaves.

Americans love machines more than life itself.

Why does the older generation hate its children with such vehemence?

In *The Graduate,* as in upper-middle-class America generally, parents relate to their children in a somewhat vampiresque way. They feed on the child's accomplishments, sucking sustenance for their pale lives from vicarious enjoyment of his or her development.

Perhaps Americans enjoy the mass impersonal killing of people who cannot fight back because they themselves suffer mass impersonal injuries from mechanical forces against which they, too, are powerless.

Any challenge to the technological-over-social priority threatens to expose the fact that Americans have lost their manhood.

Americans continually find themselves in the position of having killed someone to avoid sharing a meal which turns out to be too large to eat alone.

Americans become unhappy and vicious because their preoccupation with amassing possessions obliterates their loneliness.

Americans have created a society in which they are automatically nobodies, since no one has any stable place or enduring connection.

We have become a dangerously irritable people.

If one examines the quotations I have excerpted from the Slater volume (and these are a fair sample of his own dangerous irritability), one finds that America is, or Americans are, dying of despair, drowning in excreta, enjoying mass killing, suffering from genocidal proclivities, hating life, hating all children, loving machines more than life, seeking rapists, becoming alienated, slaves, vampires, castrates, nobodies, unhappy, vicious, dangerously irritable. And all this while wearing monotonous facial expressions! What an achievement!

But this isn't all. Professor Slater seems to be so overly attached to the word "rage" that he simply cannot find a synonym for it—"panic and rage . . . enraged fascination . . . suburbanites would be enraged . . . degree of rage . . . comparable rage . . . what so enrages their elders . . . raging against the consequences of their own inclinations." Methinks he himself rageth too much.

As my nominee for the Grand Prize for the Most Apocalyptic Paragraph of the Decade, I submit Professor Slater's peroration:

> If the old culture is not rejected then its adherents must be prepared to accept a bloodbath such as has not been seen in the United States since the Civil War for genocidal weapons will be on one side and unarmed masses on the other.[22]

Slater's "scientific" predictions of a new Fall of Man, with an exact chronology, is in the tradition of those seventeenth century philosophers and mathematicians who believed that one could predict, with exactitude and through mathematical reasoning, all possible developments in the human experience. This was a time (as Professor Louis Bredvold called it) of "the invention of the Ethical Calculus." One of its earliest proponents was, of course, Descartes and his *esprit de géométrie,* by which one could move from irrefutable axioms to absolutely certain conclusions about everything human. Hobbes also dreamed of creating a Utopia by a mathematico-physical method.[23] Other philosophers of the period, like Leibniz and Erhard Weigel, fell victim to this *furor mathematicus,* the idea that one could solve political questions by the geometrical method or algebraic fancy. Even the otherwise impertubable John Locke was derailed by these fanciful speculations. Later, Jeremy Bentham (one of the early utilitarians whose philosophy Dickens found so repellent[24]) emerged as another philosopher-reformer who, in the guise of proclaiming the greatest good for the greatest number, was in reality offering a despotic calculus to imprison the poor and turn the downtrodden into a small Benthamite profit.[25] In a sense Bentham was a forerunner of our twentieth century revolutionaries and quasi-revolutionaries whose felicific calculus created the concentration camp universe of Stalin and Hitler.

Where Slater cannot find exact numbers to confirm his own ethical calculus, he exploits cautionary phrases to make the same reasonable-sounding points—"so often," or "more and more people." As in: "more and more people feel with a larger and larger part of themselves that the destruction of mankind as a failed species might be a sound idea." Can political discourse be conducted on a level where such "intuitions" circulate as truth? It is such misuse of the English language, as I have already warned, which led to the debasement of political debate and discourse in the 1950s, the Joe McCarthy period, when fascism and concentration camps were said to be "just around the corner" and all freedom lovers were supposed to be trembling in a prison cell. Now in the 1970s, it begins again.

Writers like Slater, Hacker, and Reich (and there are, alas, others) seem to confirm a point Norman Podhoretz made recently.

> I would say that the state of consciousness within the intellectual community itself is in a parlous condition today. I would go so far as to say it is in a pathological condition. I think the pathology—it is a pathology of the spirit—derives precisely from the inability or the unwillingness of the intellectuals as a class to understand themselves as part of the common run of mankind, to understand their own implication in the common run of human experience. . . . I think the intellectuals have been trained to believe that they transcend the common destiny by virtue of the power of their minds.[26]

I would like to offer two pieces of documentation to support Podhoretz's argument. Professor Slater says that when America "is filled with intense color, music, and ornament, deodorants will be the old culture's last-ditch holdouts." And he continues:

> It is no accident that hostility to hippies so often focuses on their olfactory humanity.[27]

Somehow, for Professor Slater, not taking a bath assumes the character of a holy purification rite—"olfactory humanity," indeed!

The second item deals with an article by Professor Louis Kampf of MIT (where, I am told, he has gone so far over to the progressive left that he is known to his colleagues as "Unser Kampf"). Kampf attempts to describe literature as "a weapon in the hands of imperialism" and asks, "Is [the] counterrevolutionary acceptance of fate [in tragedy] something we are supposed to teach as a received value?" He relates how, as head of MIT's English department, he finds the "Western masterpieces" boring, and he doubts whether he will ever again teach Proust. He then describes how a young man in one class, which had been the scene of much shouting of slogans, rose, undressed and sat down again naked. The discussion continued until:

> A female student shouted, "Bullshit! There is a naked man sitting next to me. We're all thinking of him yet no one is saying a word." So for the next two hours we discussed why he had taken off his clothes, and how that related to our being in class and to the books we were reading. It was the only lively discussion we had all semester.[28]

I wonder whether the phrase "pathology of the spirit" is too much of an understatement. I wonder whether the academic community can survive such empty and abysmal rhetoric among academic intellectuals who teach the social sciences and humanities at some of our most distinguished universities. What kind of students are being graduated? Can there be transmitted to students who benefit from the teachings of Philip Slater, Charles Reich, Louis Kampf, Andrew Hacker, a love of learning, a respect for scholarship? Even a respect for the English language?

As a people we have survived McCarthyism of the right and one trusts that we shall survive Slaterism of the left and all those fashionable credos which have attempted to turn Americans into candidates for straitjackets. Still, one must ask in sadness, and even desperation, whether a country and its culture, can survive such a decadent onslaught on thought and rationality.

> Covered with ashes, tearing my hair, my face scored by clawing, but with piercing eyes, I stand before all humanity recapitulating my shames without losing sight of the effect I am producing, and saying: "I was the lowest of the low." Then imperceptibly I pass from the "I" to the "we." When I get to "This is what we are," the trick has been played and I can tell them off. I am like them, to be sure; we're in the soup together. However, I have a superiority in that I know it and this gives me the right to speak. You see the advantage, I am sure. The more I accuse myself, the more I have a right to judge you. Even better I provoke you into judging yourself, and this relieves me of that much of the burden.
>
> Albert Camus, *The Fall*, 1956

> The idea of collective guilt is a delusion.
> Michael Halberstam, "Are You Guilty of Murdering Martin Luther King?" *New York Times Magazine*, 1968

> To make comparisons with evils of the past and to attempt to guide present action in their light, sometimes [leads] to an acceptance of the dogma of collective responsibility in its most pernicious form. It is bad enough to hold all members of a group collectively responsible for actions of some individual members of that group unless the members of the group were aware of those actions, and in a position to control them or at least condemn them. But it is monstrous, and a source of great and continuous cruelty in world history, to hold a present generation responsible for the sins of omission and commission of its ancestors. . . .

The very doctrine of collective responsibility and/or guilt is self-defeating in its moral absurdity, since the descendants of the victims of any action justified by the dogma can invoke it to initiate a contemporary massacre.

　　　　　　　　　　Sidney Hook, "The Human Costs
　　　　　　　　　　　　of Revolution," Survey, 1968

8

"The American People Are Guilty"

The American people are guilty.

GUILTY of what? Like Kafka's Joseph K., guilty of everything that is mean, bad, horrific. Everything. The guilt is supposed to apply to everything and to everybody who is an American. Not to plead guilty, not to accept this burden of guilt, is only to confirm the guilt. This is not an individual guilt, such as would accrue after an arrest for drunken driving and a court sentence for the crime. This is collective responsibility for what every American does both in and out of government.

Here we have Professor Ashley Montagu's charge: " 'We are as responsible for the death of one of humanity's greatest leaders, Martin Luther King, as if we had pulled the trigger ourselves.' "[1]

And the *New Yorker*'s rhetorical accusation: "Each of us had to ask himself just how deeply implicated he himself is, by his actions or inaction in murder. If Calley is guilty, who is *not* guilty?" (Italics in original.)[2]

Time magazine has announced, "that America and Americans must stand in the larger dock of guilt and conscience for what happened at My Lai seems inescapable."[3]

Dotson Rader has put it this way, "When the young can internalize and accept as probable an early death, when they can welcome it and seek it out like terminal patients in unendurable pain, then everyone in this country is guilty, for the young contracted the disease of nihilism from the old."[4]

The Very Reverend Francis B. Sayre, Jr., has said that the reason for the " 'paroxysm in the nation's conscience

[is] simply that Calley is all of us. He is every single citizen in our graceless land.'" Interestingly enough, Dr. Herbert Marcuse has rejected this collective guilt denunciation—"Blatantly false, and a great injustice to the Berrigans, to all those who have, at the risk of their liberty and even their life, openly and actively fought the genocidal war."[5]

Eldridge Cleaver has written, "That white America could produce the assassin of Dr. Martin Luther King is looked upon by black people—and not just those identified as black militants—as a final repudiation by white America of any hope of reconciliation."[6]

I could go on citing similar statements which pin the guilty label on America, the American people, the System, or the Establishment. However, usually it is pinned on the American people—white, of course. A longer list of such quotations would clearly indicate that the Big Lie of America's guilt is based, primarily, on a general contempt for the American people.

Second, the generalized ascription of guilt is an attempt to rob Americans of a sense of the legitimacy of their existence, or, in a political sense, the legitimacy of their dissent from the minority left. When Henry Brandon attacks the American worker as "too fat and conservative" for refusing to be influenced by SDS, Brandon is seeking to rob the American worker of his legitimate right to ignore SDS revolutionism; Brandon is saying a worker has no right to be "fat and conservative," that this privilege is reserved only for non-workers.

Third, the idea of collective guilt excludes the possibility of any virtue attending upon the American people. Is there such a thing as collective innocence, collective goodness? The whole point of collective guilt is that it is total; it excludes no one from its rhetoric; it overrides anything and everything; there is no hope for salvation, or redemption; the verdict—extinction—is irreversible and beyond any appeal.

Fourth, the concept of collective guilt is yet another example of the primitive mind at work. Dr. Michael Halberstam has diagnosed primitive man in a primordial culture as knowing little to explain natural phenomena and so tending "to see all events as related to the sum of his group's morality." For Dr. Halberstam, total guilt feelings are "self-directed and self-terminated" and have "little to do with reality situations."[7]

Fifth, if the American people could only be persuaded of their collective guilt, those who purvey the monstrous Big Lie will then be able to impose their ideas of a restructured society on the country. There is an echo here from the history of other fanaticisms on the progressive left. Indeed, the accusers are saying with the Abbé Gabriel Bonnet de Mably:

Si notre avarice, notre vanité, et notre ambition sont des obstacles insurmontables à un bien parfait, subissons sans murmurer la peine que nous méritons [if our avarice, our vanity and our ambition are insurmountable obstacles to the perfect good, let us submit without a murmur to the punishment which we deserve]. (My translation.)[8]

Sixth, the concept of societal guilt is one which emerges from Sigmund Freud, particularly in chapter 8 of his *Civilization and Its Discontents,* and which has been so politicized as to have lost all meaning. The increasing sense of guilt in modern society, Freud says, is largely unconscious. But according to Professor Roger W. Smith it may well serve certain very conscious purposes: namely, coercion. The phrase "unconscious guilt," far from being an explanation, is really "a metaphor of reconstruction, a weapon of war in the struggle to shape political society." For Professor Smith, the Freudian idea of societal unconscious guilt is "part of the machinery necessary to carry out the central implication of Freud's political thought—the reconstruction of society by an elite."[9] He continued:

Felt discontent, anxiety, and suffering can be channeled into a sense of guilt, which can, in turn, be used to alter society. If, however, one sets up a notion of objective interest, one can go beyond the

> pain men feel to the pain they do not know. A distinction between false consciousness and genuine consciousness becomes necessary and in effect creates the basis for domination of society by an elite. . . .
>
> The citizen, who has now become a patient, can be expected, however, to offer resistance to the treatment of his unconscious maladies. . . . Freud finally comes to the conclusion, in *Civilization and Its Discontents*, that since society will not see that it is sick, and would resist treatment in any case, the only hope for society lies in its being coerced into receiving therapy. Elsewhere, Freud notes that therapy is, in essence, interminable.[10]

It could be argued that Freud was not quite the elitist-ideologist Professor Smith makes him out to be, determined to force upon society a most unwanted reformation.[11] Still, I think there is no escaping the fact that Freud saw in his "unconscious guilt" metaphor a special way of carrying out his reconstruction.

I hope it is obvious that in citing Professor Smith's view of Freud, I am not remotely suggesting that the founder of psychoanalysis was a purveyor of the Big Lie of a whole people's guilt. This is not what Freud was saying. He was speaking as a scientist, and the final paragraphs of *Civilization and Its Discontents* convey his sense of modesty about his conclusions. After all, the concept of guilt is one which has also been analyzed in theological terms—by Miguel de Unamuno, among others. There is a large difference between guilt in a theological sense, the sense of "original sin," and its exploitation politically. In the one, we seek a personal redemption which may be attainable; in the other, we see a calculated political attempt to reduce a people to a cringing, whipped mass whom nothing can save, except a final Armageddon. Unamuno writes in his *Tragic Sense of Life*:

> The fact that society is guilty aggravates the guilt of each one, and he is most guilty who most is sensible of the guilt. Christ, the innocent, since he best knew

the intensity of the guilt, was in a certain sense the most guilty. . . .

And the fact that guilt is collective must not actuate me to throw mine upon the shoulders of others, but rather to take upon myself the burden of the guilt of others, the guilt of all men; not to merge and sink my guilt in the total mass of guilt, but to make this total guilt my own; not to dismiss or banish my own guilt, but to open the doors of my heart to the guilt of all men. . . . The fact that society is guilty aggravates the guilt of each member of it.[12]

Freud, too, was aware of the role which the guilt sense played in civilization and in which religion acted as a mediating force:

Religions . . . claim to redeem mankind from this sense of guilt, which they call sin. From the manner in which, in Christianity, this redemption is achieved—by the sacrificial death of a single person, who in this manner takes upon himself a guilt common to everyone—we have been able to infer what the first occasion may have been on which this primal guilt, which was also the beginning of civilization, was acquired.[13]

An incisive comment on the concept of guilt has come from Professor Glenn Tinder, who said that "the sense of guilt, like the fear of death, depends on a consciousness of oneself as a distinct being. . . . The development of selfhood, however, is necessarily at the same time the development of a sense of personal responsibility. By becoming a person, one becomes vulnerable to conscience."[14] This definition precisely sets itself off from the guilt purveyors' sweeping denunciations of the American people. For them, the people are a mass, not a collectivity of persons. As a mass, they have become invulnerable to conscience pangs—and if they are invulnerable how does an American then differ from a nazi concentration camp commandant? Their accusers will not grant to American mankind, as they would and do to other peoples, "a consciousness of oneself as a distinct being."

The guilt purveyors are selective in their retributive statements. Professor Tinder said that "the sociological emphasis upon environment has led to the notion that guilt is something suffered, rather than freely incurred, and that man is thus intrinsically innocent."[15] It is here that one can note the duplicity of the accusation. When it is convenient, the environment can be blamed so that man is not responsible for his acts; when it is politically or intellectually inconvenient, then man is held responsible for the world's evil. The latter is always more dramatic, and hence more congenial to pseudo-religious apocalyptics, for it amounts to a conspiratorial theory of society. Karl Popper called it "a kind of inverted theism, an inverted belief in gods whose whims and wills rule everything and look after everything. It comes from abandoning God and then saying: 'Who is in his place?' "[16]

Dr. Hannah Arendt has put her finger on the fallacy of collective guilt: its denial of a common humanity, what she called "the unitary origin of the human race." Because of man's behavior to other men, and the knowledge of evil potentialities in men, "the result has been that they have recoiled more and more from the idea of humanity and become more susceptible to the doctrine of race which denies the very possibility of a common humanity." To accept the idea of humanity "implies the obligation of a general responsibility which they do not wish to assume." Dr. Arendt wrote:

> For the idea of humanity, when purged of all sentimentality, has the very serious consequence that in one form or another men must assume responsibility for all crimes committed by men and that all nations share the onus of evil committed by all others....
>
> In political terms, the idea of humanity, *excluding no people and assigning a monopoly of guilt to no one,* is the only guarantee that one "superior race"

after another may not feel obligated to follow the "natural law" of the right of the powerful, and exterminate "inferior races unworthy of survival." (Italics added.)[17]

Elsewhere, Dr. Arendt has called attention to more topical aspects of this problem:

> We all know, for example, that it has become rather fashionable among white liberals to react to Negro grievances with the cry, We are all guilty, and "black power" has proved only too happy to take advantage of this "confession" to instigate an irrational "black rage" ... confessions of collective guilt are always the best possible safeguard against the discovery of the actual culprits.[18]

There is another, a seventh reason, for this imposition of collective guilt on Americans: to turn them into a mass deserving of mass punishment. If the American people are "guilty," then the violence used against them and their institutions is not an example of impersonal victimization, but merely a fulfillment of nemesis, of retributive justice. The idea of mass guilt and mass punishment, one of the most vicious inventions of modern revolutionary intellectualdom, explains why workers and peasants have been the primary victims of cruelties and privations without parallel in the actually non-revolutionary sector of the world in the name of The Revolution. It is taken for granted that Lenin, Stalin, Fidel Castro, even Nkrumah, must necessarily cajole, coerce, and ultimately punish the so-called liberators of mankind before they can become true liberators. Since man is a refractory animal, he makes the fulfillment of utopian designs difficult, well-nigh impossible. He is "objectively" guilty; therefore, he must be punished. We are all sinners, of course, but for the totalitarian mind, some are more sinful than others (e.g. white construction workers who are transformed into a collective of wrongdoers as the culture critic moves quickly into the role of avenger). In other words, by placing the guilt on a mass—the American people—everything becomes permissible even if "the delinquent accepts the responsibility for his deviant actions and is willing to admit that his deviant actions involve an injury or hurt."[19] After all, the injury is not in essence an injury, since all resulting pain and suffering are merely the accompaniment of a vast exercise in justice.

Che Guevara was a revolutionary ready to wipe out most of humanity to achieve his Utopia. In Daniel James' biography, Guevara says:

> Rivers of blood will have to flow. The blood of our people is our most sacred treasure, but it must be spilled in order to save more blood in the future. What we affirm is that we must follow the road to liberation, even if it costs millions of atomic victims.[20]

The collective guilt concept is also related to the putative failure of the American system of democracy, which I have dealt with earlier. But this is an ambivalent failure. On the one hand, the people are betrayed by the System, on the other hand, the hateful guilty people are responsible for the evil of the System. By introducing the convenient concept of collective guilt, the culture critic can both be with the people and against them; he can exercise his total capacities for love and hate; he can adore the innocent collectivity like Rousseau, and he can thunder against the sinful mass like Calvin. Which is stronger—the love which is blind or the hate which is irrational? One sociologist has noted the powerful element of loathing for the people. Professor Bennett W. Berger observed "many on the left really hate 'the people,' hate, at the very least, Mr. and Mrs. Middle America, and get their greatest kicks from making them uptight with apocalyptic rhetoric."[21]

Although they pose as lovers of the people, members of the radical left, or whatever they may call themselves, have little regard for human beings; they prefer to think of the regrettably inert millions as an undifferentiated mass.

Here is one disciple of populist love, in a characteristic moment of sweet pity and sympathy:

> Look again [Charles Reich wrote] at a "fascist"—tight lipped, tense, crew cut, correctly dressed, church-going, an American flag on his car window, a hostile eye for communists, youth, and blacks. He has had very little of love, or poetry, or music, or nature, or joy. He has been dominated by fear. He has been condemned to narrow-minded prejudice, to a self-defeating materialism, to a lonely suspicion of his fellow men. He is angry, envious, bitter, self-hating. He ravages his own environment. He has fled all his life from consciousness and responsibility. He is turned against his own nature; in his agony he has recoiled upon himself. He is what the machine left after it had its way.[22]

Guilty—Guilty—Guilty, Your Honor. Are there any extenuating circumstances? Perhaps the poor slob just does not understand. But not for him is there any love or forgiveness. Not for him is there any conceivable apologia or rationalization. Not for him is there a word about his "olfactory humanity." So it is that Dr. Alexander Heard, who acted as adviser to President Nixon on campus unrest, could say in a memorandum, "The strain of idealism in college students helps to explain the intensity of beliefs and the vigor of actions rooted in those beliefs. Student behavior that to some seems simply 'unpatriotic' may be intended by the student as the highest form of patriotism."[23] As Professor Robert Nisbet said in a sharp reply:

> Of course it is scarcely conceivable that a Presidential Commission on the subject of working-class delinquency or criminality would have taken idealism as its point of departure. But when it comes to the delinquent or criminal behavior of the children of the rich, or at least the well-off, we are treated to a disquisition on their virtues that places them

somewhere between St. Francis of Assisi and the
Anabaptists of the 16th century. . . .

. . . Despite its ritualistic denunciations of violence, the [President's] Report [on campus unrest] sets this [campus] violence into a perspective which serves both logically and psychologically to justify and to encourage it.[24]

Guilt has, thus, a double standard, and although every effort is made to disguise this, the hypocrisy and finally the ethical meaninglessness or nihilism breaks through. Professor Kenneth Minogue has dealt with what he has called "the fashionable idea of national guilt," which gives the appearance of "intellectual profundity, but its real effect is to destroy moral judgment altogether." As he put it:

If everybody is guilty, then, logically, no one is guilty. . . . Either behavior is explained in scientific terms as the effect of causes, in which case it makes no sense to add such terms as "guilt" at all, or else the behavior is treated as the moral decision of the people directly involved, in which case responsibility cannot be extended beyond this circle.[25]

If there are "guilty elements" in American life, which explain the behavior of some soldiers at My Lai, there has been a switch "from a moral judgment to a scientific one, transferring the guilt across the ledger from the moral judgment to a scientific one."[26] In that case, there needs to be an inquiry into the "causes" of these "guilty elements" and then into the further causes and on into an infinite regress. As Professor Minogue put it rather wryly:

Having moved the guilt from the few American soldiers involved, I shall find no place to terminate my attribution of guilt until I come to—what? The apes? The missing link? The regrettable events in the Garden of Eden? It becomes very easy to see why the doctrine of original sin has been so attractive to generation after generation of men.[27]

He cites Marx's third thesis on Feuerbach as dealing with the kind of culture critics whose philosophical *Leitmotif* (as commonplace today as in earlier periods of intellectual folly) amounts to this: "I reject as evil the society in which I live." The Marxist thesis reads as follows:

> The materialist doctrine that men are products of circumstances and upbringing, and that, therefore, changed men are products of other circumstances and changed upbringing, forgets that it is men that change circumstances, and that the educator himself needs educating. Hence this doctrine necessarily arrives at dividing society into two parts, of which one is superior to society (in Robert Owen, for example).

What Marx is telling us is that (as Professor Minogue explicates the passage) "the social critic . . . is choosing to be part of, and not part of, society according to his caprice. And in each case, he employs a different logic of explanation, in the one case, determinist, and in the other case, indeterminist, or moral." In other words, once more the confusion between moral and scientific modes of explanation, and an easy escape into double standards.

The point of Minogue's argument is to demonstrate the illogicality of extending moral terms like "innocence" or "guilt" beyond a world "of persons making choices." Is it a serious matter if words are "capriciously misused in this way"?

> I believe that it is, for words are not merely the stipulative tools of communication, but also represent investments of thought and emotion. It is true, of course, that people do not always do what is logically possible to them. . . . Nevertheless, it will certainly happen that some among these people who begin by debasing moral terms, in order to luxuriate in a sense

of vicarious guilt, will end up ceasing to regard themselves as responsible for their actions.[28]

We are dealing here with more than the issues involved; we are also concerned with the danger to the language of politics, and therefore to the means of civilized discourse. George Orwell's classic warning to the last generation of ideologues is still relevant:

> [Such] political language—and with variations this is true of all political parties from Conservatives to Anarchists—is designed to make lies sound truthful and murder respectable, and to give an appearance of solidity to pure wind. . . .
> . . . if thought corrupts language, language can also corrupt thought.[29]

The Big Lie that the American people are "guilty" is a piece of what has been called "Herrenvolkism." It is a part of the treason of an intellectual faction which seeks to barbarize the American mind, by asserting a seigneurial disgust with men and women whom they have expelled from a common fellowship. Or perhaps it is they who have expelled themselves from this fellowship.

What remains for us who repudiate the concepts of collective guilt and collective innocence[30] is to examine the statement of Lord Robert Blake, the eminent historian and biographer, and to follow its precepts:

> A person's duty is to behave according to the moral principles of his creed in a given situation in the present. He is more likely to reach a right decision if he is guided by rational consideration on its merits of the problem which confronts him than if he allows himself to be influenced by the dark atavism of pre-Christian mythology.[31]

[Mandelstam] would say that he wanted to be with everybody else, and that he feared the Revolution might pass him by, if in his shortsightedness, he failed to notice all the great things happening before our eyes. It must be said that the same feeling was experienced by many of our contemporaries, including the most worthy of them, such as Pasternak. My brother, Evgeni Yakovlevich, used to say that the decisive part in the subjugation of the intelligentsia was played not by terror and bribery (though God knows, there was enough of both) but by the word "Revolution" which none of them could bear to give up. It is a word to which whole nations have succumbed and its force was such that one wonders why our rulers still needed prisons and capital punishment.

                                      Nadezhda Mandelstam, *Hope against Hope:*
                                                             A Memoir, 1970

The hand of Vengeance sought the bed
To which the purple tyrant fled;
The iron hand crush'd the tyrant's head,
And became a tyrant in his stead.
                                      William Blake, "I Saw a Monk
                                of Charlemaine," in *Jerusalem*, 1803

Alone, alone about a dreadful wood
Of conscious evil runs a lost mankind,
Dreading to find its Father lest it find
The Goodness it has dreaded is not good;
Alone, alone, about our dreadful wood.

Where is that Law for which we broke our own,
Where now that Justice for which Flesh resigned

*Her hereditary right to passion, Mind
His Will to absolute power? Gone. Gone.
Where is that Law for which we broke our own?*
                    W. H. Auden, "For the Time Being:
                        A Christmas Oratorio," 1944

9

"America Needs a Violent Revolution"

America needs a revolution, a people's revolution, above all, a violent revolution, to save herself and to change the world.

I

THERE IS no surer way to attract a reading or listening audience than to intone that America needs a revolution, that a revolution in America is long overdue, and, best of all, that we are in the midst of a revolution. It is one of those words which, in Professor Harold Lasswell's phrase, is endowed with "halo effects."

President Nixon has announced that he is dedicated to "the New American Revolution [which] can be a revolution as profound, as far-reaching, as exciting, as that first revolution almost 200 years ago." He was, of course, talking about "a peaceful revolution in which power will be turned back to the people."[1] President Kennedy told an assembly of Latin American diplomats in 1962 that " 'those who make peaceful revolution impossible will make violent revolution inevitable.' "[2] President Johnson, while he was the New Frontier's vice-president, announced that Americans were "the authentic revolutionaries of the world" and, later, as president, he called for "a peaceful revolution in the world."[3]

Revolutions come in all shapes and sizes—the Green [agricultural] Revolution, the Automation Revolution, the People's Revolution, the Cultural Revolution, the Academic Revolution, the Great Proletarian Cultural Revolution, the Sex Revolution, the Campus (or Student)

Revolution, the Revolution of Rising Expectations, the Communications Revolution, Women's Lib Revolution, the Black Revolution, the African Revolution, the Paperback Revolution, the Consumer Revolution. Attach the word "revolution" to any noun and one can be sure of some kind of favorable response. (A gaudy, multicolor catalogue of interior decoration and home design, Section 6 of the *New York Times,* 26 September 1971, began with this sentence, "America is undergoing its own brand of cultural revolution.") On the other hand, to refer to a counterrevolution is to ensure a hostile response. Nobody wants to be a counterrevolutionary, even those who seek freedom, say, as the Czechs or Hungarians. They tried to persuade the Soviet Union that they were really making their own revolution, not a counterrevolution, but to no avail.

By and large this rhetorical passion for the word "revolution," particularly in its presidential expression, burns with a clear, gemlike flame only in America. I have not heard prideful affirmations from British prime ministers, French presidents, German chancellors, Italian presidents, Japanese premiers that they are "the authentic revolutionaries of the world." In a world where we have noted many revolutions—the English, French, Mexican, Bolshevik, Turkish, Chinese, Yugoslav, Cuban, Vietnamese, Nazi, Fascist, Algerian—it may be said (although this is disputed) that America had one classic revolution. Still, the historian Charles A. Beard used to refer to the Civil War as "the second American Revolution"; and for Professor Zbigniew Brzezinski, America is now in the middle of a third revolution. Between the Civil War and New Deal occurred the second American Revolution, although he concedes that "to call it a revolution is admittedly to stretch the definition of revolution."[4]

Obviously, the New Left, young and old, do not mean "peaceful" when they urge a revolution in America, and they most certainly do not mean that the revolution is to wait until the majority of the American people indicate they do in fact want a violent revolution. Indeed, the striking hallmark of a real revolution is that so often a clear majority of the people oppose it.

Let me first begin this dissection of this last and most central of the nine Big Lies by quoting a definition from Dr. Marcuse:

> By "revolution" I understand the overthrow of a legally established government and constitution by a social class or movement with the aim of altering the social as well as the political structure. This definition excludes all military coups, palace revolutions, and "preventive" counterrevolutions (such as Fascism and Nazism) because they do not alter the basic social structure.[5]

Professor Marcuse's essay asserts that "to claim an ethical and moral right, a revolutionary movement must be able to give rational grounds for its chances to grasp real possibilities of human freedom and happiness, and it must be able to demonstrate the adequacy of its means for obtaining this end."[6] Now it is quite clear from the context, that by "overthrow" Dr. Marcuse means a violent overthrow since he has indicated elsewhere in his writings, which I have quoted, that he expects an existing political order to use violence to prevent its being overthrown. He is, secondly, also saying that there is only one kind of revolution—socialist, since he excludes fascist or rightist revolutions as "counterrevolutionary" and since the aim of his revolution is the overthrow of an existing capitalist system which is anti-revolutionary.

In this essay, as in many other of his essays, Dr. Marcuse shows a curious reticence about what should come after the destruction, after the holocaust. It is a reticence to be found among other revolutionaries in this country. The Communist Party of the United States of America is a little clearer as to what should happen after the revolution —their model is the Soviet Union and its foreign policy. Our revolutionaries, like Dr. Marcuse, however, are quite critical of Russia and, like Daniel Cohn-Bendit, look upon Soviet communism as "obsolete." This is not the place to enter into a long analysis of Marcuse's work.[7] I cite his language because it so reflects the temper of the self-defined revolutionaries to be found in America today, particularly in academic circles. And that temper demands destruction of America in order to produce a new and better world. An editorial in a New Left publication warned that "to students and organizers in the new movements, these older radicals seem suspiciously accommodated to the society that must be destroyed."[8] But these exhortations are in the large, never with details; as William Blake wrote:

> He who would do good to another must do it in
>   Minute Particulars.
> General Good is the plea of the scoundrel,
>   hypocrite and flatterer.[9]

Now it will be argued that this society is so rotten and so hopeless that anything will be an improvement, and because it is so decadent and obsolete there is no need to spell out, to blueprint the future, to write in advance the decrees by which the New Society will be run. For some people, America is really "finished" as it is for Richard Huelsenbeck (an émigré from nazi Germany who lived in New York for thirty-four years as a practicing psychiatrist, having had an earlier career as a Dadaist), who fled to Switzerland after delivering his farewell address:

> America is a tragic land, and the Americans are a tragic people. Their grandiose try to found a free society has failed, and now they are in an unsolvable conflict.[10]

But then we can also read Vladimir Dedijer in a letter to Sartre saying:

> The future of the world depends so much on the American New Left. Nowhere are the social contradictions deeper, and nowhere does a rebel have a greater opportunity to demonstrate the firmness of his

convictions than here. Therefore it is the greatest country in the world.[11]

The French philosopher-critic, Jean-François Revel, believes that "a true radical . . . can only be pro-American, for the United States is the hotbed of world revolution." This is the thesis of Revel's book *Without Marx or Jesus:*

> If I compare the United States today with what it was in 1950 there is no comparison, *n'est-ce pas?* —the economic progress, the progress of blacks in political and cultural life, in the university—yes, the United States is now one of the least racist countries in the world. You were forced to pass through this crisis. Europe didn't have this problem.[12]

Whether or not America has become the arena of the permanent revolution, the overriding question which revolution-mongers like Dr. Marcuse and his disciples will not—or cannot, or dare not—answer is what happens after the revolution. Lenin, as I pointed out earlier, complained that Marx hadn't shown what would happen after the "proletariat" had seized power. We now *know* what happens because there have been several revolutions since 1918 which foreclosed reform. Proudhon argued against Marx's belief that reform was impossible without a revolution, that revolutionary action was necessary "as a means of social reform." As Martin Buber has declared, referring to Proudhon's famous letter to Marx:

> [Proudhon] divined the tragedy of revolutions and came to feel it more and more deeply in the course of disappointing experiences. Their tragedy is that as regards their positive goal they will always result in the exact opposite of what the most honest and passionate revolutionaries strive for, unless and until this has so far taken shape *before* the revolution that the revolutionary act has only to wrest the space for it in which it can develop unimpeded. (Italics in original.)[13]

Not even Marx was certain that violence was needed to effect major changes in capitalist societies. In fact, he said at a public meeting at The Hague in 1872:

> We know that the institutions, manners and customs of the various countries must be considered, and we do not deny that there are countries, like England and America . . . where the worker may attain his object by peaceful means.[14]

And although Marx was conceding that the worker could "attain his object" within the existing system, he did not in fact show what might be attained, or what would be desirable as a post-revolutionary system, but offered only an early variant of the "all power to the people" platform.

One of the "explanations" for revolutionary violence in America in recent years has been that the system will not be changed until it is somehow exploded from within, that try as one will, patiently and peacefully, nothing is changed. So we are asked by a New Left spokesman to sympathize with "the impotence, irrelevance, and despair attendant on the realization that what one feels, believes, and demands are neither shared nor acted upon by the overwhelming majority of one's society."[15] As I read this *cri de coeur* of the New Left, I began to feel that, indeed, it must be a deplorable injustice that a vast majority of the heterogeneous American people prefer (in Michael Oakeshott's words) "the familiar to the unknown . . . the tried to the untried, fact to mystery, the actual to the possible, the limited to the unbounded, the near to the distant, the sufficient to the superabundant, the convenient to the perfect, present laughter to utopian bliss."[16] As Hugh Gaitskell, the late leader of British socialism, used to insist:

> The right to dissent is not something that can be made to depend on the fewness of those who dissent. It must be allowed to a majority.[17]

I have earlier cited Dr. Marcuse's view of an American revolution. Arthur I. Waskow, a Fellow of the Institute for

Policy Studies, has issued his manifesto which sounds analytical but, again, tells us precisely nothing. His scenario proceeds along these lines:

There are three major strands of "opinion and action" in American radicalism today. First, radical liberals who believe that they can effect some changes by rallies or political campaigns, but who regard "more basic change" as impossible. Second, the "chaotics" who agree that basic change is impossible, but, yet, believe it is necessary; so they don't bother to seek new laws or a classic revolution but instead opt for "chaos," not for "perverse or crazy reasons, but out of deep despair over the impossibility of changing America." Believing that only a small percentage of white America and no more than half of black and brown America "can break out of a system that oppresses half the world," they know a revolution is out of the question. Waskow quotes one of the "chaotics": " 'An American revolution? America isn't entitled to a revolution. . . . The world revolution is the only one that counts!' " Third, the Waskowites who seek "a real transformation of America—call it 'revolution' if you like, but remember that its proponents do not mean violence. They mean the creation of a participatory democracy where the people govern their own institutions at the bottom." The Waskowite (or "transformationist") problem is posed thus: "not till there are serious signs of transformation in the heart of the working class and the middle class can their argument look real." A deepening crisis, in the opinion of the third group, will lead to total collapse. The existing crisis thus far has only affected marginal people—"blacks, students, Chicanos"; next come the working class, the middle class, the suburbanites, and these will "get moving."[18] (To do what?) Again, we have here revolutionism in the name of categories—blacks, students, Chicanos, browns, workers, and suburbanites—as if there are overriding monochromatic "class loyalties" and none of the multiple, cross-cutting loyalties which inform the people in any democracy. And, of course, there is always the omnipresent, brooding Leninist construct—the people, the masses, the proletariat, the working class which will not make a thoroughgoing revolution because they are victims of "economism" and "trade union consciousness"; you can buy them off with a penny when there's a world to be born. If Lenin looked upon the Russian masses as utterly untrustworthy, and the peasants as victims of the "idiocy of rural life," how much less trustworthy would be the American people, with trade unions, economic associations, religious institutions, literacy, communications, bank-savings, and, worst of all, a presumably brainwashed faith in their country? The people?—No!

The followers of Waskow's third grouping trouble me—who are they? Are they Panthers, Weathermen? Are they Castroites, Maoists, Dubcekists, or are they perhaps an underground faction in the Americans for Democratic Action? The Waskowites make perfectly valid criticisms of America—poor and insufficient housing, unemployment, deficient medical care, pollution, high taxes, inflation, bloated military appropriations. But, as I said earlier, unless you call it "revolution," nobody will listen and you might be expected to go and do something about it, even to give up those ghastly creature comforts of the miserable "consumer society" which (as a poster declared in May 1968 during the Sorbonne uprising) "must perish of a violent death . . . Imagination is seizing power." The Waskowites confirm something Irving Howe has said and this is why they are so intriguing:

> Certain people of the New Left insist on expressing fundamental socio-political and moral attitudes towards American society and yet find themselves curiously reticent about expressing a fundamental socio-political attitude towards Communist countries.[19]

The credo of all the revolutionary *groupuscules* in the Western world is that by overthrowing capitalism and democracy, the new man will be created. So let us look around at the scenes where capitalism has been overthrown. Is there a new man in Russia, in China, in North Vietnam, in Cuba? What is new man about Brezhnev, Mao, Le Duan, Fidel Castro, except in the rose-colored spectacles of a gaggle of foolish intellectuals? What can new men say in Moscow, Peking, Hanoi, Havana, if they have to keep their mouths shut? After fifty years of the Russian Revolution, where and what is the new man?

Any analyst of the intellectual temper of our time must ask this question: Why this passion for revolutionism when so much of its achievements (by the admission of the achievers) has cost so much? The apologists for revolutionism—particularly for the Russian Revolution—have made statements which, in the light of the anti-Stalin revelations, make frightful reading. For example, Simone de Beauvoir happily quotes Maurice Merleau-Ponty's explanation of Stalin's terror:

> In 1936, in a Soviet Russia isolated, threatened and unable to preserve the Revolution except at the price of monolithic severity, all opposition assumed the objective aspect of treason.[20]

Just like that—and that "objective aspect" took the lives, by mistake it turns out, of how many Soviet citizens—ten, fifteen, twenty million?[21] Jean-Paul Sartre has been even more direct:

> Russia is not comparable to other countries. It is only permissible to judge it when one has accepted its undertaking, and then only in the name of that undertaking.[22]

Of course, with such a Sartrean imperative, there can never be any acceptable judgment about the Soviets, since who is to be judge of the adequacy or fullness of the "acceptance of the undertaking"? But why not China, Albania, Yugoslavia, Mongolia, as well? The utter irrationality of Sartre's proposition can be seen by substituting the word "God" for "Russia." The most serious indictment of revolutionists in America (as, indeed the world over, including the ideologues from St. Germain des Prés or the Sierra Maestre) is that, fundamentally, their revolutions, whether they call themselves left or right, are against people. They are the anti-people revolutions, *and they are intended as such.* Sometimes, the sentiment is a bit of a put-on, as when James Forman told off a dominantly New Left white audience: " 'We're going to liberate you whether you like it or not.' "[23] Fascists believe that, too. Drieu La Rochelle once explained to the followers of the French fascist, Jacques Doriot:

> Saving France means saving the French, all the French, even those who do not want to be saved, who let themselves go, who ask only to be left alone.[24]

In Brazil, intellectual elites often quote the phrase, " 'We must make the revolution before the people do.' "[25]

The anti-people revolution is by its nature uninterested in public opinion or the opinion of the people in whose name the revolutionaries speak. In fact, these revolutionaries flout public opinion with the same ideologized insouciance as do fascists. Dr. Marcuse said this quite plainly, "the triumph and end of introjection: the stage where the people cannot reject the system of domination without rejecting themselves, their own repressive instinctual needs and values." He continued:

> The semi-democratic process works of necessity against radical change because it produces and sustains a popular majority whose opinion is generated by the dominant interests in the *status quo.* As long as this condition prevails, it makes sense to say that *the general will is always wrong*—wrong inasmuch as it objectively counteracts the possible transformation of society into more humane ways of life. . . .
> . . . In the dynamic of corporate capitalism, *the fight for democracy thus tends to assume anti-democratic forms.* . . .
> . . . capitalist mass-democracy is perhaps to a higher degree self-perpetuating than any other form of government of society; and the more so the more it rests, not on terror and scarcity, but on efficiency and

wealth, and on the *majority will* of the underlying and administered population. (Italics added.)[26]

We must expect, then, that under a Marcusian utopian leadership, the general will and the majority will would play no role in governance. The people will have to learn to get along with the "vanguard of the proletariat," for it alone knows what is to be done independent of general will, majority will, attitudes and desires of the people. As Max Stirner once put it (with the same "dialectical logic"), " 'A people cannot be free otherwise than at the individual's expense.' "[27] From Lenin to Marcuse, from the Jacobins to the contemporary revolutionaries, there is no true or deep interest in bettering the lives of the people for whom they made, or will make, the revolution. Leon Trotsky once described the Jacobins:

> They spared no human hecatomb to build the pedestal for their Truth. . . . The counterpart to their absolute faith in a metaphysical idea was their absolute distrust of living people. (Ellipsis in quote.)[28]

George Paloczi-Horvath (whom I quoted earlier in a more critical vein) expressed his feeling about revolutionaries, of whom he had been one for a brief and unhappy period:

> They fell in love so deeply with the generation of tomorrow, with the mankind to come, that there was hardly any love left for those who happened to live in today's world. They were brought up in a manner which only filled their hearts with cold and abstract feelings, and they thought that the generation of the day after tomorrow could be happy even if it was conceived in suspicion and fear.[29]

The need for an American revolution—violent and fundamental, bloody and cleansing—is, according to its exponents, a matter of sheer survival for the country. Here a few questions intrude themselves: Does Russia also need a revolution? After all, Russia's political and social structure has changed less since 1918 than that of probably any other country in the world.[30] Shouldn't a country which is as resistant to change as the Soviet Union be a moral target of American revolutionaries, too? What about China, Albania, Cuba—should there not also be a cleansing revolution there? Other countries are allowed to suffer on with just one revolution, that vaunted "final conflict"; but not America. In fact, we are told, America really hasn't had a *real* revolution. For Dr. Hannah Arendt, it was the French Revolution that "has made world history"—whatever that means—while the American Revolution "has remained an event of little more than local importance." Admittedly it may be difficult to picture George Washington as a sans-culotte and Benjamin Franklin as a vengeful Jacobin, but it is surely a piece of European ethnocentrism to regard the American Revolution as some minor event, simply because it lacks what Professor Richard B. Morris has called "a proletarian character." Replying to Dr. Arendt, Professor Morris wrote:

> Revolutions seldom if ever recruit their leaders from the lower classes but normally propel to the fore people with middle-class aspirations who for one reason or another find the door to opportunity or security closed. Such was the case in both the American and French Revolutions.
>
> Both revolutions were started by elites. . . .[31]
>
> . . . Both stressed legality. Both affirmed the rights of man and the sacredness of private property. . . .
>
> . . . The trouble is that recent commentators . . . have refused to give to the American Revolution any dimension other than that of a political movement of liberation, whereas they have invested the French Revolution with all the trappings of class war. . . .
>
> . . . . If in its origins and common purposes the American Revolution was an anti-colonial war fought for independence and national identity, it was also marked by liberative currents, class conflicts and egalitarian urges. . . .

"America Needs a Violent Revolution" / 181

> ... The American Revolution [is] not an event in American history alone but a turning point in world history, not a single crisis settled in a brief span of years but a broad movement of liberation which has not yet run its course.[32]

Part of the fascination with revolutionism is that few of its exponents need know anything about government, administration, organization, legislation, or just simply what politics is about.[33] Professor Nathan Glazer, in a recent personal memoir, explained how one of the important influences in his "deradicalization" was a year he spent in Washington, in the Housing and Home Finance Administration:

> I learned, to my surprise, that most of the radical ideas my friends and I were suggesting had already been thought of, considered, analyzed, and had problems in their implementation that we had never dreamed of.... I learned that the difficulty with many radical ideas lay in the fact that so many varied interests played a role in government, and that most of them were legitimate interests. It was a big country, and it contained more kinds of people than were dreamed of on the shores of the Hudson.[34]

In a different sense, the Glazer "deradicalization" is a criticism of those who still insist on carrying a license in the Radical Anti-Establishment Neo-Marxist Union. I refer to Michael Harrington, who relishes, like so many of his troubled colleagues, orating in the large without ever specifying what we do next, what we do after the revolution.[35] Mr. Harrington was a consultant to a Washington task force that eventually wrote the Economic Opportunity Act of 1964. He describes how, at his first meeting with Sargent Shriver, he told him that "the billion dollars the White House planned to invest in the project was 'nickels and dimes.'" Reviewing the Harrington book, which was subtitled *A Radical Program for a New Majority,* Professor Daniel Bell wrote this penetrating comment:

I think that Harrington does not know how to spend a billion dollars, and that all his hortatory earnestness is of little help in doing so. For example, despite the subtitle, there is *no* program in this book. The gap between the intellectual and the technocrat, indeed, is that the former has little notion of how to turn *ideas* into a *program*. (Italics in original.)³⁶

Most of the oratorical radicals in America who went through the Stalinist decades and who still claim to be Marxists have done little postgraduate work in doctrine and dogma, not even to update themselves. Among such self-defined "neo-revolutionaries" (to remain a member in good standing of the Radical Anti-Establishment Neo-Marxist Union, the prefix "neo" hyphenated is *de rigueur*) as Marcuse, Jürgen Habermas and Erich Fromm, it is agreed that "exploitation and overt class-struggle are no longer the driving force of social change in developed capitalist societies."³⁷ Philip Rahv (editor of *Modern Occasions*, a breakaway from *Partisan Review*) is an example of a neo-Marxist who, as Talleyrand is reported to have said of the courtiers around Louis XVIII, has "learned nothing and forgotten nothing." In an editorial critical of the New Left, Rahv said that it "still lacks a relevant theory of revolutionary change and a strategy of action." Lenin's requirements for a genuine revolution were cited: a split and paralyzed ruling elite; an alienated people; a revolutionary party able to exploit the first two conditions. None of these three conditions exists, said Rahv, and then he added:

> However, only political philistines will conclude that this lack offers definite proof that the conditions of revolution will *never* come into existence. (Italics in original.)³⁸

What a brilliant *aperçu*, and what touching loyalty to the old barricades! If plain political history constitutes "philistinism," he will make the most of it. There has not been a revolutionary situation in America for more than half a century. Admittedly, there is precious little likelihood of one developing in the foreseeable future—but don't you dare, you philistine, suggest that it could *never* happen. Why? Because the neo-Marxist Professor Rahv finds that "in a purely objective sense, the American system of neo-capitalism ["neo" here means not that capitalism has become any better—by Rahvian definition, it cannot—but that it has become worse *and smarter*] has long been ripe for fundamental structural change." What does this jargon mean? What is "fundamental structural change"—communism, socialism, fascism, vegetarianism, praetorianism? Is it a clear idea or just a ringing phrase? It is not that Professor Rahv doesn't know how to be precise when he wants to indulge in a bit of sharp, polemical criticism. He has been, at times, one of the best literary critics in the United States, but when it comes to "a relevant theory of revolutionary change and a strategy of action" which the New Left is supposed to be lacking, what does he himself have to offer? Nothing, except that to explode bombs is as bad as it is to eat people, and to give the inevitable quotation from Trotsky.

Ideology in the literary avant-garde gets curiouser and curiouser. In the same issue of *Modern Occasions,* Saul Bellow quoted the editor of *Partisan Review,* William Phillips, as saying—the coincidences mount—that the New Left has no theory, no program.

> I am convinced that only an antitheoretical, antihistorical, non-Marxist, unstructured movement like that of the youth today could have created a new left force in the West.

This sentence, as Bellow dryly said, "in its idiocy, is really rather touching. . . . When in doubt he still quotes Trotsky."[39] Bellow's entire critique of Phillips could easily serve as a refutation of Rahv. In their passion to be eternally young and radical, both men try to demonstrate in themselves that there is no generation gap, that they are forever young in heart. Alas, it calls for an intellectual regression to the kind of historico-philosophic speculation that has nothing to do with what has happened in the last fifty years. My objection to Rahv's epithet of "political philistines" against those who believe that the conditions of revolution will "never" come into existence, is not so much to the "never" as to his failure to suggest what other conditions for revolution, besides Lenin's, might arise in his political world. Are Lenin's three conditions the only possible combination? Must they appear all at the same time and in the same immeasurable measure?

The problem with Rahv—and this certainly is not confined to him alone—is that his paradigm for revolution is what has been described as "the Great Stereotype of 1917 and [an] obstinate failure to recognize that the October Revolution was the product not of any ineluctable historical necessity but of the ability of a dedicated band of men, led by a great revolutionary strategist and tactician, to seize a unique opportunity."[40] This is not to suggest that Rahv is pro-Soviet; he is not. Nor that he is propounding some subtle line for a proletarian revolution; he is not. He, like so many others, will not let go the dream of the "great stereotype." He insists on a conformity to a unique historical event, which combined accident, contingency and one man's genius, by calling it the future. Like some blind and backward-looking Lincoln Steffens, he cries out: I have seen the past and it works.

Rahv is still pursuing the true Left position as did the Surrealists in those forgotten years between 1920 and 1936 when they sought to combine "its intellectual, artistic, and moral preoccupations with the aims and methods of international communism."[41] André Breton was quoted at the time as saying, "We are possessed by a will to total subversion." As one historian has described them:

> [The Surrealists] extolled all forms of anti-social behavior—crime, drug-addiction, suicide, insanity—as so many expressions of human freedom and revolt. They preferred the criminal to the political militant since crime seemed to be a self-sufficient act implying no fresh determinations. As an indispensable preliminary to the reconquest of liberty,

they called for a crime on an international scale: a second "Terror" or a new wave of barbarian invasions from the East.

The Surrealists of this period were contemptuous of communism. Louis Aragon in 1924 said of the Russian Revolution that "measured by the yardstick of ideas, it is nothing more than a trivial ministerial crisis." There was even a "Vietnam" experience for the Surrealists, the outbreak of hostilities between the French Army under Pétain and the Riffs in Morocco.

> It was "le grand choc" which suddenly clarified a highly ambiguous intellectual position. Their admiration for Eastern and particularly for primitive peoples, their hatred of militarism and of the "professional patriots," the academic intellectuals who celebrated France's civilizing role abroad—all directed their sympathies towards Abd-el-Krim. Nineteen of the group put their signatures to Henri Barbusse's protest: *"Appel aux Travailleurs Intellectuels. Oui ou non condamnez-vous la guerre?"*

There was long hair, and an identification with the working class:

> Breton appeared one morning at the Café Cyrano with a workman's cap over his long curls to demonstrate his solidarity with the proletariat. André Masson recalling the atmosphere of the group's meetings, admits: "When I was present at these things I kept saying to myself: 'But I'm dreaming. I must be dreaming.' "[42]

And this was all before the dawning of hallucinogenic drugs. They even dallied with a slogan on behalf of the Riffs—"revolutionary defeatism."

American radicals like Rahv and Phillips were, like so many others, fooled once. Then they learned, ever so reluctantly, not to be taken in again by doctrinaires posing as revolutionary mystics. Yet now, like some of their younger contemporaries, they are determined to stay "with it," no matter how foolish, to understate it, they may appear. But at least they have learned about the price one pays for the revolution and its broken dreams. There are others who haven't learned, who somehow cannot learn. It is to them I want to turn now.

II

> Every kind of socialism is Utopian, most of all scientific socialism. Utopia replaces God by the future. Then it proceeds to identify the future with ethics; the only values are those which serve this particular future. For that reason Utopias have always been coercive and authoritarian. . . . One of [Marx's] phrases . . . forever withholds from his triumphant disciples the greatness and the humanity which once were his: "An end that requires unjust means is not a just end."
>
> Albert Camus, *The Rebel*, 1956.

Some years ago, Professor Arthur P. Mendel took a look at the rise and fall of "scientific socialism" which he defined as the "illusory fusion of science and ethics." One reason for its fall was modern science which "provides a dramatic example of the separation of politics from scholarship, of validation by objective proof instead of scholastic quotations and [exegesis] of sacred texts," and the direction of which "undermines the very foundations of scientific socialism by promoting uncertainty, indeterminacy, relativism and subjectivism."[48] Yet scientific socialism did serve a function:

> The great service of scientific socialism was to explain the necessity of present sacrifice and to assuage the conscience of those forced, usually by conditions in underdeveloped economies, to sacrifice the very

stratum of society that they supposedly served, the deprived masses.⁴⁴

The rise of scientific socialism was due to the prevalence in the late nineteenth century of "vulgar positivism, a theory of knowledge that favored the easy formulation and uncritical acceptance of allegedly scientific laws of history by assuming an essential affinity between the study of human society and the study of nature."

Second, and more important, was the failure of earlier radical movements in Western Europe in the 1840s and in Russia during the "populist" 1870s, and the consequently powerful attraction for defeated rebels of doctrines preaching inevitable success. Professor Mendel says:

> The effect of that failure is seen in the progression of Marx's own career, from the voluntaristic idealism of his philosophical notebooks, through the mid-century debacle to the long, arduous research in the British Museum in order to construct a myth that would make History do for the rebels what they had failed to do for themselves.⁴⁵

Third, the fact of economic backwardness helped strengthen the idea of scientific socialism since its principal function is to support rapid industrialization. And if rapid industrialization is the ideal—and this was a passionately held idea among men like G. V. Plekhanov (" 'we indeed know our way and are seated in that historical train that speeds us to our goal' "), and Nicholas Berdiaev (" 'everything that fosters the productive forces is progressive; everything that impedes them is reactionary' "), and P. B. Struve, Sergei Bulgakov and other early Russian Marxists⁴⁶—then the high costs of industrialization and urbanization were not only insignificant sacrifices but also indispensable prerequisites. In time, of course, these early Russian Marxists repudiated their Marxism. They turned towards "neo-Kantian idealism" which they believed gave precedence to "the existing human generation over the claims of scientific history." Bulgakov insisted, " 'Progress

is not a law of historical development, but a moral task.' "
Berdiaev admonished:

> The paths to the future are many and diverse, and there cannot be here any exact sociological prediction, since there are no historical laws according to which the ideal of a better future will be realized by some futuristic necessity.[47]

What Russia's early Marxists realized when they turned away from Marxism was that there was an unbridgeable chasm between Utopianism and politics. Professor Talmon has brilliantly expressed the difference between the two concepts:

> Politics is concerned with very intractable material —and by that I mean men. ...
> Utopianism on the other hand, signifies that one assumes as possible (or expects as inevitable) an ultimate condition of absolute harmony, in which individual self-expression and social cohesion, though seemingly incompatible, will be combined. In other words, Politics is concerned with the careful manipulation of concrete data of experience, by reference to the logic and to the limitations inherent in any given historical situation; whereas Utopianism postulates a definite goal or preordained finale to history. ... [W]hile starting out with the wish to secure to man the means of full self-expression, Utopianism ends with a determination to impose a wholly impersonal pattern. *It tends in other words to replace history by sociology.* (Italics added.)[48]

When progressive intellectuals engage in transcendental chatter without ever specifying who, in their wonderlands, will collect the garbage and clean out the overflowing septic tank, they exemplify what William James called "faith-tendencies [which] are extremely active psychological forces, constantly outstripping evidence." James even set up a model of what he called the "faith-ladder":

1. There is nothing absurd in a certain view of the world being true, nothing self-contradictory;
2. It *might* have been true under certain conditions;
3. It *may* be true, even now;
4. It is *fit* to be true;
5. It *ought* to be true;
6. It *must* be true;
7. It *shall* be true; at any rate for *me*.
   (Italics in original.)[49]

The faith-ladder was never more in evidence than today among our revolutionary intellectuals, hanging on all seven rungs. Never mind that the evidence of the proletarian revolutions of our time shows the fearful price exacted for the perpetuation in power of elites, who in their ruthlessness make the military-industrial complex in America seem like an association of scoutmasters. They are cousins in temperament to Luther, who said, "The road to heaven lies through hell," as he encouraged the bloody repression of the Peasants' Revolt in 1525. They are the blood brothers of Marat, who said, "who cannot see that I want to cut off a few heads to save a great number?" Never mind that a half century after the Bolshevik Revolution there were still bread lines in the Soviet Union—by public admission of one of the highest Soviet officials.[50] Never mind that probably ten million or more people have fled East Germany, Hungary, Bulgaria, Czechoslovakia, Poland, the Soviet Union, China, North Vietnam, North Korea, and Tibet where anti-people revolutions have occurred. Never mind that "the contrast between rich and poor . . . in respect to income is greater in the East [European communist states] than in most other countries, greater even than in the United States."[51] Never mind that "what is striking in Russia today is that the country is still backward not only in comparison with the West but also with most of the satellite countries."[52] Never mind. None of this matters to those who still look upon Russia or, perhaps, Mao's China as models of the modernizing revolution.

These persons on the progressive socialist left to whom

I am referring are not, remotely, communists, or fellow travelers, or Soviet dupes. They represent the new class of the contemporary intelligentsia—the revolutionists. A revolutionist is someone whose revolutionism is not so powerful as to impel him to leave his native country, which he publicly castigates, to live in another where a "successful" (by his own definition) revolution has already occurred. His mind is provincial, his character and heart irresponsible. He preaches his own garrison statism, trying to modernize Bentham's moral calculus of the "pleasure-pain" principle of utility by an infusion of revolutionism and incantatory Marxist chiliasm. And when you are a revolutionist, you can say anything and all things will be forgiven you. Here is Paul Goodman, only a few years ago, not with Cold War rancor but with the understanding charity reserved for a Great Social Experiment, explaining Stalin's starvation of untold millions in the 1930s, not as deliberate, but rather as caused by "a centralized agricultural program which happened to be *inept* and so forth." (Italics added.)[53] "Inept"—that's all there is to say about Stalin's "final solution" for millions of Russian farmers! "Inept" is a one-way adjective which may excuse a governmental failure if committed in the name of the New Jerusalem, the Golden Age of the New Socialist Man—but you can never use the phrase "inept and so forth" when you sit in judgment on, say, the Great Depression or racial discrimination in the United States. Goodman, I think, might have agreed with the Bakunin who said:

> I do not believe in constitutions or in laws. The best constitution would leave me dissatisfied. We need something different. Storm and vitality and a new lawless and consequently free world.[54]

Since the Russian Revolution, there have been an endless number of apologists for Lenin, Stalin, Khrushchev, Mao who have said and written things that are simply appalling in their anti-humanist implications. Here are the ineffable Beatrice and Sidney Webb writing in 1923, "Much is subsequently forgiven to a revolution which succeeds; or which, to the active spirits of the rising generation, appears to satisfy the national needs."[55]

Or here is the *New Statesman* in 1936 writing about the Soviet purges:

> The truth about the plot for which Zinoviev, Kamenev and the others were executed, we do not know . . . very likely there was a plot [but] let us see this matter in perspective. . . . A social revolution is accompanied both by violence and by idealism. Its success must be judged primarily by the permanent achievement of its economic aims . . . there may be regrettable aspects . . . the power of the GPU and the increasing control of the Soviet bureaucracy are, historically speaking, of secondary importance. (Ellipses in quote.)[56]

"Historically speaking, of secondary importance"—what prescience about Russian politics in the next thirty-five years! In less than two decades, in 1956, Khrushchev arose and delivered his "secret" speech on Stalin. So, historically speaking, it turned out that the power and control of the state were of rather primary importance. Too late, though, because all that could be done for the victims of Stalin's purges was to grant to a selected few a posthumous rehabilitation.

It needs to be recalled that the influence of left intellectualdom was never so apparent in America as during World War II (that is, after the nazi invasion of the USSR). It was an influence not confined to intellectual circles alone. It penetrated *Life,* the jewel of the Luce empire. A special issue, 29 March 1943, was irreproachably dedicated to " 'Soviet-American cooperation.' " The *Life* editorial conceded that Russians " 'live under a system of tight, state-controlled information.' " And then came this chilling passage:

> But probably the attitude to take toward this is not to get too excited about it. When we take into ac-

count what the U.S.S.R. has accomplished in 20 years of its existence we can make allowances for certain shortcomings, however deplorable. . . . If the Soviet leaders tell us that the control of information was necessary to get this job done, we can afford to take their word for it. (Ellipsis in quote.)

And *Life* even described the NKVD, the initials at the time for the dread secret police, as " 'a national police similar to the FBI' " whose job is " 'tracking down traitors.' "[57]

G. D. H. Cole, the Fabian Socialist and radical humanist, wrote in 1942 that it was " 'much better [to] be ruled by Stalin than by a pack of half-witted and half-hearted Social-democrats.' "[58] Some years earlier, he had written:

> Much of the suppression of liberty in the Soviet Union of which we are told so much in the capitalist press . . . goes along with a tremendous enlargement of liberty in new democratic non-capitalist forms. Great suppression of personal liberties was unavoidable if the new order were to survive at all. Already, I believe, the Soviet Union is feeling its way towards the restoration of many of those liberties which had to be curtailed [this was at the height of the purges] and as soon as the Soviet leaders were [sic] able to feel even a reasonable degree of security against external intervention we shall find that they are not merely putting back the liberties they have restricted but establishing a new and higher kind of liberty, hitherto unknown in the world—a liberty extending to every section of the people, and women equally with men. (Ellipses in quote.) [59]

Merleau-Ponty, whom I quoted earlier, in January 1950 admitted the existence of forced labor in the USSR but added:

> If the communists accept the camps and the oppression, it is because they await the classless society. . . . Never did a Nazi embarrass himself with ideas such as the acknowledgment of man by man, internationalism, classless society. It is true that these ideas are not faithfully carried by today's communism . . . but they are still part of it. . . . We have the same values as a communist. . . . The USSR is *grosso modo* on the side of the forces which fight against the forms of oppression we know. (Ellipses added.) [60]

Grosso modo; in the large; not in the "minute particulars."

Nonsense of this sort was quite pervasive in the United States. Henry A. Wallace, a man who could easily—by one heartbeat—have become president of the United States, parroted this drivel:

> Some in the United States believe that we have overemphasized what might be called political or Bill-of-Rights democracy. . . . Its extreme form leads to exploitation. Russia, perceiving some of the abuses of excessive political democracy, has placed strong emphasis on economic democracy. . . . Carried to an extreme, all power is centered on one man. (Ellipses in quote.) [61]

As Dwight Macdonald wrote at the time, "Only Wallace could compress so much falsification, confusion and evasion into so short a space. . . . the Russian economic system is a slave system precisely because there is no political democracy (and who but Wallace would split democracy in half and expect the two halves to live?)" [62]

My point in recalling these inanities of the last few decades about revolution and communism is not to open up old arguments but to observe that the same kind of compressed confusion is being purveyed today in the name of revolution and socialism by people in the professions, in the social sciences, and by the radical chic aristocrats.

Of course, it is not communism nor is it, necessarily, pro-Soviet propaganda. But their approach to politics is a form of paleo-radicalism; call it, if you will (they do), neo-radicalism.[63]

III

> But am I so unreasonable as to see nothing at all that deserves commendation in the indefatigable labours of this [national] assembly? I do not deny that among an infinite number of acts of violence and folly, some good may have been done. They who destroy everything certainly will remove some grievance. They who make everything new, have a chance that they may establish something beneficial. To give them credit for what they have done in virtue of the authority they have usurped, or which can excuse them in the crimes by which that authority has been acquired, it must appear, that the same things could not have been accomplished without producing such a revolution.
>
> Edmund Burke,
> *Reflections on the Revolution in France,* 1790

Let us now examine a serious yet typical disquisition on revolution and counterrevolution by a prominent American publicist, Robert Heilbroner. As Ezra Pound, in his *Cantos,* found that the perfect society existed in eighteenth century China, so Heilbroner has found his dream society in China of the late twentieth century.

Heilbroner is concerned with the process of economic development among the new nations, and with the realities of the development process in contrast to the popular view of "the revolution of rising expectations." He has suggested four realities:

> The revolutionary aspect of development will not be limited to the realm of ideas, but will vent its fury on

institutions, social classes, and innocent men and women.

The ideas needed to guide the revolution will not only be affirmative and reasonable, but also destructive and fanatic.

Revolutionary efforts cannot be made, and certainly cannot be sustained, by voluntary effort alone, but require *an iron hand,* in the spheres both of economic direction and political control. (Italics added.)

The fourth and most difficult of these realities to face is the probability that the political force most likely to succeed in carrying through the gigantic historical transformation of development is some form of *extreme national collectivism or Communism.* (Italics added.)

The first two "realities" tell us nothing more serious than that the sun sets in the West. The following two "realities" tell us a great deal—to start the modernizing process in a successful direction, there must be a dictator (what else is "an iron hand"?) and communism. Whereas most societies "attempting to make the Great Ascent" are floundering, there are "a very few nations, all of them communist, [which] have succeeded in reaching into the lives and stirring the minds of precisely that body of the peasantry which constitutes the insuperable problem elsewhere." Heilbroner continues:

In our concentration on the politics, the betrayals, the successes and failures of the Russian, Chinese, and Cuban revolutions, we forget that their central motivation has been just such a war *à l'outrance* against the arch-enemy of backwardness—not alone the backwardness of outmoded social superstructures but even more critically that of private inertia and traditionalism.[64]

196 / ANTI-AMERICAN MYTHS

This passage I would say makes Heilbroner, by club rules, a leading member among *les terribles simplificateurs*. In the first place, Russia was *not* a backward industrial nation except in the naive minds of gullible victims of Soviet propaganda. As Harry Schwartz has described it:

> The Russian revolutions of 1917 came, not at the end of a long period of stagnation and decay, but rather after more than half a century of the most rapid and comprehensive economic progress. The average annual rate of growth of industrial output in Russia between 1885 and 1889, and again between 1907 and 1913, substantially exceeded the corresponding rates of growth during the same period in the United States, Great Britain, and Germany. Between 1890 and 1899, industrial production in Russia grew on the average over 8 per cent each year. . . .
>
> During the last half century of Czarist rule, the figures. . . . clearly indicate, Russia went a good way toward ending its former economic backwardness. *In this period was laid much of the foundation upon which the Soviet Union was later to build its own rapid economic expansion.* (Italics added.)[65]

Dr. Szamuely has pointed out that, in 1913, Russia "was already overtaking France as the world's fourth industrial power." Russia held second place in the world in oil production; third place in railway construction; third place in cotton manufacture; fourth place in machinery building.[66] And I might add, for Heilbroner's edification, that there were strikes, even general strikes, under tsarism, a phenomenon which has disappeared with the disappearance of free trade unions in the land of "the iron hand."[67]

Heilbroner confessed to being unsure whether "the vise of the past" has been loosened in China or Cuba, and added:

> It may well be that Cuba has suffered a considerable economic decline, in part due to absurd planning, in part to our refusal to buy her main crop.

This statement has an interesting built-in double standard. As Americans, we are expected to do a little for Cuba's sugar crop, but the Cubans are to do nothing at all about Castro's "absurd planning" except to cheer. Castro doesn't have to worry about any responsibility for "absurd planning." As I have previously suggested, in describing a progressive revolution, one always uses temperate adjectives. This shows objectivity in criticism—"absurd planning," or Paul Goodman's phrase, "millions died in Russia because of a centralized agricultural program which happened to be inept." But speak of poverty in America—and the adjectives must roar like thunder. Bourgeois democracy is always at fault because its economic disasters are "structural," but for a revolutionary regime evils are merely "absurd" or "inept"; their economic disasters are only unfortunate aberrations from the true road.

As for China, said Heilbroner, its economic record "is nearly as inscrutable as its political turmoil, and we may not know for many years whether the Chinese peasant is today better or worse off than before the revolution." But if after a score of years we still don't know whether the Kuomintang was better, or worse, than the Chinese communists, then why is it so horrendous to be a counter-revolutionary? For that pernicious possibility Heilbroner has an answer:

> Yet what strikes me as significant in both countries is something else. In Cuba it is the educational effort that . . . has constituted a major effort of the Castro regime. In China it is the unmistakable evidence . . . that the younger generation is no longer fettered by the traditional view of things. The very fact that the Red Guards now revile their elders, an unthinkable defiance of age-old Chinese custom, is testimony how deeply change has penetrated into the texture of Chinese life.

And now, to the climax of Heilbroner's hymn to the modernizing revolution:

It is this herculean effort to reach and rally the great anonymous mass of the population that is *the* great accomplishment of Communism—even though it is an accomplishment that is still only partially accomplished. (Italics in original.)

We are back to the *esprit de géométrie,* the ethical calculus, for we are measuring again. How do you measure the "partially accomplished"? By reference to increasing literacy? Taiwan's educational effort under Chiang Kai-shek has been far more sensational than Cuba's (although I am unsure I could measure that difference). Is "the great anonymous mass of the population" in communist countries ever to be consulted as to whether it wants to be reached and rallied? What does one mean by "reaching and rallying"? If there is to be consultation, how and by whom? And if a one-party regime is imposed in order to reach and rally this anonymous category of unpersons, is the regime to last forever, even if it turns out that the anonymous ones do not really want to be reached and rallied? For Heilbroner, the backward areas of the world won't change until "some shock treatment like that of Communism has been administered to them." He concedes that the present all-out effort by communist shock therapists may have fallen short of its goal, but how much better it is than "the timidity of the effort to bring modernization to the peoples of the non-Communist worlds." (A few sentences further it turns out that this is not "timidity" at all, but rather evil American approval for the suppression of modernizing movements as being "communist.") Isn't it conceivable that even the illiterate masses and their timid or American-dominated leaders have heard of the failures of planned economies and the admitted excesses of the Great Modernizers like those of Stalin, and are unwilling to commit their present existence to dictatorships in the name of tomorrow? Might it be that they would rather not be reached and rallied, thank you?

But the masses do not matter to Heilbroner and to fellow victims of the revolutionist delusion. They affirm that man should not be an individual but rather should live exclusively in society, and be exclusively a part of the whole; "a functional process within the life of the whole, devoid of any meaning except in terms of the whole." Thus, writes Professor Drucker:

> As Kierkegaard foresaw a hundred years ago, an optimism that proclaims human existence as existence in society leads straight to despair. And this despair can lead only to totalitarianism. For totalitarianism— and that is the trait that distinguishes it so sharply from the tyrannies of the past—is based on the affirmation of the meaninglessness of life and of the nonexistence of the person. Hence the emphasis in the totalitarian creed is not on how to live, but on how to die; to make death bearable, individual life had to be made worthless and meaningless, the optimistic creed, that started out by making life in this world mean everything, led straight to the Nazi glorification of self-immolation as the only act in which man can meaningfully exist. Despair becomes the essence of life itself.[68]

Heilbroner confirms this Kierkegaardist view when he concedes that the cost of a communist revolution from above "has been and will be horrendous"—that communism "is certainly not a benign agent of change"—that Stalin "may well have exceeded Hitler as a mass executioner"—that "free inquiry in China has been supplanted by dogma and catechism"—that "even in Russia nothing like freedom of criticism or of personal expression is allowed"—and, last, but not least, that "the economic cost of industrialization in both countries has been at least as severe as that imposed by primitive capitalism." But, like a good ideologue, what Heilbroner gives with his right hand, he takes back with his left:

> Yet one must count the gains as well as the losses. Hundreds of millions who would have been confined to the narrow cells of changeless lives have been liberated from prisons they did not even know ex-

isted. . . . Above all, the prospect of a new future has been opened. It is this that lifts the current ordeal in China above the level of pure horror.

We are busy with the measuring rod again, counting the gains and losses. But who does the counting? How does one measure gains versus losses when *millions of human beings* are involved in a campaign subjecting them to being "reached and rallied"? And if what is happening in the Chinese ordeal is "pure horror," how does one know that this miracle of Maoist modernization is soaring "above the level of pure horror"? How high is up?

I go on because it is an extraordinary intellectual performance, characteristic in many ways of the temper of our time. Now we are back again at Heilbroner's right hand. He doesn't know how "one measures the moral price of historical victories or how one can ever decide that a diffuse gain is worth a sharp and particular loss," but then one must calculate "what is likely to happen in the absence of the revolution whose prospective excesses hold us back. . . . what is the likelihood of bringing modernization without the frenzied assault that communism seems most capable of mounting." Now comes the sleight of the left hand. This time he used as his ethical calculator, Barrington Moore, Jr., who, he said, "has made a nice calculation that bears on this problem." Taking as the weight in one pan the thirty-five to forty thousand persons who lost their lives because of the Terror during the French Revolution, Moore suggests that this total wasn't much greater than the probable death rate from preventable starvation and injustice under the *ancien régime*. So the scales balance.

In his high-minded dedication to these reassuring equations, Moore has claimed:

> One has to weigh the casualties of a reign of terror against those of allowing the prevailing situation to continue, which may include a high death rate due to disease, ignorance—or at the other end of the scale, failure to control the use of powerful technical

devices. (The 40,000 deaths a year in the United States due to automobile accidents come to mind here. What would we think of a political regime that executed 40,000 people a year?) [69]

Thus are accidents and executions put on the same moral plane! In other words, Moore sees no moral difference between the deliberate execution of forty thousand people willed by a tyrant or monopolistic party dictatorship, and the chance death of the same number caused by drunken or faulty driving. Professor Hook has dealt sharply with Moore's equalizations:

> Once we permit assumptions of this grim kind to stand, then the door is open to any fanatical savior or wilful political adventurer to try to introduce a reign of terror in order to eliminate the errors and accidents and evils that are bound up with ordinary human bungling. . . .
> There is a surprising moral callousness in some of the assessments of the costs of the Russian revolution which stems from a failure to realize that any social action that is willed carries with it a degree of responsibility that cannot be ascribed to actions that are not willed. The question is not of miscalculating the effects of a specific policy. The error consists in what is being taken as the basis of calculation. [70]

In this connection, one may also go on to ask: on what basis do we compare the history of Western modernization with communist modernization? Do we (or can we) really know what the actual costs are of a communist revolution —know, that is, in the same way that we know our own economic history; in the same way that Karl Marx was able to know the horrors of the dark, satanic mills by studying the accessible reports (the same reports that led to eventual reform) of the English factory inspectors filed in the British Museum? What little knowledge we do have about communist industrialization we gather either through refugees or from the communist leaders (and, sometimes, by the studies of Sovietologists). After all, it was the Soviet leadership itself which informed the world that for a quarter century the land had been ruled by a bloodthirsty tyrant, Stalin, and then, subsequently, for almost a decade by a "harebrained" schemer (Khrushchev) who, so they said, had turned Russia into a land of bread lines.

Let me give one example, reported by Tibor Szamuely, as to how ignorant we really are (except, perhaps, for foreign embassies) about life in the Soviet Union. From July 1941 to December 1947, "an all-embracing system of food-rationing existed in Russia." To lose one's ration card (Dr. Szamuely was living in the USSR during this time) meant starvation. Yet not once during those years was the word "rationing" ever mentioned in newspapers or on radio. "The existence of rationing," he wrote, "was acknowledged in public for the first time on the day it was abolished."[71] What do we really know about food shortages, slum housing, illegal strikes, riots, crime, arbitrary arrests, labor camps? None can deny that a tremendous economy operates in the Soviet Union, one which produces intricate space weaponry. But what access do we have to *their* Pentagon Papers, or their economic reports which can be subjected to analysis? What do we really know about Mao's China—other than that one day President Nixon was photographed in living color at Peking's Gate of Heavenly Peace? We know little more than what we are told is going on by Edgar Snow or Chester A. Ronning whose dithyrambs from China and elsewhere,[72] recall the wild enthusiasm of the Webbs when they discovered that Soviet communism was "a new civilization."

The argument for communist revolutions is that they are *the* modernizing force for backward countries. Could not such an argument serve just as well as the perfect endorsement of South Africa's apartheid regime? A whitecontrolled, racist South Africa has been modernizing with conspicuous success for the last quarter century. South Africa's population is about 7 per cent of all Africa, its land only 5 per cent of the entire continent; yet it generates more power, and produces twice as much steel, as the rest of Africa combined. It has the largest electrified rail network outside Europe, the Soviet Union and Japan; half of Africa's automobiles are in South Africa. Her domestic production has risen from $7 billion to over $13 billion from 1960 to 1968. Manufacturing accounts for 31.4 per cent of the total, while agriculture contributes 9.5 per cent and mining 11.3 per cent. South Africa's industrial revolution has meant that nearly half of her African population is now employed in cities. In most domestic requirements, this once backward country is self-sufficient. In fact, she is an industrial exporter competing with Japan and Western nations in the African market, and offering surplus capital to invest abroad. One could contend—and I add that I was in South Africa in 1965 and was barred from reentry thereafter because of my generally critical news reports and articles—that South African blacks enjoy the highest standard of living of any African people. As for literacy, that touchstone for honest-to-culture communist revolutionary achievements—for G. D. H. Cole, the Webbs, Chester Ronning and Robert Heilbroner—four out of five black South Africans between the ages of seven and twenty-one can read; in the rest of Africa, four out of five *cannot*. Each year in South Africa eighty-six thousand *new* industrial jobs open up.[78]

Is, then, "apartheidism" the modernizing force for the Great Ascent? In all this fetishism about industrialization, where does South Africa fit in? To be sure, the Zulus, the Xhosas, the Swazis, the coloreds, the Asians—the country's overwhelming majority—lack elementary human rights as do the peoples of the Soviet Union and China, particularly the cultural and religious minorities. But why should this matter so long as South Africa is emerging from Boer agricultural backwardness into the sunlight of modernization? Heilbroner's modernization calls for "an iron hand," which there surely is in South Africa. Would not opposing South Africa's "iron hand" slow modernization and thus injure the chances for a better world not only for the three million whites but also the fourteen million non-whites? How can one oppose South Africa's modernization by a minority over a majority without opposing similar economic modernization in African one-party states or in China herself? Are dictatorships in modernizing countires justifiable only when the people involved are of the dictator's own race or color? Is, then, Franco's dictatorship defensible, because it only affects Spaniards and he too is modernizing?

My South African analogy, by way of rhetorical questions, can be faulted. After all, there is a tremendous amount of foreign investment in South Africa, which is not the case in Africa above the Limpopo. The argument might well be made that it would be more correct to compare the internal situation of blacks with that of whites in South Africa. If the external comparison is invalid, certainly the internal examination is valid. Blacks in South Africa, I have reported, are unpersons.[74] The non-whites are the underclass; and if one ignores their lack of civil representation and autonomy, their situation is no better or worse than the underclasses of countries within the Soviet bloc or for that matter within the Soviet Union itself. Milovan Djilas has made this point about the domination of what he calls the "new class of owners and exploiters." Djilas has written:

> The use, enjoyment and distribution of property is the privilege of the party and the party's top men....
> ... Liberalization and decentralization are in force only for Communists....
> To divest Communists of their ownership rights would be to abolish them as a class.[75]

If despite South Africa's modernization, men of good will and democratic passion are fighting South Africa's unconscionable racism, why is violation of human rights by communism's "new class" morally bearable? If this is yet another rhetorical question, I may be permitted to give my own rhetorical answer.

No price is too high for economic modernization by communist countries. It is the logic of history. "Barracks" socialism is more certain to do the job than a free form of social democracy. Extinction of human values is tolerable in a revolutionary society since one can be sure that things are always improving in what is fundamentally a People's Park of Culture and Rest. That Hungarians, East Germans, Poles, Yugoslavs, Tibetans, Cubans, Chinese abominate "war" socialism—and that they must either be walled in or terrorized into enduring it—merely attests to the genuineness of the socialism for which there are two fundamental criteria: *(1)* a permanent economic crisis which is always being solved by The Plan—increasing imports from capitalist countries is the usual solution—and which is always being sabotaged by "unreliable elements"; and, *(2)* a permanent state of war between the dictatorship and the people.

Heilbroner with his "shrewd hair-splitting or prudent reservations" (to use Albert Camus' phrase in another context) makes it clear that while for him communism "may indeed represent a retrogressive movement in the West, where it should continue to be resisted with full energies, [it] may nonetheless represent a progressive movement in the backward areas, where its advent may be the only chance these areas have of escaping misery." In other words, he is willing to impose on these peoples dictators who act like fascists in the name of a communist revolution. Following the overthrow of Kwame Nkrumah, onetime darling of the "iron hand" economic modernizers, Benjamin A. Bentum, former secretary of the Ghana Trades Union Congress, said:

> Those liberal intellectuals in America and Great Britain who consumed tons of newsprint defending Nkrumah as essential to the economic development of Ghana should look upon what Nkrumah left us— the 7 million people of Ghana. Let those in the West who defended Nkrumah and acted as his apologists, paid and unpaid, today explain the total failure of Ghana's economy.[76]

And a Ghanaian journalist, Edward Agyeman, writing in the *Daily Graphic* (Accra) denounced "white liberals [who] since the Ghana coup have created doubts as to the real intentions of those self-appointed proponents of African freedom."

Although they knew in their hearts that freedom
... was non-existent in Ghana, they never raised
a finger because it was Ghanaian suppressing Ghanaian so that was perfectly right. . . . The double-standard nature of whatever school of thought they
stand for has definitely unfurled their hidden belief
that democracy and real freedom are the exclusive
rights of the white man and that African society is
such that only dictatorship is suitable.[77]

In several places in his article, Heilbroner quotes approvingly from Professor C. E. Black's excellent book, *Dynamics of Modernization*. I wish he had quoted this passage:

Never before has human life been disposed of so
lightly as the price for immediate goals. Nationalism, a modernizing force in societies struggling for
unity and independence, easily becomes a force for
conservatism and oppression once nationhood is
achieved.[78]

Submitting reluctantly to the labyrinthine dictates of history, Heilbroner envisions an imperative uniform development for the new nations—a communist revolution. Underlying all this icy historical determinism, these schematic, formalist placebos, this *déformation professionelle* which devises deceptive parallels between past and present in order to prove the unprovable, is a disbelief that democracy can ever *really* become a way of life in these disadvantaged countries,[79] a disbelief that, indeed, democracy is much of a way of life even where it does exist. Why should American ideologues like Heilbroner feel that the great revolutionary passion is the only way? Professor Hirschman has drawn attention to the basic intellectual shortcoming:

The idea of revolution as a prerequisite to any
progress draws immense strength from the very limited human ability to visualize change and from the

fact that it makes only minimal demands on that ability.⁸⁰

But there is also the need for the myth, the Sorelian myth. It is another tragic temperamental trap, and has been defined as "a conviction based not necessarily on empirical fact but on faith, a confidence impervious to the remonstrations of critical reason. . . . It is the transformation of the elite doctrine into a melioristic creed that generates the elusive and seductive glow of the myth."⁸¹

IV

The emancipation of the working class is the work of the working class itself.

> Karl Marx and Friedrich Engels,
> *The Communist Manifesto,* 1848

Richard Hofstadter once remarked that our decades would be known to later historians as "the Age of Rubbish." The prevalence of the Sorelian myth among the left progressives substantiates the insight. The combination of cant and confusion that today passes for political thought is disseminated far and wide without let or hindrance. No Big Lie—perhaps we should call it the Metaphor of Apocalypse—is so big that it cannot somewhere find a publisher, eager to print the latest example of Spenglerian catastrophism. For example:

> The societies in which we now live are not fit to live in. The United States is an imperialist and racist nation. . . . The universities, which ought to serve the people, instead play an important role in sustaining the imperialist and racist social order. . . . In Central and Eastern Europe, even though a form of socialism has been achieved, alienation and bureaucracy are still part of man's everyday life. . . .

... A true community is composed of individuals who live and work in a common situation.[82]

Well and good, one can understand the Hyperbole, written in the spirit of "stop the world, I want to get off." But what does the last sentence actually mean? What is "a common situation"? Do the intellectuals go down "to the people," as in China, according to Chester Ronning?

Professor Megill, the author of this exercise in "new democratic theory," is described as a "politically active" assistant professor at the University of Florida who, earlier, studied in Budapest with a group of philosophers associated with the late Georg Lukács. Dr. Megill regards himself as a "new democrat" or a modern revolutionary—that is, he rejects what he calls the "dialectical materialists" which is his way of *not* saying Soviet communism, and he also rejects the liberal democrats. His speculations on revolution include:

(1) Groups which can become part of a revolutionary movement—blacks in America, intellectuals in Eastern Europe—must avoid the temptation of assimilation offered them by their respective governments. "If black power is transformed into black capitalism and black cultural nationalism, no economic change will take place," he writes.

(2) Integration of dissidents into society would not lead to development of social institutions "in which workers will control the means of production. Alienation and isolation will increase and take on new forms."

(3) In advanced industrial nations, the strategy of basing a revolutionary movement upon the unqualified opposition to the State won't work. Small, well-organized "vanguard" parties like Lenin's will not succeed in advanced industrialized countries.

(4) Liberal democracies and, to an extent, socialist systems, have learned that "it is more effective to promote revolutionaries on an individual basis within the system than to fight against them as an organized movement." Marcuse calls this "repressive tolerance." Pareto might call this "circulation of the elites."

(5) So long as members of the "revolutionary move-

ment" are not required to act "in a counterrevolutionary manner, the members of the movement can openly accept positions within society." This is called "the guerrilla strategy of participation in society while opposing the social order." (Thus a progressive professor can take a university job only if he plots revolution.) Megill never quite defines just what it is that the guerrilla does—arson, bank robberies, cop shootouts, signing petitions, Votes for Gene, Bobby, Teddy or Dump the Humph, or engages in "days of rage"? What we do get are phrases like these:

> The guerrilla in the advanced industrialized countries must be part of a movement. He must also seek to create an environment which permits him to live and work in society while taking part in the revolutionary movement. The guerrilla strategy is not a romantic dream but is a necessity dictated by the dual threats of integration and repression being used by those in authority....
> ... To build a movement today requires organizing revolutionary forces within existing institutions....
> The goal of the movement must be no less than a revolutionary transformation of society. Economic and social institutions must be brought under control of the workers.

(6) Megill merely raises the question of the kind of revolutionary movement and organization which can exist in an advanced industrialized country but offers no blueprint—"all of these questions are being seriously discussed in the movement."

(7) "In black America the language and organizational form of armed revolution are becoming increasingly relevant." As for white America—Professor Megill gets into a hopeless muddle with his simpleminded categories—"it would be naive for white America to speak of an armed revolution, when it is white America which is oppressing the blacks and is waging a war of aggression in many parts of the world."

(8) The split infinitive coda to this symphony of revolution: "A new era of history has begun, and a new movement to radically change the world is a reality."[83]

What we have here is a sort of Régis Debray manual for America, although written less romantically and less openly subversive of the existing order. "The workers must, step by step, take control of the means of production," said Debray. Debray, too, was against the dialectical materialists, except he called them "Trotskyist" and "Stalinist bureaucracies." Debray was also concerned about integration and assimilation of the revolutionary. He quoted Fidel Castro as saying, " 'The city is a cemetery of revolutionaries and resources.' " As Debray wrote: "The city-dweller lives as a consumer. As long as he has some cash in his pocket, it suffices for his daily needs. Of course it is not really enough, but with the affluence of the Yankees and the corruption that follows in their wake, more can be earned without too much difficulty." He quotes Fidel Castro once more: " 'Who will make the revolution in Latin America? Who? The people, the revolutionaries, with or without a party.' " Although a vanguard is needed to make a revolution, it need not be a Marxist-Leninist Party, said Fidel. In fact, Debray continued, *"the guerilla force is the party in embryo."* (Italics in original.)[84]

Barrington Moore, Jr., has made the point that there "has never been any such thing as a long-term revolutionary mass movement in an urban environment. . . . there has never been a long-term urban revolutionary movement that has succeeded."[85] Urban revolutionary movements are driven in a reformist direction, he says. And to Professor Moore the possibility of revolution is, alas, ruled out for the next two or three decades and for the 1972 Marcuse, the possibility is a century off.[86] What possibility of revolution does exist? For the self-styled revolutionaries, there remains only a sort of Lin Piao countryside-urban confrontation: the peoples of the Third World (in itself, of course, a superficial fiction) against the imperialists of the advanced industrialized countries. (How "Lin Piao-ism" will be fitted into a Nixon-Mao rapprochement should be interesting to see in view of Lin's reported disappearance.)

I have dealt with the Megill book because it reflects the mock seriousness of academic revolutionism, and its failure to come to grips with the embarrassing fact that, despite all the rhetoric, to parrot all the nineteenth century clichés about the "idiocy" of industrial life in America hardly seems credible to the masses in industrial life. It shares the Big Lie that America needs a revolution: that is a cardinal tenet, and remains an inextinguishable *idée reçue* in all the groves of academe. Among the revolutionists, it is taken for granted that the evils in America are systemic, no longer episodic. America is in a quagmire from which it cannot emerge; and if it were able, it should not be allowed to do so. By and large, things always seem to be improving in certain faraway countries; in America things are always going from bad to worse to indescribably worse, if that is possible. Even to believe that anything could conceivably get better in America—short of a violent revolution—is to demonstrate a benighted, counterrevolutionary chauvinism. All the countries of the world, particularly those which go by the name "revolutionary" or "people's republics" or "people's democracies," are privileged to have their faults and virtues judged by the standards of history. America is the one country in the world which is to be judged by the standards of sociology. This double standard of judgment, of course, makes it impossible ever to grant America the benefit of either doubt or credit for good intentions. To view a nation through history is to allow the nice possibility of a melioristic future. To judge a nation by sociology is to inhibit an agreeable comparison of its hopeful present with an inglorious past. In short, whatever America does, for whatever reason, America is *Amerika* and *Amerika* is wrong.

Unlike the other 143 countries in the world, only America is to be judged by the exacting and unattainable standards of a Utopia. If there is full, high-wage, plenty-of-overtime employment in America for a decade, then capitalism is merely buying off the workers so that they will not rebel. When unemployment comes, that is the *real* capitalism. If the gross national product rises and consumer income with it, it merely reflects the materialism of America civilization. If the gross national product falls slightly, it is the beginning of the end, thank God! If President Nixon loses two Supreme Court nominees and one Supersonic Transport vote, it does not mean much because the power elites didn't regard it as important enough to make a real thing about it, and anyway, has anything changed much? It was better to vote for Nixon than for Humphrey, because as president, Nixon will bring fascism to America sooner. (This strategy in Weimar Germany was, it will be recalled, expressed by the German Communist Party as *nach Hitler, kommen wir*—after Hitler, we will take over). Then when Nixon is elected and re-elected president, whatever he does is "no worse" than anything Humphrey or George McGovern might have done as president. General Motors "runs America"; but if the United Auto Workers shuts down General Motors for a few months, it proves that its workers are regrettably "trade union conscious," otherwise they'd be tearing the factories down brick by brick. What the United Auto Workers, with its brainwashed membership, is doing is "helping GM perpetuate its stranglehold on America." If black candidates are elected, with white support, it is only because "the whites are terrified of black power" or they insidiously prefer a black to handle the black ghetto. If black candidates are defeated, it proves the "honkyism" of the American voter. Angela Davis is acquitted by a jury—and it's due to the pressure of the international working class; naturally. Had she been convicted—fascism.[87]

Racism, tribalism, communalism, religious hate—all are the burden of India, Pakistan, Nigeria, Sudan, Japan, Ceylon, Australia, Britain, Yugoslavia, Algeria (with its Berbers), Spain (with its Catalans and Basques), Latin America (and its Indians), the Soviet Union and China (and their repressed minorities). The world crackles with hate, with racial and nationalistic and irredentist passions —but only America is racist.[88] (What distinguishes America from the rest of the world is that most Americans happen to be ashamed of their prejudices, while almost everybody else is busy explaining the rationale of racial and religious discrimination, and why it is impossible to end them overnight.) Ask a Singhalese sometime to explain his feelings about a Tamil, or a Sudanese Arab about a Sudanese black Christian, or a Japanese about the Eta people, or an Egyptian about a Copt, an Afrikaner about a Bantu, a Hausa about an Ibo, and listen to what they say! And I could list dozens more of such tragic complexes of community hate and human rivalry. But "only in America..."

There is a logic to this superiority of all countries, but particularly revolutionary countries, over America. It is pithily summarized in an essay about Sartre by François Bondy:

> Sartre holds the view that a state run on revolutionary principles must be judged on the basis of its "project" and its essential need to defend itself against a hostile world; that the logic of this state and its interests must always be borne in mind, whereas bourgeois states must be judged only by their errors, shortcomings, and crimes, all of which are in fact not accidental and curable but are the product of an original sin and can be removed only by a violent, purifying total revolution.[89]

In order that everything should be reduced to the same level, it is first of all necessary to procure a phantom, a monstrous abstraction, an all-embracing something which is nothing, a mirage—and that phantom is the public. . . .

A public is neither a nation, nor a generation, nor a community, nor a society, nor these particular men, for all these are only what they are through the concrete; no single person who belongs to the public makes a real commitment. . . .

A public is everything and nothing, the most dangerous of all powers and the most insignificant: one can speak to the whole nation in the name of the public, and still the public will be less than a single real man, however unimportant.

Soren Kierkegaard, *The Present Age,* 1846

But if intellectuals today have no right to accuse the people, there is a class of people whom they can and must judge—themselves. From the point of view of the community the only justification of the intellectual is that he persists, under the stress of circumstances, in being a free, conscious, reasoning individual when others lose themselves in the crowd. The duty that no intellectual can shirk without degrading himself is the duty to expose fictions and to refuse to call "useful lies," truths. To accomplish this duty, it is not necessary for him to think that he possesses the truth. The will to question can suffice.

Nicola Chiaromonte, "The Will to Question," *Encounter,* 1953

It is fancied that everything should be reduced to the same level. It is first of all necessary to procure a phantom, a monstrous abstraction, an embracing something which is nothing, a mirage—and that phenomenon: the public....

A public is neither a nation, nor a generation, nor a community, nor a society, nor these particular men, for all they are only what they are through the public; no single person — who belongs to the public makes a real commitment....

A public is everything and nothing, the most dangerous of all powers and the most insignificant: one can speak in the whole nation in the name of the public, and still the public will be less than a single real man, however numerous it....

Søren Kierkegaard, *The Present Age*, 1846

But if intellectuals truly have no right to accuse the people, there is at times of peoples whom they can and must judge themselves, from the point of view of the community: the only justification of the intellectual is that he considers, under the stress of circumstances, in being a free, clearsighted, reasoning individual when others lose themselves in the crowd. The duty of the intellectual can exist without depending on it the duty to expose fictions and to refuse to call "useful lies" truths. To accomplish this duty, it is not necessary for him to think that he possesses the truth. The will to question can suffice.

Nicola Chiaromonte, "The Will to Question," *Encounter*, 1958

Reply to James A. Wechsler

James A. Wechsler, Esq.,
Editor, Editorial Page,
New York Post.

Dear Jimmy:

A few days after the *New York Times Magazine,* 6 June 1971, published my brief first outline of the Big Lies about America, you wrote a critical column. I thought, at the time, of writing a letter to the *Post* but then decided to reply to your column in this book, which is a fuller treatment of the whole problem of mendacity in our ideologized life today.

Since you questioned my bona fides, I must begin by recalling something Dean Acheson said during the Joe McCarthy era when he was asked about some particularly upsetting smears by Senator McCarthy:

> I accept the humiliation of defending myself against imputations that I should not have been called upon to answer at all.

The gravamen of your polemic against me reduces itself to that old fellow traveler stratagem—how can one talk about slave labor in Russia when there are lynchings in the South, or how can we talk about an iron curtain over Eastern Europe when we have passport barriers of our own. As I well remember, you used to regard such tricks of evasion as contemptible.

Your argument amounts to the following main points. I recapitulate them:

(*1*) You do not deny the falsehoods about America which I listed in my article (and which are amplified in this book); you merely describe them as "falsehoods luridly circulated by some academicians and apostles of the New Left."

(*2*) By "debunking" these falsehoods, I have ended up, you say, "producing a distortion of [my] own, a sophisticated version of the Nixon 'what's-right-with-America' speech that carries the same flat flavor of Rotarian self-righteousness now permeating *Commentary* and some other journals. In a sense the half-truth seems to have become the retort proper to the large lie."

(*3*) You imply that because of alleged "obsession" with the New Left, even when it has become "a frustrated fragment," I have relaxed my "assault on injustice and inhumanity within the U.S."

(*4*) You imply that because I have voiced my concern about "Marcusian doomsayers" who preach that America is a fascist country, I am somehow "unresponsive to the concern voiced by serious men about the disdain for the Bill of Rights prevailing at the loftiest levels in Washington." (I do not see how one follows from the other. Can one not voice concern about Marcuse and his influence and also voice concern about the disdain for the Bill of Rights separately, or does one have to demonstrate continuously that one is worried about the Bill of Rights before criticizing Marcuse?)

(*5*) When Walter Cronkite sounds the alarm over the administration-backed campaign against independent journalism, you say, "His is not the voice of frenetic anti-Americanism." (Who ever said it was? Do I share the guilt of those extremists who wildly charged Cronkite with "anti-Americanism"?)

(*6*) "Such issues are not dissolved by dismissing our intolerances as 'episodic,'" you wrote. (I had contrasted "episodic" with "systemic," pointing out, namely, that discomforting, anti-freedom episodes in American life were not built into the democratic system.)

(*7*) I am "a prizefighter picking on pushovers," you say, for listing as a Big Lie the commonplace assertion by

New Left voices that "America is guilty of genocide." You concede that it is "intermittently necessary to expose" such deceitful utterances but the "great moral issue . . . involves our role in Vietnam." It is in that connection, you say, that the word "genocide" has been used—and "loosely." And then you add that nowhere in my "sermons to the moral illiterates" do I discuss the Vietnam war—"a remarkable evasion in a tract that purports to deal with the despoiling of the American image." You forget that six years ago, you recommended highly in the *New York Post* an article I had written after my second trip to Vietnam. You said it ought to be read by Secretary of State Rusk since I had told the unpalatable truth about "our continuing slide into military and political defeat" in Southeast Asia.[1] Reread that column of yours, and my article, and tell me if it was fair to talk about my "remarkable evasion."

(8) About the other Big Lies I discussed, all you can say is that I score "effective debating points." My whole argument was evidently only an "exercise in self-approval." And you add, "To expose the far-out 'Big Lies about America' does not resolve our responsibility to face the truth about America. . . . Cheerleading is not the answer to authentic America anxiety." (But none of us may have "the answer" to authentic anxieties. My "cheerleading" amounted only to reiterating modestly E. M. Forster's "two cheers for democracy." This strikes me as both truer and more helpful than retreating into three despairing sighs at the sight of any social problem.)

There is an element in the intellectual temper of our time which is especially dispiriting. It is the assumption on the part of many that only *they* care for the health of the body politic; that *they* constitute a kind of medicare monopoly; that everybody else is really part of the sickness. I am pleased that, for all your criticisms, you at least made this concession:

> No one could detect from Beichman's essay that he is a man who really cares about justice or discerns any sickness in the national spirit.

Surely it must have occurred to you to wonder how a person who cares about justice would suddenly go over to a position which is concerned only with certain excesses in the intellectual temper of contemporary America, and nothing else. Does it show a lack of concern with justice when I argue against the lies about America which circulate among our leading authors and academics and some politicians? What I was writing about in the *New York Times* and in this book is why the apocalyptic pronouncements—and not only by "Marcusian doomsayers . . . moral illiterates . . . and bearers of double-think," to use your phrases—have become part of the conventional wisdom of a large part of our intellectual community and of an important sector of public opinion, particularly young people. America has become an object of demonology among progressives and left intellectuals, a sort of stinking horror in the nostrils of world humanity. I put in a small demurrer. While America may not be Utopia, surely it is not Gehenna.

I know the ideological dangers of a fanaticized time when everybody wants simple labels. To write as I have is to risk the misunderstanding of my politics which you have exhibited. To say, as I have, that Big Lies are being disseminated about America is *not* to say that there is nothing wrong with America. On the contrary, if the Big Lies were debunked we might get down to the business of making America a better country, a more civilized place in which to live. What we are suffering from is what George Kennan had in mind when he said that "exaggeration of admittedly existing evils has regularly formed the initial basis for fanatical political movements, including the totalitarian ones." Is Kennan's statement an exercise in self-approval or of Rotarian self-righteousness?

My concern about the Big Lies should simply have signified that I have not lost my sense of hope, even my optimism, about this country, its institutions and its people. I persist in holding to a decent respect for the opinions of my countrymen, for their intentions and their achievements. They do not constitute for me some "mirage" of the public, or the people, some "monstrous abstraction" in the name of which love or hate can be exuded. I mention this because Professor Marcuse had to deal with this problem recently on a radio broadcast, and his personal embarrassment is revealing:

> When . . . Professor Marcuse, who had insisted that he loved and understood America, was pressed to specify which aspects of American life he found attractive, he fumbled for an answer, said he loved the hippies, with their long hair, and after some more fumbling, mentioned the beautiful American scenery, threatened by pollution. Despite an obvious effort, he could think of no other items. It was a quintessentially Dostoevskian spectacle of a man brilliantly at home in the world of abstractions, generalizations and political theories, but hopelessly blind to the actual details of human existence.[2]

What your column did not deal with I take the liberty now of posing to you in a series of questions:

Do you think America is hopeless?
Is America going to get worse?
Must it keep getting worse?
Do you think everything we are doing in this country is wrong?
Do you think America is irremediably going downhill?
Do you think America needs a bloody revolution?
Do you think the American worker is a reactionary, a "honky"?
Do you think that Bomber Left violence is to be "understood" and indulged?
Do you think Nixon and Agnew are fascists or that they are leading the country to a fascist dictatorship?
Do you think American democracy has failed, that it is doomed to fail, that it will fail?

You tell me that my Big Lies are only a cover-up to evade discussing "the tragic absence of moral leadership or direction." But any genuine exchange between us depends on whether your answers to each foregoing question is Yes or No. Some leading intellectuals and academics in America believe that the only valid or relevant answer to these questions is Yes. This total ideological response is, as I believe I have amply demonstrated, less an intellectual conclusion based on rational, clear, and compelling analysis, than the trap of a temperament which revels in despair, alienation, and the prospect of a great crash.

A temperamental trap, too, is the notion that it is enough —indeed it is the truest badge of the noble heart—for a liberal to be constantly intoning that he wants evil to disappear and wishes so much for things to "get better." Who does not? Except in the hopeless case of a handful of ideological misfits, the problem for democrats—and this necessarily means for reformers—is always to clarify important differences in political method and social values. What is it that we truly want? How can we best unite— or agree to cooperate—to obtain certain benefits or rewards, to induce in our organized social relationship certain readjustments and reorientations? To state that our society has earnest problems that have to be confronted is to state nothing: it is the old cant of a useless liberal and radical ritual. Our true task as committed intellectuals in a democracy begins when we move from rhetoric to re-evaluation—where have things gone wrong? What social forms have we outgrown? How can old institutions be adapted to new needs? When may we move swiftly, or prudently, or with due deliberate speed? Why is one path of reform or innovation to be preferred to another? What mix shall we create of authority and freedom? These are the eternal questions in the political conversation of mankind. I am not prescribing any set of correct answers, nor even the tone of voice in which the great debate should be conducted. But I have, over and over again, warned of a serious danger in our culture—namely, that form of political neurosis which feeds on total ideologies and all-or-nothing psychologies.

In his classic book on *Ideology and Utopia* Karl Mannheim once said:

> The distruct and suspicion which men everywhere evidence towards their adversaries, at all stages of historical development, may be regarded as the immediate precursor of the notion of ideology. But it is only when the distrust of man toward man . . . becomes explicit and is methodically recognized, that we may properly speak of an ideological taint in the utterances of others. We arrive at this level when we no longer make individuals personally responsible for the deceptions which we detect in their utterances, and when we no longer attribute the evil that they do to their malicious cunning.[3]

When I talk about the Big Lies, I am not constructing an ideological plot of my own. I am saying that these are calculated lies, sometimes cunning, sometimes malicious, not lies arising out of some structured ideology. A large number of those whom I quote in this book as purveyors of the Big Lies are not communists, fascists, nor even Marxists or Leninists. The whole point of the attack on America is that it is, in any grand or systematic sense, nonideological, in some cases rather anti-ideological. The purpose of my book is to argue that we are dealing with an unusual phenomenon: a mood of destruction rather than a rationale for revolution or reform.

Spin the globe and ask: What has turned out well—that is, in the real everyday interests of the people involved—since the end of World War II? Soviet Russia with the horrors of Stalinism, not to mention the earlier Bolshevik revolution? The Chinese revolution? Cuba, Algeria, Nkrumah's Ghana, Sukarno's Indonesia, Sekou Touré's Guinea, bleeding Nigeria, starving Bangladesh, a Czechoslovakia in thrall? Is this Rotarian self-congratulation to say that the only countries where there is a chance to get along and live in hope for a better day happen to be the Western democracies and Japan? What would transpire, do you think, if the Soviet Red Army removed its eighty thousand troops from Czechoslovakia and removed the threat of "fraternal socialist" intervention against Poland and Hungary? How long would Marxism-Leninism (*i.e.*, Stalinism-Khrushchevism-Brezhnevism) last in Eastern Europe without the overhanging menace of Soviet occupation troops?

Yet America today is held in disesteem because the popular ethos is not "socialist." These American voices who have made "socialism" into a bitch goddess of political success remind me of Tolstoy's doctor in *The Death of Ivan Ilyitch*. For the dying man, there was only one important question—would he live or die? To the doctor, however, this was an "inappropriate question . . . it was not the one under consideration; the real question was to decide between a floating kidney, chronic catarrh or appendicitis. It was not a question of Ivan Ilyitch's life or death, but one between a floating kidney or appendicitis."[4] Your attack on me reminded me of Ivan Ilyitch's doctor. It did not deal with the most serious crisis of values in the country—the desertion by a substantial minority of what we like to think of as highly motivated people from the standards of democracy. America's problem is not the Department of Justice, which may dislike the Bill of Rights. Only a few weeks after your column, the United States Supreme Court reaffirmed the doctrine of freedom of the press in the case of the *New York Times* and the Pentagon papers. Has the right to freedom of association been tampered with? Is freedom of religion endangered?

If you read the prose of the young lawyers' section of the American Bar Association, you will note an extraordinary amount of double-talk about how we-are-almost-but-not-quite-on-the-road-to-but-there-is-still-time in the area of civil liberties. Of course, there is "currently an anti-libertarian climate in the United States which properly can be labeled 'repressive.'" It is not complacency to say that there is *always* in America an anti-libertarian climate, as there is in Canada (see my chapter on fascism), in Britain, France, Italy. And each threat to civil liberties in America is always "more dangerous" than at any time in history including the time before, in this case, the McCarthy period. And the Committee on Protection of Civil Liberties and Civil Rights finally has to conclude that "while this situation is not yet at a crisis point, our civil liberties problems are serious enough for us to conclude that we are dangerously close."[5] But we are a far, far cry from what it was like in the closing days of the Weimar Republic, about which Golo Mann wrote:

> What an intellectual Babylon of voices, that Weimar Republic! . . . Philosophers demonstrating that there was no longer time for any philosophy, sociologists unmasking all creeds, values, and moral standards . . . legists affirming that the very notion of natural justice was a hoax and that any positive law, duly codified, was as good as another—far too many people assiduously sawing off the branch on which other people or they themselves were sitting. There was then, I should say, too much intellectual freedom in Germany; and all of a sudden there was none.[6]

Should we look on America as a repressive society because Abbie Hoffman's primer on "socially useful" crime had difficulty finding a publisher, a distributor, and advertising space? It then ended up being reviewed for a full page in the *New York Times Book Review* by Dotson Rader, whose manifestos to revolution and violence (which I quote in some of my chapters) are sold at any newsstand at any airport in America. Hoffman, who seems to be playing the role of the Fagin of the coming American Revolution, is author of a volume entitled *Steal This Book*. It tells you how to make stink bombs, obtain false identification papers, "how to sell your hungry body to several universities at the same time," and describes "the newest techniques in the art of shoplifting or 'inventory shrinkage' as it is referred to in the trade." Rader, whose *New York Times* review I am quoting, thunders:

> Everyone in publishing and distribution and in the press who has aided and abetted the restriction of Abbie Hoffman's freedom to be heard ought to be

deeply ashamed. . . . A kind of fearsome censorship by tacit understanding within allied industries has been established. And everyone's freedom has been lessened because of it.[7]

I wonder what your reaction would be, or that of the *New York Times*, had Hoffman proposed some scheme for stealing the *New York Post* or the *New York Times* off the newsstand or when it is dropped off in bundles. After all, is there so much difference between shoplifting merchandise and newspapers?[8] My concern is that the Abbie Hoffmans and other confidence tricksters of the "revolution," the "moral illiterates" from whom I have quoted chapter and verse, are doing precisely everything they can *to preclude peaceful change and reform*. It is always more exciting to an audience when some noble savage strips on the stage, tweaks somebody's beard and denounces aged radicals as reactionary Establishmentarians, and then outflanks them with some really revolutionary pronouncement. But it is all guerrilla theater. Nothing happens other than to distract and divert people from real issues. And even Mao Tse-tung, turning dramatically to President Nixon, has given the New Left something to brood about—like never trust anybody over seventy. The New Left can now sweat out its "Stalin-Hitler pact."

This love of "revolutionism" which I dealt with in chapter 9, I regard as far more serious than your concerns about Walter Cronkite. It is more serious because the people in this country, having been treated to a seigneurial contempt from their betters, are far more likely to accept a Nixon leadership in the future than a liberal leadership.[9] (This sentence, written in June 1971, appeared in the hardcover edition published in March 1972, well before the Democratic presidential convention and the landslide election of 1972.) The basic temperamental infatuation with "revolutionism" was cogently described by Edmund Burke as he observed Jacobin events across the Channel:

> Plots, massacres, assassinations, seem to some people a trivial price for obtaining a revolution. A cheap,

bloodless reformation, a guiltless liberty, appear flat and vapid to their taste. There must be a great change of scene; there must be a magnificent stage effect; there must be a grand spectacle to rouse the imagination, grown torpid with the lazy enjoyment of sixty years' security, and the still unanimating repose of public prosperity.[10]

To my mind, the real revolution (if we must play word games) in the world today is what goes on in America. It is this which affords me a measure of hope amidst all your gloom and foreboding. Even Jean-François Revel, the author of *Without Marx or Jesus,* no defensive tract of United States institutions, sees America as the vanguard of what he calls "the second world revolution." Interestingly enough, his argument is that America's revolutionary method is dissent—"a revolutionary judo without precedent"—plus free access to information.[11]

You see, despite what you say or think about my political and social views, I have not lost my faith that in a pluralistic, democratic society there are terminal dates before which one can do something to make things better. No society can live by daily terminal dates; or, rather, it can under a dictator, but in no other way. Whatever streak of utopianism once possessed me has been tempered by having worked for so long in the trade union movement in America and then having observed, at first hand, labor movements in Asia, Africa and Latin America. Among the painful things one learns—and few things are more painful than having to change one's mind—is that there is nothing wrong—nothing shameful, nothing guilty—in wanting higher wages, shorter hours, and the satisfaction of telling off the boss. I like the way Professor Talmon once expressed it:

> I would utter one word of warning to those who might react against Utopianism so strongly as to adopt a contemptuous, sneering attitude towards human beings, to say that they are such a rotten lot that they do not deserve anything to be done for them, and to

deny the possibility of constructive change and genuine progress.... We must try to do good—but with a full and mature knowledge of the limitations of Politics. Bertrand Russell once told us, in another context, that we had to proceed in the spirit of unyielding despair.[12]

I think America, despite the "Marcusian doomsayers," is a great moral force in the rest of the world, even taking Vietnam into account. Alan Paton spoke along these lines at the 1971 Harvard University Commencement:

Your tribulations are known to the whole world. Some of us in the outside world derive satisfaction from them.... It is foolish of us to gloat when you appear to fail to solve them, for are we any better, any wiser than you? Therefore you must regard yourselves as the testing ground of the world, and of the human race. If you fail, it will not be America that fails, but all of us.[13]

The American realities I have been trying to understand have something to do with a pathological condition in which the only way you can ensure a mass audience is to spin out fantasies, proclaim Big Lies as the Truth, in which one can write the most disgusting descriptions about people in America (I have quoted some of these descriptions in the preceding chapters) as if they were a sort of slouching slobocracy. And I am sure the Big Liars regard your readers as comprising the phantom public which troubled Kierkegaard a century ago. Despite all evidence to the contrary, Don Quixote insisted that the barber's basin was the helmet of Mambrino. Don Quixote's was a private fantasy world; but people who seek America's dehumanization are turning their private fantasies into public exhibitions.

I am concerned with the quality of life in America, the tone of its culture, the content of the public dialogue. Perhaps, with the Vietnam disaster behind us, we can cherish Talleyrand's immortal line after the downfall of Napoleon:

"To be great once more, France must cease to be colossal." To write a defense of America is not to utter half-truths against Big Lies—although, it will be recalled, Arthur Koestler once wrote, "In this war [World War II] we are fighting against a total lie in the name of a half-truth." The half-truth was certainly safer and morally superior to Hitler's Big Lie. Amidst all the Big Lies—and there are many more than the nine which I have dealt with—it is time we began to tell at least one Big Truth about the United States: that it is a country in which one has the right to hope, and this general hope can with good reason even be shared by ethnic minorities. During the 1930s, a plethora of books about Great Britain, including one book (as *The Times Literary Supplement* pointed out) "by a future President of the United States [John F. Kennedy's *Why England Slept*] predicted the imminent defeat of Britain. . . . Such books were still on the shelves in 1940 when these same people stirred themselves in the greatest renaissance of national spirit that modern history records."[14]

All is not quite lost because somebody tried to apply pressure to the Columbia Broadcasting System and the national press to be nice to the Pentagon. You will recall that a decade ago, President Kennedy was accused of news management by many editors who were fearful of government suppression of news. I wrote at the time that the grave "news management" issue was a "phony."[15] The Nixon administration is doing what comes naturally to any national administration, pressuring and manipulating the media in the same way the Kennedy and Johnson administrations did before. After all, it should not be forgotten that in August 1962, FBI agents cross-examined correspondents about Pentagon stories; that earlier, in April 1962, FBI agents cross-examined reporters in the middle of the night about their stories on the steel industry during President Kennedy's fight against the steel price rise.

The question is not that government seeks at times to narrow the sector of the freedoms guaranteed by the Bill of Rights. That is to be expected, whether the president is a Lincoln, Kennedy or Nixon. The real question is whether, as a people, we have the will, the desire and the passion to resist all encroachments on a system—old, imperfect, changing, but precious—of democratic rights and liberties, hard won in the struggle of generations. I am persuaded that we have, and that this passion for freedom in our people is not diminished by presidents, vice-presidents, attorneys general or the Pentagon. For me the basic threat to the cause of freedom comes from those who, enjoying full civil rights and economic opportunity, argue that American democracy is a fraud.

Why you see this differently I cannot say.

ARNOLD BEICHMAN

Milton Village, Mass.
30 September 1971.

P.S. Tell me what you think of your fellow columnist who has written: "We are losing our freedoms. We are losing them more rapidly, more insidiously during these Nixon years than at any time since the first World War... we are experiencing a tyranny over the mind of man that is virtually without precedent in modern times." I am talking about Harriet Van Horne; a "Marcusian doomsayer," also? She has, in the columns of the *New York Post*, 15 November 1971, compared the U.S. with South Africa.

Epilogue

If my preoccupation with some of the main currents in the contemporary intellectual scene and the dispiriting level of our public political discourse has not been an attractive or a regaling one, it is because my theme has not been the "greening" but rather the lynching of America. Did ever a country since nazi Germany so deserve an unhappy end? Can anything but obloquy and oblivion be more fitting for genocidal fascists, violent materialists, insensitive philistines, dangerous paranoids, and hopeless counterrevolutionaries? But these, as I hope successfully to have argued, are (in the Shakespearean phrase) "lies, and lies, and lies." A school of falsification has grown up in the land, and with the help of ideological passion, its spokesmen—sincere, eloquent, deluded—have been gathering supporters as if to a movement or a political party. I have quoted much in these pages, but perhaps no passage is more important than this final one from Nietzsche, and it applies —alas!—as much to the ideologues of our day as to the fanatics of his own.

> The most common lie is that which one lies to oneself; lying to others is relatively an exception. Now this wishing-*not*-to-see what one does see, this wishing not to see *as* one sees, is almost the first condition for all those who are *party* in any sense: of necessity, the party man becomes a liar. . . .
> . . . The man of faith is not free to have any conscience at all for questions of "true" and "untrue": to have integrity on *this* point would at once destroy him. The pathological condition of his perspective

232 / ANTI-AMERICAN MYTHS

> turns the convinced into fanatics. . . . Yet the grand pose of these *sick* spirits, these epileptics of the concept, makes an impression . . . the fanatics are picturesque; man prefers to see gestures rather than to hear *reasons*. (Italics in original.)

Still, we hope to have heard the reasons why the party lie cannot ultimately persuade, why the grand pose of the epileptics of the concept will not impress for long, why the picturesque gesture of the fanatic must give way to conscience and integrity. For as Nietzsche himself went on to say, "at every step one has to wrestle for truth. . . . the service of truth is the hardest service."[1]

Notes

Introduction to the Original Edition

1. In 1959 the United States State Department signed a cultur agreement with the Soviet Union. "Both parties will encourage exchanges as may be agreed between them of delegations representing organizations devoted to friendship and cultural ties, labor, trade union, youth *and other non-governmental organizations in the Soviet Union* and the United States for the purpose of exchanging experience and knowledge of the cultural and social life of both countries." (Italics added.) "Agreement between the United States of America and the Union of Soviet Socialist Republics for Cooperation in Exchanges in the Scientific, Technical, Educational and Cultural Fields in 1960-61," TIAS 4362, section XII, part 3, in *United States Treaties and Other International Agreements,* compiled ... under the direction of the Secretary of State, vol. 10, part 2, 1959 (Washington, D.C.: Government Printing Office, 1960), p. 1946. Now it is obvious that when the United States government signed this agreement in November 1959, it was propagating a fiction. There are no "non-governmental organizations" in the Soviet Union, particularly trade unions. In a one-party state, there are no autonomous, voluntary organizations. (Lionel Trilling has written that "it is characteristic of a well-developed ideology that it can diminish or destroy the primitive potency of fact.") U Thant once said that while he believed in "human dignity . . . in fundamental freedoms like freedom of expression, freedom of thought, freedom of belief, freedom of conscience, freedom of association and the freedom to choose your own lawmakers [nevertheless] this conviction does not shut me off from the knowledge that *there are hundreds of millions of people who believe otherwise.* I am absolutely aware of this fact." (Italics added.) In a press conference, 17 September 1962, *UN Note,* no. 2662. To make such a statement after anti-

communist uprisings in Germany, Poland, Hungary, Tibet and resistance movements in Franco Spain is to ignore the need to prove "hundreds of millions of people believe otherwise." U Thant said what he did for many reasons, one of the most cogent being that he was at this time the Acting Secretary General of the United Nations and had not yet been confirmed by the United Nations General Assembly to a full term.

2. "It is a necessary condition of rationality that a man shall formulate his beliefs in such a way that it is clear what evidence would be evidence *against* them and that he shall lay himself open to criticism and refutation in the light of any possible objection. But to foreclose on tolerance is precisely to cut oneself off from criticism and refutation. It is gravely to endanger one's own rationality by not admitting one's own fallibility." (Italics in original.) Alasdair MacIntyre, *Marcuse* (London: Fontana/Collins, 1970), p. 91.

3. In communist countries, the problem of lie and truth was described by Miklos Gimes, a leading communist, executed for his part in the 1956 Hungarian Revolution: "Slowly we had come to believe, at least with the greater, the dominant part of our consciousness, that there are two kinds of truth, that the truth of the Party and the people can be different and can be more important than the objective truth and that truth and political expediency are in fact identical. This is a terrible thought, yet its significance must be faced squarely. If there is a truth of a higher order than objective truth, if the criterion of truth is political expediency, then even a lie can be 'true,' for even a lie can be momentarily expedient; even a trumped-up political trial can be 'true' in this sense for even such a trial can yield important political advantage. And so we arrive at the outlook . . . which poisoned our whole public life, penetrated the remotest corners of our thinking . . . paralyzed our critical faculties and finally rendered many of us incapable of simply sensing or apprehending truth." *Béke és Szabadság*, 3 October 1965, quoted in Michael Polanyi, "Beyond Nihilism," *Encounter*, March 1960, p. 42.

4. "Counter-culture, as currently used, refers to norms and patterns of behavior, emerging institutions (such as rock festivals and communes), and beliefs and artistic traditions that have coalesced to provide an opposing alternative to the cultural templates of the main culture. It is a term broadly applied to radical students, hippies, motor cycle gangs, the homosexual Gay Power movement, women's liberation groups, the Maoist Revolutionary Youth Movement factions, the Black Panthers, the Puerto Rican

Young Lords and lower-class White Patriots. . . . The core of the counter-culture is the sector which carries through most completely the transvaluation of values. . . . Many of the counter-culture's characteristics derive from needs and wishes to reject completely the arrangements of the main culture." Michael Lerner, "Anarchism and the Counter-Culture," in *Anarchism Today*, edited by D. E. Apter and James Joll (London: Macmillan, 1971), p. 37. Another definition declares that "the counter-culture consists of nothing but the principle of negation of which it has made a cult. It deeply distrusts any form, any norm, any kind of structured present. It seeks perpetual restlessness, dynamism without pause, destination, or fulfillment. . . . Thus no norm of human conduct, no ordering orientation, no moral obligation, no structure of society flows from the counter-culture . . . one should rather speak of an anticulture." Gerhart Niemeyer, "The 'New Left'" in E.A., Goerner, ed., *Democracy in Crisis: New Challenges to Constitutional Democracy in the Atlantic Area*. International Studies of the Committee on International Relations, University of Notre Dame. (Notre Dame, Ind.: University of Notre Dame, 1971), pp. 24 and 25.

5. The peace ballot in Britain in 1935 obtained majorities in favor of reducing armaments and also in favor of collective force against aggressor countries. Neville Thompson, *The Anti-Appeasers* (London: Oxford University Press, 1971). See also John F. Naylor's *Labour's International Policy: The Labour Party in the 1930s* (London: Weidenfeld and Nicolson, 1969) which describes how Labour's intellectual left, led by Stafford Cripps and Aneurin Bevan, opposed rearmament advocated by the trade union leaders, Ernest Bevin and Walter Citrine.

6. An underground newssheet called the *Chronicle of Current Events* has been coming out in Russia with bimonthly regularity since April 1968. Open letters, political essays, petitions, protests and even novels are typewritten in many copies, passed from hand to hand in this *samizdat* publication. Each person who receives a *samizdat* tract is responsible for typing and distributing additional copies. Charlotte Saikowski, "No Channel," *Christian Science Monitor*, 25 July 1970.

7. Theodore Roszak, *The Making of a Counter Culture: Reflections on the Technocratic Society and Its Youthful Opposition* (Garden City, N.Y.: Doubleday, 1969), p. 162. The "underground press" has been described as "generally written by the alienated for the alienated. . . . Taken in quantity, the papers' ritualized reports . . . are about as dull as the stock-market quota-

tions." Jesse Kornbluth, ed., introduction to *Notes from the New Underground: An Anthology* (New York: Viking, 1968), p. xiv.

8. The phrase is even used by the right-wing press; e.g., *National Review Bulletin*, 13 April 1971, p. 852, and the *National Review*, 8 October 1971, p. 1130.

9. "Blind," of course, is not the only adjective which seems to couple so harmoniously with "anti-communism." Jack Newfield is against "mechanistic anti-communism" and "irrational anti-communism." (How about anti-mechanistic anti-communism?) Professor John Kenneth Galbraith is against "knee-jerk anti-communism" and one asks how about "non-knee-jerk anti-communism"? And, naturally, there is always "obsessive anti-communism." The need by progressives to use these adjectives arises from a distaste for identifying communism with totalitarianism despite a half century of bolshevism and all the exposés (not least, Nikita Khrushchev's).

10. Robert L. Heilbroner, "Counterrevolutionary America," *Commentary* 43, no. 4 (1967): 33.

11. Alain Touraine, *The May Movement: Revolt and Reform*, translated by Leonard F. X. Mayhew (New York: Random House, 1971), p. 354. In an even more recent publication of the New Left, a writer on women's liberation says: "Contrary to everything insinuated from just about every propaganda source, including your programmed mother. . . ." Marge Piercy, "Women's Liberation: Nobody's Baby Now," *Defiance* 1 (1970): 154.

12. Eugen Loebl, formerly Czechoslovakian deputy minister for foreign trade and director of the State Bank, now an émigré, has described "planning" in this fashion, "In Czechoslovakia, the government had an absolute monopoly of economic and political power. The form of ownership was partly responsible for this. Being the one owner, the government ran the whole economy and couldn't do it otherwise than by directing enterprises to planned targets. So we found what central directive planning really means. We found that when all activities are concentrated in one planning body it is impossible to make use of the intellectual potential of the country, and the economy operates very ineffectively. Worse, we found that such a system forbids creative thinking at lower levels and so creates an antihumanistic society. From these experiences we discovered that the effectiveness of a modern economy and society depends on the intellectual level on which it is run." Quoted in François Duchêne, ed., *The Endless Crisis: America in the Seventies* (New York: Simon and Schuster, 1970), p. 247.

13. Vernon Bogdanor and Robert Skidelsky, ed., introduction

to *The Age of Affluence, 1951-1964* (London: Macmillan, Papermac edition, 1970), p. 11.

14. *Ibid.*, p. 12. Max Weber has argued, "To take a practical political stand is one thing, and to analyze political structures and party positions is another. When speaking in a political meeting about democracy, one does not hide one's personal standpoint; indeed, to come out clearly and take a stand is one's damned duty. The words one uses in such a meeting are not means of scientific analysis but means of canvassing votes and winning over others. . . . It would be an outrage, however, to use words in this fashion in a lecture or in the lecture-room. . . . the qualities that make a man an excellent scholar and academic teacher are not the qualities that make him a leader to give directions in practical life or, more specifically, in politics." "Science as a Vocation," in *From Max Weber*, translated, edited, and with an introduction by H. H. Gerth and C. Wright Mills (New York: Oxford University Press, A Galaxy Book, 1958), pp. 145, 150.

15. Leon Trotsky once wrote (from exile, of course), "The Fabians were indignant when the revolutionary proletariat withdrew freedom of activity from 'educated' society, but they think it quite in the order of things when a bureaucracy withdraws freedom of activity from the proletariat." *The Revolution Betrayed: What Is the Soviet and Where Is It Going?*, translated by Max Eastman (New York: Pioneer, 1945), p. 304. "When the sugar crop fails," wrote Goronwy Rees, "torture the poets." *Encounter*, July 1971, p. 43.

16. *New York Times*, 22 May 1971. The text is an example of the "universal falsehood" in politicized culture since it implies that the repressive system in Russia is abnormal "Stalinism" and that somehow a certain amount of freedom now exists in what were once Stalinist countries. Long ignored, of course, was the crushing of freedom for all Cubans, not merely poets, by the Castro regime. The text of the statement addressed to Castro is worth reading:

We hold that it is our duty to inform you of our shame and anger.

The deplorable text of the confession signed by Heberto Padilla can only have been obtained by means that amount to the negation of revolutionary legality and justice.

The contents of this confession, with its absurd accusations and delirious assertions, as well as the pitiable parody of self-criticism to which Heberto Padilla and Comrades Belkis Cuza, Dias Martinez, César López and Pablo Armando Fernández submitted to at the seat of the National Union of Cuban Writers and Artists, recall the most sordid moments of the era of Stalinism, with its prefabricated verdicts and its witch-hunts.

[It is] with the same vehemence that from the very first day was ours in defending the Cuban revolution, which seemed to us exemplary in its respect for the human being and in its struggle for liberation, that we exhort you to spare Cuba dogmatic obscurantism, cultural xenophobia and the repressive system imposed by Stalinism on the socialist countries and of which events similar to those now occurring in Cuba were flagrant manifestations.

The contempt for human dignity implied in the act of forcing a man into ludicrously accusing himself of the worst treasons and indignities does not alert us because it concerns a writer but because any Cuban comrade—peasant, worker, technician or intellectual—can also become the victim of similar violence and humiliations.

We would want the Cuban revolution to return to what made us consider it as a model in the realm of socialism.

17. Quoted in Leo Sauvage, "Discovering Castro's Cuba," *New Leader*, 28 June 1971, p. 8. (See note 16 above for text of letter.) Sauvage continues, "yet to which point in this paragon of revolution did they wish to return? From the fall of 1959 . . . to the present day, Castro has pursued a consistently sordid neo-Stalinism: political purges and arrests among the old anti-Batista fighters; government takeover of the press and trade unions; militarization of education and labor; elimination of civil liberties and of virtually every freedom—including, despite a much-touted tolerance for abstract art, the freedom of intellectual expression." *Ibid.* He quotes from an article by Susan Sontag, titled "Some Thoughts on the Right Way (for us) to Love the Cuban Revolution," in which she proclaimed that " 'the Cuban revolution is astonishingly free of repression,' that it had 'not begun eating its children' and had 'no intention of doing so.' " *Ramparts*, April 1969, quoted in "Discovering Castro's Cuba," p. 8. Miss Sontag has since said she "strongly regretted" having signed the anti-Castro statement. *The Village Voice*, 4 November 1971, pp. 1, 28.

18. Saul Landau, "Cuba: The Present Reality," an interview with the editor and members of the editorial board, *New Left Review*, no. 9 (1961), pp. 14, 15, 17, 18, 20, 22. Elizabeth Sutherland was writing about this time that Fidel Castro "seems, first of all, utterly devoted to the welfare of his people—and his people are the poor, not the rich." *Manchester Guardian Weekly*, 7 December 1961, p. 2.

19. Susan Sontag, "Posters: Advertisement, Art, Political Arti-

fact, Commodity," introductory essay, in *Art of the Revolution: Castro's Cuba, 1959-1970*, compiled by Dugald Stermer (New York: McGraw-Hill, 1970), pp. xiii, xv, xviii.

20. As for the end of Stalinism, Roger Garaudy, French communist dissident, has described the present Soviet leadership as having been "formed by Stalinism and put in position in Stalin's time on the basis of the criteria of the epoch [and developing] into a reactionary neo-Bonapartism and a dictatorship of the army." Quoted in U.S., Congress, Senate, Government Operations Committee, *International Negotiation*, hearings before the Subcommittee on National Security and International Operations, 92nd Cong., 1st sess., pt. 6, 30 April 1971, pp. 164-65. Isaac Deutscher, no bitter-end hater of the Soviets, in one of his last books said that " 'the bureaucracy has been unable to free the country from the absurdities and rigidities of its method of government. Its rule, though preferable to Stalin's autocracy, is still misrule. It is immensely wasteful; and it deadens or weakens all progressive impulses within the social organism.' " In his *Russia, China and the West*, quoted in a review by Donald Zagoria, *American Political Science Review* 65 (1971): 541. Zagoria, himself, said, "crypto-Stalinism is stronger than ever in the Soviet Union." *Ibid*.

21. "Second Report on the Situation of Political Prisoners and their Relatives in Cuba," *Report of the Inter-American Commission on Human Rights*, Document OEA/Ser. L/V/II.33, Organization of American States (17 November 1970), 44.

22. Fritz Stern, *The Politics of Cultural Despair: A Study in the Rise of the Germanic Ideology* (Berkeley: University of California Press, 1961), pp. xii, xviii, xix, 268. For a brilliant comparative analysis of the university turmoil, see Professor Stern's "Reflections on the International Student Movement," *American Scholar* 40 (1970/71): 123-37.

23. Quoted in François-Bondy, "Jean-Paul Sartre," in *The New Left: Six Critical Essays*, edited by Maurice Cranston (New York: The Library Press, 1971), p. 52, note 1. Sartre's views have deeply influenced Robert Heilbroner. See my chapter 9.

Chapter One

1. Herbert Marcuse, *University Review*, no. 15 (1971), p. 4; Charles A. Reich, *The Greening of America: How the Youth Revolution Is Trying to Make America Livable* (New York:

Random House, 1970), pp. 300, 8; Philip Green, *New York Times Magazine*, 20 September 1970, p. 97.

2. Philip Slater, *The Pursuit of Loneliness* (Boston: Beacon, 1970), p. 147. (The author fails to specify where and how this choice—if the poor syntax implies a choice—is to be presented.) Mel Wulf, "The Growing Threat to Civil Liberties," *New Politics* 8, no. 3 (1970): 52, 53; Alfred Kazin, in *Horizon*, July 1962; Andrew Kopkind, "Are We in the Middle of a Revolution?" *New York Times Magazine*, 10 November 1968, p. 62; Tom Hayden, quoted in Anthony Howard, "Mis-Trial," a review of *Trial*, in *New Statesman*, 23 April 1971, p. 568; John Tytell, "Papers of the Movement," a review of *The New Left: A Documentary History*, edited by Massimo Teodori, *Catholic World*, May 1970, p. 95; Dotson Rader, "On Revolutionary Violence," *Defiance* 1 (1970): 208; Kenneth Lamott, *Anti-California: Report from Our First Parafascist State* (Boston: Little, Brown, 1971); *Black Panther*, 30 August 1969, quoted by Seymour Martin Lipset as having an article entitled "Zionism (Kosher Nationalism) + Imperialism = Fascism" in which Zionism is described several times as a variety of fascism, in his *Revolution and Counterrevolution: Change and Resistance in Social Structures* (New York: Basic Books, 1968), p. 392, note 12; *Los Angeles Times*, 13 March 1970; Daniel Sisson, "The Dialogue: Youth and Society," in *The New Politics: Mood or Movement?*, edited by James A. Burkhart and Frank J. Kendrick (Englewood Cliffs, N.J.: Prentice-Hall, 1971), p. 86. In similar vein to these writers, Sartre, after a visit to the Soviet Union in 1954, found "complete freedom of criticism" in Russia but, without visiting the United States, he said there was only "pre-Fascism in America." Quoted in Bondy, "Sartre," p. 55.

3. Dr. James Cheek, commencement address at the Agricultural and Technical College of North Carolina, Greensboro, 7 June 1971, mimeographed, pp. 10, 13. A National Opinion Research Center Survey in 1971 found that "the so-called white backlash against blacks is virtually nonexistent" and that 70% of American voters would vote for a black candidate for president as against 38% in 1958. *Christian Science Monitor*, 17 December 1971.

4. Bertram M. Gross, "Friendly Fascism: A Model for America," *Social Policy*, November/December 1970, pp. 44, 46. Walter Lippmann thinks "the country's too big for national fascism [but] I think there will be local fascism." *Sunday Globe* (Boston), 17 October 1971, p. A-3.

5. *The Communist*, August 1933, p. 734, quoted in Theodore

Draper, "The Ghost of Social-Fascism," *Commentary* 47, no. 2 (1969): p. 41, note 25.

6. Henry Ashby Turner Jr., "Fascism and Modernization," *World Politics* 24, no. 4 (July 1972): 563. Professor Turner's acute analysis brings to mind the French communist who said during the Stalin-Tito confrontation, "'when I say that Tito's regime is comparable to that of Franco, I am not playing with words. I can prove by Marxist analysis that the Yugoslav regime is a fascist regime.'" Quoted in K. A. Jelenski, "The Literature of Disenchantment," *Survey*, no. 42 (1962), p. 117.

7. N. Kogan, "Fascism as a Political System," in *The Nature of Fascism*, edited by S. J. Woolf, Reading University Studies on Contemporary Europe, Studies in Fascism, 2 (London: Weidenfeld and Nicolson, 1968), pp. 11-18 (See also Dante Germino's review of this work in *American Political Science Review* 64 [1970]: 614-15); Franz Neumann, *Behemoth: The Structure and Rise of National Socialism, 1933-1944* (New York: Octagon Books, 1963), pp. 400-58. Neumann also writes: "National Socialism has no theory of society as we understand it, no consistent picture of its operation, structure, and development. It has aims to carry through and adjusts its ideological pronouncements to a series of everchanging goals." *Behemoth*, p. 38.

8. Howard H. Lentner and Thomas J. Lewis, "Revolutionary Terrorism in Democratic Society," *Freedom at Issue*, no. 7 (1971), p. 13.

9. *Ibid.*, p. 4.

10. Roger Neville Williams, "Strong-Arm Rule in Canada," *New Republic*, 30 January 1971, p. 15.

11. "Anti-Terror Law Lapsing In Canada" was the headline in the *New York Times*, 30 April 1971. Police state, indeed! Prime Minister Trudeau is not only a man of firmness but also a man with a fine sense of irony. In signing an agreement in Moscow, 20 May 1971, he said it was an effort to affirm Canada's independent foreign policy in the face of what he called the "overpowering presence of the United States of America." To make such a statement in a country whose Red Army had overpowered popular resistance in Poland, Hungary, Czechoslovakia and East Germany is a sure example of Gallic wit.

12. In his *Schriften zur Ideologie und Politik* (Neuwied: Luchterhand, 1967), p. 644, quoted in David Kettler, "The Vocation of Radical Intellectuals," *Politics and Society* 1, no. 1 (1970): 46.

13. Quoted in Hubert H. Humphrey, "Damned If You Do, Dead If You Don't," a review of *Democracy's Dilemma: The To-*

talitarian Party in a Free Society by Benjamin E. Lippincott, *Book Week*, 26 December 1965, p. 2.

14. Alain Touraine, *The May Movement: Revolt and Reform*, translated by Leonard F. X. Mayhew (New York: Random House, 1971), p. 266.

15. *Ibid.*, p. 269. In the Fall semester of 1968, the erstwhile president of Columbia University, Dr. Andrew Cordier, formerly a high United Nations official, was arraigned by leaders of Students for a Democratic Society as the man who had "murdered" Patrice Lumumba during the time Cordier had been in the Congo representing the United Nations. Candlelight marches to "mourn" Lumumba (eight years after his assassination!) and mass meetings were held on the campus to dramatize Cordier's "complicity." The only visible faculty reaction to this Goebbels-like exercise in the Big Lie was a letter of exculpation in the college daily by Arthur Lall, a former Indian diplomat teaching at Columbia. When I expressed my curiosity to a senior professor at Columbia at this faculty silence in the face of such a monstrous act of character assassination, he replied that some accusations are so contemptible "we should apply the Oxford method—ignore them." Several weeks later, Cordier, attending a campus press reception, was confronted by forty SDS members, one of whom presented him with a "subpoena" to stand trial for "crimes against the students and residents of Morningside Heights." When some of the guests laughed, an SDS leader faced around to them and said: "Some of you may laugh at this but this man is a criminal." *Columbia Spectator*, 22 November 1968. No "mature political judgment," I suppose, to use Professor Touraine's euphemism.

16. V. I. Lenin, *What Is to Be Done? Burning Questions of Our Movement* (New York: International Publishers, New World Paperbacks, 1969), p. 39.

17. For these quotations, my analysis, and what follows I am grateful to Theodore Draper and his article, "Ghost of Social-Fascism," pp. 29-42.

18. *Ibid.*, pp. 34-35. The concept of "naked" was the basis of a communist *bon mot* in the 1930s—"Fascism is capitalism gone nudist." In that benighted period, nudity had not yet become a synonym for liberation.

19. The 1931 report to the Eleventh Plenum of the Communist International, prepared by Manuilsky, did not mention Hitler once but there were pages and pages on the need to destroy the social democrats. A mere four months before Hitler actually came to power, Kuusinen said " 'the *main blow*' " must be directed against " 'social-fascism and the reformist trade-union bureau-

cracy.'" (Italics in original.) Quoted in Draper, "Ghost of Social-Fascism," pp. 36-37.

20. Engels in a letter to Eduard Bernstein in 1882, quoted in Sidney Hook, "The Fallacy of the Theory of Social Fascism," in *The Anxious Years*, edited by Louis Filler (New York: Putnam's, 1963), pp. 320-21.

21. *Ibid.*, pp. 328-29.

22. Draper, "Ghost of Social-Fascism," p. 36.

23. Karl Marx and Friedrich Engels, *Correspondence, 1846-1895*, a selection with commentary and notes, translated by Dona Torr. New ed. (London: Lawrence and Wishart, 1936), p. 437.

24. Howard Zinn, "Speaking of Books: Historian as Citizen," *New York Times Book Review*, 25 September 1966, p. 36.

25. B. F. Skinner, *Walden Two* (New York: Macmillan, Macmillan Paperbacks Edition, 1966), p. 232.

26. C. Wright Mills, *The Power Elite* (New York: Oxford University Press, 1957), p. 4.

27. John Bunzel, *Anti-Politics in America: Reflections on the Anti-Political Temper and Its Distortions of the Democratic Process* (New York: Knopf, 1967), p. 105, note 2.

28. Quoted in Ernst Nolte, *Three Faces of Fascism*, translated from the German by Leila Vennewitz (New York: Weidenfeld and Nicolson, 1965), p. 7.

29. V. I. Lenin, *Sobranie sochinenii*, vol. 17 (Moscow: 1925), p. 89, translated and quoted in Nomad, *Aspects of Revolt*, p. 123.

30. Benjamin R. Barber, "The Revolution as Reality: Common Men and the Future of Democracy," *Modern Occasions*, Spring 1971, p. 342. The shrewdness of Professor Barber's observation is confirmed in a study by Seymour Martin Lipset and Richard B. Dobson showing how a number of leading liberals supported Mussolini fascism, including the *New Republic*, which in the late 1920s urged a "sympathetic hearing" for fascism because it promoted "national cohesion and national welfare." "The Intellectual as Critic and Rebel: With Special Reference to the United States and the Soviet Union." In *Daedalus* 101 (Summer 1972), p. 170.

31. Joachim Fest, "The Romantic Counter-Revolution of Our Time," *Encounter*, June 1971, pp. 59-60. More precisely, Marcuse has written that "as long as [the semi-democratic process] prevails, it makes sense to say that the general will is always wrong. . . ." *An Essay on Liberation* (Boston: Beacon, 1970), p. 65.

32. For a harrowing report of Soviet concentration camps as they exist today, see Peter Reddaway in the London *Observer*, 3 January 1971. Anatoly T. Marchenko wrote in his first person narrative of six years spent in Soviet labor camps, 1960 to 1966,

that "today's Soviet camps for political prisoners are just as horrific as in Stalin's time. A few things are better, a few things worse. . . . I would like this evidence of mine concerning the Soviet camps and prisons for political prisoners to come to the attention of humanists and progressive people in other countries—those who stick up for political prisoners in Greece and Portugal and in Spain and South Africa. Let them ask their Soviet colleagues in the struggle against inhumanity: 'And what have you done in your country to stop political prisoners from being, say, "reformed" by starvation?'" *My Testimony*, translated by Michael Scammell (London: Pall Mall, 1969), p. 3.

33. *New York Times*, 16 June 1971, Op-Ed page.

34. Robert Conquest, *The Great Terror: Stalin's Purge of the Thirties* (New York: Macmillan, 1968).

35. Note this entry in the Ciano diaries, 4 December 1939: "I showed the Duce the report of an Italian. . . . the only foreigner permitted to live in Posen [Poland]. . . . With a simplicity which accentuates the horror of the facts, he describes all that the Germans are doing: unmentionable atrocities without reason. The Duce himself was indignant; he advised me to see to it that by indirect channels the American and French newspapers get the contents of the report. The world must know." Galeazzo Ciano, *The Ciano Diaries, 1939-1943*, the complete unabridged diaries, edited by Hugh Gibson (Garden City, N. Y.: Doubleday, 1946), p. 175.

36. Text of address by Senator Mondale, 7 May 1971, mimeographed, p. 9. Harriet Van Horne, a "Marcusian doomsayer" columnist, has written: "It's significant that the only two countries in which the free press is under attack from its elected government are South Africa and the USA. . . . There are other parallels, including South Africa's secret police and controlled courts." *New York Post*, 15 November 1971.

37. See my interview with Mrs. Mvubelo, *Christian Science Monitor*, 19 July 1971, p. 15.

38. If Senator Mondale is really concerned about improving the lot of the American Negro, I would commend to him "The Blacks and the Unions," by Bayard Rustin, *Harper's Magazine*, May 1971, pp. 78-81, and "America's Race Paradox: The Gap between Social Progress and Political Despair," by Nathan Glazer, *Encounter*, October 1968, pp. 9-18.

39. The case is cited as *Tinker v. Des Moines School Dist.*, 393 US 503, opinion delivered by then Associate Supreme Court Justice Abe Fortas.

Chapter Two

1. Corpses of thousands of Polish officers, who had been captured by the Russians in 1939 and kept in prisoner-of-war camps, were discovered in the Katyn Forest near Smolensk by the Germans. Scholarly examination of evidence has led to the conclusion that the murder of fifteen thousand Polish officers was committed by Soviet security forces. Adam B. Ulam, *Expansion and Coexistence: A History of Soviet Foreign Policy, 1917-67* (New York: Praeger, 1968), pp. 343-44. See also Milovan Djilas, *The New Class: An Analysis of the Communist System* (New York: Praeger, 1957), pp. 26-27.

2. "Malaya accused Communist China today of genocide and the denial of fundamental human rights in Tibet. The Tibetans' 'identity as a distinctive Buddhist race is in danger of extinction because of the policy of genocide pursued by their oppressors,' the Malayan Minister of Internal Security, Dr. Ismail bin Abdul Rahman, told the [United Nations] General Assembly." *New York Times,* 4 October 1962. On 15 June 1970 Aleksandr I. Solzhenitsyn protested in an open letter the confinement to a mental hospital of Zhores Medvedev. The Nobel prize-winning novelist told the Moscow intelligentsia to whom his letter was addressed: "It is time to understand that the imprisonment of some persons in madhouses because they have minds of their own is *spiritual murder,* a variation on the gas chambers, and even more cruel. . . ." *New York Times Magazine,* 7 November 1971, p. 116.

3. In mid-June 1940, Stalin sent ultimata to Lithuania, Latvia and Estonia demanding, first, the dissolution of their respecive governments to be replaced by governments satisfactory to the Soviet Union. Second, the Red Army was to be admitted at once to garrison each of the three nations. The three countries surrendered. "Free elections" were called and the three new parliaments "unanimously" demanded entry into the Soviet Union. Moscow has "persistently endeavored to achieve Russification of Lithuania, Estonia and Latvia by encouraging migration of Russions to the Baltic area and by trying to force domination of Russian language and Russian culture." *New York Times,* 21 June 1971.

4. In John Wear Burton, ed. *Nonalignment* (London: Deutsch, 1966), p. 135.

5. Susan Sontag, in "What's Happening to America," *Partisan Review* 34 (1967): 57-58. Bayard Rustin has written: "Take the question of white racism. Simply telling white people that they

are racist is dangerous and counter-productive . . . it's a copout for whites who are titillated and delighted to be abused and called racists. And thus Stokely Carmichael can come back to the United States and demand (and receive) $2,500 a lecture for telling white people how they stink." *ADA World*, September 1970. Also see Malcolm X, *The Autobiography of Malcolm X* (New York: Grove Press, 1966), p. 176. "Book after book showed me how the white man brought upon the world's black, brown, yellow and red people every variety of the sufferings of exploitations."

6. Earl Ubell, *Village Voice*, 21 November 1968, quoted in Mitchell Goodman, *The Movement towards a New America* (New York: Knopf, 1970), p. 155. The misuse of the word "genocide" is not confined to Left-Liberals. Even that usually precise wordsmith, William F. Buckley, has slipped. Witness this sentence: "But irrespective of whether one agrees with the general goals of [John Birch] Society's members, as I emphatically do, genocidal assaults upon the membership of the Society and on candidates who refuse to condemn all members of the Society, are unreasonable and undiscriminating." William F. Buckley, "Goldwater and the John Birch Society," *National Review* (19 November 1963), p. 430.

7. *New York Times*, 28 June 1968, p. 39.

8. James Baldwin, in "A Question of Commitment," *New York Times Book Review*, 2 June 1968, p. 2. In a recent "rap" session with Margaret Mead, Baldwin said that "what this generation [of blacks] . . . is saying, is they realize that you, the white people, white Americans, have always attempted to murder them." *A Rap on Race* (Philadelphia: Lippincott, 1971), p. 11. *No Name in the Street* (New York: Dial, 1972), pp. 191 and 192.

9. Quoted in Louis J. Halle, "Bringing about Change: A Matter of Manners?" *New Republic*, 23 November 1968, p. 21.

10. Published by International Publishers, Communist party subsidiary.

11. Colin McGlashan, "Patmos Legacy," review of *The Rediscovery of Black Nationalism* by Theodore Draper, *New Statesman*, 23 April 1971, p. 566. The reviewer's intellectual powers as an observer are exemplified by his ability to see the American Negro's salvation in communism—after all we have learned from the lips of communist leaders themselves about what communism does to man's "sense of dignity."

12. Slater, *Pursuit of Loneliness*, pp. 33, 128.

13. Much of this analysis is based on a brilliant piece of reportage by Edward Jay Epstein, "The Panthers and the Police: A

Pattern of Genocide?" *New Yorker*, 13 February 1971, pp. 45-77. I must here record my admiration for another example of brilliant reporting on the Black Panther phenomenon—Gail Sheehy's book, *Panthermania: The Clash of Black Against Black in One American City* (New York: Harper & Row, 1971). The book deals with what she calls the "Panther Myth."

14. Some 300 newspapers and news agencies subscribe to the *New York Times* news service and about 200 to that of the *Washington Post*.

15. Epstein, "Panthers," p. 45.

16. *Ibid.*

17. Robert L. Bartley, "Those 28 Panthers—and the Press," *Wall Street Journal*, 17 March 1971. Bartley concedes only that Epstein had merely dotted "i's" and crossed "t's" of what was supposedly known about Garry's hyperbole about police genocide.

18. Arnold Beichman, interview with Epstein, *Christian Science Monitor*, 11 March 1971, p. 17.

19. Epstein, "Panthers," p. 77.

20. Anne Roe, *The Making of a Scientist* (New York: Dodd, Mead, 1953), p. 240.

21. Slater, *Pursuit of Loneliness*, p. 147. A few years ago Kenneth Tynan, then the drama critic for the *Observer*, wrote something quite typical of the "better-red-than-dead" brigade: " 'Suppose one were confronted with an outright choice between nuclear annihilation and the Communist hegemony. The hero nowadays would be the man who elected to live under the new regime hoping to change it; and the coward would be the man who preferred . . . to lie down and die.' " Quoted in "People," *Time*, 7 July 1961.

22. Personal Communication, 17 December 1971. Rosenthal is managing editor of the *New York Times*. The full text after the paragraph I have already quoted reads:

"When I was a reporter, I had no problems at all about this. The journalism of objectivity—or the nearest possible approach to objectivity—gave me no problems because I felt it filled an essential social need. There are many young newspapermen today who feel the same way. There are others, who come out of the current atmosphere of advocacy in colleges or who are affected by it later on in their careers, who do have problems about it. They run into trouble in a paper like ours when consciously or unconsciously their advocacy is clearly reflected in their stories. One of three things happen. They submit grudgingly to the principle of objectivity and make themselves and their editors unhappy. They decide that advocacy is what they really want and leave—this happens very rarely indeed. Or, in most cases, they come to see that the journalism of objectivity does indeed perform a social good and while they remain advocates personally, they do not try to inject it into their copy.

"The problem of advocacy is still with us and probably always will be with us. At the time of the Chicago Convention [1968] when emotions were particularly high, it did present a problem. On specific other occasions such as the trial of the Chicago Seven, we ran into it again. But I do have a feeling that for the time being at least the problem is diminishing, rather than increasing, at least on *The Times*."

Chapter Three

1. "Although about 220 Americans died in violent civil strife in the 5 years before mid-1968, the rate of 1.1 per million population was infinitesimal compared with the average of all nations of 238 per million, and less than the European average of 2.4 per million. These differences reflect the comparative evidence that, from a world wide perspective, Americans have seldom organized for violence. . . . These comparisons afford little comfort when the tumult of the United States is contrasted with the relative domestic tranquillity of developed democratic nations like Sweden, Great Britain, and Australia, or with the comparable current tranquillity of nations as diverse as Yugoslavia, Turkey, Jamaica, or Malaysia. In total magnitude of strife, the United States ranks 24th among the 114 larger nations and colonies of the world. In magnitude of turmoil alone, it ranks sixth." Hugh D. Graham and Ted R. Gurr, *Violence in America: Historical and Comparative Perspectives*, a report to the National Commission on the Causes and Prevention of Violence, June 1969, prepared . . . for the President's Commission (New York: New American Library, A Signet Book, 1969), p. 776. An important analysis of America's homicide rate is by Raymond D. Gastil, "Homicide and a Regional Culture of Violence," *American Sociological Review* 36, June (1971): 412-27. He argues that high US murder rates are related primarily to the persistence of Southern cultural traditions developed before the Civil War and subsequently spreading over much of the country.

2. Jimmy Breslin wrote admiringly about Rep. Bella Abzug's 1970 Congressional campaign in New York and climaxed his report with this loving paragraph: " 'There she is in the purple dress, that's Bella Abzug, she's against Israel,' a little guy from the Jewish Defense League began yelling at a rally on the East

side the other night. Bella grabbed a young guy who had driven her to the meeting. 'Hit that bastard in the mouth for me,' she said, 'I can't do it where people see me.'" *New York Magazine*, 5 October 1970. Great stuff, Jimmy, but what would you have said if it was a construction worker giving such an order, the honky fascist beast?

3. Pacifica's radio station in Houston, Texas, was bombed a couple of times recently and the FBI "on the basis of informers' tips" arrested the radical right bombers. Nicholas C. Criss, "Bombers to the Right of Them," *Nation*, 11 January 1971, p. 42. I have the impression that the FBI seems to do much better at nabbing right-wing terrorists than left terrorists.

4. "Any decrease in the perceived likelihood of retribution tends to increase the likelihood and magnitude of civil violence." Ted Gurr, "Psychological Factors in Civil Violence," *World Politics* 20 (1968): 265.

5. Quoted in "The Two Wars," *Activist* 11, no. 1 (1970): 33. The publication, a student political quarterly, describes itself as "recognized by the Oberlin College Faculty and its filial Student Senate as a student-operated educational organization." In the same issue, an anonymous article declares: "Bombings, if they are to be ultimately effective, must occur regularly and visibly. They must disrupt the flow of life in the cities and become a genuine threat to the transport system of the country. They must create an atmosphere in which the government is seen as no longer being able to provide for the domestic tranquillity. . . . At the height of revolutionary violence (and government inability to end it) the progressive forces will emerge as the sole force capable of restoring law and order." "Toward a Theory of Armed Struggle," *ibid.*, p. 18.

6. Quoted in Julia K. Ellison. "The Radical Consciousness of Dr. Spock: The Baby Doctor Is Still Counselling Dissent," *Harvard Crimson*, 26 April 1971, p. 3.

7. Wayne O'Neil, "The MLA's MVE Award for 1968," *College English* 32, no. 3 (1970): 290, quoted in *Public Interest*, no. 23 (1971), p. 132.

8. Tytell, "Papers of the Movement," p. 95.

9. Richard Poirier, "The War Against the Young: Its Beginnings," in his *The Performing Self: Compositions in the Languages of Contemporary Life* (New York: Oxford University Press, 1971), p. 154. One of the editors of *Partisan Review*, the professor-critic is much concerned to keep "with it." In what must be considered an abuse of the critical imagination, he said that critics of the university militants were engaged in a "war

against youth" and that it was time that America had a "cultural revolution." *Ibid.*, p. 144.

10. Robert Lekachman, "The Brighter Side," *New Leader*, 28 April 1969, p. 7.

11. *New Statesman*, 5 September 1936.

12. Herbert Marcuse, *Five Lectures: Psychoanalysis, Politics, and Utopia*, translations by Jeremy J. Shapiro and Shierry M. Weber (Boston: Beacon, 1970), p. 103.

13. Stephen Saltonstall, "Toward a Strategy of Disruption," in Burkhart and Kendrick, *New Politics*, p. 72, reprinted from "Students and Society," *Center Occasional Paper* 1, no. 1 (1967), a publication of the Center for the Study of Democratic Institutions in Santa Barbara, California. How reminiscent of nazi Germany, where judges were authorized to punish "according to the healthy sentiment of the people."

14. Tom Hayden, in "The New Radicalism: Round IV," *Partisan Review* 33 (1966): 54.

15. *An End to Political Science: The Caucus Papers*, edited by Marvin Surkin and Alan Wolfe (New York: Basic Books, 1970), p. 91.

16. Jay Martin, "The Politics of Terror," *Partisan Review* 38 (1971): 102. Here in this quotation we find another example of whatever-America-does-America-is-wrong. If the media ignore the "alternate life-styles within the current society," it proves that the power elite and its kept press are suppressing legitimate and important news. But if the media report the "alternative life-styles" and if the media, as has become the usual case, sympathizes with the "alternative life-styles," why then it only shows that the media is "swallowing up" the "alternative life-styles" and that the "liberated zones" of the counter-culture are "almost immediately 're-enslaved' by the mass media."

17. Joseph Adelson, "Investing the Young," *Commentary* 51, no. 5 (1971): 45, 46.

18. "Violence is necessary, it is as American as cherry pie," is the way Brown put it originally. In his *Die Nigger Die!* (New York: Dial, 1969), Brown writes "America's very existence offends me."

19. Robert Coles, "Black Anger," a review of *Soul on Ice* by Eldridge Cleaver, *Atlantic*, June 1968, p. 107. Arthur Waskow adopted Cleaver into the Old Testament tradition referring to "the *shofet* Eldridge Cleaver (who went into exile like Moses)." *The Freedom Seder: A New Haggadah for Passover* (New York: Holt, Rinehart & Winston, 1970). *Shofet* is a Biblical judge not, as Waskow updates the word to mean, a "revolutionary leader."

Canonization of a revolutionary is not unusual in contemporary revolutionary rhetoric. It is part of the operational code of the revolutionary claque to invoke Christianity, God, Judaism, Jesus Christ in justification of their secular redemptionist crusade. *The Communist Manifesto* becomes the Sermon on the Mount. Here, for example, is an aria from a recent Passion of Che Guevara: "In the cult of Che, that element [of the untrue and the irrational] is his identification with Christ. Because he fought for the poor and because he chose to be sacrificed in his prime, he gives a mystical feeling that he died for *us*, for all humanity. Clearly, he killed other men. Clearly, he hated his enemies. Clearly, his beliefs stemmed from political doctrines loathsome to many. Clearly, he advocated and used tactics that were sometimes dubious or inhuman. . . . Yet clearly, he transcends all these facts. He appears as larger than a human being, as somebody approaching a saviour." (Italics in original.) Andrew Sinclair, *Guevara* (London: Fontana/Collins, 1970), p. 91. Robespierre promulgated the "pure cult of the Supreme Being" decree because he couldn't stand atheists. In his speech "On the Cult of the Supreme Being (May 7, 1794)," quoted in *Robespierre*, compiled by George Rudé (Englewood Cliffs, N.J.: Prentice-Hall, A Spectrum Book, 1967), pp. 68-73.

20. *New York Times*, 2 November 1970.

21. David Cartwright, *Evergreen Review*, no. 66, April 1969, quoted in Rader, "On Revolutionary Violence," *Defiance* 1 (1970): 204-5. "The contemporary term 'underground press' stems from the rush of anti-establishment newspapers in the early 1960s when most underground papers reflected the American drug culture. Since drugs were, and are, illegal, the name 'underground press' caught on and held." Robert J. Glessing, *The Underground Press in America* (Bloomington: Indiana University Press, 1970), p. 3. There were an estimated 457 so-called underground newspapers in 1968. Glessing, *Underground Press*, p. 6.

22. Dotson Rader, "On Revolutionary Violence," p. 203. As another example of this frenetic, meta-rational rhetoric, here is a sample from the *Harvard Crimson:* "Terrorism could help restore the understanding of transcendence. Blowing up buildings destroys the product. . . . The very virtue of terrorism, in fact, is that it allows a spontaneous release of frustrations caused by capitalism." Richard E. Hyland, *Harvard Crimson*, special supplement, 22 October 1969. "The only reason I wouldn't blow up the Center for International Affairs is that I might get caught," he also wrote. Almost two years later, he was arrested and jailed in Mexico, charged with working with the Comando Armado del Pueblo

(People's Armed Commandoes), described as a Mexican Marxist urban guerrilla group. The *Times* (Los Angeles), 29 September 1971, reported that at the time of his arrest, Hyland was enrolled as a student in the University of the Americas, Mexico City. Final disposition of his case was not known at this writing.

23. Berthoff's letter was published in the *Harvard Crimson*, 1 April 1971. This passage was quoted in the 21 April 1971 issue.

24. George Paloczi-Horvath, *Youth Up in Arms: A Political and Social World Survey, 1955-1970* (New York: McKay, 1971), pp. 334, 335-36. He also discloses that at the end of 1970, "dissent by young people was treated virtually as a crime in the majority of the countries in the United Nations Organization." *Ibid.*, p. 323. No source for this disclosure is given.

25. H. G. Wells, *The New Machiavelli*, in the Collected Essex edition, vol. 3 (London Benn, 1926), p. 115.

26. "'The Father of the Student Rebellion?' Herbert Marcuse talks to Robert McKenzie," *Listener*, 17 October 1968, p. 499.

27. Marcuse, *Five Lectures*, pp. 89-90. Professor Marcuse's influence on campus revolutionaries was expressed some years ago by a University of Buffalo graduate student: "'Do you know why the demonstrations and protest movements succeeded? Because we didn't play by the rules of the game. Our movement wasn't organized democratically. . . . It was our unrepressed intolerance and thorough anti-permissiveness that brought our actions success. But who gave us the intellectual courage to be intolerant and unpermissive? I think Herbert Marcuse more than anyone. He is the New Left's Professor.'" Quoted in Lionel Abel, "Seven Heroes of the New Left," *New York Times Magazine*, 5 May 1968, p. 135.

28. Richard Hofstadter and Michael Wallace, eds., *American Violence: A Documentary History* (New York: Knopf, 1970), p. 29.

29. Adelson, "Inventing the Young," pp. 43-44.

30. Carl Oglesby, "Vietnamese Crucible: An Essay on the Meanings of the Cold War," in *Containment and Change*, edited by Carl Oglesby and Richard Shaull (New York: Macmillan, 1967), p. 146.

31. H. Mark Roelofs, "Legitimation Through Ideological Commitment," abstract of paper presented at the American Political Science Association Convention, September 1970, mimeographed.

32. Quoted in Lewis S. Feuer, *The Conflict of Generations: The Character and Significance of Student Movements* (New York: Basic Books, 1969), p. 527. Professor Feuer attributes the *Catechism* to Bakunin. However, according to Michael Confino, it would appear that this 1869 document was written by Nechayev

alone. See James Joll, "Anarchism—A Living Tradition," in Apter and Joll, *Anarchism Today*, p. 215. Nechayev is the subject of a fascinating chapter in Franco Venturi, *Roots of Revolution: A History of the Populist Movements in 19th Century Russia* (New York: Knopf, 1961), pp. 354-88.

33. Professor Eugene Genovese has written that the "doctrine of absolute morality and absolute political truth has provided the ideological foundation for every form of totalitarianism that we have faced or are now facing." Letter in *New York Review of Books*, 19 December 1968, p. 36.

34. Joll, "Anarchism," in Apter and Joll, *Anarchism Today*, p. 218. Barbara Tuchman describes in some detail Europe's assassins during the late nineteenth and early twentieth centuries, and their highborn supporters. She tells the story of Laurent Tailhade, a French poet, who when he heard of the bombing of the Chamber of Deputies in 1893 and the wounding of some of its members, exclaimed, *"Qu'importe les victimes si le geste est beau?* [what do the victims matter if it is a beautiful gesture?]." For him, the future anarchist society meant that the aristocracy would be one of intellect and "the common man will kiss the footprints of the poets." A few months later, a bomb exploded in a restaurant where he was eating; he lost the sight of one eye. *The Proud Tower: A Portrait of the World before the War 1890-1914* (New York: Macmillan, 1966), pp. 63-113.

35. Claire Sterling, "Ma-Ma-Maoisti Close Italian Universities," *Reporter*, 2 May 1968, p. 22; Marc Kravetz, a long-time activist in the French National Student Federation, quoted in Steven Kelman, "Student Confrontation at Alghero," *New Leader*, 9 June 1969, p. 13. It may well be sophistry to talk about violence accomplishing "a lot" or "a little." In practical terms, how does one measure either quantity? Professor Robert Paul Wolff has written that the occupation of Columbia in Spring 1968 leads to certain general conclusions—"First, the total harm done by the students and their supporters was very small in comparison with the good results which were achieved." "On Violence," in *Obligation and Dissent*, edited by D. W. Hanson and R. B. Fowler (Boston: Little, Brown, 1971), p. 250. What Wolff means by "total harm" and "the good results" is difficult to ascertain from the text of his essay.

36. Arnold Beichman, "Where Does Columbia Go From Here?", *New York Magazine*, 12 May 1968, p. 22.

37. Eugen Weber, *Varieties of Fascism* (New York: Van Nostrand, 1964), p. 29.

38. Ivan Turgenev, *Fathers and Sons*, translated by Constance Garnett (New York: Modern Library, n.d.), pp. 60, 56-57.

39. Ivo K. Feierabend and Rosalind Feierabend, "Aggressive Behaviour within Politics, 1948-1962: A Cross-National Study," in *Conflict and Violence in Latin American Politics*, edited by F. J. Moreno and B. Mitrani (New York: Crowell, 1971), p. 344.

40. Albert O. Hirschman, *Journeys toward Progress: Studies of Economic Policy-Making in Latin America* (New York: Greenwood, 1968), p. 257.

41. "Whatever threatens the supremacy of the apparat threatens the Soviet system." Zbigniew Brzezinski and Samuel P. Huntington, *Political Power: USA/USSR* (New York: Viking, 1968), p. 415.

42. Karl Mannheim theorized about "symbols or symbolic activities that serve as substitutes for real activities." He based himself on Kurt Lewin, who described a young feeble-minded child who wants to throw a ball a long way. Although he fails, he is happy because he finds a substitute in the vigorous movement he has made. This type of child was called a "gesture-child" because he is satisfied with gestures when other children are striving for concrete goals. (Kurt Lewin, *A Dynamic Theory of Personality*, chapter 6.) Mannheim extended this concept to incorporate the "gesture-adult who exists on substitute goals and being satisfied with gestures and symbols." *Man and Society in an Age of Reconstruction: Studies in Modern Social Structure* (New York: Harcourt, Brace, 1954), pp. 131, 132.

43. AP dispatch in *Chicago Tribune*, 22 June 1972; Waisberg decision, *National Review*, 21 July 1972, p. 774.

44. *Commentary* (August 1972), p. 82.

45. A. L. Goodhart, "Munich Terrorism and the Hope of Peace," *Times* (London), 13 September 1972.

46. Daniel Bell, "Sensibility in the 60's," *Commentary* 51, no. 6 (1971): 73.

Chapter Four

1. Edgar Z. Friedenberg described the majority of Americans as "honkies." Letter in *New York Review of Books*, 23 July 1970, p. 46. This epithet originally described pejoratively central European immigrants. Recently, Negroes used it to refer to as a synonym for racists. Professor Friedenberg has argued that "what is wrong with America may be characteristic of mass democracy

itself." "The Revolt Against Democracy," *Change in Higher Education*, May/June 1969, p. 16.

2. A. H. Raskin, "The Working Man Has Become a Snob," *Saturday Evening Post*, 18 May 1968, p. 10. Bayard Rustin, on the other hand, has argued, "Thus today the trade-union movement has been relegated to reactionary status, even though it is actually more progressive than at any time in its history—if by progressive we mean a commitment to broad, long-term social reform in addition to the immediate objectives of improving wages and working conditions." In "The Blacks and the Unions," *Harper's Magazine*, May 1971, p. 81.

3. Roszak, *Making of a Counter Culture*, p. 3.

4. Edward Hyams, "Whatever Happened to Socialism?", *New Statesman*, 14 May 1971, p. 666. Walter Lippmann has written, "The stereotype of Labor as Emancipator selects the evidence which supports itself and rejects the other. And so parallel with the real movements of working men there exists a fiction the Labor Movement in which an idealized mass moves towards an idealized goal." *Public Opinion* (New York: Macmillan, 1960), p. 152. As an example of what Lippmann might be talking about, Staughton Lynd recently wrote that "the poor, when they find voice, will produce a truer, sounder radicalism than any which alienated intellectuals might prescribe." *Dissent*, 12 (1965): 328.

5. Bertrand Russell, *Freedom versus Organization, 1814-1914* (London: Allen & Unwin, 1952), p. 215.

6. Friedrich Engels, *Selected Writings*, edited by W. O. Henderson (Baltimore: Penguin Books, 1967), pp. 96-97. One can understand Engels' bitterness in view of the fact that his prophecies of revolution in England had utterly failed to come true: "If the English middle classes have not come to their senses by that time [1852 or 1853]—and there is no reason to anticipate any change of heart in that quarter—then a revolution is to be expected. And it will be more violent than any previous revolution. The English working classes driven to desperation . . . will turn to incendiarism. Popular fury will reach an intensity far greater than that which animated the French workers in 1793. The war of the poor against the rich will be the most bloodthirsty the world has ever seen. Even if some of the middle classes espouse the cause of the workers—even if the middle classes as a whole mended their ways—the catastrophe could not be avoided. . . . These are all conclusions that can be drawn *with absolute certainty*. They are *based on facts* which cannot be disputed—facts of historical developments and facts of human nature. It is particularly *easy to forecast* future events in England because in

that country every aspect of social development is so plain and clear-cut [italics added]. The revolution *must* come [italics in original]. The workers are moving from minor guerilla skirmishes to demonstrations and armed conflict of a more serious nature." *The Condition of the Working Class in England,* translated and edited by W. O. Henderson and W. H. Chaloner (Stanford, Calif.: Stanford University Press, 1968), pp. 334-35, 336. Marx, himself, said in 1866, "The trade unions have hitherto paid too much attention to the immediate disputes with Capital. They have not yet fully understood their mission against the existing system of production. They have kept aloof from the general social and political movement." In M. Beer, *A History of British Socialism II* (London: 1929), page 219. Quoted by Edward Andrew, "Work and Freedom in Marcuse and Marx," *Canadian Journal of Political Science,* June 1970, p. 251. Also see Lenin, *Imperialism: The Highest Stage of Capitalism* (New York: International Publishers, 1935), pp. 95-96.

7. In his *Intimate Journals,* translated by Christopher Isherwood (Hollywood: Marcel Rodd, 1947), p. 41, quoted in César Graña, *Bohemian versus Bourgeois: French Society and the French Man of Letters in the Nineteenth Century* (New York: Basic Books, 1964), p. 121.

8. The original quotation is from Jean-Marc Coudray, *Mai 68: La brèche* (Paris: Fayard, 1968), quoted in Daniel Cohn-Bendit and Gabriel Cohn-Bendit, *Obsolete Communism: The Left-Wing Alternative,* translated by Arnold Pomerans (New York: McGraw-Hill, 1968), p. 107.

9. Sanche de Gramont, "The French Worker Wants to Join the Affluent Society, Not to Wreck It," *New York Times Magazine,* 16 June 1968, p. 62.

10. *New York Times,* 11 May 1970. For even stronger statements on the "honky" American people, see Slater and Reich in my chapter 7.

11. Based on Max Nomad, *Aspects of Revolt,* pp. 42-43.

12. In his *Oeuvres* (Paris: 1907), vol. 2, p. 311, quoted in Nomad, *Aspects of Revolt,* p. 143.

13. Herbert Marcuse, *An Essay on Liberation* (Boston: Beacon, 1969), p. 17.

14. Quoted in Bertram D. Wolfe, *Three Who Made a Revolution* (Boston: Beacon, 1962), p. 156. Wolfe adds, "Lenin's sole change was to strike out the word 'people' and substitute 'proletariat.'" *Ibid.* Mussolini once said, " 'You know I am no worshipper of the new god, the masses. At any rate, history proves that social changes have always been brought about by minorities, by

a mere handful of men.'" In his *Reden* (Leipzig: 1928), quoted in Mannheim, *Ideology and Utopia*, p. 134, note 25.

15. *Bolshevik*, no. 16 (August 1946), pp. 50-53, quoted in W. W. Kulski, "Classes in the Classless State," *Problems of Communism* 4, no. 1 (1955): 21. Quite a departure from Lenin's view of the status of workers after the revolution in which the national economy would be so organized that "technicians, managers, bookkeepers as well as *all* officials, should receive no higher wages than 'workingmen's wages,' all under the control and leadership of the armed proletariat." (Italics in original.) V. I. Lenin, *State and Revolution*, 2d ed. (New York: International Publishers, n. d.), p. 44.

16. Quoted in Rustin, "Blacks and the Union," p. 81.

17. Paul Goodman, *People or Personnel: Decentralizing and the Mixed System* (New York: Random House, 1965), p. 40. Goodman now calls himself a "neolithic conservative," whatever that is.

18. Lenin, *What Is to Be Done?* pp. 31-32. Lenin, Engels, all those revolutionaries who were disillusioned with the proletariat were perfectly justified in their lack of confidence in that class to make a revolution and to accept the essential sacrifices in the present for a possible post-revolutionary paradise in the future. A leading English labor official at the end of the nineteenth century spoke to this point: "We are evolving Socialism through co-operation and through the municipalities taking over gas and water and the control of the streets. We are going still further in the same direction, but for generations to come shall still have employers and workpeople, *and I am not going to starve myself or to ask workpeople to starve themselves, for the idea that their grandchildren might be well off . . . I want a little of that well-off business myself,* and if I cannot get it by any other system I am going to make the best of the system we have." (Italics added.) Election speech by James Mawdsley, secretary of the Spinners' Union, 28 June 1899. Quoted in P. F. Clarke, *Lancashire and the New Liberalism* (Cambridge: At the University Press, 1971), p. 43.

19. Theodore Draper said that the Cuban revolution "was essentially a middle class revolution which has been used to destroy the middle class." In "Castro's Cuba: A Revolution Betrayed," *New Leader*, 27 March 1961, section 2, p. 7.

20. "Nothing is more unpleasant than a virtuous person with a mean mind," Walter Bagehot once wrote. Someone who might have fitted this description, as far as workers at least were concerned, was Richard Cobden who "demanded freedom from the

working man [yet] opposed the reduction of the number of hours in the factories; and even if this opposition cannot be explained by his hostility to the intervention of parliament in the labour contract, it is impossible to reconcile his demand for freedom with his profound hatred and contempt for workmen's associations. Trade unions are for him based upon the principle of brutal tyranny and monopoly. With these implications, it is easy to see why the [Anti-Corn-Law] League utterly failed to convert the working man." Guido de Ruggiero, *The History of European Liberalism*, translated by R. G. Collingwood (Boston: Beacon, Beacon Paperback, 1959), p. 127. Bagehot, of course, admired Cobden and would have shuddered at anyone using his aphorism against the man he called "a sensitive agitator."

21. Marcuse, *Essay on Liberation*, p. 55.

22. In his "On the New Left," *Studies on the Left* 2, no. 1 (1961): 70-71, quoted in Lewis S. Feuer, *Marx and the Intellectuals: A Set of Post-Ideological Essays* (Garden City, N. Y.: Doubleday, Anchor Books, 1969), pp. 217-18.

23. C. Wright Mills, *Power, Politics and People: The Collected Essays*, edited and with an introduction by Irving Louis Horowitz (New York: Oxford University Press, 1963), p. 256. American intellectuals have for years enjoyed quoting President Eisenhower's scriptural injunction to "guard against the acquisition of unwarranted influence, whether sought or unsought, by the military-industrial complex." In the same farewell address is this injunction, long forgotten: "We must also be alert to the equal and opposite danger that public policy could itself become the captive of a scientific-technological elite."

24. For an example of this kind of ideological attack on American labor see Ronald Radosh, *American Labor and United States Foreign Policy* (New York: Random House, 1969).

25. "The AFL-CIO executive council, under George Meany's leadership, continues to make more sense on international problems than any other of our major institutions, civilian or governmental." *National Review Bulletin*, 8 July 1961. Same issue, three pages further on: "The AFL-CIO and ADA react orgasmatically to any attack on the free enterprise system." Also, see Arnold Beichman, "I say NR [National Review] is Anti-Labor," *National Review*, 7 October 1961, pp. 227-28.

26. J. K. Galbraith, *The New Industrial State* (Boston: Houghton Mifflin, 1967), p. 291.

27. Quoted in "Galbraith: An Ambassador's Journal," *Harvard Crimson*, 30 April 1971, p. 3.

28. Irving Kristol, "Writing About Trade Unions," *New York Times Book Review,* 1 February 1970, p. 6.

29. The postal strike highlighted an interesting split between the workers and the students: "At least half a dozen times yesterday afternoon a crowd of striking postal workers in front of the General Post Office was approached by young people who offered solidarity with the strikers in the name of the peace movement or student radical groups. And in each instance the uninvited supporters were screamed at, taunted and sent packing by the strikers who made it clear that they saw no connection between their labor dispute for more pay and any other struggle." *New York Times,* 24 March 1970. "Rank-and-File Opposition, UAW Moves Gingerly on Student Strike Aid," read a headline reporting on the United Auto Workers during the Fall 1970 strike. *Christian Science Monitor,* 14 October 1970.

30. Edward Banfield, in *Voting, Interest Groups and Parties,* edited by Bradbury Seasholes (Glenview, Ill.: Scott, Foresman, 1967), p. 130.

31. *Commentary* (August 1972), p. 82.

32. *American Political Science Review* 66, no. 1 (March 1972): 200.

33. Che Guevara, *Che Guevara Speaks,* edited by George Lavan (New York: Grove, Evergreen Black Cat, 1968), pp. 128-29.

34. V. I. Lenin, *Sochineniia,* 4th ed. (Moscow: 1951), vol. 31, p. 233, quoted in *Revolutionary Russia,* edited by Richard Pipes, Russian Research Center Studies, 55 (Cambridge, Mass.: Harvard University Press, 1968), p. 340.

35. Karl Marx and Friedrich Engels, *The Communist Manifesto* . . . edited by Samuel H. Beer (New York: Appleton-Century-Crofts, 1955), p. 22.

36. Interview in *TV Guide,* 27 September 1969, quoted in Edith Efron, *The News Twisters* (Los Angeles: Nash, 1971), p. 180.

37. Andrew Hacker, *The End of the American Era* (New York: Atheneum, 1970), pp. 6, 31.

Chapter Five

1. Robert Paul Wolff, review of *The Making of a Counter Culture* by Theodore Roszak, *New York Times Book Review,* 7 September 1969, p. 3.

2. Allan C. Brownfeld, "The Irrelevance of American Politics," *Yale Review* 60, no. 1 (1970): 1-13. The author argues that both parties have become hard to distinguish because they

"are addicted to the liberal formula which entered our political life at the time of the New Deal." *Ibid.*, p. 3. On this, see note 12.

3. Robert Paul Wolff, "Beyond Tolerance," in *Critique of Pure Tolerance* by R. P. Wolff, Barrington Moore, Jr., and Herbert Marcuse (Boston: Beacon, Beacon Paperbacks, 1969), p. 16. For another antithetical view of party nominating conventions see Herbert McClosky, "Are Political Conventions Undemocratic?" in *The Radical Left: The Abuse of Discontent,* edited with introductions by W. P. Gerberding and Duane E. Smith (Boston: Houghton Mifflin, 1970), pp. 296-311, and particularly his postscript on the 1968 Democratic Convention, *ibid.*, pp. 310-11.

4. "[The living system] is the way people actually behave, the way they actually think and feel, the way they actually deal with each other. It includes both the formal and the informal activities. The living system represents how things are, not merely how they are supposed to be." Chris Argyris, "Some Causes of Organizational Ineffectiveness within the Department of State," Department of State, Center for International Systems Research, *Occasional Paper*, no. 2 (Washington, D. C.: 1967), p. 2.

5. Anthony Sampson, *Anatomy of Britain* (London: Hodder and Stoughton, 1965), p. 624.

6. *New York Times*, 28 May 1971.

7. Wolff, "Beyond Tolerance," in *Critique of Pure Tolerance,* pp. 51-52.

8. Alpheus Thomas Mason, "Understanding the Warren Court: Judicial Self-Restraint and Judicial Duty," *Political Science Quarterly* 81 (1966): 560.

9. Gurr, "Psychological Factors in Civil Violence," p. 269.

10. Mills, *Power, Politics and People*, p. 227.

11. Richard Pipes, "Russia's Politics: Fatigue for the Elite," *Interplay* 4, no. 2 (1971): 5.

12. S. I. Benn and R. S. Peters, *Social Principles and the Democratic State* (London: Allen & Unwin, 1965), p. 347. However, some U. S. political scientists have argued that "the belief that the two American parties are identical in principle and doctrine has little foundation in fact. Examination of the opinions of Democratic and Republican leaders shows them to be distinct communities of co-believers who diverge sharply on many important issues." Herbert McClosky, Paul J. Hoffman, Rosemary O'Hara, "Issue Conflict and Consensus Among Party Leaders and Followers," *American Political Science Review* 54 (1960): 425-26.

13. Seymour Martin Lipset, *The First Nation: The United States in Historical and Comparative Perspectives* (New York: Basic Books, 1963), p. 44.

14. Richard Flacks, "Strategies for Radical Social Change," *Social Policy*, March/April 1971, p. 14.

15. Bunzel, *Anti-Politics in America* (New York: Random House, Vintage, 1966). At this writing, Dr. Bunzel is president of San Jose College in California.

16. James Madison, *The Federalist, Number X, New York, November 24, 1787*, in *The Federalist: A Commentary on the Constitution of the United States* . . . by Alexander Hamilton, John Jay, and James Madison, edited by John C. Hamilton (Philadelphia: Lippincott, 1904), p. 104.

17. Quoted in Richard Hofstadter, *The Idea of a Party System: The Rise of Legitimate Opposition in the United States, 1780-1840*. Jefferson Memorial Lectures (Berkeley: University of California Press, 1969), p. 2.

18. "Political parties in democratic systems are the outgrowth of the concentration of power in popularly elected bodies and the expansion of the electorate. They are the descendants of the uninstitutionalized factions of eighteenth-century politics." Brzezinski and Huntington, *Political Power: USA/USSR*, p. 236.

19. John Stuart Mill, "Coleridge," in his *Essays on Politics and Culture*, edited with an introduction by Gertrude Himmelfarb (Garden City, N. Y.: Doubleday, Anchor Books, 1963), p. 138.

20. "There is no subject in which we must proceed with more caution, than in [tracing the history of the arts and sciences]; lest we assign causes which never existed and reduce what is merely contingent to stable and universal principles." David Hume, "Of the Rise of the Arts and Sciences," in his *Philosophical Works*, edited by Thomas Hill and Thomas Hodge Grose (1882; reprint ed., Aalen, Sweden: Scientia, 1964), vol. 3, *Essays, Moral, Political and Literary*, vol. 1, p. 176.

21. Quoted in Duchêne, *Endless Crisis*, p. 143.

22. For example, Stanley Aronowitz, identified as an official of an experimental school in New York City has written, *"But political democracy is not enough*. The old Marxists and liberals overconcentrated on political power as the sole end. . . . Nor is industrial democracy the whole thing. . . . I am a libertarian communist, critical of Lenin's and Trotsky's positions, which overconcentrate on political power. My view is that socialism consists of direct democracy in all the institutions, direct popular control, people repossessing their own lives and thus removing alienation." (Italics in original.) *Social Policy*, November/December 1970, p. 12.

23. Thomas R. Dye and L. H. Zeigler, *The Irony of Democ-*

racy: An Uncommon Introduction to American Politics (Belmont, Calif.: Wadsworth, 1971), pp. 191-92.

24. Quoted in Isaac Deutscher, *The Prophet Armed: Trotsky: 1879-1921* (London: Oxford University Press, 1954), p. 518.

25. Merle Fainsod, *How Russia Is Ruled*, rev. ed., Russian Research Center Studies, 11 (Cambridge, Mass.: Harvard University Press, 1963), p. 60.

26. The pluralistic society of the United States is "a community in which group conflicts do not normally pose the threat of violent upheavals. The difficulty is that no one can quite say how the United States got that way, but two major considerations may be suggested. One is that the dividing lines of American society have become so numerous and intertangled, the pluralism has become so complex, that no clear-cut divisions of loyalty and interest can be found; the community has not been thoroughly unified but its division has been confused by a process of multiplication. . . . The second consideration is that individual loyalties have not only been scattered among a variety of groups, but that some of them—including in most cases the ultimately decisive loyalties—have been detached from smaller entities and lodged in the national community itself." Inis L. Claude, Jr., *Swords into Plowshares: The Problems and Progress of International Organization*, 3rd ed. rev. (New York: Random House, 1964), p. 400.

27. Grant McConnell, *Private Power and American Democracy* (New York: Knopf, 1966).

28. Mark Kesselman, review of *Private Power and American Democracy* by Grant McConnell, *Political Science Quarterly* 82 (1967): 318.

29. Quoted in Bertram Wolfe, "*Das Kapital* One Hundred Years Later," *Antioch Review* 26 (1966/67): 433. He also quotes Abba Lerner as saying, "Marxists must be described as people who concentrate on destroying what we have without considering what we will get in its place." *Ibid.*, p. 433-34.

Chapter Six

1. Alfred North Whitehead, *Adventures of Ideas* (Cambridge: At the University Press, 1935), p. 84.

2. Professor Fritz Stern once noted, "It is curious that intellectuals . . . often exaggerate the precariousness of intellectual life and of human creativity, protesting that it is doomed to extinction because of the rising masses, because of affluence or poverty, philistinism or creeping conformity. Is the intellectual enterprise

so feeble and intellect so vulnerable or corruptible?" "The Political Consequences of the Unpolitical German," *History,* no. 3 (New York: Meridian Books, 1960), p. 120.

3. "No modern nation has ever constructed a foreign policy that was acceptable to its intellectuals," Irving Kristol has written, in "American Intellectuals and Foreign Policy," *Foreign Affairs* 45 (1966/67): 596. Charles Frankel points out that "international affairs are peculiarly susceptible to galloping abstractions . . . intellectuals, more than most other groups, have the power to create, dignify, inflate, criticize, moderate or puncture these abstractions." In "The Scribblers and International Relations," *Foreign Affairs* 45 (1965/66):2.

4. Milovan Djilas, "Liberal Marx Is Not Democracy," *Freedom at Issue,* no. 7 (1971), p. 2.

5. N. S. Khrushchev, report on Soviet Communist party's draft program, *New York Times,* 1 August 1963.

6. John W. Aldridge, *In the Country of the Young* (New York: Harper's Magazine Press Book, 1969), p. 97.

7. Hacker, *End of the American Era,* pp. 4, 5, 6, 35.

8. Norman Podhoretz, "Roots of Conflict between Labor and Intellectuals," *New America,* 28 February 1971, p. 4.

9. Hacker, *End of the American Era,* p. 73.

10. The skeptic "robs us of certainty only by so defining it as to make certain that it cannot be obtained." A. J. Ayer, *The Problem of Knowledge* (Hammondsworth, Eng.: Penguin Books, 1962), p. 69.

11. Hacker, *End of the American Era,* pp. 76, 95, 113, 4, 9, 34.

12. Martin Kilson, "The Left and the Politics of the Dispossessed," review of *Racism and the Class Struggle: Further Pages from a Black Worker's Notebook* by James Boggs, *Modern Occasions,* Spring 1971, p. 444.

13. Hacker, *End of the American Era,* pp. 173, 180 in note.

14. *Christian Science Monitor,* 21 June 1971.

15. Samuel Butler, *Erewhon and Erewhon Revisited,* introduction by Lewis Mumford (New York: Modern Library, 1927), *Erewhon,* pp. 208-09.

Chapter Seven

1. Paul Jacobs, in "What's Happening to America," *Partisan Review* 34 (1967): 28. Dr. Marcuse has written that American society is "an explosion of insanity." He said, "the problem is

not: 'Who are the madmen?' It is the society that is insane." In panel discussion, "Democracy Has/Hasn't a Future," p. 102.

2. Harold Rosenberg, in "What's Happening to America," p. 45.

3. Nat Hentoff, "A Sanity Test for Self and Society," *Evergreen Review*, no. 60, November 1968, p. 53. He also wrote, "so long as so many of our institutions remain part of America's expanding war machine, the mass paranoia that is infecting our society may not only be 'normal,' but our only hope for survival." *Ibid.,* p. 51. Dr. H. Jack Geiger quotes a left therapist as saying that "paranoia is a state of heightened awareness. Most people are persecuted beyond their wildest delusions. Those who feel at ease are blind. Depression is the result of intolerable alienation and deprivation. . . . Schizophrenia is an experience saner than normality—in this mad world." *Social Policy*, August/September 1970, p. 12.

4. Susan Sontag, in "What's Happening to America," p. 53.

5. Norman Mailer, *The White Negro* (San Francisco: City Lights Books, 1959), p. 6. This was originally published in *Dissent* 4, no. 3 (1957): 276-93. More recently, Mailer said that "the center of America might be insane" and "I think American society has become progressively insane because it has become progressively a technological society." In "Democracy Has/Hasn't a Future," p. 101.

6. Theodore Roszak, "The Disease Called Politics," in *Seeds of Liberation*, edited by Paul Goodman (New York: Braziller, 1964), pp. 450, 453, 446.

7. *New York Times*, 17 April 1971.

8. Allen Ginsberg, "Renaissance or Die," in *Notes from the New Underground*, edited by Jesse Kornbluth (New York: Viking, 1968), pp. 54-55.

9. Paul Williams, "The Hippies Are Gone: Where Did They Go?" in *ibid.,* p. 270.

10. Jack Newfield, "This Movement: This New Left," *Defiance* 1 (1970): 17, 21. Insanity can also be regarded as "progressive." All one needs to do is insert a "halo" adjective before the noun and presto! you're sane. For example, Frantz Fanon describes a young independent nation as it sets out on its road to national development as "possessed by a kind of creative madness." *The Wretched of the Earth*, preface by Jean-Paul Sartre, translated by Constance Farrington (New York: Grove, Evergreen Black Cat, 1968), p. 95. Thus what is pure Dionysian frenzy in one context may become, paradoxically, purgative Apoleonian perfection in another; it all depends on the adjective.

11. Harry Schwartz, "The Ideologically Naked," a review of *Democracy Is Not Enough* by John Scott, *New Leader*, 25 April 1960, p. 26.

12. Quoted in an advertisement, *Atlantic*, June 1971, p. 8. The answer, *ibid.*, p. 87.

13. Quoted in Bunzel, *Anti-Politics in America*, p. 32.

14. It is not the first time, of course, that it has been noted that left, right and center frequently sound alike. For example, note the rhetoric in this right statement: " 'No one who has watched closely what has been going on in our public school system in America these past two decades can escape the feeling that something drastic—and rather terrible—has happened to it. What is more, it is difficult to believe that it has happened by accident, that there has not been a planned, slyly executed and almost successful attempt to deliberately under-educate our children in order to make them into an unquestioning mass who would follow meekly those who wish to turn [and here right and left part company] the American Republic into a socialist society.' " Rosalie M. Gordon, "What Happened to Our Schools?" in a pamphlet entitled *America's Future, Inc.* (New Rochelle, N. Y.: 1956), quoted in Bunzel, *Anti-Politics in America*, p. 74.

15. Alexander Campbell, "As Others See Us: Would You Want Your Daughter To Marry an American?" *Modern Occasions*, Spring 1971, p. 426.

16. Bell, "Sensibility in the 60's," *Commentary* 51, no. 6 (1971), p. 70. The novelists he has in mind include: Joseph Heller, J. P. Donleavy, Bruce Friedman, Thomas Pynchon, Terry Southern.

17. Slater, *Pursuit of Loneliness*, p. xii; Reich, *Greening of America*, p. 152; Paul Goodman, quoted in Rader, "On Revolutionary Violence," p. 194; Tom Seligson, "America's Future: The High School Revolutionaries," *Defiance* 1 (1970): 30. This kind of reportage has an historical parallel—the travel account written by Frances Milton Trollope, mother of Anthony Trollope, of her travels in the United States. Published in 1832 under the title *Domestic Manners of the Americans*, her travel journal was a best-seller in America—because of its scorching attack on the country and its inhabitants. It contained such generalizations as: " 'I never saw a people so totally divested of gaiety; there is no trace of this feeling from one end of the Union to the other.' " Quoted in Helen Reeder Cross, " 'I Hate America,' " *History Today*, March 1970, p. 170. One of Mrs. Trollope's fiercest critics wrote: "No one could have been worse adapted by nature of learning whether a nation was in a way to survive [than Frances Trollope]. . . . If a thing were ugly to her eyes, it ought to be ugly

to all eyes—and if ugly, it must be bad. What though a people had plenty to eat and clothes to wear, if they put their feet up on the tables and did not reverence their betters? The Americans were to her rough, uncouth, and vulgar—and she told them so. . . . She was neither clearsighted nor accurate; and in her attempts to describe morals, manners, and even facts, was unable to avoid the pitfalls of exaggeration." The author of that passage was Anthony Trollope and it is to be found in his *Autobiography*. Here, quoted in Cross, "'I Hate America,'" p. 173.

18. Ray L. Birdwhistell, "Kinesics: Inter- and Intra-Channel Communications Research," *Social Science Information* 7, no. 6 (1968): pp. 22-25. What is a matter of undoubted scientific fact is that anthropologists concede that it "is difficult, if not impossible, to validate the representativeness of their minute sample of observed or reported behavior of specific persons in the mass societies of the United States, India or China." See E. Adamson Hoebel, "Anthropological Perspectives on National Character," *Annals of the American Academy of Political and Social Science* 370 (1967): 5. Professor Don Martindale has written: "Despite repeated approaches, a sociology of national character remains to be developed." "Sociology of National Character," *ibid.*, p. 35. See also David Reisman, "Some Questions about the Study of American National Character in the Twentieth Century," *ibid.*, pp. 36-47.

19. The *Malleus Maleficarum* was a manual prepared in the fifteenth century to aid inquisitors of the church in finding witches.

20. Edmund Wilson, "Mencken's Democratic Man," in his *Shores of Light: A Literary Chronicle of the Twenties and Thirties* (New York: Farrar, Straus and Young, 1952), p. 294.

21. Cyril Connolly, *Enemies of Promise and Other Essays: An Autobiography of Ideas* (Garden City, N.Y.: Doubleday, Anchor Books, 1960), p. 41. Also see Michael Lerner, "Respectable Bigotry," *American Scholar* 38 (1968/69): 606-17.

22. Slater, *Pursuit of Loneliness*, pp. 147-48.

23. Louis I. Bredvold, "The Invention of the Ethical Calculus," in *The Seventeenth Century: Studies in the History of English Thought and Literature from Bacon to Pope* by Richard Foster Jones, and others (Stanford, Calif.: Stanford University Press, 1965), pp. 165-80.

24. F. R. Leavis, "'Hard Times': The World of Bentham," in *Dickens the Novelist* by F. R. Leavis and Q. D. Leavis (London: Chatto and Windus, 1970), pp. 187-212.

25. For this unconventional, yet most scholarly, view of Bentham, I am grateful to the pioneering researches of Professor

Gertrude Himmelfarb, particularly "The Haunted House of Jeremy Bentham," in her *Victorian Minds* (New York: Knopf, 1968), pp. 32-81, and "Bentham's Utopia: The National Charity Company," *Journal of British Studies* 10, no. 1 (1970): 80-125.

26. Norman Podhoretz, "Roots of Conflict between Labor and Intellectuals," *New America*, 28 February 1971, p. 4. Mr. Podhoretz represents sidewalk psychoanalysis on *my* side; I deplore psychoanalysis as a political tactic on any side.

27. Slater, *Pursuit of Loneliness*, p. 105. Were it not for the fact that this image and the rhetoric is so congruent with everything that goes before and after, I might have been tempted to regard this as a hyperbolic put-on.

28. Louis Kampf, "The Trouble with Literature," *Change in Higher Education* 2, no. 3 (1970): 30-34.

Chapter Eight

1. Quoted in Max Geltman, "Reflections on Violence," *National Review*, 21 May 1968, p. 514.

2. In "Notes and Comments," *New Yorker*, 10 April 1971, p. 29.

3. *Time*, 5 December 1969.

4. Rader, "On Revolutionary Violence," p. 203.

5. Francis Sayre, quoted in Herbert Marcuse, "Reflections on Calley," *New York Times*, 13 May 1971, Op–Ed Page. Marcuse, *ibid*. "To be sure," adds Dr. Marcuse, "in a 'metaphysical' sense, everyone who partakes of this society is indeed guilty—but the Calley case is not a case study in metaphysics." *Ibid*.

6. Eldridge Cleaver, "Requiem for Nonviolence," in *New Politics* by Burkhart and Kendrick, p. 73, reprinted from his *Post-Prison Writings and Speeches*, edited by Robert Scheer (New York: Random House, 1969).

7. Michael Halberstam, "Are *You* Guilty of Murdering Martin Luther King?" *New York Times Magazine*, 9 June 1968, pp. 54, 27.

8. Quoted in J. L. Talmon, *The Origins of Totalitarian Democracy* (New York: Praeger, 1960), p. 55.

9. Roger W. Smith, "The Political Meaning of Unconscious Guilt," in *Guilt: Man and Society*, edited by R. W. Smith (Garden City, N.Y.: Doubleday, Anchor Books, 1971), pp. 186, 191. Freud said there were two origins "of the sense of guilt: one arising from fear of an authority, and the other, later on, arising from fear of the super-ego. . . . the sense of guilt is an expression of

the conflict due to ambivalence, of the eternal struggle between Eros and the instinct of destruction or death." *Civilization and Its Discontents* (New York: Norton, 1962), pp. 74, 79.

10. Smith, "Political Meaning of Unconscious Guilt," pp. 191-92.

11. The apposite passage in Freud reads, "And as regards the therapeutic application of our knowledge, what would be the use of the most correct analysis of social neuroses, since no one possesses authority to impose such a therapy upon the group? But in spite of all these difficulties, we may expect that one day someone will venture to embark upon a pathology of cultural communities." I am not sure that here Freud meant actual coercion, although this might have been implied. *Civilization and Its Discontents*, p. 91.

12. Miguel de Jugo y Unamuno, *The Tragic Sense of Life in Men and in Peoples*, translated by J. E. Crawford Flitch, with an introductory essay by Salvador de Madariaga (London: Macmillan, 1926), pp. 291, 290.

13. Freud, *Civilization and Its Discontents*, p. 83.

14. Glenn Tinder, *The Crisis of Political Imagination* (New York: Scribner's, 1964), p. 74.

15. *Ibid.*, p. 215.

16. K. R. Popper, "Towards a Rationalist Theory of Tradition," *Rationalist Annual*, 1949, p. 40.

17. Hannah Arendt, "Organized Guilt and Universal Responsibility," in *Guilt: Man and Society*, pp. 266-67.

18. Hannah Arendt, "Reflections on Violence," *Journal of International Affairs* 23 (1969): 25.

19. Gresham M. Sykes and David Matza, "Techniques of Neutralization: A Theory of Delinquency," in *Guilt: Man and Society*, p. 144.

20. Quoted by J. Bowyer Bell, *The Myth of the Guerrilla* (New York: Knopf, 1971), p. 218.

21. Bennett W. Berger, "Strategies for Radical Social Change: Symposium," *Social Policy*, November/December 1970, p. 20. For a full-scale analysis on the bigotry found among "elite, liberal students . . . directed at the lower middle class," see Michael Lerner, "Respectable Bigotry," *American Scholar* 38 (1968/69): 606-17.

22. Reich, *Greening of America*, p. 297.

23. Alexander Heard, chancellor of Vanderbilt University, in a memorandum to President Nixon, 19 June 1971, mimeographed, pp. 14-15.

24. Robert A. Nisbet, "*An Epistle to the Americans:* The

Counter-Culture and Its Apologists: 1," *Commentary* 50, no. 6 (1970): 42. James Harrington once wrote about the "virtuosi" who were soon to found the Royal Society, that "they had an excellent facility of magnifying a Louse and diminishing a Commonwealth." *Political Writings: Representative Selections,* edited with an introduction by Charles Blitzer (New York: Liberal Arts, 1955), quoted in the introduction, p. xxviii.

25. K. R. Minogue, "On the Fashionable Idea of National Guilt," *American Scholar* 39 (1969/70): 212. Dr. Robert Waelder has shown how "moral aspirations can outreach themselves in the attitude of extreme liberalism to crime and the criminal." He argues that today a lawbreaker "appears to be fully exonerated as a victim of circumstance . . . and society is seen as responsible." Conditioning by circumstance is an impermissible plea for "judges, the government, the upper classes and even the victim [of the lawbreaker] himself." Arguing that such a position is logically untenable, Dr. Waelder writes, "If all behavior is determined to the exclusion of all culpability and responsibility, neither the lawmaker nor society can be called to account; neither exhortation nor condemnation makes any sense whatever. If, on the other hand, there is sense in attaching blame to society for its acts of commission, the same ought to apply to the lawbreaker, too. The fact that, in this modern view, the lawbreaker is treated on the assumption of complete determinism, while society is treated on the assumption of freedom of choice, merely reflects the will to condemn society." "Protest and Revolution against Western Societies," in *The Revolution in World Politics,* edited by Morton A. Kaplan (New York: Wiley, 1962), pp. 6-7.

26. Minogue, "Fashionable Idea of National Guilt," p. 213.

27. *Ibid.,* p. 217.

28. Marx, quoted in *ibid.*; Minogue, *ibid.*

29. George Orwell, "Politics and the English Language," in his *Inside the Whale and Other Essays* (Hammondsworth, Eng.: Penguin Books, 1962), pp. 157, 154.

30. "The rules of the game are that the left-wing student is an idealist with the right to express his idealism however he wishes and, because he is an idealist and young, he must not be treated as a responsible adult but rather must be granted amnesty." Arnold Beichman, "As the campus civil war goes on, will teacher be the new drop-out?" *New York Times Sunday Magazine,* 7 December 1969.

31. Robert Blake, "Anglo-Saxons worry too much about guilt," *Times* (London), 22 January 1972, p. 10.

Chapter Nine

1. "Text of President's Message to Congress on Federal Budget for Fiscal Year 1972," *New York Times*, 30 January 1971.
2. Quoted in Arthur M. Schlesinger, Jr., *A Thousand Days: John F. Kennedy in the White House* (Boston: Houghton Mifflin, 1965), p. 789. Harvey Wheeler, a Fellow of The Center for the Study of Democratic Institutions, says America is in a "pre-revolutionary situation." *New York Times*, 31 October 1971, p. 17.
3. Lyndon B. Johnson, *A Time for Action: A Selection from the Speeches and Writings, 1953–64*, introduction by Adlai E. Stevenson (New York: Washington Square, An Atheneum Book, 1964), pp. 118, 166.
4. Zbigniew Brzezinski, *Between Two Ages: America's Role in the Technetronic Era* (New York: Viking, 1970), p. 199. I do not mean to treat so cavalierly this brilliant analysis of America in the technetronic era. Professor Brzezinski is really suggesting that America is the arena of the "permanent revolution."
5. Herbert Marcuse, "Ethics and Revolution," in *Obligation and Dissent*, p. 260.
6. *Ibid.*, p. 261.
7. Sharply critical analyses of Dr. Marcuse are to be found in Cranston, "Herbert Marcuse," in *The New Left*, pp. 85-116; MacIntyre, *Marcuse;* and George Kateb, "The Political Thought of Herbert Marcuse," *Commentary* 49, no. 1 (1970): 48-63. Of course, there is nothing quite like reading Marcuse himself.
8. From the Editors, "After the Election," *Studies on the Left* 5, no. 1 (1965): 20.
9. William Blake, *Jerusalem*, in his *Complete Writings: With All the Variant Readings*, edited by Geoffrey Keynes (New York: Random House, 1957), p. 687.
10. Richard Huelsenbeck, "Reflections on Leaving America for Good," *American Scholar* 39 (1969/70): 85.
11. Vladimir Dedijer, "American Left Carries the Hope of the World: A Letter to Jean-Paul Sartre," *New York Times*, 4 February 1971, Op–Ed Page. From such compliments as Dedijer's, heaven save us. His recent volume, *The Battle Stalin Lost: Memoirs of Yugoslavia, 1948–1953* (New York: Viking, 1971) is written in a now passé dialect known as "Communese" which can be used to cover the derelictions of Stalinism ("distortions in Soviet society") while exposing in "this mad America the witchhunt conducted against communism." See my review, *Christian Science Monitor*, 11 February 1971.

12. Quoted in John L. Hess, "Frenchman Says True Radicals Must be Pro-American," *New York Times,* 13 April 1971. In his book, Revel writes, "America in 1971 is a mobile entity. It crosses all lines, not only financial, social and familial lines, but also cultural and moral lines. And, containing as it does a diversity of cultures and contradictory moral systems, it generates collective and individual crises with constantly increasing frequency. It is precisely these crises—which are numerous, permanent and always new—that comprise a modern revolution; that is, a revolution as it is realized in societies that are too complex, and insufficiently hierarchical and centralized, to be changed overnight by a single coup and in a single direction. Crisis has become America's second nature. But, in order to realize this fact, one must live it; and that is why the rest of the world perceives only dimly the true dynamism of present-day America." *Without Marx or Jesus* (New York: Doubleday, 1971), pp. 262-63.

13. Martin Buber, *Paths in Utopia,* translated by R. E. C. Hull, introduction by Ephraim Fischoff (Boston: Beacon, Beacon Paperback, 1966), p. 44.

14. Quoted in Hans Kelsen, *The Political Theory of Bolshevism: A Critical Analysis,* University of California Publications in Political Science, 2, no. 1 (Berkeley: University of California Press, 1948), p. 41.

15. The Editors, "After the Election," p. 20.

16. Michael Oakeshott, *Rationalism in Politics and Other Essays* (New York: Basic Books, 1962), p. 169.

17. *Guardian* (Manchester, Eng.), 24 October 1960, quoted in R. T. McKenzie, *British Political Parties: The Distribution of Power within the Conservative and Labour Parties,* 2d ed. (New York: Praeger, 1964), p. 622.

18. Arthur I. Waskow, "Patterns of American Protest," *New York Times,* 4 May 1971, Op-Ed Page.

19. Irving Howe, *On the Nature of Communism and Relations with Communists,* League for Industrial Democracy, Occasional Paper, Looking Forward, 5 (New York: League for Industrial Democracy, n.d. [1966]), p. 13.

20. Quoted in Simone de Beauvoir, *The Prime of Life,* translated by Peter Green (Cleveland: World, 1962).

21. For these estimates see Robert Conquest, *Great Terror,* Appendix A "Casualty Figures."

22. Jean-Paul Sartre, "Merleau-Ponty," in his *Situations,* translated by Benita Eisler (London: Hamish Hamilton, 1965), p. 266.

23. Quoted in Walter Goodman, "When Black Power Runs the New Left," *New York Times Magazine,* 24 September 1967, p.

125. Forman, formerly executive secretary of the Student Non-Violent Coordinating Committee, was addressing the National Conference for New Politics, Chicago, September 3, 1967. Walter Goodman's report of the convention was subtitled, "Yessir, Boss, Said the White Radicals," *ibid.*, p. 28. His report reminded me of a Jules Feiffer cartoon where for seven frames a bearded black berates a white in frightful language. In the eighth frame, the white, grinning foolishly but happily, pays the black some money and inquires if he can come back next week at the same time for more of the same.

24. Quoted in Eugen Weber, *Varieties of Fascism: Doctrines of Revolution in the Twentieth Century* (Princeton, N. J.: Van Nostrand, Anvil Original, 1964), p. 36.

25. Quoted in Samuel Huntington, *Political Order in Changing Societies* (New Haven: Yale University Press, 1968), p. 359.

26. Marcuse, *Essay on Liberation*, pp. 65-66.

27. Johann Kaspar Schmidt (pseudonym: Max Stirner) in his *Einzigne und sein Eigentum* (Leipzig: Reclam, 1892), quoted in Leopold Labedz, "Students and Revolution," *Survey*, no. 68 (1968), p. 7. Che Guevara put it this way, "In the future, individualism ought to be the efficient utilization of the whole individual for the absolute benefit of a collectivity." *Venceremos!: The Speeches and Writings of Ernesto Che Guevara*, edited, annoted, and with an introduction by John Gerassi (New York: Macmillan, 1968), p. 115.

28. In his *Nashi Politicheskie Zadachi* (Geneva: 1940), p. 95, quoted in Deutscher, *Prophet Armed*, p. 91. Of course, when Trotsky became the prophet armed, he forgot about the Jacobins, arguing that even though the Bolsheviks were in the minority, they represented the proletariat of the future, for "in certain conditions the part is incomparably greater than the whole," as he expressed it in his *History of the Russian Revolution*. Maxim Gorky, who had known Lenin for many years, wrote from St. Petersburg during the revolution that Lenin "has no pity for the mass of people . . . Lenin does not know the people. . . . The working classes are to Lenin what minerals are to the metallurgist." (Ellipses in original.) Quoted in Lewis S. Feuer, "Lenin's Fantasy: The Interpretation of a Russian Revolutionary Dream," *Encounter*, December 1970, p. 34.

29. George Paloczi-Horvath, "A Meeting of Two Young Men," in *Bitter Harvest: The Intellectual Revolt behind the Iron Curtain*, edited by Edmund Stillman, introduction by François Bondy (London: Thames and Hudson, 1959), p. 92. This passage reminds me of Montaigne's description of Alexander, tyrant of Pherae

who "could not bear to hear tragedies played in the theatre for fear that his citizens might see him groaning at the misfortunes of Hecuba and Andromache, he who, without pity, had so many people cruelly murdered every day." *The Complete Works of Montaigne,* ed. Donald M. Frame (Stanford, Calif.: Stanford University Press, 1957), pp. 523-24.

30. Tibor Szamuely, "The Quest for Soviet Man: Russia Fifty Years After—I," *Spectator,* 20 October 1967, p. 455.

31. Richard B. Morris, *The American Revolution Reconsidered* (New York: Harper & Row, 1967), p. 48. C. Wright Mills put it somewhat differently: " 'Marx was basically wrong. Look, it is obvious that the proletariat doesn't make history, no matter how much you want to stretch historical facts. At certain points in history it has been more active than at others, but clearly an elite has made and still makes world history. . . . Now in all the overdeveloped societies, with the intricate control of the mass media, it is up to intellectuals who have a conscience to do what must be done.' " Quoted in Sam Landau, "C. Wright Mills: The Last Six Months," *Ramparts,* August 1965, p. 48.

32. Morris, *American Revolution Reconsidered,* pp. 49, 54, 84, 85.

33. Lenin knew little about government, administration and organization, as he made quite clear when he wrote, before he seized power, "With such *economic* prerequisites it is perfectly possible, immediately, within twenty-four hours after the overthrow of the capitalists and the bureaucrats, to replace them, in the control of production and distribution, in the business of *control* of labour and products, by the armed workers, by the whole people in arms. . . . The whole of society will have become one office and one factory, with equal work and equal pay. . . . The more complete the democracy, the nearer the moment when it begins to be unnecessary. The more democratic the 'state' consisting of armed workers, which is 'no longer a state in the proper sense of the word,' the more rapidly does *every* state begin to wither away." (Italics in original.) Lenin, *State and Revolution,* pp. 83-84. If Lenin knew little about administration and government, he did know what was important—politics and power. As Archilochus is quoted: " 'The fox knows many things but the hedgehog knows one big thing.' " In Isaiah Berlin, *The Hedgehog and the Fox: An Essay on Tolstoy's View of History* (London: Weidenfeld and Nicolson, 1967), p. 1.

34. Nathan Glazer, "On Being Deradicalized," *Commentary* 50, no. 4 (1970): 75.

35. Michael Harrington, *Toward a Democratic Left* (New York: Macmillan, 1968). Harrington tells an anecdote of the 1930s. One day the phone rang in a union office and a woman's voice announced, "This is Mary Jones at the drugstore. We've just kicked the manager out and started a sit-down strike. What do we do next?"

36. Daniel Bell, "How Do We Climb Down from Pisgah?", review of *Toward a Democratic Left: A Radical Program for a New Majority*, by Michael Harrington, *New Leader*, 20 May 1968, p. 22. Leon Trotsky, a little earlier than Professor Bell, was also aware of "the fatal discrepancy between ideology and practical living social reality. The intelligentsia, however, has been taking this glaring evidence of its own poverty of thought as justification of its unabashed haughtiness. . . . In fact, the intelligentsia substituted itself for political parties, classes and the people themselves. It has lived through entire cultural epochs—for the sake of the people. It has marked out the roads of development—again for the people. Where has all this titanic work taken place? In the imagination of this same intelligentsia." "Concerning the Intelligentsia," *Partisan Review* 35 (1968): 591. (First published, 1912, in *Kievskaya Mysl*.)

37. "The Laws behind Disorders: Hunting the Spectre That Is Haunting the World," review article of (among other titles) *Marx und die Revolution* by Ernest Bloch and others, *Times Literary Supplement*, 19 March 1971, p. 309.

38. Philip Rahv, "What and Where Is the New Left," *Modern Occasions*, Winter 1971, pp. 159-60. There are, of course, other possible requirements for revolution. Professor J. L. Talmon points out that social revolution "has not proved feasible without war." The French Revolution "established its hold in conditions of war; the Russian Revolution was a by-product of war; the Chinese Revolution was the result of war. The 1848 Revolutions, on the other hand, failed because there was no war." *Utopianism and Politics*, p. 18. Eric Hoffer says, "We are usually told that revolutions are set in motion to realize radical changes. Actually it is drastic change which sets the stage for revolution. The revolutionary mood and temper are generated by the irritations, difficulties, hungers, and frustrations inherent in the realization of drastic change." *The Ordeal of Change* (New York: Harper & Row, 1963), p. 4.

39. In his "Radical Styles," *Partisan Review* 36 (1969): 397, quoted in Saul Bellow, "Culture Now: Some Animadversions, Some Laughs," *Modern Occasions*, Winter 1971, p. 166. "*Partisan Review*, once the champion of Kafka, Joyce and Eliot—indeed

the very locus of American intellectual values—was [now] publishing articles on the glories of Camp and underground films, along with encomiums by its own editors on the artistic power of the Beatles," wrote Robert Brustein, dean of the Yale School of Drama. "If an Artist Wants to Be Serious and Respected *and* Rich, Famous and Popular, He Is Suffering from Cultural Schizophrenia," *New York Times Magazine,* 26 September 1971, p. 85.

40. "How Not to Start a Revolution," a review of *Armed Insurrection* by A. Neuberg (pseudonym), *Times Literary Supplement,* 29 January 1971, p. 115. This is the first English translation (London: New Left Books, 1970) of the revolutionary handbook, *Der bewaffnete Aufstand,* first published in 1928 by the Comintern.

41. Robert S. Short, "The Politics of Surrealism, 1920-36," *Journal of Contemporary History* 1, no. 2 (1966): 3.

42. *Ibid.,* pp. 6, 7, 8. The entire article is worth reading because it prefigures some of the moral problems of the radical and the artist in the Age of Revolutionism.

43. Arthur P. Mendel, "The Rise and Fall of 'Scientific Socialism,'" *Foreign Affairs* 45 (1966/67): 107, 108. He quotes Joseph Schumpeter's definition of Marx's scientific socialism as "'preaching in the garb of analysis.'" *Ibid.,* p. 98.

44. *Ibid.,* p. 110. A third condition could be the exposé of Stalinism by official Soviet spokesmen. If scientific socialism could not only produce but allow such a tyrant to rule for so long as a personal dictator what happens to the "scientific" attribute? In this connection, see interview with Palmiro Togliatti in *Nuovi Argomenti,* reprinted in Columbia University, Russian Institute, *Anti-Stalin Campaign and International Communism* (New York: Columbia University Press, 1956), pp. 120-21.

45. Mendel, "'Scientific Socialism,'" p. 98.

46. Quoted in *ibid.,* p. 99. Professor Mendel's excellent work on the early Russian Marxists and their changing theories is titled *Dilemmas of Progress in Tsarist Russia: Legal Marxism and Legal Populism,* Russian Research Center Studies, 43 (Cambridge, Mass.: Harvard University Press, 1961).

47. Mendel, "'Scientific Socialism,'" p. 102; Bulgakov quoted in *ibid.,* p. 102, note 9; Berdiaev quoted in *ibid.,* p. 102.

48. Talmon, *Utopianism and Politics,* p. 8.

49. William James, "Faith and the Right to Believe," in his *Writings,* comprehensive ed., edited, with an introduction, by John J. McDermott (New York: Random House, 1968), p. 737. Cf. Miguel de Unamuno: "The maddest dreams of the fancy have some ground of reason, and who knows if everything that the

imagination of man can conceive either has not already happened, or is not now happening or will not happen some time, in some world or another? The possible combinations are perhaps infinite. It only remains to know whether all that is imaginable is possible." *Tragic Sense of Life,* p. 143.

50. Adam Ulam quotes a member of the Soviet Presidium, as reported in an official Soviet publication in 1965, following Khrushchev's ouster: " 'We heard the slogan [that we must] catch up and overcome in the near future the United States in per-capita production of meat and milk. We heard slogans about fulfilling the Seven-Year Plan in three or four years, [slogans] that we live well now and tomorrow we shall live better. But what did we have in fact?—Bread lines!' " *Plenum of the Central Committee of the CPSU, March 24-26, 1965* (Moscow: 1965), p. 36, quoted in Ulam, *Expansion and Coexistence,* p. 686. The speaker is P. Ye. Shelest. Bread lines, this primitive form of rationing, the kind of rationing which has disappeared in Western democracies—half a century after the Revolution—bread lines! Imagine what the Soviet press would be saying if bread lines were reported in a Western capitalist democracy.

51. Hannah Arendt, "Thoughts on Politics and Revolution," *New York Review of Books,* 22 April 1971, p. 17.

52. Arendt, "Reflections on Violence," *Journal of International Affairs* 23, no. 1 (1969): 21-22. She is discussing Solzhenitsyn's novel, *The First Circle,* which she writes, "shows how attempts at a rational economic development were wrecked by Stalin's methods, and one hopes that this book will put to rest the myth that terror and the enormous losses in human lives were the price that had to be paid for rapid industrialization of the country." *Ibid.,* pp. 21-22, note 34. Schumpeter takes a somewhat different view, still analogous to that of Dr. Arendt: "For the really terrible point about the Stalin regime is not what it did to millions of victims but the fact *that it had to do it if it wished to survive.* In other words, those principles and that practice are inseparable." (Italics in original.) *Capitalism, Socialism, and Democracy,* 3d ed. (New York: Harper & Row, 1950), p. 362, note 10.

53. Goodman, *People or Personnel,* pp. 121-22.

54. Mikhail Bakunin, quoted in Mannheim, *Ideology and Utopia,* p. 218.

55. Sidney Webb and Beatrice Webb, *Decay of Capitalist Civilization,* 2d ed. (London: Fabian Society, and Allen and Unwin, 1923), p. 78.

56. In an editorial, *New Statesman*, 5 September 1936, quoted in Alfred Sherman, "The Days of the Left Book Club," *Survey*, no. 41 (1962), p. 81.

57. Quoted in Paul Willen, "Who 'Collaborated' with Russia?", *Antioch Review* 14 (1954): 264, 265. *Life* followed the Webbs' verdict about the secret police: "there is now, we think, little or no sign of general disapproval [of the GPU] among the four-fifths of the people who are manual workers in industry or agriculture either of its continued existence or of its vigorous activities." Sidney Webb and Beatrice Webb, *Soviet Communism: A New Civilization*, 3d ed. in one volume (London: Longmans, Green, 1947), p. 483. (This book was first published in 1935, following the Webbs' 1932 visit to Russia.) How in a dictatorship with a controlled press can anyone know anything about "four-fifths" of the people or "one-fifth"?

58. In *Europe, Russia and the Future* (London: Gollancz, 1941), quoted in Alfred Sherman "Days of the Left Book Club," p. 75. Following the brutal Soviet invasion of Hungary, Cole wrote that the risks of a "fascist" victory in Hungary in the fall of 1956 justified Soviet intervention because "despite [communism's] immoralism, it has shown itself also a great liberating force through the extension of education and social services to the masses previously excluded from them. It is, therefore, likely to become liberalized, even against its will." *New Statesman*, 20 April 1957, quoted in Sidney Hook, "Moral Judgments and Historical Ambiguity: A Socialist View," *Problems of Communism* 6, no. 4 (1957): 48.

59. In *Peace and Friendship*, proceedings of the Second National Congress of Peace and Friendship with the USSR, 1937, p. 150, quoted in Sherman, "Days of the Left Book Club," p. 78.

60. In an unsigned editorial, *Les Temps Modernes*, January 1950, quoted in Jelenski, "Literature of Disenchantment," p. 117. As Romain Rolland once said, " 'Give an intellectual any ideal and any evil passion and he will always succeed in harmonizing the twain.' " *Above the Battle*, translated by C. K. Ogden (Chicago: Open Court Publishing Co., 1916), p. 162, quoted in Lewis S. Feuer, "The Political Linguistics of the 'Intellectual': 1898-1918," *Survey*, no. 78 (1971), p. 117.

61. In his speech at the Soviet Friendship Rally in Madison Square Garden 8 November 1942, quoted in Dwight Macdonald, *Henry Wallace: The Man and the Myth* (New York: Vanguard, 1948), p. 101.

62. *Ibid.*, p. 102.

63. I have consciously omitted inane statements made by American liberals. Anybody, however, who is interested can refer to Frank A. Warren III, *Liberals and Communism: The "Red Decade" Revisited* (Bloomington, Ind.: Indiana University Press, 1966), and Eugene Lyons, *The Red Decade: The Stalinist Penetration of America* (Indianapolis: Bobbs-Merrill, 1941).

64. Heilbroner, "Counterrevolutionary America," pp. 31, 32. Since I will quote extensively from the article in this chapter, I am dispensing with further footnotes, but subsequent citations can be found, pp. 32-34. That time has not altered Heilbroner's views can be seen as, in 1971, he wrote that he had no doubt at all that he was correct "in believing the efforts of Castro and Mao heroic, whether successful or not." In a review of *Politics and the Stages of Growth* by W. W. Rostow, *New York Times Book Review*, 1 August 1971, p. 20. Professor Richard L. Walker, director of the Institute for International Studies at the University of South Carolina, estimates that from 1949 to 1971, the Chinese communist regime had caused the deaths of more than 32 million Chinese. (This includes the "political liquidation" campaigns and deaths in forced labor camps and frontier territorial development.) Professor Walker credits the Chinese leaders with achieving remarkable progress but he argues that "those who wish to rationalize public assassination, purges of classes and groups or slave labor as a necessary expedient for China's progress are resorting to the same logic which justified a Hitler and his methods for dealing with economic depression in the Third Reich." U. S. Congress, Senate Committee on the Judiciary, Subcommittee to Investigate the Administration of the Internal Security Act and Other Internal Security Laws, *The Human Cost of Communism in China*, by Richard L. Walker, 92d Cong., 1st Sess., 1971, committee print, p. iv, table, "Casualties to Communism in China," 16, xi. Dr. Walker's statistics of the communist death toll were cited by *Time* (23 August 1971) as "classic examples of the unverifiable statistic." For a recent critique of the uban revolution ("an almost unmitigated economic disaster" and "the wreckage of the early years of the regime set back Cuba's economic development for years"), see Lowry Nelson, *Cuba: The Measure of a Revolution* (Minneapolis: University of Minnesota Press, 1972).

65. Harry Schwartz, *Russia's Soviet Economy*, 2d ed. (New York: Prentice-Hall, 1954), pp. 63, 64. Also, see Fainsod, *How Russia Is Ruled*, pp. 20-30, for more on Russian industrial development under Tsarism.

66. Tibor Szamuely, "The Impact on the Outside World: Russia Fifty Years After—3," *Spectator*, 3 November 1967, p. 528.

67. In 1912, 1913 and 1914, well over two thousand strikes occurred each year. The annual number of strikers approximated one million. Schwartz, *Russia's Soviet Economy*, p. 68.

68. Peter F. Drucker, "The Unfashionable Kierkegaard," in his *Men, Ideas & Politics: Essays* (New York: Harper & Row, 1971), p. 60. No doubt this is the kind of sentiment Kierkegaard might have been reprobating: "All production is appropriation of nature by the individual within and through a definite form of society. . . . Man is in the most literal sense of the word a *zoon politikon*, not only a social animal, but an animal which can develop into an individual *only in society*. Production by isolated individuals outside of society . . . is as great an absurdity as the idea of the development of language without individuals living together and talking to one another." (Italics added.) Karl Marx, *A Contribution to the Critique of Political Economy*, translated from the 2d German ed. by N. I. Stone, with an appendix containing Marx's introduction to the *Critique* recently published among his posthumous papers (Chicago: Kerr, 1904), introduction, pp. 273, 268.

69. Barrington Moore, Jr., "Tolerance and the Scientific Outlook," in *Critique of Pure Tolerance*, p. 76.

70. Sidney Hook, "The Human Costs of Revolution," *Survey*, no. 66 (1968), pp. 135, 134.

71. Szamuely, "Quest for Soviet Man," p. 454. Professor Jerome M. Gilison has argued, "use of the Soviet press is a standard technique of Sovietology, but it is hardly to be considered a source of accurate information on conditions in Soviet society. . . . Of course, if a theme is repeated frequently [in the Soviet press], one may justifiably suppose that the problem is relatively widespread, but from such a technique one never derives more than a *supposition*." (Italics in original.) In a review of *The New Class Divided: Russian Science and Technology versus Communism* by Albert Parry, *American Political Science Review* 61 (1967): 538.

72. A sense of *déjà vu* overwhelmed me as I read Dr. Ronning's paragraph that "by 1966 many influential Chinese, including bureaucrats, university professors, party cadres, and even army officers led by Liu Shao-chi, yielded to the temptation to revert to the old Chinese tradition which would have put in power a new elite class." *New York Times*, 7 June 1971. It was like rereading those fulsome explanations by pro-Soviet Western paranymphs defending Stalin's purge trials in the 1930s. Shouldn't Dr. Ronning, after all we've learned about totalitarian justice from the

communists themselves, offer some evidence, if any exists, for his allegations? Were there even any trials? Or read this kindly analysis by Dr. Ronning about a more on-the-spot version of Heilbroner's "reaching and rallying" concept of Chinese communism: "Harmony is as important in modern time as it was in ancient China. Today, however, harmony is maintained by all the people of China working together in close cooperation for the benefit of all. To keep in touch with the people, intellectuals spend part-time in doing manual labor, which was most undignified to the scholars of the past." *New York Times*, 11 July 1971. I suppose forcing intellectuals to parade around the streets wearing dunce caps and self-abasing placards comes under the old Chinese concept which Dr. Ronning quotes so happily as characterizing today's China: *"T'ien hsia i chia* [under Heaven one family]." It never fails to astonish that one is expected to have a skeptical attitude about democracy as nothing more than a "lesser evil" but a similar skeptical attitude about communism is frequently regarded as "red-baiting," "Cold War propaganda," or being "anti-historical." This double standard and tolerance of intolerance recalls a letter Proudhon wrote Marx: " 'Let us not fall into the contradiction of your countryman Martin Luther who, after having overthrown the catholic theology, immediately set about founding a protestant theology of his own amid a great clamor of excommunications and anathemas. . . . Because we stand in the van of a new movement let us not make ourselves the protagonists of a new religion, even if it be a religion of logic, a religion of reason.' " In a letter, 17 May 1846, quoted in Buber, *Paths in Utopia*, p. 12.

73. Selwyn Lloyd, "South Africa: Time for Reappraisal," *South African Scope*, March/April 1971, p. 10; George W. Shepherd, "The New South Africa," *Worldview*, June 1971, pp. 9-12.

74. Arnold Beichman, "South Africa: Future Tense," *Columbia University Forum*, Fall 1965, pp. 29-33.

75. Djilas, *New Class*, pp. 39, 60, 63, 45.

76. Benjamin A. Bentum, in a speech at the International Labor Conference, 50th, Geneva, 14 June 1966, in *Trade Unions in Chains* (Accra: 1966), p. 20.

77. *Daily Graphic* (Accra), 26 June 1966, p. 5.

78. C. E. Black, *The Dynamics of Modernization: A Study in Comparative History* (New York: Harper & Row, 1966), p. 27.

79. Does Heilbroner's view of "democracy" differ very much from that of the old South's John C. Calhoun? "It is a great and dangerous error to suppose that all people are equally entitled to liberty. It is a reward to be earned, not a blessing to be gra-

tuitously lavished on all alike;—a reward reserved for the intelligent, the patriotic, the virtuous and deserving;—and not a boon to be bestowed on a people too ignorant, degraded and vicious, to be capable either of appreciating or enjoying it. . . . The progress of a people rising from a lower to a higher point in the scale of liberty, is necessarily slow;—and by attempting to precipitate it, we either retard, or permanently defeat it." (Ellipsis in quote.) In "A Disquisition on Government," in his *Works* (New York: Appleton, 1851-56), vol. I, pp. 1, 2, 4, quoted in Carl L. Becker, *The Declaration of Independence: A Study in the History of Political Ideas* (New York: Knopf, 1964), p. 250.

80. Hirschman, *Journeys toward Progress*, pp. 254-55. An excellent example of what I called in my introduction, "one-way adjectives," is to be found in an amusing paradigm called "The Semantics of Problem-Solving." Using four cells, Professor Hirschman separates derogatory from laudatory terms, horizontally, and remedial from ideological approaches, vertically. *Ibid.*, p. 248.

81. James H. Meisel, *The Myth of the Ruling Class: Gaetano Mosca and the "Elite,"* with the first English translation of the final version of *The Theory of the Ruling Class* (Ann Arbor: University of Michigan Press, 1958), pp. 5, 9. The Sorelian myth also applies to the view "that socialism is especially meritorious in promoting economic development in [less advanced] countries." Professor Abram Bergson, whom I'm quoting, has sought to demonstrate by a comparison of the Soviet Bloc countries (COMECON) and OECD countries of the West that "socialism . . . does no more than hold its own with capitalism. Possibly capitalism is the superior system." In "Development under Two Systems: Comparative Productivity Growth since 1950," *World Politics* 23 (1971): 580, 593.

82. Kenneth A. Megill, *The New Democratic Theory* (New York: Free Press, 1970), pp. 136, 137. A similar impression in language is to be found in Raymond Williams, who writes, "A society in which revolution is necessary is a society in which the incorporation of all its people, *as whole human beings,* is in practice impossible without a change in its fundamental form of relationships. The many kinds of partial 'incorporation'—as voters, as employees, or as persons entitled to education, legal protection, social services and so on—are real human gains, but do not in themselves amount to that full membership which is the end of classes. . . . Revolution remains necessary . . . not only because some men desire it, but because there can be no acceptable human order while the full humanity of any class of men is

in practice denied." (Italics in original.) *Modern Tragedy* (Stanford, Calif.: Stanford University Press, 1966), pp. 76-77.

What is a "whole human being"? Where is such a creature to be found? Is Professor Williams a "whole human being"? There are no answers, except more words: "The reality of full membership is the capacity to direct a particular society, by active mutual responsibility and co-operation, on a basis of full social equality. And while this is the purpose of revolution, it remains necessary in all societies in which there are, for example, subordinate racial groups, landless landworkers, hired hands, the unemployed, and suppressed or discriminate minorities of any kind." *Modern Tragedy*, p. 77.

83. Megill, *New Democratic Theory*, pp. 156-58, 160-63.

84. Régis Debray, *Revolution in the Revolution?: Armed Struggle and Political Struggle in Latin America*, translated from the author's French and Spanish by Bobbye Ortiz (New York: Monthly Review Press, 1967), pp. 36-39, 70-71, 106; Castro quoted, pp. 69, 98.

85. Barrington Moore, Jr., "Revolution in America?" *New York Review of Books*, 30 January 1969, p. 8.

86. Herbert Marcuse, *Counter-Revolution and Revolt* (Boston: Beacon, 1972), p. 134.

87. In a brilliant commentary after the Angela Davis acquittal, Bernard Levin wrote: "Those who thought, and stridently declared, that the conviction of Miss Davis was certain can hardly be expected, being who and what they mostly are, to admit now that their argument was baseless and had nothing to do with justice but everything to do with politics. What they can, I think, be asked to do is to estimate the chances of a similar acquittal for those accused of 'political' offenses in the countries which are governed by regimes professing the same philosophy as Miss Davis. More; they can be asked to say whether it is often the case that, when a Russian dissident is tried, Russian newspapers and television are permitted to report extensively and continually the arguments of the defense, whether protest meetings, marches and petitions are allowed there, and whether the defendants can freely choose their counsel, cross-examine the prosecution witnesses and call what evidence they please to their defense.

"It is no use saying to me that the standards of Russian justice are irrelevant to a consideration of the American kind. In the first place, those who declare that America is a tyranny ought to be continually reminded what a tyranny actually is, with particular examples, and in the second place it is the standards of Russian justice that Miss Davis, who proudly proclaims herself a Communist, wishes to see prevail in America, and indeed throughout the world. There would be no acquittals for anyone put on trial for such offenses in an America run by her and her kind, whether the evidence justified a conviction or not, and those who are even now brainlessly echoing her claim that she was fighting for, or even that she desires, anything recognizable as freedom for Americans of any color are, whether they realize it or not . . . echoing a lie." *Times* (London), 6 June 1972.

88. "Those who are discouraged by the slow pace of racial integration in the United States may gain solace from the realization that this is the first time in world history that peoples of such disparate backgrounds have sought to solve the problem of living together in an advanced society." Black, *Dynamics of Modernization*, p. 87.

89. Bondy, "Sartre," in *New Left*, p. 53.

Reply to James A. Wechsler

1. Arnold Beichman, "As the Cookie Crumbles in Vietnam," *Columbia University Forum*, Spring 1965, pp. 5-10. Reprinted in *The Dirty Wars: Guerrilla Actions and Other Forms of Unconventional Warfare* (New York: Delacorte Press, 1968), pp. 271-79. I wrote, *inter alia* that "in Vietnam we are talking about a kind of war that no fleets armed with no-matter-how-many Polaris systems and Minuteman can win."

2. Simon Karlinsky, "Dostoevsky as Rorschach Test," *New York Times Book Review*, 13 June 1971, p. 23.

3. Karl Mannheim, *Ideology and Utopia: An Introduction to the Sociology of Knowledge*, translated from the German by Louis Wirth and Edward Shils (New York: Harcourt, Brace & World, A Harvest Book, 1936), p. 61.

4. L. N. Tolstoy, "The Death of Iván Ilyitch," in his *Iván Ilyitch, and Other Stories*, translated by Nathan Haskell Dole (1887; reprint ed., New York: 1960), p. 121.

5. "A.B.A. Unit of Young Lawyers Sees Threats to U.S. Liberties," *New York Times*, 9 July 1971.

6. Golo Mann, "The Intellectuals: Germany," *Encounter*, June 1955, p. 47.

7. Dotson Rader, review of *Steal This Book*, by Abbie Hoffman, *New York Times Book Review*, 18 July 1971, p. 19. Cheering crime in the name of revolution is nothing new. The *New York Review* on its cover, 24 August 1967, published a diagram showing how to make a Molotov cocktail as illustration of articles

by Andrew Kopkind and Tom Hayden. The opening sentences of the issue were: "The Movement is dead; the Revolution is unborn. The streets are bloody and ablaze." In the 1880s, John Most, the German-American anarchist, published a pamphlet, *Revolutionäire Kriegewissenschaft* (Revolutionary War Science). It was a handbook on explosives with hints on how to start fires safely. Max Nomad, *Aspects of Revolt* (New York: Bookman Associates, 1959), p. 213.

8. This question of private property has intrigued even Arthur Schlesinger. For example, some time ago in a discussion, Professor Marcuse asked: "Do you consider the forcible occupation of buildings and the invasion of private property a part of the democratic process?" To which Professor Schlesinger replied: "Yes." In a panel discussion, "Democracy Has/Hasn't a Future . . . a Present," *New York Times Magazine*, 26 May 1968, p. 101. Affirm now, explain later.

9. After the pseudo-revolutionary uprisings in France in May 1968, De Gaulle called for new elections for the National Assembly. The results in June 1968 gave the Gaullist forces an absolute majority in the new parliament, and the left, in comparison with 1967, had been routed. As Anthony Hartley writes: " 'the May events' looked backwards toward historical episodes and nineteenth century ideologies which, while they called forth powerful echoes in the French mind, were hardly relevant to an advanced industrial society. To replace the rigid centralized structure of the French state by a kind of anarcho-syndicalism was no solution." *Gaullism: The Rise and Fall of a Political Movement* (New York: Outerbridge and Dienstfrey, 1971), pp. 286-87. For a brilliant explanation of the 1972 election and the Nixon landslide, see Seymour Martin Lipset and Earl Raab, "McGovern's Little Mistake; From Party to Faction," *Commentary*, 54: 7 (January 1973).

10. Edmund Burke, *Reflections on the Revolution in France*, edited by F. G. Selby (London: Macmillan, 1906), p. 71.

11. Quoted in *Time*, 22 February 1971, pp. 18-19.

12. J. L. Talmon, *Utopianism and Politics*, with a foreword by T. E. Utley (London: Conservative Political Centre, 1957), p. 21.

13. Alan Paton, the South African novelist and anti-apartheid leader, in a speech before the Harvard alumni, 17 June 1971, mimeographed, p. 7.

14. In a review of *End of the American Era* by Andrew Hacker, *Times Literary Supplement*, 28 May 1971, p. 607.

15. Arnold Beichman, "The Unmanageable Issue behind 'Managed News,'" *Columbia University Forum*, Spring 1963, pp. 4-10.

Epilogue

1. Friedrich Nietzsche, *Werke* (Leipzig: Naumann, 1897-1904), Bd. 8, *Der Antichrist,* sections 55, 54, 50, quoted in Walter Kaufmann, *Nietzsche: Philosopher, Psychologist, Antichrist,* 3rd ed. (Princeton, N.J.: Princeton University Press, 1958), pp. 354, 355, 356.

Selected Bibliography

I. Books

Aldridge, John W. *In the Country of the Young.* New York: Harper's Magazine Press Book, 1969.

Bell, J. Bowyer. *The Myth of the Guerrilla: Revolutionary Theory and Malpractice.* New York: Knopf, 1971.

Black, C. E. *The Dynamics of Modernization: A Study in Comparative History.* New York: Harper & Row, 1966.

Bogdanor, Vernon, and Skidelsky, Robert. *The Age of Affluence, 1951–1964.* London: Macmillan, Papermac, 1970.

Brzezinski, Zbigniew. *Between Two Ages: America's Role in the Technetronic Era.* New York: Viking, 1970.

Brzezinski, Zbigniew, and Huntington, Samuel P. *Political Power: USA/USSR.* New York: Viking, 1968.

Bunzel, John. *Anti-Politics in America: Reflections on the Anti-Political Temper and Its Distortions of the Democratic Process.* New York: Knopf, 1967.

Burton, John Wear, ed. *Nonalignment.* Papers from . . . discussions held by the Friends Peace and International Relations Committee in London, 1963. London: Deutsch, 1966.

Cohn-Bendit, Daniel, and Cohn-Bendit, Gabriel. *Obsolete Communism: The Left-Wing Alternative.* Translated by Arnold Pomerans. New York: McGraw-Hill, 1968.

Connolly, Cyril. *Enemies of Promise and Other Essays: An Autobiography of Ideas.* Garden City, N.Y.: Doubleday, Anchor Books, 1960.

Debray, Régis. *Revolution in the Revolution? Armed Struggle and Political Struggle in Latin America.* Translated from the author's French and Spanish by Bobbye Ortiz. New York: Monthly Review Press, 1967.

Drucker, Peter F. "The Unfashionable Kierkegaard." In his *Men, Ideas & Politics: Essays.* New York: Harper & Row, 1971.

Duchêne, François. *The Endless Crisis: America in the Seventies.* A confrontation of the world's leading social scientists on the problems, impact and global role of the United States in the next decade. A seminar under the auspices of the International Association for Cultural Freedom. New York: Simon & Schuster, 1970.

Dye, Thomas R., and Zeigler, L. H. *The Irony of Democracy: An Uncommon Introduction to American Politics.* Belmont, Calif.: Wadsworth, 1971.

An End to Political Science: The Caucus Papers. Edited by Marvin Surkin and Alan Wolfe. New York: Basic Books, 1970.

Fainsod, Merle. *How Russia Is Ruled.* Rev. ed. Russian Research Center Studies, 11. Cambridge, Mass: Harvard University Press, 1963.

Feuer, Lewis S. *The Conflict of Generations: The Character and Significance of Student Movements.* New York: Basic Books, 1969.

———. *Marx and the Intellectuals: A Set of Post-Ideological Essays.* Garden City, N.Y.: Anchor Books, 1969.

Galbraith, J. K. *The New Industrial State.* Boston: Houghton Mifflin, 1967.

Goodman, Mitchell, ed. *The Movement towards a New America.* New York: Knopf, 1970.

Goodman, Paul. *People or Personnel: Decentralizing and the Mixed System.* New York: Random House, 1965.

Graham, Hugh D., and Gurr, Ted R. *Violence in America: Historical and Comparative Perspectives.* A Report to the National Commission on the Causes and Prevention of Violence, June 1969, prepared for . . . the President's Commission. New York: New American Library, A Signet Book, 1969.

Hacker, Andrew. *The End of the American Era.* New York: Atheneum, 1970.

Hartley, Anthony. *Gaullism: The Rise and Fall of a Political Movement.* New York: Outerbridge & Dienstfrey, 1971.

Hirschman, Albert O. *Journeys toward Progress: Studies of Economic Policy-Making in Latin America.* New York: Greenwood, 1968.

Hofstadter, Richard. *The Idea of a Party System: The Rise of Legitimate Opposition in the United States, 1780-1840.* Jefferson Memorial Lectures. Berkeley: University of California Press, 1969.

Hofstadter, Richard, and Wallace, Michael, eds. *American Violence: A Documentary History.* New York: Macmillan, 1967.

Huntington, Samuel P. *Political Order in Changing Societies.* New Haven: Yale University Press, 1968.

Kelsen, Hans. *The Political Theory of Bolshevism: A Critical Analysis.* University of California Publication in Political Science, 2, no. 1. Berkeley: University of California Press, 1948.

Lenin, V. I. *Imperialism: The Highest Stage of Capitalism.* A Popular Outline. Rev. Translation. New York: International Publishers, 1935.

Lippmann, Walter. *Public Opinion.* New York: Macmillan, 1960.

Lipset, Seymour Martin. *The First Nation: The United States in Historical and Comparative Perspectives.* New York: Basic Books, 1963.

―――. *Revolution and Counterrevolution: Change and Resistance in Social Structures.* New York: Basic Books, 1968.

McConnell, Grant. *Private Power and American Democracy.* New York: Knopf, 1966.

MacIntyre, Alasdair. *Marcuse.* London: Fontana/Collins, 1970.

Malcolm X. *The Autobiography of Malcolm X.* With the assistance of Alex Haley. New York: Grove Press, 1966.

Marcuse, Herbert. *An Essay on Liberation.* Boston: Beacon, 1969.

―――. *Five Lectures: Psychoanalysis, Politics, and Utopia.* Translations by Jeremy J. Shapiro and Shierry M. Weber. Boston: Beacon, 1970.

Megill, Kenneth A. *The New Democratic Theory.* New York: Free Press, 1970.

Mills, C. Wright. *Power, Politics and People: The Collected Essays.* Edited and with an introduction by Irving Louis Horowitz. New York: Oxford University Press, 1963.

Morris, Richard B. *The American Revolution Reconsidered.* New York: Harper & Row, 1967.

Nelson, Lowry. *Cuba: The Measure of a Revolution.* Minneapolis: University of Minnesota Press, 1972.

Neumann, Franz. *Behemoth: The Structure and Rise of National Socialism, 1933-1944.* New York: Octagon Books, 1963.

Nomad, Max. *Aspects of Revolt.* New York: Bookman Associates, 1959.

Oakeshott, Michael. *Rationalism in Politics and Other Essays.* New York: Basic Books, 1962.

Paloczi-Horvath, George. *Youth Up in Arms: A Political and Social World Survey, 1955-1970.* New York: McKay, 1971.

Reich, Charles A. *The Greening of America: How the Youth Revolution Is Trying To Make America Livable.* New York: Random House, 1970.

Revel, Jean-François. *Without Marx or Jesus*. New York: Doubleday, 1971.
Roszak, Theodore. *The Making of a Counter Culture: Reflections on the Technocratic Society and Its Youthful Opposition*. Garden City, N.Y.: Doubleday, 1969.
Schwartz, Harry. *Russia's Soviet Economy*, 2d ed. New York: Prentice-Hall, 1954.
Skinner, B. F. *Walden Two*. New York: Macmillan, Macmillan Paperbacks, 1966.
Slater, Philip. *The Pursuit of Loneliness: American Culture at the Breaking Point*. Boston: Beacon, 1970.
Stern, Fritz. *The Politics of Cultural Despair: A Study in the Rise of the Germanic Ideology*. Berkeley: University of California Press, 1961.
Talmon, J. L. *The Origins of Totalitarian Democracy*. New York: Praeger, 1960.
Thompson, Neville. *The Anti-Appeasers*. London: Oxford University Press, 1971.
Tinder, Glenn. *The Crisis of Political Imagination*. New York: Scribner's, 1964.
Touraine, Alain. *The May Movement: Revolt and Reform*. Translated by Leonard F. X. Mayhew. New York: Random House, 1971.
Trilling, Lionel. *Sincerity and Authenticity*. Cambridge: Harvard University Press, 1972.
Ulam, Adam B. *Expansion and Coexistence: A History of Soviet Foreign Policy, 1917-67*. New York: Praeger, 1968.
Weber, Eugen. *Varieties of Fascism*. New York: Van Nostrand, 1964.
Weber, Max. *From Max Weber: Essays in Sociology*. Translated and edited by H. H. Gerth and C. Wright Mills. 1958. Reprint. New York: Oxford University Press, 1970.

II. Articles in Books

Arendt, Hannah. "Organized Guilt and Universal Responsibility." In *Guilt: Man and Society*, edited by R. W. Smith. Garden City, N. Y.: Doubleday, Anchor Books, 1971.
Bondy, François. "Jean-Paul Sartre." In *The New Left: Six Critical Essays*, edited by Maurice Cranston. New York: The Library Press, 1971.
Bredvold, Louis L. "The Invention of the Ethical Calculus." In *The Seventeenth Century: Studies in the History of English*

Thought and Literature from Bacon to Pope by Richard Foster Jones, and others. Stanford, Calif.: Stanford University Press, 1965.

Cleaver, Eldridge. "Requiem for Nonviolence." In *The New Politics: Mood or Movement?* edited by James A. Burkhart and Frank J. Kendrick. Englewood Cliffs, N. J.: Prentice-Hall, 1971.

Cranston, Maurice. "Herbert Marcuse." In *The New Left: Six Critical Essays*, edited by Maurice Cranston. New York: The Library Press, 1971.

Feierabend, Ivo K., and Feierabend, Rosalind. "Aggressive Behaviour within Politics, 1948-1962: A Cross-National Study." In *Conflict and Violence in Latin American Politics*, edited by F. J. Moreno and B. Mitrani. New York: Crowell, 1971.

Ginsberg, Allen. "Renaissance or Die." In *Notes from the New Underground*, edited by Jesse Kornbluth. New York: Viking, 1968.

Himmelfarb, Gertrude. "The Haunted House of Jeremy Bentham." In her *Victorian Minds*. New York: Knopf, 1968.

Hook, Sidney. "The Fallacy of the Theory of Social Fascism." In *The Anxious Years*, edited by Louis Filler. New York: Putnam's, 1963.

Joll, James. "Anarchism." In *Anarchism Today*, edited by D. E. Apter and James Joll. London: Macmillan, 1971.

Kogan, N. "Fascism as a Political System." In *The Nature of Fascism*, edited by S. J. Woolf. Reading University Studies on Contemporary Europe, Studies in Fascism, 2. London: Weidenfeld and Nicolson, 1968.

Lerner, Michael. "Anarchism and the Counter-Culture." In *Anarchism Today*, edited by D. E. Apter and James Joll. London: Macmillan, 1971.

Marcuse, Herbert. "Ethics and Revolution." In *Obligation and Dissent*, edited by D. W. Hanson and R. B. Fowler. Boston: Little, Brown, 1971.

Moore, Barrington, Jr. "Tolerance and the Scientific Outlook." In *Critique of Pure Tolerance* by R. P. Wolff, Barrington Moore, Jr., and Herbert Marcuse. Boston: Beacon, Beacon Paperbacks, 1969.

Niemeyer, Gerhart. "The 'New Left' ". In *Democracy in Crisis: New Challenges to Constitutional Democracy in the Atlantic Area*. International Studies of the Committee on International Relations, University of Notre Dame. Notre Dame, Ind.: University of Notre Dame Press, 1971.

Oglesby, Carl. "Vietnamese Crucible: An Essay on the Meanings of the Cold War." In *Containment and Change*, edited by Carl Oglesby and Richard Shaull. New York: Macmillan, 1967.

Poirier, Richard. "The War against the Young: Its Beginnings." In his *The Performing Self: Compositions and Decompositions in the Languages of Contemporary Life*. New York: Oxford University Press, 1971.

Roszak, Theodore. "The Disease Called Politics." In *Seeds of Liberation*, edited by Paul Goodman. New York: Braziller, 1964.

Saltonstall, Stephen. "Toward a Strategy of Disruption." In *The New Politics: Mood or Movement?* edited by James A. Burkhart and Frank J. Kendrick. Englewood Cliffs, N.J.: Prentice-Hall, 1971.

Sartre, Jean-Paul. "Merleau-Ponty." In his *Situations*, translated by Benita Eisler. London: Hamish Hamilton, 1965.

Sisson, Daniel. "The Dialogue: Youth and Society." In *The New Politics: Mood or Movement?*, edited by James A. Burkhart and Frank J. Kendrick. Englewood Cliffs, N.J.: Prentice-Hall, 1971.

Smith, Roger W. "The Political Meaning of Unconscious Guilt." In *Guilt: Man and Society*, edited by R. W. Smith. Garden City, N.Y.: Doubleday, Anchor Books, 1971.

Sontag, Susan. "Posters: Advertisement, Art, Political Artifact, Commodity." Introductory Essay. In *Art of the Revolution: Castro's Cuba, 1959-1970*, compiled by Dugald Stermer. New York: McGraw-Hill, 1970.

Sykes, Gresham M., and Matza, David. "Techniques of Neutralization: A Theory of Delinquency." In *Guilt: Man and Society*, edited by R. W. Smith. Garden City, N.Y.: Doubleday, Anchor Books, 1971.

Williams, Paul. "The Hippies Are Gone: Where Did They Go?" In *Notes from the New Underground*, edited by Jesse Kornbluth. New York: Viking, 1968.

Wolff, Robert Paul. "Beyond Tolerance." In *Critique of Pure Tolerance* by R. P. Wolff, Barrington Moore, Jr., and Herbert Marcuse. Boston: Beacon, Beacon Paperbacks, 1969.

III. Articles in Periodicals

Adelson, Joseph. "Inventing the Young." *Commentary* 51, no. 5 (1971): 43-48.

Andrew, Edward. "Work and Freedom in Marcuse and Marx." *Canadian Journal of Political Science* 3 (1970): 241-56.

Arendt, Hannah. "Reflections on Violence." *Journal of International Affairs* 23 (1969): 1-35.

———. "Thoughts on Politics and Revolution." *New York Review of Books,* 22 April 1971, pp. 8-20.

Bell, Daniel. "Sensibility in the 60's." *Commentary* 51, no. 6 (1971): 63-73.

Bellow, Saul. "Culture Now: Some Animadversions, Some Laughs." *Modern Occasions,* Winter 1971, pp. 162-78.

Berger, Bennett W. "Strategies for Radical Social Change: Symposium." *Social Policy,* November/December 1970, pp. 18-20.

Birdwhistell, Ray L. "Kinesics: Inter- and Intra-Channel Communications Research." *Social Science Information* 7, no. 6 (1968): 9-26.

Blake, Robert. "Anglo-Saxons worry too much about guilt.", *Times* (London), 22 January 1972, p. 10.

Brownfeld, Allan C. "The Irrelevance of American Politics." *Yale Review* 60, no. 1 (1970): 1-13.

Campbell, Alexander. "As Others See Us: Would You Want Your Daughter to Marry an American?" *Modern Occasions,* Spring 1971, pp. 422-33.

"Democracy Has/Hasn't a Future . . . a Present." A panel discussion. *New York Times Magazine,* 26 May 1968, p. 30.

Djilas, Milovan. "Liberal Marx Is Not Democracy." *Freedom at Issue,* no. 7 (1971), p. 2.

Draper, Theodore. "The Ghost of Social-Fascism." *Commentary* 47, no. 2 (1969): 29-42.

Epstein, Edward Jay. "The Panthers and the Police: A Pattern of Genocide?" *New Yorker,* 13 February 1971, pp. 45-77.

Fest, Joachim. "The Romantic Counter-Revolution of Our Time." *Encounter,* June 1971, pp. 58-61.

Feuer, Lewis S. "Lenin's Fantasy: The Interpretation of a Russian Revolutionary Dream." *Encounter,* December 1970, pp. 23-35.

Flacks, Richard. "Strategies for Radical Social Change." *Social Policy,* March/April 1971, pp. 7-14.

Friedenberg, Edgar Z. "The Revolt against Democracy." *Change in Higher Education* 1, no. 3 (1969): 1-7.

Gastel, Raymond D. "Homicide and a Regional Culture of Violence." *American Sociological Review* 36 (1971): 412-27.

Geiger, H. Jack. "Hidden Professional Roles: The Physician as Reactionary, Reformer, Revolutionary." *Social Policy,* March/April 1971, pp. 24-33.

Goodman, Walter. "When Black Power Runs the New Left." *New York Times Magazine,* 24 September 1967, p. 28.

Gross, Bertram M. "Friendly Fascism: A Model for America." *Social Policy*, November/December 1970, pp. 44-52.

Halberstam, Michael. "Are *You* Guilty of Murdering Martin Luther King?" *New York Times Magazine*, 9 June 1968, p. 27.

Halle, Louis J. "Bringing about Change: A Matter of Manners?" *New Republic*, 23 November 1968, pp. 19-22.

Heilbroner, Robert L. "Counterrevolutionary America." *Commentary* 43, no. 4 (1967): 31-38.

Himmelfarb, Gertrude. "Bentham's Utopia: The National Charity Company." *Journal of British Studies* 10, no. 1 (1970): 80-125.

Hook, Sidney. "The Human Costs of Revolution." *Survey*, no. 66 (1966), pp. 129-37.

Huelsenbeck, Richard. "Reflections on Leaving America for Good." *American Scholar* 39 (1969/70): 80-85.

Hyams, Edward. "Whatever Happened to Socialism?" *New Statesman*, 14 May 1971, p. 666.

Jelenski, K. A. "The Literature of Disenchantment." *Survey*, no. 41 (1962), pp. 109-19.

Kampf, Louis. "The Trouble with Literature." *Change in Higher Education* 2, no. 3 (1970): 27-34.

Karlinsky, Simon. "Dostoevsky as Rorschach Test." *New York Times Book Review*, 13 June 1971, p. 1.

Landau, Saul. "Cuba: The Present Reality." An interview with the editor and members of the editorial board. *New Left Review*, no. 9 (1961), pp. 3-7.

Lekachman, Robert. "The Brighter Side." *New Leader*, 28 April 1969, pp. 3-7.

Lentner, Howard H., and Lewis, Thomas J. "Revolutionary Terrorism in Democratic Society." *Freedom at Issue*, no. 7 (1971), p. 3.

Levin, Bernard. "Angela Davis: Heads She Wins, Tails They Lose." *Times* (London), 6 June 1972.

Lippmann, Walter, *Globe* (Boston), 17 October 1971, p. A-3.

Lipset, Seymour Martin and Earl Raab, "McGovern's Little Mistake: From Party to Faction," *Commentary* 54: no. 7 (1973).

Mann, Golo. "The Intellectuals: Germany." *Encounter*, June 1955, pp. 42-49.

Martin, Jay. "The Politics of Terror." *Partisan Review* 33 (1966): 95-103.

Mason, Alpheus Thomas. "Understanding the Warren Court: Judicial Self-Restraint and Judicial Duty." *Political Science Quarterly* 81 (1966): 523-63.

McCracken, Samuel. "Radical Untruth." *Commentary*, August 1972, pp. 80-82.

Mendel, Arthur P. "The Rise and Fall of 'Scientific Socialism.'" *Foreign Affairs* 45 (1966/67): 98-111.

Minogue, K. R. "On the Fashionable Idea of National Guilt." *American Scholar* 39 (1969/70): 211-18.

National Opinion Research Center. "Surveys Find White Backlash Ebbing in U.S." *Christian Science Monitor*, 17 December 1971.

Newfield, Jack. "This Movement: This New Left." *Defiance* 1 (1970): 11-23.

Nisbet, Roger A. *"An Epistle to Americans:* The Counter-Culture and Its Apologists: 1." *Commentary* 50, no. 6 (1970): 40-54.

Piercy, Marge. "Women's Liberation: Nobody's Baby Now." *Defiance* 1 (1970): 135-62.

Pipes, Richard. "Russia's Politics: Fatigue for the Elite." *Interplay* 4, no. 2 (1971): 5-8.

Polanyi, Michael. "Beyond Nihilism." *Encounter*, March 1960, pp. 34-43.

"A Question of Commitment." *New York Times Book Review*, 2 June 1968, p. 2.

Rader, Dotson. "On Revolutionary Violence." *Defiance* 1 (1970): 194-212.

Rahv, Philip. "What and Where Is the New Left." *Modern Occasions*, Winter 1971, pp. 157-61.

Raskin, A. H. "The Working Man Has Become a Snob." *Saturday Evening Post*, 18 May 1968, p. 10.

Rustin, Bayard. "The Blacks and the Unions." *Harper's Magazine*, May 1971, pp. 78-81.

Sauvage, Leo. "Discovering Castro's Cuba." *New Leader*, 28 June 1971, pp. 8-14.

Seligson, Tom. "America's Future: The High School Revolutionaries." *Defiance* 1 (1970): 25-71.

Sherman, Alfred. "The Days of the Left Book Club," *Survey*, no. 41 (1962), pp. 75-86.

Short, Robert S. "The Politics of Surrealism, 1920-36." *Journal of Contemporary History* 1, no. 2 (1966): 3-25.

Solzhenitsyn, Alexander. "Open Letter: This Is How We Live." *New York Times Magazine*, 7 November 1971, p. 116.

Sontag, Susan. "Discipline for a Wayward Writer." *Village Voice*, 4 November 1971, p. 1.

Stern, Fritz. "Reflections on the International Student Movement." *American Scholar* 40 (1970/71): 123-37.

Turner, Henry Ashby Jr. "Fascism and Modernization," *World Politics* 24, no. 4 (July 1972): 563.
Tytell, John. "Papers of the Movement." A review of *The New Left: A Documentary History* edited by Massimo Teodori, *Catholic World*, May 1970, pp. 94-95.
"What's happening to America." *Partisan Review* 34 (1967): 51-58.
Willen, Paul. "Who 'Collaborated' with Russia?" *Antioch Review* 14 (1954): 259-83.
Wolfe, Bertram. *"Das Kapital* One Hundred Years Later." *Antioch Review* 26 (1966/67): 421-41.

Name Index

An * following page number indicates that an author is quoted, but not identified on that page.

Abd-el-Krim, 185
Abel, Lionel, 77
Acheson, Dean, 217
Adams, John, 105
Adelson, Joseph, 63, 69-70
Agnew, Spiro, 30, 85, 221
Agyeman, Edward, 205
Aldridge, John W., 123
Alsop, Stewart, 142
Aragon, Louis, 185
Arendt, Hannah, 160-61, 180
Armstrong, Karleton Lewis, 75-76

Bagehot, Walter, 112
Bakunin, Mikhail, 69, 71, 83, 85, 96, 190
Baldwin, James, 46
Banfield, Edward, 93
Barber, Benjamin, 33
Barbusse, Henri, 185
Batista, Fulgencio, 35, 88
Baudelaire, Charles, 84
Beauvoir, Simone de, 8, 177
Beard, Charles A., 170
Beichman, Arnold, 29-30, 36, 72-73, 106-07, 219; Beichman's Law, 141
Bell, Daniel, 77-78, 143, 181-82
Bellow, Saul, 143, 183

Beltov, N. *See* Plekhanov, G. V.
Bendit, Daniel Cohn.
  See Cohn-Bendit, Daniel
Benn, S. I., 104-05*
Bentham, Jeremy, 150, 190
Bentum, Benjamin A., 205
Berdiaev, Nicholas, 187, 188
Berthoff, Warner, 66
Berger, Bennett W., 162
Berrigan, Daniel, and
  Berrigan, Philip, 156
Birdwhistell, Ray, 145-46
Black, C.E., 206
Blake, Robert, 166
Blake, William, 172
Blanqui, Auguste, and
  Blanquism, 30, 75, 85
Bondy, François, 213
Bourassa, Robert, 23
Brandon, Henry, 90, 156
Bredvold, Louis, 150
Breton, André, 184, 185
Brezhnev, Leonid I., 176
Brewster, Kingman, 4
Browder, Earl, 26, 27
Brown, H. Rap, 64
Brownfeld, Allan C., 101
Brustein, Robert, 77
Brzezinski, Zbigniew, 170
Buber, Martin, 173

299

Buckley, William F., 91
Bukharin, Nikolai, 115
Bulgakov, Sergei, 187
Bunzel, John, 32-33, 107
Buonarroti, Filippo, 85
Burke, Edmund, 109, 124, 226-27
Butler, Samuel, 132-33

Calley, William Laws, Jr., 155, 156
Campbell, Alexander, 142-43
Camus, Albert, 205
Carmichael, Stokeley, 46
Cartwright, David, 65*
Castro, Fidel, 8, 9, 35, 88, 122, 161, 176, 197, 210
Cheek, James, 17
Chiang Kai-shek, 198
Clark, Mark, 49, 50
Cleaver, Eldridge, 50, 63-64, 76, 156
Cohn-Bendit, Daniel, 75, 84, 171
Cole, G.D.H., 192, 203
Coles, Robert, 64
Connolly, Cyril, 147
Conquest, Robert, 35
Cronkite, Walter, 218, 226
Cross, James, 23
Cruise O'Brien, Conor, 42

Daley, Richard, 110
Daniel, Yuli, 120
Davis, Angela, 212
Davis, Rennie, 21
de Beauvoir, Simone.
  See Beauvoir, Simone de
Debray, Régis, 89, 210
Dedijer, Vladimir, 172
de Gaulle, Charles.
  See Gaulle, Charles de
de Gramont, Sanche.
  See Gramont, Sanche de

de Mably, Gabriel Bonnet.
  See Mably, Gabriel Bonnet de
Descartes, René, 150
de Unamuno, Miguel.
  See Unamuno, Miguel de
Dickens, Charles, 150
Djilas, Milovan, 122, 204
Doriot, Jacques, 73, 178
Dowd, Douglas, 58, 67
Draper, Theodore, 27, 29
Drieu La Rochelle, Pierre, 73, 178
Drucker, Peter F., 199
Duras, Marguerite, 8

Eisenhower, Dwight D., 102
el-Krim, Abd.
  See Abd-el-Krim
Engels, Friedrich, 7, 28, 30, 70, 83, 87, 88, 96, 116
Epstein, Edward Jay, 48-51

Fainsod, Merle, 115
Fairlie, Henry, 5
Feirabend, Ivo, and
  Feirabend, Rosalind, 74*
Fest, Joachim, 33-34
Firbank, Ronald, 147
Flacks, Richard, 105-06, 107
Forman, James, 178
Forster, E.M., 219
Franco, Bahamonde Francisco, 204
Freed, Fred, 97
Fremont-Smith, Eliot, 44
Freud, Sigmund, 157-58, 159
Fromm, Erich, 182
Fuentes, Carlos, 8

Galbraith, John Kenneth, 91-92, 93
Gaitskell, Hugh, 174
Garry, Charles R., 47-49
Gaulle, Charles de, 26

Name Index / 301

Ginsberg, Allen, 139-40
Glazer, Nathan, 181
Gompers, Samuel, 27
Goodhart, A.L., 76-77
Goodman, Paul, 87, 145, 190, 197
Gramont, Sanche de, 64
Gramsci, Antonio, 9
Green, Philip, 16
Gross, Bertram, 17-19, 133
Guevara, Che, 95, 96, 162
Gurr, Ted, 104

Habermas, Jürgen, 182
Hacker, Andrew, 97, 124-33, 151, 152
Halberstam, Michael, 156-57
Hall, Gus, 12
Hamilton, Alexander, 84, 105
Hampton, Fred, 49, 50
Harrington, Michael, 181-82
Hayden, Tom, 16, 32, 61
Heard, Alexander, 163
Heilbroner, Robert, 5, 6, 194-200, 203, 205, 206, 24-42
Hentoff, Nat, 138
Hersey, John, 44
Hirschman, Albert O., 74*, 206
Hitler, Adolf, and Hitlerism, 4, 17, 19, 28, 29, 30, 35, 44, 91, 150, 199, 212, 229
Hobbes, Thomas, 150; Hobbesian nightmare, 107
Hoffman, Abbie, 225-26
Hoffman, Nicholas von.
    See von Hoffman, Nicholas
Hofstadter, Richard, 68-69, 207
Hook, Sidney, 28-29, 201
Horne, Harriet Van.
    See Van Horne, Harriet
Howe, Irving, 77, 176
Huelsenbeck, Richard, 172
Humphrey, Hubert H., 212
Hyams, Edward, 82-83

Ionesco, Eugene, 131

Jackson, George Lester, 64
Jacobs, Paul, 137
James, Daniel, 162
James, William, 188-89
Joll, James, 71-72
Johnson, Lyndon B., 169, 229

Kafka, Franz, 155
Kamenev, Lev B., 191
Kampf, Louis, 152
Karlinsky, Simon, 19-20*
Kazin, Alfred, 16
Kempton, Murray, 87, 90
Keniston, Kenneth, 63
Kennan, George, 220
Kennedy, John F., 142, 169, 229
Kennedy, Robert F., 36
Kesselman, Mark, 116
Khrushchev, Nikita S., 122-23, 191, 202
Kierkegaard, Søren, 199, 228
Kifner, John, 48, 49
Kilson, Martin, 129
King, Martin Luther, 155, 156
Kissinger, Henry, 30
Koestler, Arthur, 229
Kogan, N., 20
Kopkind, Andrew, 16, 32
Kristol, Irving, 91, 92-93
Kuusinen, Otto, 27

La Guardia, Fiorello Henry, 108, 111
Lamott, Kenneth, 17
Landau, Saul, 8
Laporte, Pierre, 23
La Rochelle, Pierre Drieu.
    See Drieu La Rochelle, Pierre
Lasswell, Harold, 169
Latham, Earl, 95
Le Duan, 176
Ledru-Rollin, Alexandre, 75

Leibniz, Gottfried Wilhelm, 150
Lekachman, Robert, 60
Lenin, V.I., and Leninism, 26, 33, 95, 96, 105, 116, 161, 173, 175-76, 179, 184, 208
Lin Piao, 210-11
Lindsay, John V., 110, 111
Lippmann, Walter, 18, 23, 87-88
Lipset, Seymour Martin, 105
Locke, John, 150
Loebl, Eugen, 113
Lovejoy, Arthur O., 25
Lowenstein, Allard, 21
Lowi, Theodore, 108
Lubell, Samuel, 131
Lukács, Georg, 24-25, 131, 208
Luther, Martin, 189
Lynd, Staughton, 75, 98

Mably, Gabriel Bonnet de, 157
McCarthy, Eugene, 103
McCarthy, Joe, and McCarthyism, 37, 50, 151, 152, 217, 224
McConnell, Grant, 115-16
McCracken, Samuel, 76, 94
Macdonald, Dwight, 193
McGovern, George, 81, 212
Madison, James, 108
Mailer, Norman, 138
Malraux, André, 3
Mandelstam, Osip E., 10
Mann, Golo, 225
Mannheim, Karl, 223
Mao Tse-tung, 122, 176, 200, 202, 210, 226
Marat, Jean Paul, 189
Marcuse, Herbert, 15, 31, 34, 60, 66, 67, 68, 86, 90, 120, 133, 156, 171, 173, 178-79, 182, 208, 210, 218, 221; "Marcusian doomsayers," 218, 220, 228, 230
Marighella, Carlos, 64

Martin, Jay, 62*
Marx, Karl, and Marxism, 7, 28, 83, 87, 90, 91, 94, 96, 97, 116, 122, 128, 165, 173, 174, 187-88, 201
Mason, Alpheus T., 103
Masson, André, 185
Meany, George, 62, 81, 92
Megill, Kenneth, 207*, 208-10, 211
Mencken, H.L., 147
Mendel, Arthur P., 186-87
Merleau-Ponty, Maurice, 177, 192-93
Merton, Robert, 125
Mill, John Stuart, 111-12
Mills, C. Wright, 32-33, 90-91, 104
Minogue, Kenneth, 163-65
Mitchell, John, 224
Mondale, Walter F., 36-37
Montagu, Ashley, 155
Moore, Jr., Barrington, 200-01, 210
Moore, Paul, 139
Moravia, Alberto, 8
Morris, Richard B., 180-81
Mussolini, Benito, 19, 26, 33, 35
Mvubelo, Lucy, 36

Nechayev, Sergei G., 71
Neumann, Franz, 20
Newfield, Jack, 140
Niebuhr, Reinhold, 141
Nietzsche, Friedrich Wilhelm, 71, 231-32
Nisbet, Robert, 163-64
Nixon, Richard, and Nixon administration, 30-31, 49-50, 51, 63, 81, 85, 101, 163, 169, 202, 210, 211, 218, 226, 229
Nkrumah, Kwame, 89, 122, 161, 205

Name Index

Oakeshott, Michael, 174
O'Brien, Conor Cruise.
   See Cruise O'Brien, Conor
O'Dwyer, William, 111
Oglesby, Carl, 70*
O'Neil, Wayne, 59
Orwell, George, 95, 98, 166
Ossowski, Stanley, 95
Owen, Robert, 194

Padilla, Herberto, 8, 10
Paloczi-Horvath, George, 66-67, 179
Pareto, Vilfredo, 208
Paton, Alan, 228
Patterson, William L., 46
Pétain, Henri Philippe Omer, 185
Peters, R.S., 104-5*
Phillips, William, 183, 185
Pipes, Richard, 104
Plekhanov, G.V., 187
Podhoretz, Norman, 126, 151
Poirier, Richard, 59
Popper, Karl, 160
Pound, Ezra, 194
Proudhon, Pierre Joseph, 85, 173

Rader, Dotson, 16, 65,* 67, 155, 225
Raeff, Marc, 121
Rahv, Philip, 77, 182-84, 185
Rákosi, Matyas, 66
Raskin, A.H., 81
Raskin, Marcus, 61
Reich, Charles, 15, 77, 133, 144, 145, 151, 152, 163
Resnais, Alain, 8
Reston, James, 103
Reuther, Walter P., 120
Revel, Jean-François, 173, 227

Richardson, Elliott, 21-22
Robespierre, Maximilien, 31
Rochelle, Pierre Drieu La.
   See Drieu La Rochelle, Pierre
Rockefeller, Laurance S., 67
Roelofs, H. Mark, 71
Rollin, Alexandre Ledru-.
   See Ledru-Rollin, Alexandre
Ronning, Chester A., 202, 203, 208
Roosevelt, Franklin D., 19
Rosenberg, Harold, 138
Rosenthal, A.M., 53
Rossiter, Clinton, 103
Roszak, Theodore, 77, 82, 139
Roy, Claude, 8
Russell, Bertrand, 83, 228

Saltonstall, Stephen, 61*
Sampson, Anthony, 103
Sarraute, Nathalie, 8
Sartre, Jean-Paul, 8, 10, 12, 177, 213
Sayre, Jr., Francis B., 155
Sayre, Wallace, 110
Schmidt, Johann Kaspar.
   See Stirner, Max (pseud.)
Schwartz, Harry, 141, 196
Scott, John, 141
Seligson, Tom, 145
Shirer, William L., 16
Sieyès, Abbé, 75
Sinyavsky, Andrey, 10, 120
Sisson, Daniel, 17
Skidelsky, Robert, 7
Skinner, B.F., 32, 33
Slater, Philip, 16, 47, 52-53, 144, 145, 146-51, 152
Smith, Eliot Fremont.
   See Fremont-Smith, Eliot
Smith, Roger W., 157-58
Snow, Edgar, 202
"Soledad Brothers," 64
Solzhenitsyn, Alexander, 34-35

Sontag, Susan, 8, 9-10, 11, 12, 42-43, 138
Sorel, George, 70; Sorelian myth, 207
Spock, Benjamin, 58
Stalin, Joseph, and Stalinism, 8, 10, 24-25, 27, 35, 41, 60, 91, 120, 122, 145, 150, 161, 177, 190, 191, 199, 202
Steel, Ronald, 18
Stendhal (pseud.), 86
Stern, Fritz, 11-12
Stevenson, Adlai, 102
Stirner, Max (pseud.), 179
Strasser, Gregor, 34
Struve, P.B., 187
Sukarno, 89, 122
Szamuely, Tibor, 196, 202
Szulc, Tad, 64

Taine, Hippolyte, 83
Talleyrand-Périgord, Charles Maurice de, 228
Talmon, J.L., 188, 227-28
Tenzer, Morton J., 45
Tinder, Glenn, 159-60
Tkachev, P.N., 86, 96
Tolstoy, L.N., 60, 224
Touraine, Alain, 6, 25-26, 75
Trotsky, Leon, 179
Trudeau, Pierre Elliott, 22-23
Turgenev, Ivan S., 73
Turner, Jr., Henry Ashby, 19-20
Tytell, John, 16, 59

Ulam, Adam, 276, n. 50

Ubell, Earl, 44
Unamuno, Miguel de, 158-59

Van Horne, Harriet, 30, 230
Voltaire, François Marie Arouet, 132
von Hoffman, Nicholas, 50
Vorster, J.B., 36

Wagner, Robert F., 111
Waisberg, Harry, 76
Wallace, George, 29, 87, 90, 91, 102, 103
Wallace, Henry A., 193
Washington, George, 108
Waskow, Arthur I., and "Waskowites," 174-75
Waugh, Jack, 130
Weber, Max, 125
Webb, Beatrice, and Webb, Sidney, 190, 202, 203
Wechsler, James A., 217-30; arguments recapitulated, 217-18
Weigel, Erhard, 150
Welch, Robert, 142
Wells, H. G., 67-68
Whitehead, Alfred North, 120
Williams, Paul, 140
Wilson, Edmund, 147
Wolfe, Bertram, 116
Wolff, Robert Paul, 101-03
Wulf, Mel, 16

Zink, Jeffrey, 85
Zinn, Howard, 31
Zinoviev, Grigori E., 27, 191

Subject Index

Academics and Academicians. *See* Elites; Intellectuals; Intellectuals in America; New Left; Progressives

ADA. *See* Americans for Democratic Action (ADA)

Adjectives, use of. *See* Language, and one-way adjectives, concepts

Algiers Motel Incident (Hersey), 44

Alienation: in America, 121; in communist countries (Megill), 207; as dissociation in writers (Bell), 143; and integration of dissidents, 208; and political power, 52; in Russia, 121-22

Ambiguity. *See* Intellectuals in America, ambiguities, double standard, and paradoxes of

America: valid criticisms of, 12, 114, 176; destruction of, demanded (*see* Revolution, America's need for); economy in, 123; intellectuals' attitudes towards (*see* Intellectuals in America, attitudes of, towards America); as moral force, 227-28; and moral equality (Hacker), 129; praised by leftists (Dedijer; Revel), 172-73; judged by sociology, utopianism, 211; as tragic (Huelsenbeck), 172. *See also* Democracy, in America; "Fascism" in America; Insanity in America, of Americans; Revolution, in America

American Bar Association, Young Lawyers Section, Committee on Protection of Civil Liberties and Civil Rights. *See* Committee on Protection of Civil Liberties and Civil Rights

American Revolution, 170; compared with French, 180-81; "New American" (Nixon), 169; second and third, 170. *See also* Revolution, in America

American workers. *See* Workers and working class in America

Americans: denied as "distinct beings," 160; denied dissent, 156; intellectuals' attitudes towards (*see* Intellectuals in America, contempt of, for Americans); as materialistic (*see* Materialism and materialistic values); preferences of (Oakeshott), 174; psychoanalyzed, 140-42. *See also* Dehumanization of Americans; Genocide, by Americans; Insanity in America, of Americans; Middle class; Workers and working class in America

Americans for Democratic Action (ADA), 92

Anarchism and Anarchists, 71-73. *See also* Bomber Left; Bomber Right

Anti-politics, 107-12; dangers of, 108 (Mill), 111-12

Apartheid: in America (Mondale), 36; as modernizing force, 202, 203; in South Africa, 36-37, 202-04

Apparat: need for, in revolutions, 74-75

Arkansans, 142-43

Art, Cuban. *See* Cuba, art in

Assassinations, political, 63-64, 65; of John F. Kennedy, 142; of Martin Luther King, 155, 156; at Olympic Games, 76

Avant-garde. *See* Elites; Intellectuals; Intellectuals in America; New Left; Progressives

Barbarization of Americans. *See* Dehumanization of Americans

Big Lies: categorized, 12; growth of, 47; and ideology, 223; intent of, 52; and news media, 47-51. *See also* "Fascism" in America; Genocide, by Americans; Insanity in America, of Americans; Materialism and materialistic values; Political System; Revolution; Utopias and utopianism; Violence; Workers and working class in America

Bill of Rights, 7, 218, 224, 229, (Mason) 103; Bill-of-Rights democracy (Wallace), 193

Black Panthers, 17; "genocide" against, 47-52

Black power, 208, 212; and collective guilt (Arendt), 161

Blacks in America, 128, 129, 173, 212. *See also* Racism and race relations, in America

Bomber Left, 57-78 *passim;* anarchistical, 72; lacking *apparat,* 74; indulgence, and defense of, 57-63, 69-70, 74

Bomber Right, 57

Capitalism: in "bourgeois republic" (Khrushchev), 122-23; and democracy (Marcuse), 178; "pluralist" (Wolff), 103

Catechism of the Revolutionist (Nechayev), 71

Censorship. *See* Freedom, of the news media, in America; News management issue; Underground press, in Russia

China: communism in, 6, 197-98, 199-200; "reaching and rallying" in (Heilbroner), 197-98. *See also* Mao Tse-tung in "Name Index"

Chinese Revolution, 195

Christian Science Monitor, 48

Civil rights, 224-25; in Cuba, 10; as deterrent to revolution, 103-04; and Adlai Stevenson, 102; of student protesters, 66; violence as a part of, 68; and Waisberg's judgment, 76

Civilization and Its Discontents (Freud), 157-59
Class and class struggle: in America, 94-95, 128; and American, French Revolutions (Morris), 180; and dictatorship (Lenin), 33; as interest-group politics (Wolff), 103
Class Structure in the Social Consciousness (Ossowski), 95
Classless society. *See* Communism, and the classless society (Merleau-Ponty); Communism, and elites ("new class")
Collective guilt. *See* Guilt, collective
Colombia (country), 74
Columbia Broadcasting System, 142, 229
Columbia University. *See* Student protest movement, at Columbia
Comintern Congress: of 1922, 26-27; "Stalinist," 28
Commentary, 218
Committee on Protection of Civil Liberties and Civil Rights, 225
Communism: and alienation (Megill), 207; and the classless society (Merleau-Ponty), 193-94; human costs of, 35, 177, 190-93; costs of, versus gains, 199-202; criteria of genuineness, 205; and elites ("new class"), 204; its "reaching and rallying" (Heilbroner), 198; as "reality" of modernization, 6, 195, 198; and Surrealism, Surrealists, 184-85; in the West contrasted to backward countries, 204-05. *See also* China; Mao Tse-tung in "Name Index"; Russia; Stalin, Joseph, and Stalinism in "Name Index"
Communist International. *See* Comintern Congress
Communist Party of France, 75
Communist Party of the Soviet Union, 104
Communist Party of the United States, 18-19, 171
Counter-culture, 4; ideology of (Bell), 77
Counterrevolution: in communist countries, 68, 170; and fascism, (Fest) 33-44, (Marcuse) 171; effects of word "counterrevolution," 170
Cuba, 7-10, 196, 197; art in, 9. *See also* Castro, Fidel, in "Name Index"
Cuban Revolution, 8-9, 88, 195
Culture, 3; "progressive culture," 12; as revolutionary, totalitarian politics, 32
Culture critics. *See* Elites; Intellectuals; Intellectuals in America; New Left; Progressives

Death of Ivan Ilyitch (Tolstoy), 224
Defiance, 65
Dehumanization of Americans: dehumanizing descriptions, 140-41, 144-45, (Reich) 144, 163, (Slater) 144, 148-49

Democracy: in America, affirmed, (Hacker) 129, (Loebl) 113; in America, denied, (Hacker) 131, (Wolff) 101; in America, failure of, 162, (Huelsenbeck) 172; in America, in Russia compared (Wallace), 193; and decentralization (McConnell), 115-16; intellectuals' discontent with, disbelief in, 52, 97, 206, 224; Khrushchev on, 122-23; Marcuse on, 178-79; "participatory" (Waskow), 175; "pluralist" (Wolff), 103

Democrats and Republicans, 103, 104-05

Depression, economic: virtue of (Aldridge), 123

Despair: totalitarianism from (Kierkegaard), 199; violence from, in America *(Defiance)*, 65

Developing nations. *See* New nations

Dictatorship:: of the bourgeoisie (Khrushchev), 123; in Ghana, 205-06; as modernizing force, 195, 203-04; of the proletariat, (Guevara) 95, (Lenin) 96; in South Africa, 203; use of, (Skinner) 32, 33, (Lenin) 33. *See also* Castro, Fidel; Hitler, Adolf, and Hitlerism; Stalin, Joseph, and Stalinism in "Name Index"

Dissent: allowed to majority (Gaitskell), 174; denied by "collective guilt," 156; as "revolutionary" (Revel), 227; as standard of health in democracy (Paul Moore), 139

Divorce, in America, 130-31

Double standard. *See* Intellectuals in America, ambiguities, double standard, and paradoxes of

Dynamics of Modernization (Black), 206

Eastern Europe, economy in, 122

Economic depression. *See* Depression, economic

Education: in Cuba, 197; in Cuba, Taiwan compared, 198. *See also* Literacy; Schools

Elections, in America, 101-05; presidential primaries, 102-03; uselessness of (Wolff), 101-02

Elites: ambivalence of, 83-84; in American, French Revolutions (Morris), 180; and analysis of American political system, 107; in Brazil, 178; as "new class," 204; "elitist society" no longer possible, 124; "power elite" (Mills' concept), 32-33; to reconstruct society (Freud), 157-58; and Sorelian myth, 207; "split and paralyzed" (Lenin), 182. *See also* Intellectuals; Intellectuals in America; New Left; Progressives

Erewhon (Butler), 132-33

L'esprit de géométrie (Descartes' concept), 150, 198

Ethical calculus, 31, 150, 198; Bentham's moral calculus, 190; "measuring rod," 200; Moore's equations, 200-01

"Extra-parliamentary movements" (Flacks), 105-06

Facial expressions of Americans, 144-45; smiles, 145-46
Faction politics. *See* Interest-group politics
Faith-ladder (James), 188-89
Fantasy, fantasies, fantasizing: about America, 228; about fascism, 30; as "rhetoric of revolution" (Bell), 77; about youth (Adelson), 69-70; of youth, 71
Fascism and fascists: in America (*see* "Fascism" in America); in Canada, 23-24; and counterrevolution, (Fest) 33-34, (Marcuse) 171; and despair, 199; defined, (Kogan) 20, (Mussolini) 33, (Neumann) 20, (Turner) 19-20; fantastification about, 30; in France, 25-26, 178; intellectuals' fascination with, 33; pathology of (Barber), 33; and student protest (Fest), 33-34. *See also* Social fascism
"Fascism" in America, 15-38; Gross on, 17-19; and Hitler's Germany compared, 17, 44, 46; lack of proof, theory, of, 18-19, 20, 23, 30-31, 34; and totalitarianism in Russia compared, 31; word "fascism" qualified, 15-18, 24
Fathers and Sons (Turgenev), 73-74
Federalist Paper Number 10, 108
Federalists, 105
FLQ *(Front de la Libération du Québec)*, 23-24
Fortune, 92
Freedom: basic threat to, 230; "buttresses" of (Mason), 103-04; explicated, (Lovejoy) 25, (Whitehead) 120; at individual's expense (Stirner), 179; of the news media, in America, 21-22, 63-65, 224, 225-26 (*see also* News management issue; Underground press, in America); of speech, in America, 66; suppression of (*see* Repression); in Weimar Republic, 225
French Communist Party. *See* Communist Party of France
French Popular Party (PPF), 73
French Revolution, 26, 200-1, 226-27; compared to American, 180; Jacobins in, 179, 226-27
Front de la Libération du Québec. See FLQ *(Front de la Libération du Québec)*

General Motors Corporation, 212
Genocide, by Americans, 41-53; and Black Panthers, 47-51; government a party to, 45; as "Hitlerism," nazism, in America, 17, 44, 46; middle class, passive supporter of (Podhoretz), 126; and Vietnam war, 43, (Marcuse) 156, (Wechsler) 219; "unknowingly genocidal" (Fremont-Smith), 44-45
GPU, 191
Guerrillas and guerrilla warfare: as "the party in embryo" (Debray), 210; distinct from terrorists, 77; urban, 64, 75, 209-10

312 / ANTI-AMERICAN MYTHS

Guilt: "by category," "objective," 26; **collective** (*see* Guilt, collective); as a political weapon (R. W. Smith), 157-58; in theological terms, (Freud) 158-59, (Unamuno) 158-59

Guilt, collective, 155-66; and black power (Arendt), 161; and Calley, My Lai, 155-56, 164; concept of, denied (Marcuse), 156; denies "distinct beingness," 159; **fallacy of** (Arendt), 160-61; derived from Freud, 157-58; **illogicality of** (Minogue), 164; and ambiguity, viciousness of intellectuals, 161-62; and Martin Luther King, 155, 156; reasons for **ascription of,** 156-58, 161; use by revolutionaries, 161; and **youth (Rader),** 155

Hallucinatory writing. *See* Writing, **hallucinatory**
Hard hats, 94
Harvard Crimson, 15
Harvard University. *See* Vietnam war, **demonstrations** against, at Harvard
Health, Education and Welfare (HEW), **Department** of, 21-22
History, as standard of judgment, 211; **progressives' laws** of, 30

Ideological politics. *See* Anti-politics
Ideologues. *See* Elites; Intellectuals; **Intellectuals in America;** New Left; Progressives
Ideology: and Big Lies, 52, 223; dangers of, 222-23; journalism as, 53; and mendacity, 217; and **attack on reason** (Bell), 77; truth in relation to, 52
Ideology and Utopia (Mannheim), 223
Individual, individualism: freedom, at **expense of** (Stirner), 179; Kierkegaardist denial of, 198-99
Insanity in America, of Americans, 137-52; desirability of, in mass breakdown (Ginsberg), 139-40; desirability of, in student-professor relationship (Hentoff), 138; assembling evidence of, 138; only America paranoid, 143-44; as theme in modern novels (Bell), 143
Intellectuals: in America (*see* Intellectuals in **America**); attitudes of, towards workers, "the people," 82-85; in China, 208; and Ghana, 205-06; in Russia, 119-20, **121-22;** true role of, defined, 222; in Weimar Republic, 11
Intellectuals in America: alienation of, 122; ambiguities, double standard, paradoxes of, 34-35, 67, 113-14, 120, 162, 165, 197, 204-06, 211-12, (as elites) 83-84, (as guilt purveyors) 160, (as New Left) 32, 176; attitudes of, toward America, 35, 52, 106, 121, 211-12, 223; attitudes of, towards communism, fascism, 34-35; contempt of, for Americans, 81, 82, 84, 89-90, 97, 156, 162-63, 166 (*see also* Dehumanization of Americans); and

democracy, 52, 97, 224; fascination of, with fascism (Barber), 33; hallucinatory writing of, 143; hatred towards middle class, 123-24, 131, 162; indulgence of Bomber Left, of violence, 57-63, 66-70, 74, 75-76; influence of, 120-21, 191; and the Jamesian faith-ladder, 188-89; in agreement with Khrushchev, 122-23; lack of planning (*see* Post-revolutionary world, lack of planning for); language of (*see* Language, misuse of); and workers, trade unions, 83-84, 87, 89-90, 106. *See also* Elites; New Left; Progressives

Inter-American Commission on Human Rights, 10

Interest-group politics, 109; as class struggle (Wolff), 103; dangers of (Mill), 111-12

Jacobins, 179, 226-27

Journalism: as advocacy, manifestology, 53; and Big Lies (*see* Big Lies, and news media)

Judgment, standards of: by history, 210-11; by project, undertaking (Sartre), 177, 213; by sociology, 211; by utopianism, 211-12

Kinesics, 145-46

Labor. *See* Workers and working class; Workers and working class in America; Trade unionism and trade unions

Language, misuse of: capriciously misused (Minogue), 165-66; to distort fact, 5-6, 132; and one-way adjectives, concepts, 5-6; and use of paradox, 32; and debasement of political debate, discourse, 151; for political ends (Orwell), 166; and specific words as "absurd," 197; "and yet," 61; "blind," 5-6; "counterrevolution," 170; "creative disorder, vandalism," 32; "ethical," 10; "fascism," 15-18, 24; "genocide," 41, 219; "immeasurably," 127; "inept," 190, 197; "invariably," 131; "neo-," 182, 183; "planned" as opposed to "programmed," 6; "profound," 126; "repressive tolerance," 31, 32, 208; "revolution," 169, 170, 176; "transcendence," 10; "underground press," 5; "virtually," 124-25; "we" and "our" (Beichman's Law), 141

Lies and lying: Big Lies (*see* Big Lies); as conventional wisdom, 220; as counter-culture, 4; "in culture," 3-4, 12, 32; institutionalized lie, 3; by progressives (*see* Progressives, political conventions, rhetoric of)

Life, 50, 191-92

Literacy: in South Africa, 203

LSD, use of: as mass therapy (Ginsberg), 139-40; as revolutionary tactic, 61

Majority: and anti-people revolutions, revolutionaries, 170, 175-76 (*see also* Revolutions, as anti-people); and right to dissent (Gaitskell), 174; repression of, in communist countries, South Africa, compared, 202-04; as exercising sanctions (Hacker), 125-26. See also Middle class; Workers and working class; Workers and working class in America
Malleus Maleficarum, 146
Man Who Cried Genocide (Patterson), 46-47
Maquis, 76
Marriages, American, 130-31
The Masses (political concept). *See* The People (political concept)
Materialism and materialistic values: attacked by intellectuals, 97, 119, 123; desired in communist countries, 119-20; and French workers, 84; paradox of intellectuals in relation to, 120-21
Mayor (office of): in New York City, 110, 112
Micromegas (Voltaire), 132
Middle class, 126-27; animosity towards, 123-24, 131, 162; blacks, identifying with, 130; as leaders of revolution (Morris), 180; and party system, 114
Minimanual of the Urban Guerilla (Marighella), 64
Modernization: in China, 197-98; as argument for communism, 195, 198, 202; in communist countries, 204; and nationalism (Black), 206; "realities" of (Heilbroner), 194-95; in South Africa, 202-04
Multi-party system. *See* Two-party and multi-party system
My Lai, 155-56, 164

National guilt. *See* Guilt, collective
Nationalism: duality of (Black), 206
Negroes in America. *See* Black Panthers; Black power; Blacks in America; Racism and race relations, in America
"New class" (Djilas), 204
New Left, 16, 116, 172, 174, 178, 218, 226; paradox, ambiguity of, 32, 176; and disregard of majority will, 170; praise of (Dedijer), 172; and revolution, terrorism, 16, 59, 170; lacking theory, program, 183
New man (socialist concept), 176-77, 190
New nations: and double standard towards, 203-06; right of self-determination, 42; "realities" of communism, dictatorship, in (Heilbroner), 194-95, 206
New Republic, 50
"New sensibility" (Bell), 77
New Statesman, 47, 50
New York City, politics in, 107-13

New York Post, 219
New York Times, 48, 49, 51, 81, 92, 170, 224
New York Times Book Review, 46
New Yorker, 51, 155
News management issue, 229
News media: and Big Lies, 47, 51, 53; freedom of (*see* Freedom, of the news media, in America); and workers, 92-93
Newsday, 51
Newsweek, 49, 92
Nihilism, 155, 164. *See also* Anarchism and Anarchists
Nine Lies about America (Beichman): criticized, (McCracken) 76, (Wechsler) 17-18
NKVD, 192
Notes on Democracy (Mencken), 147
Novelists. *See* Writing, hallucinatory

Olympic Games 1972, 76
One-party system: 104; intellectuals' attitudes towards, 107, 114
Oppression. *See* Repression
Organization of American States, Inter-American Commission on Human Rights. *See* Inter-American Commission on Human Rights

Paradox. *See* Intellectuals in America, ambiguities, double standard, paradoxes of; Rhetoric, of paradox
Partisan Review, 63, 163-64
Parti populaire français. See French Popular Party
Party system: traditional opposition to, in America, 108; abolition of, in New York City, 107-13. *See also* One-party system; Two-party and multi-party system
Pentagon papers, 224; Russia's, 202
The People (political concept), 83-84, 85-86, 96, 175-76, 220-21; animosity towards, 85-86, 162 (*see also* Middle class, animosity towards; Workers and working class in America, animosity towards); and anti-people revolutions, revolutionaries, 175-76, 178-79 (*see also* Revolutions, as anti-people); in "Leninist construct," 175-76; "Power to the people," 84, 174
Planned economy: "planned" as opposed to "programmed," 6
Pluralism, 113. *See also* Democracy; Party system; Two-party and multi-party system
Political system: definition (Banfield), 93; failure of (Flacks), 105; as "system of social union" (Mill), 111-12. *See also* Anti-politics; One-party system; Party system; Two-party and multi-party system

Post-revolutionary world, 173, 176-77; lack of planning for, 72-73, 171, 173-74, 181
Power Elite (Mills), 32
PPF. *See* French Popular Party
Presidential primaries, 102-03
President's Commission on Campus Unrest, 192-93
Press (*see* News media); freedom of (*see* Freedom, of the news media, in America)
Prison brutality, 142-43
Progressives: and communist "social-fascist" line, 27-28; continuing failure of, 106; their laws of history, 30; political conventions, rhetoric of, 5-6, 12 (*see also* Language, misuse of); and "status quo," 7-8. *See also* Elites; Intellectuals; Intellectuals in America; New Left
"Project," as standard of judgment (Sartre), 177, 213
Pursuit of Loneliness (Slater), 52, 147; chrestomathy from, 148-49

Quebec, 22-23

Racism and race relations: in America, 36, 37, 161, 209, 212-13; and assassination of King (Cleaver), 156; "doctrine of race" (Arendt), 160-61; in countries other than America, 212-13; America least racist (Revel), 173; in South Africa, 36-37, 203-04; of working class, 94; whites, alone, guilty (Sontag), 42-43. *See also* Black Panthers; Black power
Radical Anti-Establishment Neo-Marxist Union, 181, 182
Radical Left. *See* New Left
Radicals and radicalism: "deradicalization" (Glazer), 181; and the "new sensibility," 77-78; three strands of (Waskow), 174-76. *See also* New Left; Student Protest Movement
Ramparts, 50
"Reach and rally": communism's accomplishment, 198, 200
Reason: attack on, 77; disbelief in (Fest), 34
Reconstruction of society, 157-58
Reform without revolution: Marx on, 174; "peaceful change" (Mason; Gurr), 103-04; precluded, 226; Proudhon on, 173
Repression: in China, 199-200; in Ghana, 206; and nationalism (Black), 206; reactionary and revolutionary compared (Tolstoy), 224; "repressive tolerance," 31, 32, 208; in Russia, 5, 34-35, 41, 191-93, 199, 204; in South Africa, 36-37, 203-04
Republican party. *See* Democrats and Republicans
Revolution: in America, 127-28, 175, 182-83, 227 (*see also* American Revolution); America's need for, 169, 172, 174, 179, 211; as anti-people, 82-97 *passim*, 170, 175-76, 178-79,

189-92, (Lenin) 33, (Marcuse) 86, (Paloczi-Horvath) 67; and an *apparat,* centralization, 74-76; against "backwardness," 195; definition of (Marcuse), 171; "domesticated" (Mason), 103-04; as "extra-parliamentary" movements (Flacks), 105-06; human costs of, 177, 189-93; Lenin's requirements for, 182, 184; materialism as incentive to, 119-20; "playacting" and "rhetoric" of (Bell), 77; as "purifying" (Sartre), 213; "moral right of" (Mason) 103-04; four "realities" of (Heilbroner), 194-95; "Great Stereotype" of, 184; tragedy of (Proudhon), 173; and its vanguard, (Castro) 210, (Guevara) 95, (Megill) 208; America as the vanguard of (Revel), 227; and effects of word "revolution," 169, 170, 176. *See also* Chinese Revolution; Counterrevolution; Cuban Revolution; Revolutionaries and Revolutionists; Reform without revolution; Russian Revolution

Revolution in the Revolution? (Debray "manual"), 210

Revolutionaries and revolutionists: as absolutists, 70; as antipeople (*see* Revolution, as anti-people); characteristics of, 190, (Nechayev) 71, (Paloczi-Horvath) 179; fantasy world of, 71; and fascination with fascism (Barber), 31; in France, 74-75; and collective guilt, 161-62; contemporary intelligentsia as, 190; and disregard of majority, 96, 178-79; and lack of political "know-how," 181-82; and lack of post-revolutionary plans (*see* Post-revolutionary world, lack of planning for); and society, the state (Megill), 208; animosity to workers (*see* Revolution, as anti-people). *See also* Bomber Left; Guerrillas and guerrilla warfare; Terrorism and terrorists

Rhetoric: of intellectuals, 152; of paradox, 32; of revolution, 77

Riffs, 185

Russia: attitudes towards, 190-93; awaiting classless society, 193; pre-1917 economy of, 196; rationing in, 202; suppression in, 5, 34-35, 41, 190-93, 199, 204. *See also* Stalin, Joseph, and Stalinism in "Name Index"

Russian Revolution, 177, 195, 196, (Aragon) 185; human costs of, 177, 190; the "Great Stereotype," 184

Samizdat, 35

Schools: as "enclaves of totalitarianism," 36-38; ghetto, 47

Scientific socialism, 186-87

SDS. *See* Students for a Democratic Society (SDS)

Smiles, 145-46

Social critics. *See* Elites; Intellectuals in America; New Left; Progressives

Social democracy, 26-29; in Great Britain (Hyams), 82-83; in Weimar Republic, 28-29
Social fascism, 26-29; Roosevelt's "new deal" as, 19
Societal guilt, *See* Guilt, collective
Society, reconstruction of. *See* Reconstruction of society
Sociology, as standard of judgment, 211-12
South Africa, 202-04; and America compared, 36-37; literacy in, 203; racism in, 36-37, 203-04
Speech, freedom of. *See* Freedom, of speech, in America
Standards of judgment. *See* Judgment, standards of
Status quo, 6-7
Student protest movement, 60, 66-68; 75; at Columbia, 29-30, 58, 72-73; defense of (Paloczi-Horvath), 66-67; and fascism (Fest), 33-34; at Harvard, 66; lacking program, 72-73; and President's Commission on Campus Unrest, 163-64; and riots, in France, 25-26, 176; and trade unions, 106-07; and workers, 30, 89-90, 156. *See also* Bomber Left
Students for a Democratic Society (SDS), 29-30, 60, 72-73, 89, 156
Suffrage. *See* Universal suffrage
Suppression. *See* Repression
Supreme Court of the United States, 37, 224
Surrealism and Surrealists, 184-85

Taiwan, 198
Tammany Hall, 108, 111
Terrorism and terrorists: and New Left (Rader), 16; "revolutionary terror" (Marcuse), 60; distinct from guerrillas, 76-77. *See also* Anarchism and anarchists; Bomber Left; Bomber Right; Student protest movement
Third World, 91, 210. *See also* New nations
Time, 49, 92
Totalitarianism and totalitarian movements: and collective guilt, 161-62; origin in despair, denial of individual (Kierkegaard), 199; origin in exaggeration (Kennan), 220; schools as "enclaves" of, 37-38. *See also* Communism; Fascism; Dictatorship
Trade unions and trade unionism: challenge to organize for, 106-07; and intellectuals, 91-92; and Lenin, 87-88; and news media, 92-93; in Russia, 196
Tragic Sense of Life (Unamuno), 158-59
Truth: Big Truth about America, 229; culture as, 3; and ideology, 52; and Jacobins (Trotsky), 179; Nietzsche on, 232

Two-party and multi-party system: in America, criticism of, 101, 103, 104, 114; attitudes of intellectuals towards, 107, 113-14; defense of, 115; as tyrannical (Rossiter), 103; virtues of, 103-04, 105. *See also* Democracy

"Unanticipated consequences," 125
Underdeveloped countries. *See* New nations
Underground press: in America, 5; in Russia, 5, (Solzhenitsyn) 34-35
United Auto Workers, 212
Universal suffrage, 85-86
Utilitarianism. *See* Bentham, Jeremy, in "Name Index"
Utopias and utopianism, 227-28; Butler's *Erewhon*, 132-33; Guevara's, 162; Hobbes', 150; Marcusean, 179; and politics, 188; Republic of Virtue, 52; Walden Two, 30, 32, 33; as standard of judgment, 211-12; utopian designs and punishment, 161; utopian promise and workers, 95-96

Vietnam war, 75-76, 219, 228; (Galbraith) 92; demonstrations against, at Harvard, 66; "genocidal war," 43, (Marcuse) 156; and HEW, 21; as moral issue, 21, 219; Surrealists' "Vietnam," 185
Village Voice, 140
Violence: as anarchistical, meaningless, 72-74; in communist, democratic countries compared, 68; indulgence of (*see* Bomber Left, indulgence of); "mystique" of, 68-69; between students and hard hats, 94. *See also* Anarchism and anarchists; Bomber Left; Bomber Right; Revolution; Student protest movement; Terrorism and terrorists

Walden Two (Skinner's Utopia), 30, 32, 33
Wall Street Journal, 49
War Measures Act (Canada), 23
Washington Post, 48, 50
Weathermen, 58-59, 89, 93
Weimar Republic, 225; communists in, and Hitler, 28-29; intellectuals in, 11-12; workers in, and Hitler, 30
White Negro (Mailer), 138
Workers and working class: in America (*see* Workers and working class in America); animosity towards, 82-83, 86-87, 95-96; as anti-revolutionary, 82-97 *passim;* under capitalism (Marx), 96; in communist countries, 86, 89, 95-96; in Cuba, 88; in France, 82, 84; in Great Britain, 82-83. *See also* Trade unions and trade unionism

320 / ANTI-AMERICAN MYTHS

Workers and working class in America: animosity towards, 82, 87, 91-92, 97, 161; as anti-revolutionary, 82-97 *passim;* denied dissent, 156; and elites, 83-84; not agent of social change, 62, 90-91; and racism, 94; and student protest movement, 29-30, 89-90, 93-94, 156; as resistant to totalitarianism, 91-92; and utopian promise, 95-96; as wrongdoers, deserving punishment, 161-62. *See also* Trade unions and trade unionism

Writing, hallucinatory, 143

Youth: in China (Heilbroner) 197; cult of (Paloczi-Horvath) 66, (Adelson) 69-70; fantasy of, 71; and collective guilt (Rader), 155; as the New Left (Phillips) 183; and nihilism (Rader), 155; as victim, revolutionary hero, (Keniston) 63, (Adelson) 69-70. *See also* Bomber Left; Student protest movement